'Although group psychotherapy and group anal  over a century, no one has written as significant development and future direction of this field as Cañete have done. I congratulate these accompli duced a work of great comprehensiveness, schola., g.......s and ....p ...... ing, which expands our understanding of the vital role of group attachment throughout the life cycle and illuminates ways in which individual and group practitioners can offer more effective treatments'.

Prof Brett Kahr, *Senior Fellow Tavistock Institute of Medical Psychology, Freud Museum's Honorary Director of Research, Visiting Professor of Psychoanalysis and Mental Health, Regent's University of London*

'This remarkable study moves the reader along to think deeply about the enormous importance of groups for what made us human, and adds a new dimension to current knowledge of our sociability as a species'.

Dr Mauricio Cortina, *Psychoanalyst, Director Attachment, Development and Human Evolution, Washington School of Psychiatry*

'A unique developmental perspective on group lives and more: Drawing on meticulous anthropological, psychosocial, organisational and clinical research, as well as on their prolific careers over four decades, the authors have produced a wonderful book in which they study the nature and evolution of group attachment, both in the group and to the group, as we travel through the whole life cycle. Fundamental reading within any discipline interested in how and why groups shape our lives and evolve over time'.

Dame Clare Gerada DBE, **FRCPsych**, *President Royal College General Practitioners*

'A fascinating integration of attachment theory and developmental group analysis that elucidates psychosocial dynamics which, as a historian, I endeavour to understand: group processes through which deeply flawed leaders transpose their problems onto their countries in ways that both feed upon and inflame citizen's own anxieties and flaws, contributing to the disparate, rigid and often authoritarian groupthink they need to stay in power. In magisterial terms, this book provides a deeply compassionate way to understand the frightening world in which we live'.

Sir Paul Preston KBE, *Professor of International History, London School of Economics*

'This readable, enjoyable and accessible text brings together a creative combination of group attachment and group-analytic perspectives on the human life cycle. It is a welcome addition to the rich bookshelf of NLGA titles and essential reading for students on all IGA courses and qualified individual and group psychotherapists alike. The authors weave learned scholarship with deep clinical experience and original case material over every age and stage of the developmental journey. We see ourselves and our patients in every chapter, with each phase and individuation challenge laid bare with uncanny insight that speaks directly to the reader'.

Prof Barry Curnow, *National Director of Training,*
Institute of Group Analysis

'This book offers an in-depth exploration of how group identity and group attachment processes influence our sense of self, as they unfold throughout our lives. Its modern recognition of how the stages of human development have evolved over time, offers an essential reminder of the fluidity of our identities and how much this is determined by the groups we belong to. I wholeheartedly recommend it to all psychotherapists and counsellors and to anyone interested in the changes of our own minds'.

Andy Cottom, *Director Westminster Therapy, Vice-*
Chair UK Council for Psychotherapy

'An excellent book by two seasoned and imaginative clinicians, who combine an exhaustive review of the literature on life-span psychosocial development and rich group-analytic and group attachment thinking to different contexts, including therapy, in all life stages. This comprehensive account of identity formation, developmental tasks and expressions of group functioning is a timely and decidedly valuable contribution to the psychoanalytic, group and attachment literature on the understanding of what shapes us, as we grow from childhood into senescence'.

Dr Tony Kaplan FRCPsych, *Consultant Child and*
Adolescent Psychiatrist

'An ambitious, innovative and timely work that takes a life-span perspective on our development as group animals. With Shakespeare's seven life stages in mind, the seven chapters explore how personal and group identity and attachment evolve from cradle to grave, including relevant implications for psychoanalytic and group-analytic theory and practice. Empirical studies and clinical narratives are combined creatively for each life stage, making this book a must read for individual and group psychotherapists and a highly recommended read for all mental health professionals'.

Dr Gwen Adshead FRCPsych, *Consultant Forensic*
Psychiatrist, Group Analyst

'For practitioners, students and theoreticians, whether working in group analysis, group relations, psychoanalysis or social psychology, this timely book plugs a significant conceptual gap created by the insufficient attention paid to group attachment and psychosocial development from a life cycle perspective. A meaningful and reasoned integration of Bowlby's attachment theory and models of group psychosocial development. With this pioneering work, developmental group analysis has now come of age'.

Peter Zelaskowski, *Group-Analytic Psychotherapist,*
Editor Group-Analytic Contexts *(2014–2021)*

'This ground-breaking book is a much-needed addition to the theory and practice of group analysis. Seven chapters combine details of each life stage with case-studies drawn from the wide-ranging experience of the authors. Bringing together group analysis, attachment and the life cycle, this exciting study distinctively combines developmental theory, qualitative research and clinical practice. It is a unique contribution to the literature that should be essential reading for present and future students, as well as individual and group practitioners'.

Revd Dr Anne Holmes, *Group Analyst, Former Tutor*
Oxford IGA Foundation Course

'You don't have to be an expert in the psychoanalytic, group-analytic or at-tachment field to benefit from the authors' deep insights into the Seven Ages of Man, knowledge gleaned from their extensive research and work with patient groups of all ages. Group attachment and human development, the core subjects of the book, are universal and the authors' means of expression are elegant, jargon-free and accessible to all'.

Mike Bailey, *Editor, Publisher, Writer, Society of Authors*

'A valuable and original contribution to group analysis and more. It high-lights not only the wide applicability of the group approach to people at dif-ferent life stages, from childhood to old age, but the way human development is intrinsic to the group process, reflected in it and enhanced by it. This book will be of particular use to all individual and group practitioners and to those studying the important relationship between life development and the group context'.

Dr Morris Nitsun, *Psychologist, Psychotherapist, Group*
Analyst, Artist, Author of The Anti-Group

A well-researched, balanced, incisive and very readable text which skill-fully integrates life-span developmental theories, clinical work across all age groups and a broader societal perspective. Essential reading for mental health professionals, social and political scientists, it deserves a wider readership as societies and communities grapple with challenging personal and group cir-cumstances in the times we live in.

Jimmy Burns Marañón OBE, *Author & Journalist,*
Chairman British-Spanish Society

'As I read, I found myself quickly moved to reflecting on my work as a therapist and trainer and, more personally, on my own life as it approaches the later stages. A real strength of this study is that it describes, beautifully and scholarly, key developmental tasks and challenges at different life periods, and how these build on each other and can be coherently integrated into a whole and meaningful existence'.

Dr Ray Haddock FRCPsych, *Consultant Psychiatrist,*
Group Analyst, Licensed Systems-Centered Practitioner

'The field of psychiatry is broad and some general psychiatrists may practise without encountering group analysis, which is why this book is such a breath of fresh air for the jobbing clinician. The authors clearly elucidate complex theoretical concepts (some deemed historically incompatible) whilst expertly illustrating them with straightforward and meaningful clinical vignettes. The patients described will be familiar to any psychiatrist. The book defines the crucial role that group attachment comes to play throughout the life cycle in an accessible and methodically educational manner'.

Dr Danny Allen FRCPsych, *Consultant General*
Adult Psychiatrist

'An engaging, fully updated and inspiring volume that uniquely integrates group analysis, attachment theory and psychosocial development throughout the life cycle. Both John Bowlby and SH Foulkes would have been delighted with the publication of this new book, which is the most far-reaching exposition of the concept and therapeutic application of group attachment since Bowlby outlined it in 1969'.

Dr Mario Marrone, *Psychoanalyst, Group Analyst,*
Founder & President International Attachment Network

'Group-analytic psychotherapy is often the treatment of choice for individuals of all ages. Yet, until this inspiring volume, a life span developmental perspective was non-existent. Drawing on their extensive training and clinical experience, and illustrated by compelling clinical vignettes, the authors integrate theory with the latest empirical research findings in group therapy and psychosocial and peer group development. This book fills a vital gap in the literature and will be useful to any health practitioner or patient interested in personal development, relationships and group processes'.

Dr Jessica Yakeley FRCPsych, *Director Portman*
Clinic, Tavistock & Portman NHS Trust, Fellow British
Psychoanalytical Society

'In reading this state-of-the-art study, I gained a fresh perspective into my professional life's work with both perpetrators and victims of abusive social and sexual behaviour. I highly recommend this book as a milestone in the understanding of both ordinary and exceptional human behaviour, and the exploration of the healing potential of group attachment'.

Dr Estela Welldon FRCPsych, *Honorary Member American Psychoanalytic Association, Founder & Honorary President International Association for Forensic Psychotherapy*

'The reader will embark on a passionate journey through the vicissitudes of human development. A most engaging and enlightening read that puts groups and group attachment at the centre stage of personal growth and creativity throughout life: a key contribution to developmental, psychoanalytic, attachment and group literature'.

Prof Carla Penna, *Psychoanalyst, Group Analyst, Former President Brazilian Association of Group Psychotherapy*

'While universalist narratives like psychoanalysis may be challenged and critiqued from postmodernist and relativist perspectives, the life cycle (the journey we all make) retains its claim to universality as does our need for attachment. This book further emphasises that we travel this journey in relationship with others through our attachments and our membership of various groups and cultures where our personalities and identities are formed. A distinctly valuable contribution to our struggle to make sense of our human condition'.

Dick Blackwell, *Associate Editor of* Group Analysis

Group Analysis throughout the Life Cycle

Arturo Ezquerro and María Cañete present a captivating journey through human development, group lives and group attachment from infancy all the way into old age. Co-constructed with meticulous anthropological, psycho-social, cultural, psychoanalytic and clinical research, as well as stirring stories and insights which contain a rare blend of common sense and inspiration, this book offers an exciting new outlook on attachment and group analysis.

Group Analysis throughout the Life Cycle first assesses psychosocial, peer group and other group developmental studies, within a broad evolutionary and cultural context, looking into changes and constancies, continuities and discontinuities, as well as overlaps that occur throughout each developmental stage. It then presents a thorough review of psychoanalytic, group-analytic and wider group literature. Each chapter also includes qualitative group-analytic research which examines clinical group phenomena that can be present in all age groups, as well as distinct phase-specific characteristics and developmental tasks, as they find expression in the therapeutic process.

Presented with frankness, self-reflective thinking and compassion, this volume will be essential reading for group analysts, psychoanalysts, psychotherapists, psychologists, psychiatrists, political scientists and sociologists in practice and in training. It will also appeal to other healthcare professionals and readers interested in human development, relationships and attachment theory.

Dr Arturo Ezquerro is a London-based consultant psychiatrist, psycho-analytic psychotherapist and group analyst, and a senior assessor and trainer at the Institute of Group Analysis. He is an honorary member of the International Attachment Network and the World Association of International Studies and is the former Head of NHS Medical Psychotherapy Services for Brent. Ezquerro has over a hundred publications in six languages, including *Encounters with John Bowlby* (Routledge).

Dr María Cañete is a consultant psychotherapist and group analyst. She trained at the Tavistock Clinic and is a senior trainer at the Institute of Group Analysis. She is a former director of NHS group psychotherapy programmes for University College, St Charles and Mile End Hospitals, London. Cañete has published widely in English, German and Spanish.

The New International Library of Group Analysis (NILGA)
Series Editor: Earl Hopper

Drawing on the seminal ideas of British, European and American group analysts, psychoanalysts, social psychologists and social scientists, the books in this series focus on the study of small and large groups, organisations and other social systems, and on the study of the transpersonal and transgenerational sociality of human nature. NILGA books will be required reading for the members of professional organisations in the field of group analysis, psychoanalysis and related social sciences. They will be indispensable for the "formation" of students of psychotherapy, whether they are mainly interested in clinical work with patients or in consultancy to teams and organisational clients within the private and public sectors.

Recent titles in the series include:

Psycho-social Explorations of Trauma, Exclusion and Violence
Un-housed Minds and Inhospitable Environments
Christopher Scanlon and John Adlam

Sibling Relations and the Horizontal Axis in Theory and Practice
Contemporary Group Analysis, Psychoanalysis and Organization Consultancy
Edited by Smadar Ashuach and Avi Berman

From Crowd Psychology to the Dynamics of Large Groups
Historical, Theoretical and Practical Considerations
Carla Penna

A Psychotherapist Paints
Insights from the Border of Art and Psychotherapy
Morris Nitsun

Group Analysis throughout the Life Cycle
Foulkes Revisited from a Group Attachment and Developmental Perspective
Arturo Ezquerro and María Cañete

For more information about this series, please visit: https://www.routledge.com/

Group Analysis throughout the Life Cycle

Foulkes Revisited from a Group Attachment and Developmental Perspective

Arturo Ezquerro and María Cañete

Routledge
Taylor & Francis Group

LONDON AND NEW YORK

Designed cover image: R.M. Nunes / Getty Images

First published 2023
by Routledge
4 Park Square, Milton Park, Abingdon, Oxon OX14 4RN

and by Routledge
605 Third Avenue, New York, NY 10158

Routledge is an imprint of the Taylor & Francis Group, an informa business

British Library Cataloguing-in-Publication Data
A catalogue record for this book is available from the British Library

ISBN: 9780367766139 (hbk)
ISBN: 9780367766122 (pbk)
ISBN: 9781003167747 (ebk)

DOI: 10.4324/9781003167747

Typeset in Bembo
by codeMantra

To our teachers, to our colleagues and, above all, to our patients

Contents

Acknowledgements

First of all, we wish to acknowledge the power of partnership:

In contrast to mathematics, in a book project collaboration like this, one plus one is not two but a complex, challenging and mutually rewarding experience. We are indeed two distinct individuals. Yet, in our working together, we have managed to share with each other the group experiences we had internalised throughout our lives. As we were navigating through this process, we irritated, frustrated and got angry with each other. But our creativity survived; we enjoyed the task, supported and cared for one another, whilst learning from each other. We have become stronger; we have grown in our relationship.

John Bowlby and SH Foulkes have been present in our minds all over the writing of *Group Analysis throughout the Life Cycle*. In different ways, both had emphasised the core of our group humanness, connections and attachments; yet, they did not quote or refer to each other's work. However, in our minds and in our writing, we have endeavoured to bring them closer together. Certainly, in our fantasy, they became the partners they had not come to be during their life-course.

Whilst working on the book, we have been stimulated by what we had learned from our tutors, trainers and supervisors, within an institutional group context, both at Tavistock Clinic and at the Institute of Group Analysis, including Peter Bruggen, Anton Obholzer, Caroline Garland, Sandy Bourne, John Steiner, Sheilagh Davies, Sebastian Kraemer, Marcus Johns, Adele Mitwoch, Harold Behr, Norman Vella, Malcolm Pines and Robin Skynner.

This volume is in many ways the product of a group enterprise. We have been inspired by key group-analytic authors who have also written about the integration of attachment thinking and group analysis, including Liza Glenn, Mario Marrone, Felicity de Zulueta, Jason Maratos and Gwen Adshead. And we have been encouraged by another group of distinguished clinicians, researchers and scholars in the fields of attachment research, psychotherapy, psychoanalysis or group analysis, including Brett Kahr, Mauricio Cortina, Jessica Yakeley, Andy Cottom, Clare Gerada, Barry Curnow, Peter Zelaskowski, Anne Holmes, Ray Haddock, Estela Welldon, Carla Penna, Dick Blackwell and Morris Nitsun. They remain a motivating force.

Outside the mental health field, we have very much appreciated the feedback received from Paul Preston, Mike Bailey and Jimmy Burns Marañón who, in their work as historians, journalists and writers, consider that the book provides a deeply compassionate way to understand the frightening world in which we live, and they render the text suitable for a wider readership, as societies and communities grapple with challenging personal and group circumstances in the face of turbulent times.

Our thanks must likewise include many other colleagues and friends. Among them, Tony Kaplan, Jane Marshall, Maureen Kendal, Rafael González-Vizoso, Peter Keller, Verónica Álvarez, Susannah Kahtan, Paul Mallett, Mark Ardern, Brian Martindale, Nicolás Caparrós, Isabel Sanfeliu, Peter Shoenberg, Niels Rygaard, Jacqueline Fogden, Graham Lane, Vicente Madoz, Peter Hildebrand, Naomi Stern and Emilio Butragueño are all noteworthy. They have read parts of the manuscript, made helpful suggestions or discussed with us different aspects of the project.

Within this group, we are especially grateful to Tony Kaplan, a creative child and adolescent psychiatrist, for his spot-on comments on young people's psychosocial development, and to Emilio Butragueño, director of Real Madrid's institutional relations for injecting us with a spirit of "never give up". Indeed, the job of building up constancy and resilience is a life-long task and, without such a conviction, Real would not have won the Champions League an absurd total of fourteen times!

At a practical level, we wish to acknowledge the assistance received in obtaining much-valued material from the Tavistock & Portman NHS Foundation Trust Library, as well as the Institute of Group Analysis & Group-Analytic Society Joint Library. Guidance from Elizabeth Nokes, in particular, has made our job considerably easier.

We would like to highlight that we are always going to be indebted to Danny Allen, a good friend and colleague, for his generous and invaluable help during the polishing up and editing stages.

Finally, this project owns a great deal to the work of two people: Susannah Frearson, Routledge's editor for mental health and psychoanalysis, whose efficiency has made the book's pregnancy process painless, and Earl Hopper, chief editor of the series, whose wealth of experience and wisdom and his leadership at the International Library of Group Analysis constitute an ongoing source of inspiration for us. In the last couple of years, we have very much enjoyed working with both of them. And we look forward to continue working with them on the second volume of the series: The Power of Group Attachment.

See you soon!

Group Analysis throughout the Life Cycle: Foulkes revisited from a group attachment and developmental perspective

London, 9 July 2022
By: Arturo Ezquerro and María Cañete

Foreword

The social unconscious with respect to persons and social systems is at the core of the group analytic perspective. Relationality is at the core of the social unconscious. And the study of attachment processes is an essential element of relational thinking. Such processes are available to observation and to various kinds of measurement. This has enabled the "scientific" study of them.

We have shifted our thinking about people in terms of instincts and drives towards thinking about them in terms of their co-constructed relationships as both ends and means for obtaining pleasure and avoiding pain in the service of life itself. However, this shift was never intended to be a renunciation of the organismic individual in favour of an appreciation of the disembodied person, or an attempt to understand the dynamics of human society disassociated from the human species.

The essential balance of sociality and physicality is the implicit starting point of this first volume of a selection of Dr Arturo Ezquerro and Dr María Cañete's theoretical, empirical and clinical essays concerning attachment thinking in the group analytic project. They focus on the dynamics of attachment at each phase of the "life trajectories" that are typical of contemporary societies. They draw on sociology, group dynamics and psychoanalysis, or in other words on the disciplines that inform the group analytic perspective.

Disciplines in which the ratio of axioms to propositions is high are characterised by ambivalent tensions and polarisations. We find this between analysts and their patients, supervisors and their students, and especially among colleagues. Our Institutes are highly vulnerable to traumatogenic processes, and sub-groupings and contra-groupings predominate. Within this context, the "attachment school of thought" has been extremely fertile and continues to be extremely fecund. Moreover, the intellectual and personal fidelities to Dr John Bowlby, the father of this school of thought, have been remarkably strong and enduring.

I would like to recount a personal anecdote that conveys something about the personality of this founding father. I first met Dr John Bowlby in 1979 at a small dinner party in North London. I was a Lecturer in Sociology but also a candidate at the Institute of Psychoanalysis, trying to navigate the stormy seas between sociology and psychoanalysis, often having to explain to my fellow candidates that sociology at the London School of Economics was not only about making a brave new world, and that group analysis at the Institute of Group Analysis was not merely an activity for delinquent adolescents and patients who had been hospitalised and needed something to do until their meds kicked in. I found myself sitting next to Dr Bowlby during drinks before dinner. I was very anxious to meet this famous "insider outsider". Tactfully putting me at my ease, he asked about my intellectual interests. I talked about my conviction that both the aspirations and the apathies of children could be traced to the experiences of their parents and even grandparents during the war and its immediate aftermath. Like the children of Shoah survivors in particular, the post-war generations were replacement children. Dr Bowlby said: "How interesting. You know, you must really trust your judgment. After all, Winnicott recognised this sort of thing only late in life; and Rycroft is still trying to grasp it". When I added that each of us had to struggle with the Oedipus complex of our parents, he said: "You sound very psychoanalytical. I no longer think in such terms, but it is generally overlooked that Freud said as much". When after dinner I persisted that it would always be a stretch for psychoanalysis to account for any form of action other than verbal exchange, and we might always need more than two people in order to negotiate the "truth value" of a verbal exchange, he replied: "I doubt that there is any kind of basic opposition among psychoanalysis, sociology, and group analysis. Each of them complements the other two". Neither my wife, Mrs Bowlby, nor our hostess, who is still a friend of mine, attempted to get us to change the subject or to converse with any of the other guests. I felt that I had been taken very seriously.

Bowlby was disappointed that silo patterns of colleagueship had come to dominate the development of psychoanalysis in Britain. He said that it was important for us to "just get on with it". What really mattered to him was the appreciation of attachment processes and their biological basis throughout life, beginning with the zygote and the uterus, and ending with the detachment of a person from those who continued to live. Repetition was hardly a matter of innate malign envy and the death instinct in the context of the Kleinian ascendency.

That said, it must be acknowledged that Dr Bowlby never cited the work of Foulkes. His publication in 1949 of an article about a group of mothers and their babies, based on the work of Bion, was published only one year after Foulkes had published *Introduction to Group Psychotherapy*. Moreover, his article was concerned with some of the same questions that were of interest to Foulkes in his work with a group of murderous mothers in which he argued that the sociogenesis of international conflict was recapitulated unconsciously in their family life. Nonetheless, Bowlby offered a bridge to group analysis. He appreciated the contributions of the socio-cultural school of psychoanalysis and was familiar with the work of sociologists who specialised in the study of the family and of socialisation more generally. Several of his professional progeny had become or were becoming group analysts, and had begun to explore attachment processes within groups and to groups as such. And during the 1980s, he presented some of his work at Scientific Meetings at the Institute of Group Analysis.

Many themes in the history of psychoanalysis and group analysis in Britain are embedded in each of the chapters of this important book. Written with verve and clarity, Arturo and María have loyally commemorated the work not only of John Bowlby, but also of their own analysts, group analysts, teachers and mentors. The study of their essays will help establish a way of thinking that is likely to become more important during the current times of social and political turmoil. This new book will become required reading for all courses on attachment and group thinking throughout the life cycle especially by students of group analysis. I particularly appreciate its extensive bibliography, which not only demarcates the field of attachment thinking and research, but facilitates the study of group analysis itself. It does not matter which of them might be regarded as "mother". Each of them is a good enough caregiver.

Earl Hopper
Series Editor

Introduction

Arturo Ezquerro and María Cañete

Genesis of the book

Group Analysis throughout the Life Cycle is a ground-breaking project on group-analytic thinking and practice, with a distinct group attachment and life-span psychosocial developmental perspective.

We (the authors) have so far enjoyed a personal and professional partnership lasting nearly four decades. Our trajectories have been largely shaped by a blend of medical, psychiatric, psychoanalytic, phenomenological, existential, psychotherapeutic and group-analytic training and experience. Over the years, we have developed a strong group-analytic identity.

We have learned that groups are at the core of human existence and provide internal, interpersonal and multi-personal experiences that are necessary for healthy development and creativity.

In our evolution as a species, the group became an adaptive social organisation in the service of survival. The group is a humanising environment *par excellence*, and can also be a therapeutic and attachment space.

At different points in our careers, we have separately conducted psychotherapy groups for children, adolescents and young adults, as well as for adults, the late-middle-aged and older adults.

We came to realise that a life-span developmental perspective made a lot of sense and enlightened our understanding of healthy and pathological processes, relationships and group phenomena. Having said that, we could not find such a perspective in the existing group-analytic literature.

In the circumstances, we proposed to Dr Earl Hopper, series editor of the New International Library of Group Analysis, that we put together a book in which we would reflect on our extensive clinical group work regarding each and every stage in the life cycle, whilst also reviewing updated research studies into age-specific psychosocial development from cradle to grave, and its relevance to attachment and to group-analytic thinking and practice.

Dr Hopper loved the idea; Routledge became interested in the project and here we are.

As the book unfolded, our intellectual excitement pushed us to investigate the nature and evolution of attachment *in* the group and *to* the group,

DOI: 10.4324/9781003167747-1

from anthropological, developmental, cultural, organisational and clinical standpoints.

Whilst we navigated through the intricacies and beauty of group attachment as a universal human attribute, we considered that the study of this subject would deserve more space in its own right. We talked to Dr Hopper and to Routledge again, and a second volume was agreed: *The Power of Group Attachment*.

In the second volume of this series, we shall put across the concept of *group attachment* as an evolving and increasingly useful construct for group analysis and other therapeutic disciplines, as well as for the understanding of human evolution, organisations, intra-group and inter-group relations and personal development. The text will expand and complement the content of the present volume.

There are many publications on the various stages of personality, psychosocial and peer group development throughout the life cycle, and on group psychotherapy for different age groups. However, these fields have largely developed separately. The two volumes of this series aim to bring them closer together.

We argue that personal development is intrinsic to the group process, reflected in it and enhanced by it. Whilst we explore the interface and mutual influences between members' personal growth and the development of the group itself, we are not specifically dealing with the traditional developmental phases in a group's life, which have been depicted in the literature largely in sequential terms: forming, storming, norming, performing and adjourning.

In our view, although these descriptions invite us to think about the developmental stages of the groups we work with, their applicability is rather limited to some small closed-group configurations. Furthermore, boundaries between such phenomena are less sequential and more dynamic than originally thought.

A group, like an individual, does not really graduate once and for all from any of the above developmental phases. As we will see below, there are changing vicissitudes, continuities and fluctuations, as well as overlaps. Development is an open-ended task in a relational context with an ever-evolving environment.

Developmental stages on the stage

As far as we are aware, this is the first publication that has assembled, in an integrated fashion, clinical samples and reviews of group-analytic psychotherapy with each of the main age groups throughout all developmental stages in the life cycle: childhood, adolescence, young (or emerging) adulthood, adulthood, late-middle age and old age.

Whilst we were organising our thoughts, we re-read William Shakespeare's insights into life-span human development. Interestingly, he co-founded his own theatre in 1599. He called it *The Globe*, as he was drawing a comparison of the world to a stage and of people to actors.

In fact, Shakespeare adopted for his Globe theatre the Latin motto *totus mundus agit histrionem* [all the world is a playhouse], which supposedly derives from *quod fere totus mundus exerceat histrionem* [because all the world is a playground], an axiom originally produced by Petronius, the first-century Roman satirical author.

The division of human life into a series of developmental stages had been a commonplace concept in art and literature, well before Shakespeare's time; he conspicuously came to exploit it in his play *As You Like It*:

> *All the world's a stage,*
> *And all the men and women merely players;*
> *They have their exits and their entrances,*
> *And one man in his time plays many parts,*
> *His acts being seven ages...*

Life can indeed be seen as a whole cycle, from birth to death – the *last scene of all*, as Shakespeare put it.

Amongst ancient writers, ideas on the number of developmental stages in the human life-span differed – three or four being the most frequent. The notion of seven ages first appeared in Europe in the twelfth century, in the context of medieval philosophical thinking and theology.

Applying to all age groups, in both reality and fiction, seven is the most significant number across most countries, religions and cultures which have, over time, co-constructed groups of seven. These include:

- the seven wonders of the ancient world,
- the seven days of the week,
- the seven deadly sins,
- the seven virtues,
- the seven colours of the rainbow,
- the seven notes on a musical scale,
- the seven palms in an Egyptian sacred cubit,
- the seven lucky gods in Japanese mythology,
- the seven steps taken by the Buddha at birth,
- the seven days of the Passover feast,
- Snow White and the Seven Dwarfs,
- and (why not?) The Magnificent Seven.

In the circumstances, we couldn't help but decide to write seven chapters.

An outline of the book

Within each of its chapters, the present volume has been mainly structured into three broad areas:

- first, psychosocial, peer group and other group developmental studies, within a broad evolutionary and cultural context, throughout the life cycle;
- second, a review of the psychoanalytic, group-analytic and wider group psychotherapy literature on each life stage;
- third, qualitative clinical group-analytic research on each particular age group.

As a whole, the book provides a comprehensive study of psychosocial and peer group development, through each and every one of the main stages in the human life cycle, and its application to group-analytic thinking and practice. Consequently, we would like to claim that this study is an important step for developmental group analysis to come of age.

Chapter 1 is entitled *Developmental Group Analysis Comes of Age*; it is the first group-analytic publication that provides a developmental perspective throughout the entire life cycle.

The chapter amalgamates in an integrated fashion the most relevant research findings on life-span psychosocial and peer group development and on group psychotherapy from childhood to old age; it pulls together the other, phase specific, chapters of this book into a succinct and coherent whole. This initial chapter is structured into three sections:

- The first explores key historical events in the evolution of psychoanalysis and group analysis, which delayed the adoption of a life-span developmental perspective; it reviews relevant literature on the origins of such perspective in the fields of psychoanalysis and attachment.
- The second provides an integrated overview of psychosocial, peer group and group attachment development throughout the life cycle; it looks into changes and constancies, continuities and discontinuities, as well as overlaps that occur throughout each of the developmental stages, from infancy to old age.
- The third examines clinical group phenomena that can be present in all different major age groups in the life-span, including children, adolescents, young adults, adults, the late middle-aged and older adults; it also compares the distinct characteristics of each of these age groups, outlining phase-specific issues and developmental tasks, as they find expression in the therapeutic group process.

This study comes to the conclusion that group psychotherapy is highly beneficial in all age groups, and that proper knowledge of the psychosocial and peer group developmental stages throughout the life cycle should be an integral part of the training, thinking and clinical work of individual and group psychotherapy practitioners and other mental health professionals.

Chapter 2 is entitled *Early Psychosocial Development: Can Children Benefit from Group-Analytic Therapy?* It scrutinises psychosocial and peer group development from infancy to adolescence, including sibling and peer relationships. These constitute a profound part of growing up and are influenced by early relationships with primary attachment figures, but can develop quite autonomously following a different developmental path. The growth-engendering and altruistic nature of peer relations is a good basis for the effectiveness of child group psychotherapy.

Psychodynamic therapy groups for children have multiple benefits:

- They operate at the formative peer group level.
- They have an integrative developmental function.
- They possess distinct therapeutic value for the child's integral adjustment and wellbeing.
- An additional advantage is that many parents (and children) look at the group as less threatening a format than individual therapy, in which the child can be perceived as being singled out.

This chapter is structured in three sections:

- First, it thoroughly studies the child's psychosocial and peer group development.
- Second, it outlines the history of group therapy for children and reviews the literature on the subject.
- Third, it provides vivid clinical vignettes of a psychotherapy group with children aged six to eleven years, which was conducted by one of the authors.

The main objectives of the chapter are:

A to provide an integrated understanding of the child's psychosocial and peer group development, for the benefit of professionals, parents, children and society by and large;
B to present a reasoned and evidence-based case for the multiple benefits of group psychotherapy with children;
C to encourage psychotherapists and other professionals (including group analysts) to run groups for children, as well as to inform their wider practice with a useful developmental perspective.

Chapter 3 is entitled *The Power and Therapeutic Potential of the Adolescent Peer Group*.

It explores the nature and implications of peer group attachment, which is powerful and fundamental to adolescent development, perhaps more so than at any other stage in the life cycle. This power can be used to enhance the beneficial effects of psychotherapy groups for adolescents, which often are the treatment of choice for a number of reasons:

- They operate at the core of peer group development and identity formation.
- They have an important reflective function.
- They are growth-engendering and allow for a reworking of attachment relationships.
- An additional advantage is that, in groups, adolescents can develop and exercise a sense of autonomy, as well as inner authority that they recognise as their own.

This chapter is structured into three sections:

- First, it studies key aspects of adolescent psychosocial and peer group development.
- Second, it reviews relevant psychoanalytic and group literature on adolescence.
- Third, it provides a qualitative case study of innovative group therapy in an in-patient adolescent unit, run on therapeutic community principles adapted to adolescence, where one of the authors worked.

The main objectives of the chapter are:

A   to offer an integrated understanding of adolescent development;
B   to inspire psychotherapists and other mental health professionals (including group analysts) who are daunted by the prospect of working with or conducting groups for adolescents, as well as to inform their wider practice with a valuable developmental perspective;
C   to encourage the reader (including parents) to discern their own (countertransferential) reactions to adolescents, optimally reconnecting to their own transit through adolescence, without negating, deriding or pathologising the dramatic expressions of this unique period.

Chapter 4 is entitled *Young Adults' Group Lives: An Increasingly Long-Winded Road to Adulthood.*

It devotes itself to a crucial period in the life cycle, described as young, early or emerging adulthood, a time of intense identity exploration and construction, with its idiosyncratic developmental, intrapsychic and psychosocial challenges. As people grow out of adolescence, they face increasing pressure to make life choices that will help them define who they are amongst their peers, in the new groups they belong to in society, and in their own minds.

The chapter reviews the specialist literature on this life stage, addressing changes in society since the 1960s, particularly in developed countries, contributing to an increasingly complex, stressful and long-winded road to adulthood. These changes vary considerably across cultural, socio-economic, personal and political contexts. Traditional milestones of adulthood, such as obtaining a stable job, getting married and having children, have become less defining, and the development of a capacity to experience oneself as a coherent, whole person within diverse interpersonal and group contexts has been emphasised as a new marker of adult status.

The exploratory, unstable and fluid quality of this life period requires a reconfiguration of individual and group attachment relationships, including a greater exposure to diversity and the development of more mature levels of intimacy. These developmental pressures can leave some young or emerging adults feeling lost and becoming vulnerable to mental health problems.

A group-analytic, qualitative clinical case study with patients aged nineteen to twenty-nine is presented, supporting previous research that incorporates a developmental perspective in therapeutic group interventions with this age group, in order to enhance young adults' competence in handling age-related tasks. Further group-analytic qualitative and quantitative research is required for the benefit of emerging adults and of society as a whole.

Chapter 5 is entitled *Adult Life in its Prime: Integrating Differences and Complex Group Configurations.*

It devotes itself to adults and their key developmental challenges and tasks which require more advanced levels of integration than in previous life stages: dealing with diversity and differences, long-term love, family and work commitments, complex group configurations, conflicts and intimate citizenship, as well as striving to achieve a sense of wholeness, balance and life satisfaction – something that is present in other developmental stages but which acquires a full dimension in adulthood.

As part of the exploration into adulthood, the chapter examines the interface and the process of integrating differences between the Tavistock (Bionian) and group-analytic (Foulkesian) approaches to group therapy, which have been largely considered antagonistic and incompatible. Relevant theories and models within the frameworks of psychoanalysis, attachment and group analysis are reviewed, including the fundamental role that group attachment plays in adult life.

A qualitative case study is presented, based on an NHS adult out-patient group for patients aged twenty-five to fifty-five, which met weekly over three years. Conducting this group was an integral component of the author's training at the Institute of Group Analysis (IGA), although the group met at the Tavistock Clinic ("next door"). The author, who became the Institute's first trainee to run such group at the Tavistock, had two supervisors simultaneously, one from each institution; hence, there was a constant tension between the two theories throughout the history of the group.

The chapter aims to encourage adults to reflect on their development. It also aims to stimulate clinicians to include a life-span developmental perspective, as an aid to the tasks of dealing with conflict and integrating differences in their training and subsequent practice; ultimately, to enjoy their personal and professional growth, as adults working with adult patients, and to develop an attitude in which the patients' well-being is prioritised over and above a particular therapeutic technique.

Chapter 6 is entitled *Late-Middle Age: Searching for a New Group Identity?*

It concentrates on another critical period in the life cycle, described as late-middle age, a time of reworking group identity and group attachment, with its specific developmental, intrapsychic and psychosocial challenges, after mastery of middle adulthood but before settling into old age.

Developmental pressures for this age group may include a struggle between the world within and the increasing risk of illness, declining intellectual and economic productivity, intergenerational issues and a feeling of having less to give. In addition, the gradual loss of statuses and of significant attachment figures and peers, as well as a heightened awareness of one's own mortality, may generate states of anxiety and isolation.

On the other hand, late-middle-aged individuals bring a wealth of experience and wisdom that can be pooled in dealing with universal themes and problems, so contributing to society and to future generations – a process that has been described as generativity.

The chapter reviews the specialist psychoanalytic and group literature on this life stage and provides empirically supported data that emphasises the fundamental role of group identity, group membership and group attachment, in assisting late-middle-aged adults to focus on their developmental challenges, to grieve their losses, to adjust to major life changes, such as retirement, and to continue growing.

A group-analytic, qualitative clinical case study with patients aged fifty-five to sixty-seven is presented, supporting the idea that personal growth is an open-ended task. The chapter concludes that late-middle age is a suitable period for group-analytic psychotherapy, since a well-functioning group can help this population explore safely, come to grips with their developmental tasks, grieve and work through their losses and difficulties, and face later life in better shape.

Chapter 7 is entitled *Group Analysis with Older Adults: Can Creativity Survive when Time is Running Out?*

It focusses on late life, a time of growth in some areas and significant decline in others, with its characteristic developmental, intrapsychic and psychosocial challenges. Older adults have a long history behind them, as well as an expectation of a shorter time to live. In contrast to young adults, who go through a process of expansion, elderly people increasingly experience reduced rather than expanded choices and capabilities, including many losses and a likely reduction of group connections and networks. They need to achieve a balance between disengagement from public roles and sufficient social involvement with, and commitment to life.

The chapter reviews relevant studies on old age development and ageism, as well as the specialist psychoanalytic and group literature on this life stage, which provides evidence for the beneficial effects of group-analytic psychotherapy and other modalities of psychodynamic group therapy with older adults.

A group-analytic, qualitative clinical research on patients aged sixty-five to ninety-five (in an NHS out-patient clinic) is presented, supporting the idea that personal growth can continue until death. The natural processes of reminiscence and life review are an important component of the therapeutic work. Meaningful reminiscing and staying in contact with the past can promote a sense of continuity, self-constancy and ego-integrity, for elderly people to re-assess and give value to their own life experiences and to themselves, as well as to come to terms with the inexorable reality of approaching death.

This chapter aims to encourage group analysts and other psychotherapy practitioners and health professionals to overcome their prejudices toward and hesitations about working with older adults. For those already working with this population, the chapter aims to help them reflect on their work, stimulate their thinking and extend their repertoire. Through an exploration of the developmental pressures and strengths of late life, the chapter also aims to challenge ageism and to encourage older adults to live as well as possible all the way to the very end.

Concluding remarks

Throughout the book, we emphasise that attachment needs are life-long, not just a matter of babies needing their mothers, or of young children and adolescents needing their parents and their peer group. Attachment (like food and sexuality) is a basic and integral part of our existence all the way from cradle to grave.

Indeed, attachment theory had its original focus on affectional bonds between infants and their parental caregivers. It gradually extended from this to adult romantic and marital relationships and to psychotherapeutic relations. It is only recently that an attachment standpoint has been incorporated into groups (see Chapter 1).

So far, only a few empirical studies have applied attachment knowledge to the analysis of group processes in general and group psychotherapy in particular, although they still lack a life-span developmental perspective. The current volume and the next volume of this series aim to plug this significant conceptual gap.

Overall, the present book contains a large amount of research, a comprehensive update of knowledge on psychosocial and group components of human development, and a wealth of clinical experience.

We have endeavoured to provide a balanced and reasoned integration of theory, research, training and clinical work throughout, whilst showing our commitment to diversity, inclusiveness and openness to different viewpoints.

Furthermore, we critically examine our own skills in dealing with a broad range of problems, as well as our limitations in understanding and managing complex situations, through which our ideas have evolved over time.

To illustrate this, vivid clinical vignettes are presented with frankness, self-reflected thinking, compassion and care for the well-being of people suffering or struggling to become attached and to grow.

Thus, the text will appeal to anyone who is interested in personal development and relationships or who has ever been a patient, as well as to psychoanalysts, group analysts, psychotherapists, psychologists, psychiatrists, other mental health professionals and social and political scientists.

We have come to the conclusion that proper knowledge of the psychosocial, peer group and group attachment developmental stages throughout the life cycle should be an integral part of the training, thinking and practice of the above professionals.

The distinct developmental and group attachment emphasis of this book, as applied to group lives in general and to group-analytic theoretical formulations and applications in particular, aims to contribute to a new outlook in the fields of attachment and group analysis.

Arturo Ezquerro and María Cañete

London, 5 March 2022

ORCID iD: Arturo Ezquerro https://orcid.org/0000-0002-9910-4576

ORCID iD: María Cañete https://orcid.org/0000-0001-7967-1103

1 Developmental group analysis comes of age

Arturo Ezquerro and María Cañete

Introduction: human development as an open-ended task

Group analysis is not only a highly beneficial and cost-effective type of psychotherapy (mainly for adults), but also a creative and democratic way of understanding human life and group relations, within which the integration of the *stranger group* as a therapeutic tool is a cornerstone (Nitzgen, 2008; Ezquerro, 2020a, 2021a). Stranger means that members are unfamiliar with each other prior to joining the group.

On the whole, group analysis has come to be a strong clinical and theoretical discipline, particularly regarding issues of interpersonal, intragroup and intergroup relations, diversity, race, gender, psychosexual development, individual and collective trauma, systemic thinking and organisational life, as well as power, politics and social thought, including the social unconscious (Hopper, 1996, 2000, 2003; Blackwell; 2005; Nitsun, 2006; Nitzgen, 2008; Dalal, 2011; Ormay, 2012; Hopper and Weinberg, 2016; Barwick and Weegman, 2018; Thornton, 2019; Parker, 2020; Ezquerro, 2020a, 2021a, 2021b).

In addition, a number of group analysts have made valuable contributions regarding important aspects of psychosocial development at different life stages (Nitsun, 1989; Pines, 1998; Evans, 2000; Ezquerro, 2017; Parker, 2020), as well as self-reflections on their personal and professional developmental journey (Hopper, 2003; Nitsun, 2015; Ezquerro, 2017, 2020b). In the following sections and subsequent chapters, we shall expand on these.

Overall, however, group analysts have so far paid insufficient attention to attachment, particularly group attachment, and to an integrated perspective on psychosocial and peer group development throughout the life cycle. Only a few group-analytic practitioners have tried to integrate Bowlby's attachment theory with group analysis.

In a landmark paper, Liza Glenn (1987) shared insights of her supervision with Bowlby and postulated that, under optimal conditions, the group matrix can be perceived as an attachment figure and secure base. In my IGA, dissertation (*Does Attachment Relate to Group Analysis?*), I stated that attachment theory gives primary status to socio-emotional bonds and provides a

DOI: 10.4324/9781003167747-2

good foundation for the theory of group analysis, which rests on the premise that the essence of human being is social (Ezquerro, 1991).

In the mid-1980s, at the Institute of Group Analysis (IGA), Earl Hopper presented a paper on The Socio-Cultural School of Psychoanalysis. John Bowlby was the discussant of Hopper's paper and responded by drawing areas of coincidence between attachment theory and this particular psychoanalytic school. Mario Marrone (1998) elaborated on these similarities and advocated attachment-based experiential group work with psychotherapists to increase their understanding of patients and themselves.

In her work as a forensic psychiatrist, Gwen Adshead (1998) emphasised the importance of the caring role that mental health professionals have to play, including enough continuity and reliability, as potential attachment figures for very damaged and violent patients who hardly had any secure attachment experience in their lives. Felicity de Zulueta (1993) looked into the traumatic roots of destructiveness and concluded that severe disruptions in the early attachment system, such as child abuse, are a fuel for future aggression and violence – attachment *gone wrong*. And Jason Maratos (1996) highlighted the relevance of attachment in the construction of our individual self and our group self.

It is striking that, in his many publications, SH Foulkes (the father of group analysis) hardly referred to attachment or human development, let alone a life-span developmental perspective. In fact, the words development or attachment do not appear in any of the indexes of his books. These terms are also absent in the index of *The Practice of Group Analysis* (Roberts and Pines, 1991), with contributions from early generations of group analysts, largely considered a blueprint of group-analytic psychotherapy.

Consequently, in the thinking, training and practice of group analysts, past and present, there has been a concerning absence of a life-span perspective on psychosocial and peer group development. In this chapter and throughout the book, we will endeavour to redress or, at least, address this.

Foulkes developed group analysis from 1940 onward, in the wider context of the Second World War. He was a German-Jewish psychiatrist and psychoanalyst who had emigrated to England as a refugee, in 1933. Whilst running a private outpatient clinic in Exeter, he decided to experiment with putting a number of his individual adult patients together in a newly created psychotherapy group.

In 1942, he was posted to the Military Neurosis Centre at Northfield Hospital, near Birmingham. He started treating groups of soldiers and, as the numbers of psychiatric casualties increased on a large scale, from 1943 to 1945, he contributed to the process of transforming the whole hospital into what has been considered the first therapeutic community.

Gradually, Foulkes designed an innovative and powerful therapeutic tool. Whilst largely based on psychoanalytic insights, his technique was not a direct application of psychoanalysis to the group but a form of ground-breaking therapy *in* the group, *of* the group, *by* the group, including its conductor (Foulkes, 1964).

This method has become a distinct therapeutic philosophy in which patients are conceived as having, alongside their problems, enough internal resources to help each other and, eventually, become a group of co-therapists (Ezquerro, 1989).

Foulkesian theory has often been criticised as vague; however, its imprecision has been seen by others as part of its strength. It can be applied to many situations: psychotherapy in small, median and large groups and in individual, couple and family therapy, as well as in education and institutional dynamics and consultations (Brown and Zinkin, 1994).

Early group analysis was strongly influenced by Freudian psychoanalysis, which was meant to be a developmental theory of the mind from the outset.

In fact, Freud (1905a) proposed a theory of human development based on a postulated active sexual life from birth, through childhood, to adolescence, and described oral, anal, phallic and genital developmental stages. It seems that he came to conceive this after working with patients with a diagnosis of hysteria, the neurotic condition *par excellence* at the time, and other unexplained psychosomatic symptoms.

Originally, Freud (1896) attributed these symptoms to childhood sexual abuse, as per the stories reported by his adult patients about their childhood experiences. His so-called *seduction theory* was born, but it would be short-lived.

On 26 April 1896, he presented his findings to the Society for Psychiatry and Neurology of Vienna. Krafft-Ebing, who chair the meeting, commented that the presentation sounded like a scientific fairy-tale (Ezquerro, 2019a).

Unfortunately, Freud surrendered to external pressure from his peer group and from the bourgeois society of the Austro-Hungarian empire, as well as to the internal pressures of his own doubts. He repudiated his initial belief and affirmed instead that his patients' reports of childhood sexual molestations were illusions or fantasies.

Consequently, Freud's interests became focussed on the *internal* world, especially on the powerful influence that unconscious mental processes have on the way a person feels, thinks and behaves and, above all, on the defensive processes that actively keep them unconscious (Bowlby, 1988a, 1988b).

The British psychoanalyst, Peter Hildebrand (1995) argued that, far too uncritically and for far too long, Freud and other psychoanalytic theorists accepted a hypothesis of continuous physical and psychosocial development from birth to young adulthood, followed by a long refractory period during mid-life and, then, a final stage of psychic and somatic deficit and social withdrawal before death.

This conception was not only oversimplified but also detached from reality, since psychosocial and somatic development in adulthood and in late life is far more complex, multidirectional and multidimensional than had been supposed by Freud and his followers (see Chapters 5–7).

The first attempts at building empirically based, psychoanalytic theories of human development across the life cycle can be attributed to Erik Erikson (1959, 1966) and John Bowlby (1958, 1969).

Erikson was a leading American developmental psychologist and psychoanalyst; he was born in Germany to a Danish-Jewish mother who fled Copenhagen when she discovered that she was pregnant out of wedlock. Erikson became widely respected and quoted across a wide range of disciplines. His theory on psychosocial development as an open-ended task and his concept of *identity crisis* (Erikson, 1963, 1971) has inspired several generations of professionals, patients and public.

Bowlby, a British psychologist, psychoanalyst and child psychiatrist, revolutionised contemporary thinking with his evolutionary-based theory of human attachment (Bowlby, 1958, 1969). He provided a comprehensive and highly coherent understanding of individual, interpersonal and group behaviour and emotion, through multiple domains across the life cycle.

In different but interrelated ways, Erikson (1959, 1966) and Bowlby (1969, 1973, 1980) constructed a life-long perspective of psychosocial development. On the one hand, Bowlby put an emphasis on the developmental influence for personality change and growth of meaningful and intimate attachment relationships from cradle to grave; on the other, Erikson on age-specific developmental tasks across what he termed the eight ages of man.

Erikson and Bowlby worked together at an interdisciplinary study group on human development, sponsored by the World Health Organization, held in Geneva between 1953 and 1956. They both seemed to function along a common wavelength, proving that psychoanalytic notions and attachment ideas do not need to be at war. In fact, Erikson tried to integrate Bowlby's insights on attachment into his own thinking:

> The baby will certainly feel secure only with one or two persons, especially at critical times. Each of the stages which I outlined coincides with an extension of the social radius of interaction: from the family to the known 'world'.
>
> Therefore, with each crisis, security has to be re-established within a wider radius, from a mother or maternal person to that of parental persons in general … to the basic family, to the neighbourhood, to the peer group, to the apprenticeship organization and so on. Each of the early securities is basic for the later one, but it has first to find its own establishment in its own social radius.
>
> Erikson, in Ezquerro (2017: 94)

According to Erikson (1966)'s theory on the stages of human development, achieving wisdom later in life involves revisiting previous crises and reviving psychosocial and group accomplishments.

Along these lines and grounded on Darwin's theory of evolution, Bowlby conceptualised attachment as both an in-built force for human connectedness and a relationship, which constitute the main basis for our sociality and is essential for both physical and emotional survival.

Attachment (like food and sexuality) is a fundamental and integral part of our existence all the way from the cradle to the grave. The strength of the instinctual component of attachment gradually allows for the establishment of meaningful, intimate and enduring relationships.

John Bowlby was no doubt a group person who conceived the human mind as a social phenomenon. Whilst he originally investigated the nature of the child's attachment to the mother within the family environment Bowlby (1951, 1953, 1958), the compass of his work included other manifestations of interpersonal attachment, and of group attachment, throughout the whole life cycle:

> Intimate attachments to other human beings are the hub around which a person's life revolves, not only when he is an infant or a toddler or a schoolchild but throughout his adolescence and his years of maturity as well, and on into old age. From these intimate attachments a person draws his strength and enjoyment of life and, through what he contributes, he gives strength and enjoyment to others.
>
> Bowlby (1980: 442)

And his standpoint on group attachment provides food for thought:

> During adolescence and adult life, a measure of attachment behaviour is commonly directed not only towards persons outside the family but also towards groups and institutions other than the family. A school or college, a work group, a religious group or a political group can come to constitute for many people a subordinate attachment 'figure', and for some people a primary attachment 'figure'. In such cases, it seems probable, the development of attachment to a group is mediated, at least initially, by attachment to a person holding a prominent position within that group.
>
> Bowlby (1969: 207)

Comprehensive and precise accounts of the genesis and development of attachment theory can be found in Bowlby (1991), Ainsworth (1991), Holmes (1993), Karen (1998), Marrone (1998), Cassidy and Shaver (2008), Van der Horst (2011), Tasca (2014), Ezquerro (2017), Marmarosh (2020), Marmarosh et al. (2020), Tasca and Maxwell (2021).

The theory has gradually been extended from its original focus on affectional bonds between infants and their parental caregivers to adult attachment across the life cycle, including couple relationships and psychotherapy (Ainsworth, 1991; Parkes, Stevenson-Hinde and Marris, 1991; Clulow, 2001; Ludlam and Nyberg, 2007; Wallin, 2007).

More recently, as we elaborate on in the second volume of this series (Ezquerro and Canete, in-press), an attachment perspective has been increasingly incorporated into group thinking. We argue that attachment inevitably goes beyond the interpersonal experience to penetrate group lives.

As outlined by Bowlby (1969) groups can come to constitute both primary and subsidiary attachments. Group attachment can apply to group processes in general (Sochos, 2015) and group psychotherapy in particular (Marmarosh, 2020).

As a concept, relational phenomenon and internalised experience, group attachment is highly relevant to everyday life, to group analysis and most other therapeutic disciplines, as well as the understanding of human evolution, organisations, intra-group and inter-group relations and personal development (Ezquerro and Canete, in-press).

Group attachment might be defined in different ways. From our perspective, it can be conceptualised as a construct that agglutinates a complex constellation of meaningful relationships, in the group and to the group, with its members and with the group-as-a-whole, with a view to maximising survival, growth and creativity (Ezquerro, 2019c).

Indeed, in the early days, most of the specialist literature concentrated on primary attachments. However, there has been an increasing interest in secondary and other subsidiary attachments. Some authors have looked at attachment theory from a systemic perspective, spelling out the reciprocal and hierarchical qualities of attachment relationships.

Antonucci (1986) described an interesting *convoy model* with three circles or group constellations of socially supportive networks, which echoes some of Erikson's formulations:

- the inner circle represents the closest and most important relationships; usually (but not always) these are attachments with parents, siblings, spouse and children;
- the middle circle represents relationships that are less close but still significantly close; these attachments are likely to be with other relatives and friends with whom one has multi-level relationships;
- the third circle is conceptualised as including people with whom one has special social or professional connections, such as colleagues and managers; these attachments are role-specific and singular, as well as important and potentially influential, but depend on temporary situations or networks and are likely to be terminated if such contexts change.

The convoy model acknowledges the power of primary attachments with highly significant others and with groups and aims to integrate these with other significant interpersonal and group experiences that people have over time, including relationships with friends, colleagues and institutions. These attachments are fundamental for the development of resilience and other capacities which help a person recover from adversity and meet new challenges during the course of life.

The systemic concept of *asymmetrical reciprocity* (Robinson, 1980) can be useful for the understanding of the power differential in parent–child relationships. This asymmetry has a counterpart in therapist–patient relationships, as well as in the complex relations that take place within education, work and other organisational group contexts. In all these situations, there are power differentials between teachers and pupils, supervisors and supervisees, managers and members and so on.

Bearing in mind the huge relevance of group attachment in the constantly evolving contexts of human group lives, we shall now examine some key aspects of psychosocial and peer group development from infancy all the way into old age.

In the following sections and chapters, we will argue that personal identity and development are intrinsic to the group process, reflected in it and enhanced by it. Whilst thoroughly exploring the interface and mutual influences between members personal growth and the development of the group itself, we shall not specifically deal with the traditional developmental phases in a group's life, as described in the literature: forming, storming, norming, performing and adjourning, which have been largely proposed as sequential stages (Tuckman, 1965).

No doubt, these stances invite to think about group development. However, their applicability is rather limited to some small closed-group configurations. Furthermore, boundaries between such phenomena are less sequential and more dynamic than originally thought. A group, like an individual, does not really graduate once and for all from any of the above developmental phases.

Real life is in fact more complex than that, as highlighted by complexity science (Stacey, 2001; Maldonado, 2005), a theme upon which we elaborate elsewhere (Ezquerro and Canete, in-press). In this chapter, we will look into continuities and discontinuities, fluctuations, changes and constancies, as well as overlaps and other vicissitudes, across life-span developmental paths. Human development is an open-ended task, in a changing relational context with an ever-evolving environment.

Psychosocial and peer group development from cradle to grave

Human development is complex, multifaceted and multidirectional. Early developmentalists tended to focus on infancy, childhood and adolescence, largely to the exclusion of other periods in the life-span.

This has changed; it is now largely accepted that, in different ways, growth and change can occur from the cradle to the grave. In connection with that, contemporary developmentalists have increasingly given weight to the entire life cycle.

Baltes et al. (2006) pointed out that there are both gains and losses within each developmental stage. With age, certain capabilities become more refined and sophisticated, whilst others involve a loss of skill and capacity.

In addition, there are shifts in how people invest their resources (in terms of motivation, energy and time) at different points in their lives. Recurring phenomena across the life-span, such as a reactivation of attachment needs, should not be regarded as regression.

It is beyond the scope of this section to cover all aspects of life-span development. Our primary focus is on psychosocial, peer group and group attachment development.

Infancy and childhood

There is a long tradition of systematic studies showing that infants are socially responsive from birth onward (Bowlby, 1958, 1969; Rutter, 1980; Stern, 1998, 2006; Music, 2014; Ezquerro 2017). They can recognise their mother's smell within hours and her voice within days and can also smile and keep a firm grasp with their hands within weeks. These responses facilitate the formation of an attachment relationship with the mother, father and other significant adults providing care, protection, warmth and affection.

In their study of early group formation in childhood, Grunebaum and Solomon (1980, 1982) postulated that, although influenced by their early attachments, infants' relationships with their siblings and peers can develop quite autonomously and follow a different pathway of psychosocial development – something that can be seen as early as six months.

By this age, babies show social reciprocity and delight in the interactions with their parents or primary attachment figures; they also begin to show surprise at their own mirror image and a rudimentary awareness of other babies. By the end of the first year of life, this incipient interest in peers clearly becomes a source of enjoyment (Trevarthen, 2005).

The development of mutuality is facilitated by the process of mimicking facial expressions – something that has been described as *imitative mirroring* (Atkins, 1983). Through these interchanges, the capacity to monitor reciprocity grows steadily alongside the development of self-recognition and awareness of peers, which unfolds through stages between six and twenty-four months.

By this age, children show a desire to share in more complex interactions such as social games, as well as the higher levels of collaboration that are required to construct joint projects; a sense of "we" begins to emerge (Tomasello, 2009). It is quite remarkable that infants and toddlers behave in a characteristic way towards their *homologues* (Pines, 1998).

In a detailed description of babies' reactions to the presence of other babies, aged eight to ten months, Atkins (1983) observed the fascinating lure that they show for one another. This manifested itself through reciprocated gratifying smiles, mutual interest in each other and in the other's activities, and even actions apparently directed towards the other.

These interactions can be interpreted in terms of the increasing awareness that infants have of their similarities to each other. No doubt, children's self-awareness is greatly enhanced through their exchanges with their homo-logues. This process has been described as *twinship mirroring* (Pines, 1998). Infants and toddlers tend to be attracted by perceptual resemblances, sensing that the other is like oneself.

Atkins (1983) concluded that little ones like other little ones (even strangers) even more than they like adults. The other is distinct, yet like oneself, and so children become aware of being themselves through both the resemblance and differentiation from other children: the seed of peer group life.

Early peer group relationships generate a unique developmental sequence and predict future social competence (Vandell and Mueller, 1980).

Play is the primary mode of interaction; it evolves from parallel play, through associative play, to cooperative play. Parallel play appears to function as a transitional bridge from solitary to group activities. Cooperative play increases significantly during the fourth year of life (Robinson et al., 2003).

Remarkably, Piaget (1953) observed children through the process of group formation. He formulated the concept of *collective monologue* for situations in which children play in close proximity and talk enthusiastically, even taking turns in vocalising, but the content of their speech does not correlate with each other (see Chapter 2).

Sometimes adolescent groups, even adult groups, go through phases of collective monologue too!

Cooperative group behaviour is deeply rooted in the make-up of the hu-man species (Axelrod and Hamilton, 1981). In evolutionary terms, a hypoth-esis of *group selection* has been proposed to explain cooperation and altruism towards non-kin members (Bowles, 2006, 2009).

This is the group equivalent to natural selection: over many hundred-thousand years, human groups with more cooperative and altruistic members had a greater chance of survival (Cortina and Liotti, 2010). And this distinct characteristic became part of our genetic endowment.

In connection with that, it is possible to observe toddlers displaying spon-taneous altruistic behaviour toward others as early as eighteen months, with-out seeking any apparent reward. At twenty-four months, they sometimes comfort others or show concern for them. In order to do this, they need to have some awareness of the emotional states of others (Warneken and Tomasello, 2006).

During the pre-school years, this incipient form of *mentalisation* gradually grows into a more sophisticated understanding of how others think and feel. As language develops, shared intentionality and perspective-taking abilities take a huge step forward. This promotes the development of empathy, which may in turn lead to an increase in cooperative and caring behaviours (Vaish, Carpenter and Tomasello, 2009).

Nota bene, Harlow (1971) observed that peer attachment behaviour and co-operative play in children appear before aggressive behaviour. This indicates that aggression can be socialised through play in the context of a peer group (see Chapter 2).

Summing up, infants show evidence of group orientation during the second half of the first year of life, whilst a more distinct sense of peer group is gradually established during the second and third year; during this period toddlers are increasingly more likely to socially imitate peers than adults (Ryalls, Gull and Ryalls, 2000).

From the age of three years, children show an increasingly active social group life. They begin to organise themselves in more structured group formations at the age of four or five. By the ages of six and seven, it is possible to see more stable groups in which increasingly advanced forms of sharing and social learning can take place, including a sense of fairness (Banny et al., 2011).

By late childhood, social cooperation has become the norm, with children being observed to engage in various forms of peer group activities over 90% of the time in the school playground. Conflicts may become more apparent between the authority of parents and teachers, on the one hand, and the new principles, norms and culture set by the group, on the other (Rubin et al., 2015).

The experience of peer group life in pre-adolescence is, more often than not, positive and fulfilling. However, bullying and scapegoating may generate a devastating feeling of isolation. Being left alone and unaided by other group members can be particularly difficult to handle (Ezquerro, 1995, 1997, 2017).

In addition, pre-adolescents need their own time and space for privacy and freedom from group exposure, which has to be integrated with an increasingly powerful drive for intimate group association.

Adolescence

Bowlby (1969, 1988a) considered that, in adolescence, the excursions and explorations from the primary attachment figures of childhood become longer in time and space.

He also pointed out that *group attachment* is specifically sought in this period. Adolescent personality development has a wider, deeper and stronger psychosocial and group nature than in children.

According to Harris (1995, 2009) and Griffin (2014), the peer group becomes essential to the adolescent's identity and wellbeing, more than in any other stage in the life cycle. On a daily basis, teenagers are influenced considerably more by peers than by adults; they are highly susceptible to the influence of their peer group in ways that are more powerful than what adults usually think of as peer group pressure. This indicates that peer group attachment is a basic component of adolescent development.

Nevertheless, recent research indicates that those adolescents who also develop satisfactory attachment relationships with a significant adult role-model (not necessarily parental) are more successful than their peers in coping with the challenges and stresses of life (Csikszentmihalyi, 2021). Thus, for optimal adolescent development, it is necessary to combine attachment with adults and peer group attachment.

Indeed, adolescent development shows broad individual variations, according to ages, stages and cultures. It is useful to differentiate early, middle and late sub-phases within adolescence (see Chapter 3).

Action is often a key note, predominantly during the early and middle subphases, not only in the teenagers themselves but also in those surrounding them, particularly those responsible for their care. Because of this pressure for action, the provision of group space for thinking and reflection is critical for adolescents, their parents and care professionals.

Authority during this life period becomes a key issue for parents and society, as well as for adolescents who need to develop and exercise a growing sense of authority that they can recognise as their own (Bruggen, 2006).

Quite often, when adolescents overstep boundaries, they may not find an authoritative adult to relate to but one who is authoritarian, angrily expressing moral outrage and external prohibition. This may prevent (or delay) the development of age-appropriate inhibitory mechanisms and self-regulation – a sense of *inner* authority.

A number of studies (Griffin, 2014; Csikszentmihalyi, 2021) have shown that adolescence is the second period of heightened brain plasticity, similar to the first three years of life. This makes adolescence not only a time of resilience and opportunity, but also a really vulnerable time; sharp fluctuations are intrinsic to it and must be understood on their own terms, not through the *lenses* of childhood or adulthood.

Teenagers have a tendency to form a group of friends with other teenagers who resemble themselves in terms of prosocial, antisocial or delinquent behaviour (Hafen et al., 2011).

They rapidly develop a capacity to connect to a peer group they feel attracted to in playful, adventurous, dramatic and, sometimes, dangerous ways. The intensity of these interactions is not present in children's groups and is not often repeated in adult groups. Loyalty and faithfulness within an adolescent peer group constitute a remarkable phenomenon (Frankel, 1998).

Adolescent peer groups offer closeness, mutual support, exploration of related conflicts, comparison and validation of personal and sexual identity and choices, and experimentation with social roles. Comparing themselves to their peers helps teenagers, particularly in late adolescence, to clarify and develop their own identities, as well as to appraise their talents and performance.

More often than not, this is a positive and growth-engendering experience. But things can go wrong: some adolescents run away from home, participate in city street gangs or religious cults, abuse increasingly harmful drugs in groups and, in some cases, become involved in self-harming or parasuicidal behaviour and may end up killing themselves.

Summing up, adolescents have a profound necessity to connect with a larger circle of meaning and relationships, as well as with a cultural and political environment. It is often said that adolescence begins with *biology* and ends with *society*. For this task to be completed successfully, a balance between individual and group attachment (including a satisfactory peer group life) is fundamental. In this way, the adolescent can gradually face the complexities of adulthood more confidently.

Emerging, young or early adulthood

Development cannot be hurried along. The road to adulthood has become increasingly complex, stressful and long-winded, due to changes in society that can be traced back to the 1960s, particularly in developed countries. Nowadays, more and more people in their twenties consider themselves to be neither adolescents nor adults, and the concept of emerging adulthood as a distinct developmental stage has been proposed (Arnett, 2015).

This is a time of more pointed personal and group identity exploration and construction, with distinct developmental, intrapsychic and psychosocial challenges (see Chapter 4). Emerging adults have increasing responsibilities, clearer identities and deeper explorations than adolescents; but they are not yet constrained by definite adult-role requirements in society.

Having said that, the characteristics of this period are neither uniform nor universal: there are different emerging adulthoods with a broad range of possible trajectories that vary significantly, depending on national, cultural, socioeconomic, personal and political context. In this chapter, and throughout the book, we shall use the terms emerging, young or early adults more or less interchangeably.

Young adults are more ready for intimacy than adolescents and develop a greater capacity to commit themselves to group affiliations and partnerships.

Erikson (1963, 1971) dealt thoroughly with this age group. In his theory, most emerging adults experience a dichotomy between *intimacy* and *isolation*, as they try to achieve a stable sense of personal identity whilst experiencing a growing desire to share their personal life with other people. A crisis might arise and, without intimacy, early adults may suffer from isolation and loneliness.

Another important concept related to close human connections is *self-expansion* (Aron et al., 2005). This is a notion that particularly applies to young adults as they enlarge and deepen their experiences, resources and understanding through the development of intimacy with friends, partners and groups.

Intimacy progresses from attraction to a close connection to ongoing commitment and breaks the isolation caused by too much self-focus. Intimacy and self-expansion are important ingredients for the healthy development of the human psyche.

Work on sexuality, which was prominent in adolescence, continues unfolding during early adulthood, a period when sexual choices and commitments become more definite and certain.

In contrast to adolescent love, which tends to be tentative and transient, love in young adulthood involves a deeper level of intimacy and is more identity focussed. In terms of work experiences, emerging adults increasingly concentrate on laying the ground for a fulfilling adult occupation, as well as exploring professional and group identity (Morgan, 2013; Arnett, 2014).

We discussed earlier that, in terms of group configurations, children and adolescents are largely involved in a school-based peer group culture. This culture evolves over time.

Undeniably, peer group involvement continues to be prominent in emerging adults; however, society and its multiple contexts become increasingly relevant to them, as they explore a wider and deeper range of group connections with work and institutions. This goes beyond the peer group experience and may include other configurations, including social, leisure, occupational, religious and political groups.

The potential of young adults is still huge and their array of choices about how to live, work and love is greater than it has ever been before and possibly greater than it will ever be again – which makes this life stage remarkably lively and intense.

There is a growing interest during young adulthood in large-group dynamics, which can be seen as a search for meaning in local and global political events. Politics leads to a discovery of one's own take on the world; what moves the psyche finds expression in political choices. Emerging adulthood is a fascinating time to tune into what has been described in the literature as the political development of the person (Samuels, 1993), and as the birth of a political self (Gaudilliere, 2021).

Adulthood

According to Earl Hopper (2000), *adult maturity* must include the development of the willingness and ability to take on the role and status of citizen. Unavoidably, this is also a group phenomenon in that people cannot take such positions if they have not ensured that citizenship is available, which is a political process.

Blumer (1969) argued that *full* adult status requires the development of *intimate citizenship*. This concept includes a plurality of public discourses and stories about how to live interpersonal and group lives in an increasingly complex world where we are confronted by an escalating series of choices and difficulties around different intimacies (see Chapter 5).

Intimate citizenship is both a personal and group notion which Blumer explored further, as he examined the development of rights, obligations, recognitions and respect around the most intimate spheres of life.

Who to live with, how to raise children, how to handle one's body, how to relate as gendered beings and how such arrangements are bound up with membership of different and complex groups and communities, bringing their own inevitable tensions and splits?

Thus, differences and conflict are ubiquitous and the *mature* citizen has to learn creative ways for dealing with them.

Adults come to serve multiple roles in multiple relationships, in a myriad of group contexts; typically more than in any other stage in the life cycle. They have to face and navigate through a striking diversity of beliefs, values, knowledge, opinions and situations. This can be an exhausting experience.

In the modern (or post-modern) world, if there is a unifying developmental theme and a key developmental task in adulthood, these might have to consist of dealing with diversity in its most comprehensive sense (Berger, 2008).

In the psychoanalytic tradition, by and large, love and work are two cornerstones of adult human life (Freud, 1905b; Garland, 2010). This entails a fundamentally developed capacity for intimacy, responsibility and autonomy, as well as an ability for making one's own decisions, tolerating uncertainty and not knowing and continuing further development as social beings.

Another hallmark of adulthood is that society expects adult citizens to enter long-term responsibilities, commitments and obligations, which will probably set them on paths that resist drastic changes in trajectory.

Having said that, in adulthood, it is also important not to lose some of the fluidity and developmental strengths of childhood, adolescence and emerging adulthood: the curiosity to engage with the world and a sense of playfulness, linked to the aptitude for being creative and developing new ideas (Lanyado and Horne, 2009).

Irrespective of any diagnosis and developmental tasks that adults might face, a common pathway is that they must tap into and identify some passions, experience the joy that comes with expressing them and have opportunities to share this joy with others (Feldman, 2018).

There must be a conscious effort to cultivate and integrate not just the logics of the mind, but also the desires of the heart.

This is what ultimately leads to a sense of balance and satisfaction in life, a developmental goal that applies to the whole life cycle but takes full dimension in adulthood.

Late-middle age

Full adult status is precious; it is linked to the concept of mastery, of having control of your life, of reaching the peak of skill and productivity, of being in your prime! Losing such a status, being no longer on the centre stage of life and facing old age can be painful. It does not happen overnight, but it is part of a life-changing process within which retirement is typically a major constituent.

Therefore, there might be merit in thinking about late-middle age as another critical period in the life cycle, a time of real or anticipated loss, of reworking personal and group identity and attachment, after mastery of adulthood but before settling into the winter of life.

Retirement tends to be seen as a negative notion based on what people are not doing, namely, that they are not working (Denton and Spencer, 2009).

However, this biased attitude must be put into question. In recent decades, retirement has increasingly been perceived as an opportunity for life review and change, for new beginnings and revised identities, including group identity.

Since there is no generally accepted definition of the term *retirement*, Hershenson (2016) proposed focusing on *statuses* and developmental tasks, to better understand late-middle age with a view to making successful adjustments.

An important developmental task for late-middle-aged adults is to create space for working through their losses, including loss of statuses, of parental and other attachment figures, declining intellectual and economic productivity and increasing risk of illness, as well as mourning for that which has not been achieved during mastery of adulthood (see Chapter 6).

In addition, they need to renegotiate and sort out hopes, expectations and goals for the new challenges ahead, and to deal with intergenerational issues and a heightened awareness of their own mortality.

Hildebrand (1995) compared the characteristics of late-middle-aged people with those in the age range of thirty-five to fifty-four. He found that the latter, particularly men, actively seek mastery; they are invested in production and competition; they strive to acquire control over the resources upon which their security and the security of their dependents are based; they tend to give priority to personal agency over community.

In contrast, people over fifty-five are more diffusely sensual and less interested in competition; they tend to reverse the priorities of younger adults and orient themselves towards community rather than personal agency.

From a more specific group perspective, Haslam, Steffens et al. (2019) suggested that, when it comes to preparing for, going through and recovering from retirement, it is essential to attend to group-identity and group-attachment processes that underpin successful adjustment. They emphasised that maintaining some existing group memberships supports a sense of self-continuity and can be a platform for new group identities and attachments.

Indeed, late-middle age is another opportunity to change and to develop new or dormant aspects of oneself, as well as a chance to experience a new freedom to do things for the simple sake of enjoyment and pleasure. In a number of group contexts, late-middle-aged individuals bring a wealth of knowledge, experience and wisdom that can be pooled in dealing with universal themes and problems, to enrich their lives and the lives of others, contributing to society and to future generations (see Chapter 6).

In this sense, Erikson's (1959, 1966) concept of *generativity*, of making one's mark on the world through creative and nurturing processes that will outlast the person, contributing to the life of future generations, seems particularly relevant to the late-middle-aged, as they experience a stronger wish to leave a legacy behind.

Through becoming involved in community groups and organisations and other forms of potential generativity, late-middle-aged adults can develop a sense of transcendence. Failure to do this may lead to feeling useless, disconnected or stagnated.

Despite the heightened vulnerability of this period, and within its many individual variations, the majority of late-middle-aged people manage to get on successfully with the developmental tasks inherent in this life stage. This helps them start to negotiate the challenges of late life in reasonably good shape (Penberthy and Penberthy, 2020).

Old age

Erikson (1966) asserted that personality changes may occur in old age as a result of new psychosocial challenges.

In his view, those who succeed experience a sense of satisfaction and accomplishment, which he termed *integrity*. These people typically feel they have realised and fulfilled many of the possibilities that came their way in life.

In contrast, other individuals look back on their lives with regret, as they may have missed important opportunities and may not have achieved their targets. These people can become anxious, angry, depressed or despondent over what they have done or failed to do with their lives; in short, they *despair*.

In society, there is a broad range of prejudices and discrimination directed at older people. This has been conceptualised under the term *ageism* (Butler, 1975) and has been considered a *psychosocial disease*, particularly in our era of rapid social and technological changes (Bengtson and Whittington, 2014).

As we are learning more about neurological and psychosocial development, we are in a better position to contest ageism.

Old age should be considered an integral part of life, with new developmental pressures, facing growth in some areas and decline in others. Chronological age alone cannot define this life stage and, in assessing older adults, it is necessary to take into account their individual and group characteristics; their physical and psychosocial well-being; their *functional age* (see Chapter 7).

The increasingly obvious prospect of one's own death usually triggers the natural process of life review, through which older adults can gain new insights into earlier relational and group contexts and function more effectively in the present.

Optimally, they may come to terms with the past and even resolve problems and conflicts they had previously struggled with, which would help them face later life with greater serenity (Latorre et al., 2015).

A number of authors have examined the developmental tasks of old age; we have selected a few:

- Peck (1968) suggested that some *redefinition of self* is required after the loss of work roles, as well as the development of *ego transcendence* to overcome preoccupation with oblivion.

- Neugarten (1977) highlighted the need to accommodate multiple declines, to review the past and to gaze into the future, including the trajectory to death, with dignity and acceptance.
- Waddell (2007) stressed the task of working through many losses and coming to terms with the forthcoming end of one's existence, whilst keeping connected with the outside world.

Research on this life stage is complex, as individual characteristics and levels of involvement vary significantly. Dementia and decline in the sense organs can have a major impact on psychosocial well-being as well as on group participation and attachment, since the senses serve as links between the individual and the external world.

Feldman (2018) looked into how different people tried to cope with ageing in different ways. Some try to continue to be as involved with the world as they were before, which might not be realistic; others disengage and may become too withdrawn; a third group pursue a middle-of-the-road approach.

From an existential perspective, Simone de Beauvoir (1970) stated that, in old age, there is only one solution and this is to go on pursuing ends that give meaning to human existence, such as dedication to other people, groups or causes and to social, political, intellectual or creative work, since life can only have value as long as one attributes value to the lives of others.

Group-analytic psychotherapy across the life cycle

From its inception in 1971, the Institute of Group Analysis IGA has offered a comprehensive four-year training in adult group psychotherapy. In order to qualify as an IGA group analyst, it is necessary to do a one-year introductory course followed by a three-year qualifying course. Apart from the requirements of academic seminars, written dissertations and personal group therapy, trainees have to conduct on their own, under supervision, a heterogeneous and slow-open mixed group with adults who are strangers to each other.

Not long ago, the IGA added a requirement that trainees must run a second training group. This provides opportunities for choosing one amongst a number of special interest groups (homogeneous or heterogeneous), including psychosis, survivors and perpetrators of sexual abuse, addictions, personality disorders, single sex, etc. This group can be conducted with a co-therapist and does not necessarily have to be with adults.

Thus, the second group opens a door for other age groups, such as children, adolescents, young adults, the late-middle-aged and older adults. However, an overwhelming majority of trainees have opted for special interest groups with adults.

The IGA librarian helped us with our thorough research on the written work of group analysts, as part of their training at the institute, but we could only find three clinical dissertations on group psychotherapy with adolescents and one with young adults; none with children, the late-middle-aged or older adults.

On the above evidence, we may say that the lack of a life-span developmental perspective in group-analytic thinking, training and clinical practice is a matter of concern. We shall now endeavour to redress or, at least, address this. We will put a greater emphasis on group psychotherapy with the age groups that have been most neglected.

Group psychotherapy with children

Various forms of child group psychotherapy have been used since the 1910s (see Chapter 2).

In short, it has proved to be growth-engendering, as well as a beneficial and cost-effective form of treatment for children, at least from the age of four years. The positive changes more widely reported include improved self-esteem, reality testing and social skills, as well as the development of self-awareness and empathy (Lanyado and Horne, 2009; Haen and Aronson, 2017; Shechtman, 2014, 2017).

Slavson (1943) originally described some of the processes through which children gradually become attached to a therapy group and develop *resonant empathy*. Interestingly, Foulkes (1977) and most group analysts have made therapeutic use of *resonance* in adult groups.

According to Slavson (1978), once a reasonably secure attachment to the group is established, the rapidity of the therapeutic progress in children can sometimes be quite astonishing, over and above the pace of change in adult groups. He further argued that group psychotherapy with children is less difficult, less protracted and the outcomes are more basic and more lasting than with adults, because the *neurotic* engrams have not been as yet crystalised and so can be altered more easily.

James Anthony (1965), a founding member of the Group Analytic Society and distinguished child psychiatrist, described a mixed therapy group for kindergarten children, aged four to six, in which play and activity supplemented language to a large extent.

Anthony observed that, by the age of four, most children have developed an ability to share symbolic meanings with other children through *social pretence*. They can spontaneously take on complementary roles which, other than their symbolic function, have no correspondence with their real-life circumstances and identities.

Play is a normal activity through which younger children can have a more rapid access to group formation. Through the play characters, children can create symbolic dialogues. Particularly in younger children, play can be the therapeutic equivalent of free association in adults.

There is empirical evidence that psychodynamic group therapy, including group-analytic psychotherapy, can help children to overcome egocentricity, learn delaying gratification, manage difficult feelings, develop symbolic thinking and explore new values, as well as to develop creativity, empathy, altruism and pro-social behaviour (Dwivedi, 1998; Lanyado and Horne, 2009; Haen and Aronson, 2017; Ezquerro, 1995, 1997, 2017; Shechtman, 2014, 2017; Marmarosh, 2020).

In the 1970s, child group therapy became an accepted and well-established form of treatment in the (British) NHS (Farrell, 1984). However, despite the blueprint left by Anthony (1965) about how group-analytic therapy with children might develop, group analysis has been largely unconcerned with psychosocial and peer group development in children, let alone with child group psychotherapy.

Out of the forty-five emblematic annual Foulkes' lectures delivered in the UK up to the year 2022, only one has devoted itself to therapeutic group work with children. That speaks for itself. The guest speaker was Claude Pigott, a French psychoanalyst, in 1989. According to him, children talk with their bodies as well as with speech and have the gift of condensing a whole situation down to its basics (Pigott, 1990).

The number of group analysts working with children and writing about it pales into insignificance, when compared with the number of group analysts working with adults and putting their experience on paper!

Amongst this minority, the general consensus is that child group therapists must provide more structure to the sessions than occurs in adult groups. It is important to encourage children to form relationships, develop a language of feelings and accept group norms with a view to co-constructing a secure base (see Chapter 2). Fostering peer relationships is an important part of child group psychotherapy.

It is generally accepted that co-therapy is desirable in children's groups, due to their high level of activity, which demands keeping an eye on all the moves, whilst preserving an analytic mode. The presence of two co-therapists, flexibly sharing both roles (looking after the safety of the group and creating thinking space), can enhance the group's therapeutic potential.

In addition, two co-therapists may symbolically represent a *parental couple* working together, a positive experience that some of the children may not have had before but that they can now internalise.

In groups with adults, who are compelled to express themselves in words, activity tends to be seen as a form of acting out and inactivity as a potential form of reflection.

In contrast to that, in groups with children, activity is part of their ordinary language and inactivity may represent a state of resistance. In children's groups there is far less verbal interpretation than in adult groups, but play and non-verbal narratives can be interpreted verbally to the child.

Play, activity and movement in the room are some of the key differences between children and adults in groups, which may partly explain why group analysts have shied away from child group therapy. Children are not supposed to sit on their chairs around a circle for ninety minutes, as adults do. The group–analytic approach focuses on verbal expression as the preferred mode of communication.

In this respect, Anthony (1965) pointed out that the main technical problem in child group psychotherapy consists not so much in interpreting activity, but in converting it into speech. In order to achieve that, group therapists need to develop a capacity to talk to children; this entails effort and practice.

It is more difficult to talk therapeutically to children than to adults because it requires a radical change in one's normal talking habits. To establish a two-way communicative process with children may require that therapists learn to speak the language of the child, which is simple, brief, direct and concrete. According to Anthony (1965), it defies artful dissimulation and circumlocution and attempts to say what it means.

In addition, therapists must become interested in what the child has to say, which may represent an unusual viewpoint of the world, seen through innocent eyes.

Above all, successful talking with children implies reciprocal communication. Anthony further observed that children usually admit the right sort of adults in, and open the door to their magical world of childhood to them.

It is vital that therapists make themselves conversant with early psychosocial and peer group development before running psychotherapy groups with children. It would be a huge mistake to generalise knowledge attained from running adult groups to children's groups because children have unique developmental needs and operate differently from how adults do.

Group psychotherapy with children also differs from that of adults in the quality and quantity of *dynamic administration*. This is akin to a parenting function, as it involves setting up the group, dealing with issues of time and space, handling boundary issues and so on.

In view of the strong tendency towards action, groups for children require even more careful advanced planning than for adults, as well as special attention to boundary activities and incidents that may impinge on the group processes (Woods, 1993; Behr and Hearst, 2005).

In connection with that, therapists conducting psychotherapy groups with children should expect to experience considerable amounts of positive and negative counter-transference feelings in quick sequence. Special attention should be paid to this, so as not to inadvertently project these feelings onto the children.

Counter-transference is also an especially relevant issue in groups with adolescents, as we will show below.

Group psychotherapy with adolescents

Unlike children, adolescents are wordy and worldly enough to perceive with reasonable accuracy the inconsistencies between what adults say they think and how they act. Ambivalence towards adults is not an unusual feature in the adolescent mind.

Group therapists (including group analysts) need to be profusely conversant with adolescent developmental processes and to understand their own counter-transference reactions in order to disentangle what belongs to them and what to the adolescent. They have to be persuasively *authoritative* and avoid superior *authoritarian* attitudes (see Chapter 3).

Teenagers have a remarkable built-in capacity for resilience. This can be observed in their exceptional ability to pick up something positive in negative events and overcome crises. Some studies (Marmarosh et al., 2020; Csikszentmihalyi, 2021) have found that teens fully recover from bad moods in about half the time it takes adults to do so, of course, with all the pros and cons inherent in that.

Mood fluctuations are a hallmark of adolescence; in this life stage, resilience and vulnerability can be two sides of the same coin. Therapists need to bear these oscillations in mind when they conduct groups with adolescents, particularly with those who may struggle to engage therapeutically.

Having said that, another important dimension in adolescence is the impact of collaborating and working therapeutically with peers in groups, which is distinctly stronger than in childhood and other life stages. The power of peer group attachment in the adolescent's mind makes group psychotherapy, more often than not, the treatment of choice for this population (Dies, 2000; Shechtman, 2014, 2017; Ezquerro, 2017, 2019b).

John Evans (1998, 2000) developed a modified group-analytic approach for adolescents, which he termed *active-analytic* group therapy. He argued that the type of purely reflective stance considered appropriate for grown-ups is simply not workable for adolescents, who are neither as articulate nor as intellectually defensive as adults. His central thesis is a pragmatic one: adolescents have to be engaged with tactics that recognise their developmental level and match their active social behaviour.

Evans (1998) maintained that a rigid non-directive approach can sometimes lead to a sort of aimless or manic distractibility, even a breakdown of group function. In his experience, the group conductor must be proactively responsive and prepared to change tack at a moment's notice, anticipating possible impulsive acts or supporting an isolated teenager.

As with children, the use of appropriate language with this population, particularly early adolescents, is crucial. When therapists use words or expressions with several layers of meaning, they can create confusion and increase tension, preventing reflection in the adolescent (Evans, 2000).

Attempting to link the here-and-now with a member's past in only one go, not realising that it may be too complex for the adolescent to grasp the connection, could make an accurate interpretation useless or counterproductive.

In adolescent groups, checking with members if a comment makes sense, and welcoming their corrections or clarifications, is a good way of contributing to the creation of a culture that can make dialogue and mutual understanding an intrinsic part of the therapeutic process.

Interventions have to be delivered flexibly. A respectful silence, or a brief appreciative acknowledgement in the face of an angry adolescent's verbal challenge, might be equivalent to a powerful interpretation. Conversely, verbal formulations may rightly be valued for their effort and concern, as much as for their acuity and depth (see Chapter 3).

As with children, group-analytic psychotherapy with adolescents, especially with the younger ones, requires more careful planning than for adult groups in terms of *dynamic administration*, since boundary incidents are commonplace. Teenagers may bring strange objects, display odd non-verbal language or keep deliberately silent at times.

Furthermore, themes of conversation tend to change rapidly, jumping from topic to topic, and non-verbal expressions often predominate. According to Billow (2004), therapists need stamina, patience and containment, to engage adolescents at both symbolic and bonding levels and promote group attachment. In many situations, holding the group emotionally is a central part of the therapy.

The handling of authority is a crucial part of group psychotherapy with adolescents (Bruggen, 1979, 2006; Ezquerro, 2017, 2019b). They have a growing ability to project their incipient and fragile sense of personal authority onto their peer group, a process through which they can develop their own views and status.

Teenagers recognise parts of themselves more easily, when they project them onto their peers in a group situation. The authority of the peer group can help them regulate the distance *from*, and *to*, the authority of parents and other adults, as well as explore new attachment relationships.

Working with adolescents in groups is usually more challenging than working with adults but perseverance pays off.

Group psychotherapy with young adults

There are overlaps between late adolescence and early or emerging adulthood. In groups with young adults, it is not infrequent to have elements of the casualness and spontaneity of adolescent groups, whilst also a more reflective and deeper level of disclosure and intimacy. There are less boundary issues than in adolescent groups but more than in adult groups (see Chapters 3–5).

The predominant culture in young adults' groups is one in which there is a mix of cautiousness and urgency. This can manifest itself through common themes: difficulties with their parents and ambivalence about couple relationships, as well as uncertainty about adopting a clear direction in their lives and consolidating their identity.

In terms of group culture, mutual trust and peer group attachment can develop quite rapidly. Developing a caring concern toward other group members is a therapeutic experience in its own right, which helps emerging adults take responsibility for themselves.

In contrast to groups with full grown-ups, in groups for young adults, the conductor must accept a leadership role that extends beyond the early phases of therapy. As the group matures, through reliance on its own strength, it replaces the authority of the leader with the authority of the group.

Young adults are more confident than adolescents to exercise their own authority. However, Johansson and Werbart (2009) found that those with greater negative past experiences need a more active involvement of the therapist in the here-and-now group sessions.

The road to adulthood has become increasingly convoluted in recent decades, affecting the mental health of a large proportion of young or emerging adults who are more vulnerable emotionally than full adults. Despite this, group analysts have paid little specific attention to this age group.

This stage is when most people accumulate almost all of their formal education, meet their future partners and the friends they will keep, and start on the careers that they will stay with for many years. It is also a period when adventures, travels and relationships are embarked on with an abandon that probably will not happen again (see Chapter 4).

From a group-attachment perspective, emerging adults deserve that society grants them a better measure of security. It is in the interests of society to look after young adults, so they become productive contributing members, making the most of their abilities for the benefit of themselves and others.

For young adults, peer group life continues to be prominent. However, they also need to explore and negotiate connections to, and memberships of, more complex group structures. As they engage with the uncertainty and changes of emerging adult life, they may become vulnerable to anxieties related to personal, professional and group identities.

Whilst a measure of group attachment is a *sine qua non* for optimal development in this and other life stages, for young adults involved in a love relationship, the partner is usually the main confidant and attachment figure.

Age-homogeneous therapy groups might be particularly indicated for some young adults struggling with developmental tasks, whilst other people of the same age may fit in better within standard adult groups.

Group psychotherapy with adults

Completing education, leaving home, finding a stable job, marrying and becoming parents are no longer the main criteria used in determining adulthood. The development of a capacity to experience oneself as a coherent whole person, within diverse interpersonal and group contexts, is now considered the main marker of adult status. This can be better achieved through meaningful interpersonal relationships and group connections.

Adulthood and its commitments usually offer more security, stability and predictability than emerging adulthood. However, there is also some closing of doors: the end of a sense of unobstructed freedom and of wide-open possibility.

In terms of obligations and duties, adulthood typically is the most demanding period in the life cycle. Adults may equally experience satisfaction and frustration, whilst juggling multiple tasks all at once – such as developing their career, paying the mortgage, raising their children, looking after their elderly parents and so on.

This can be exhausting, particularly for working mothers in societies in which there is a culture or structure of gender inequality. Sometimes, it might be necessary to prioritise a few things at the price of dropping others, with the sense of loss and pain associated with this. Some achieve a balance; others do not.

Those who had not gotten on successfully with the developmental tasks of previous developmental stages may experience regrets and become more vulnerable to depression, stress or anxiety as they navigate new challenges.

Some stressful life events such as illness in the family, bereavement, being made redundant at work, getting divorced and other separations and relationship difficulties might put unbearable pressure on a susceptible psyche or fragile personality.

Some adults may have sustained an equilibrium over many years, carrying a dormant vulnerability within them which can now be decompensated in the face of adversity. This may require psychotherapeutic treatment; group-analytic therapy might be particularly indicated.

Schlapobersky (2016) referred to the reciprocity between personal development in adults and the development of the therapy group itself. He suggested that the developmental histories and statuses of members influence, and are influenced by, the developmental stage of the group.

Groups are growth-engendering throughout the life cycle; in adulthood they may promote the achievement of a sense of wholeness in one's personality, as well as a sense of existential completeness. Group-analytic treatment aims to supply psychosocial common sense, a sense of community to a problem by letting other people openly participate in its attempted solution (Foulkes, 1964).

The need to belong to, identify with and become attached to a group is a fundamental human motivation, as it serves survival. In many ways, psychopathology is the result of insecurity, particularly when one's needs for belongingness and group attachment go unmet.

According to Schechter et al. (2018), what is essential is not simply belonging to one or more groups, but the experience of genuine connection to and secure attachment with others. Group psychotherapy with adults addresses this in many different ways.

Adult patients discuss a broad range of problems in the psychotherapy groups they belong to. Some issues are age-specific and relate to the difficulties they have in getting on with their developmental tasks as adults; other issues, as suggested earlier, are expressions of unresolved problems or conflicts they had experienced in former developmental stages.

Please see Chapter 5 of this book for a qualitative group-analytic case study with a thorough exposition of these matters.

Group psychotherapy with the late-middle-aged

The sharp increase in life expectancy during the last fifty or so years, and the complexities of the retirement process and other major life changes, have indicated that late-middle age can now be considered a phase-specific critical period in the life-span, after mastery of middle adulthood but before settling into old age.

There is much variation in how people deal with these changes. Homogeneous psychotherapy groups for the late-middle-aged can be particularly indicated in some cases. In Chapter 6, there is a detailed description of common themes and issues presented by late-middle-aged patients in groups. These include the following:

- fear of being displaced by younger people in work roles, linked to an anxiety about being unable to cope with retirement and loss of status, identity and worth;
- concerns about declining intellectual and economic productivity, including a feeling of having less to give;
- intergenerational issues;
- apprehension about an impoverished sexuality and the impact this may have on relationships;
- anxieties about an increasing vulnerability to illness and a heightened awareness of their own mortality, particularly for those who feel they have not achieved the goals they had set for themselves.

Having said that, the majority of people in this age group agree that there comes a time when the establishment of a personal sense of safety, and of secure attachment, is more important than having power at work or their sexual drives fulfilled – no matter how dominant and motivating these may have been in earlier years.

Of course, sexuality continues to play a significant role in their lives, but manifests itself differently from previous developmental stages. In psychotherapy groups, late-middle-aged members talk about sexuality in less physical and passionate a fashion than in groups with younger adults; but there are more expressions of tenderness, affection and loyalty, whilst they continue searching for sensual growth and experience on the road to old age.

In existential terms, preoccupation with death (apart from bereavement and suicide) is not a prominent issue until late-middle age. Patients within this age group tend to talk about their own mortality and about the death of people close to them (parents, partners, friends and peers) more than in any other previous developmental stage. For some, this generates an anxiety about gradually losing their peer group and becoming isolated as a result. This theme becomes increasingly more relevant in old age.

When thinking about late-middle age in group analysis, by and large, group processes have been considered an afterthought or have not been considered at all. It should be noted that, having started the practice of group-analytic psychotherapy in the early 1940s, Foulkes and his followers neglected work with late-middle-aged and older adults until the late 1980s (Roberts and Pines, 1991).

Group Analysis: The International Journal of Group-Analytic Psychotherapy did not publish any clinical paper on group psychotherapy with this population until 1989, at the end of the third decade of its existence (Ezquerro, 1989).

Recent research studies (Haslam, Lam et al., 2018; Haslam, Steffens et al., 2019) have shown that joining new groups (including therapy groups), gaining new group identities and forming new group attachments are key to successfully working through the challenges of late-middle age, including retirement. Group lives can also become an important resource further down the track into old age.

In a well-functioning group, late-middle-aged patients can explore safely, come to grips with their developmental tasks, grieve and work through their losses and difficulties, and face later life in better shape.

Group psychotherapy with older adults

Historically, there have been substantial barriers and impediments to the delivery of psychodynamic individual and group therapy for older adults.

According to Butler (1975, 2010), this is part of an extensive culture of prejudice and discrimination against this population – something that he conceptualised under the term *ageism*.

The main obstacles to the development of group psychotherapy programmes for elderly patients come not so much from advanced age, but from negative attitudes in society and from prejudiced counter-transference in the therapists themselves.

Within psychodynamic psychotherapy, prejudice and discrimination started with Freud's (1905b) assertion that people over fifty were unsuitable for psychotherapy and no longer educable. This Freudian claim was full of ageism and resulted in widespread disregard for the treatment of older adults by psychoanalytic and group-analytic practitioners, particularly in Europe, during most of the twentieth century (see Chapters 6 and 7).

Things have improved, but there is still a long way to go. In a recent research study, Saunders et al. (2021) found that older adults continue being largely under-represented in psychotherapy and psychological treatment services, and they still suffer disproportionally within established healthcare systems.

Apart from ageism, older adults have to cope with the multiple losses that are linked to the ageing process. These may include the loss of personal capabilities, relationships, functions and roles, leading to an impoverished sense of self.

Age-homogeneous psychotherapy groups can be very beneficial for elderly patients (see Chapter 7). The therapeutic gains these patients make in such groups compare favourably with the benefits they obtain when they attend standard adult groups. The main reasons for this are:

- the culture of old-age-homogeneous groups tends to be one of mutual acceptance and encouragement, which helps members show less anxiety about disclosing inner feelings and painful memories than when they are in standard adult groups;
- older adults can comfortably share and compare themes, not only in terms of common concerns, but also in the exploration of pleasures and satisfactions that are communal to members of the same age group;
- they are more caring and protective of each other and show less confrontation or strong overt reactions to fellow members than younger adults do;
- they also put less emphasis on here-and-now issues in the group, whilst focussing more on reminiscence and life review.

Although not identical, the terms reminiscence and life review tend to be used interchangeably. Both involve evoking, pondering and describing memories; life review is more therapeutically specific in that it promotes discussing what the memory means to the patient (Liu et al., 2021). Some authors have considered reminiscence to be a part of the wider process of life review (Butler, 2010).

In a well-functioning group, appropriate grieving of losses and letting go of the past might be facilitated, promoting better engagement with the current environment. The reminiscence of previously mastered challenges can also help older adults face future uncertainties with less apprehension and reflect on the legacy they will leave behind, a sense of continuing existence in a world in which some part of themselves might remain.

In particular, in age-homogeneous groups, reminiscence may lead to a feeling of interconnectedness with others and to a powerful sense of mutuality. Moreover, it can be a source of reasonably harmonious social interaction, as older adults seek to share their previous experiences with others who know what it was like.

In Chapter 7, we will expand on this and show that issues of competitiveness, rivalry and aggression, which are generally present in the early stages of adult groups, tend to be absent or manifest themselves differently in groups with elderly patients – who do not struggle for power and control openly like younger adults, but concentrate more on the identification of common problems.

The belief amongst older patients that their problems are common to their age group facilitates disclosure, which in turn reinforces the idea that they are not unique in their misfortune. By contrast, younger adults tend to believe that their problems are more unique than they really are, which inhibits self-disclosure to some extent (see Chapter 7).

In standard adult groups, an elderly patient who is significantly older than all other members can be put at risk of being left out, or might not be involved enough in some of the issues that are more relevant to younger adults. On the other hand, the same patient would have a wider range of possibilities for dealing more directly with intergenerational issues (Moss, 2017).

Although they may feel more inhibited to reveal themselves, older adults can confront more directly the inequities of ageist bias in groups with members who are younger than them and, in so doing, become active and valued members of the group. Therapists must be prepared to contest ageism in the consulting room, in healthcare services and in the wider context of society.

We discussed earlier that chronological age alone is not the defining element of older adults' identity. It is necessary to take into account their individual characteristics and group connections, their physical, emotional and psychosocial well-being – their functional age.

Broadly speaking, it can be helpful to differentiate between the *young-old* and the *old-old*. In general terms, the old–old seem more prepared to accept death than the young-old, although they fear more the process and manner of dying.

Coming to terms with the forthcoming end of one's own existence is largely considered the main and more challenging developmental task of late life. However, despite an increasing sense of time running out, horizons shrinking and options dwindling, elderly people can keep their creativity alive to the very end.

Discussion

Groups are at the core of human existence and provide internal, interpersonal and multi-personal experiences that are necessary for healthy development and creativity, throughout the entire life cycle.

A number of psychoanalytic and group-analytic authors have referred to the nature of the relationship between the individual and the group:

- Bion (1961) unequivocally stated that the individual is a *group animal* and, for integral development, needs to be part of groups.
- Foulkes (1964) claimed that, ultimately, the individual is an *abstraction* and cannot exist outside a group.
- From a more radical perspective, Caparrós (2004) suggested that the person comes to be a *group*, holding a myriad of internalised group experiences in their mind.

Inevitably, humans are born into a group. From birth, infants start to internalise group experiences, either directly or through their interactions with their attachment figures, who have mental representations of their own previous group experiences. In our evolution as a species, the group became an adaptive social organisation in the service of survival. The group is a humanising environment *par excellence* and can also be a therapeutic and attachment space (Canete and Ezquerro, 2012).

Peer group orientation clearly shows during the second half of the first year of life. From them on, to late life, the peer group plays a fundamental role in psychosocial development, identity formation, attachment and well-being. The intensity and characteristics of peer group attachment and the incorporation of other, increasingly complex, group constellations vary according to developmental stage and environmental circumstances, as thoroughly spelled out in this and subsequent chapters.

Outside home, children, adolescents and young adults take on the norms and culture prevalent in the peer groups in which they spend most of their time, and to which they need to belong and fit in. Indeed, there are intra-group biases, inter-group hostilities and other complex non-peer group processes, which become increasingly relevant in adulthood and also need to be taken into account.

Harris (2009) hypothesised that developing some long-term personality traits away from the home environment must be advantageous from an evolutionarily perspective because future success is more likely to depend on interactions with peers than interactions with parents. Moreover, evolutionary success would be enhanced by diversifying personality characteristics away from the already existing genetic similarities with parents.

When the needs for meaningful connections and attachments to groups are not properly satisfied, individuals become more vulnerable to mental health problems. Psychopathology is, above all, an expression of difficulties, disruptions or ruptures in interpersonal relationships and group lives.

A psychotherapy group is an ideal space where these ruptures can be reflected upon and repaired, in collaboration with fellow members and the therapist. Such a group, regardless of age differences, resembles and often becomes a powerful symbol of a basic peer group in ordinary development. In addition, the therapy group can be a token representation of the surrounding community and its culture.

In his sociocultural theory, Vygotsky (1978) advanced the idea that a person's unique development cannot be properly viewed and understood without seeing how that person is enmeshed within a multiple social and cultural context.

Society and culture challenge and shape us. Psychosocial and peer group development encompasses changes in our interactions with (and understandings of) one another, as well as in our knowledge and understanding of ourselves as members of society.

Erikson (1971) argued that each developmental phase presents a crisis or conflict that the individual must resolve. Although no crisis is ever fully resolved, individuals must sufficiently address the crisis of each stage in order to deal with the new demands of the next stage. The failure to master challenges that are typical of a given period decreases the likelihood of successfully negotiating future biographical transitions.

According to Quinodoz (2009), each developmental phase in the life cycle has its dramatic moments and its joys. It is important to recognise them within oneself in the present, in order to perceive the uniqueness of human existence. The majority of elderly people manage to bring together their childhood, adolescence and adulthood with sufficient harmony to give meaning to old age, and to perceive their journey as a whole and complete life story.

Group-analytic thinking can deepen life review processes, helping older adults recognise the child, the adolescent and the adult still present internally. Meaningful reminiscing and staying in contact with the past can promote a sense of continuity, self-constancy and ego-integrity, for individuals to review and give value to their life experiences and to themselves.

Life review can, in fact, promote re-integration of the individual's identity, of who they are, by re-connecting them with who they were. Continuity with the past can be a good antidote to overwhelming despair. However, reminiscence can sometimes connote defensive and nostalgic idealisation and a difficulty in letting go.

Remarkably, in our psychotherapy groups over the years (see Chapters 6 and 7), we have seen many older adults managing to resolve complex life-long conflicts or put them into perspective. They still endeavour to become attached, to grow and to consider the legacy they would be leaving behind themselves.

This chapter has delivered a wide-ranging and inclusive life-span perspective on psychosocial, peer group and group attachment development, and its relevance to mental health and group-analytic thinking and practice. These themes are thoroughly elaborated in the following chapters, which focus on each and every one of the stages in the human life cycle.

Therefore, we would like to claim that developmental group analysis has now come of age.

Conclusion

Personality structure and traits start being shaped from birth onward, or even sooner. On the whole, they are taken as largely consolidated in adulthood. However, personal development is an open-ended task.

A life-span perspective on psychosocial, peer group and group attachment development can enrich the training and practice of mental health professionals (including group analysts), social and political scientists and public, by providing them with valuable and highly relevant knowledge of the human condition. This has the potential to refine their understanding, thinking and theorising and improve their work.

Furthermore, a comprehensive group-analytic theory cannot be complete without becoming sufficiently conversant with a life-span perspective of human development. No particular single period of life governs all development. Instead, every period contains the potential for both growth and decline. People can grow and change throughout their lives.

References

Adshead G (1998) Psychiatric staff as attachment figures. *British Journal of Psychiatry* 172: 64–69.

Ainsworth MDS (1991) Attachment and other affectional bonds across the life cycle. In: Parkes CM, Stevenson-Hinde J and Marris P (eds) *Attachment Across the Life Cycle*. London and New York: Tavistock/Routledge, pp. 33–51.

Anthony EJ (1965) Group analytic psychotherapy with children and adolescents. In E. J. Anthony EJ and Foulkes SH (eds) *Group Psychotherapy: The Psychoanalytic Approach*. London: Maresfield, pp. 186–232.

Antonucci TC (1986) A hierarchical mapping technique. *Generations* 10 (4): 10–12.

Arnett JJ (2014) Emerging adulthood: The winding road from the late teens through the twenties. New York: Oxford University Press.

Arnett JJ (2015) *Oxford Handbook of Emerging Adulthood*. New York: Oxford University Press.

Aron A, Fisher H, Mashek DJ, Strong G, Li H, Brown LL (2005) Reward, motivation, and emotion systems associated with early-stage intense romantic love. *Journal of Neurophysiology* 94(1): 327–337.

Atkins RN (1983) Peer relatedness in the first year of life: the bird of a new world. *Annual of Psychoanalysis* 11: 227–244.

Axelrod R and Hamilton WD (1981) The evolution of cooperation. *Science* 211: 1390.

Barwick N and Weegman M (2018) *Group Therapy: A Group-Analytic Approach*. London: Routledge.

Baltes PB, Lindenberger U and Staudinger UM (2006) Life span theory in developmental psychology. In: Damon W and Lerner RM (Series eds) and Lerner RM (Vol ed) *Handbook of Child psychology. Vol 1: Theoretical Models of Human Development* (6th edition) Hoboken, NJ: Wiley, pp. 569–664.

Banny AM, Ames A, Heilbron N and Prinstein MJ (2011). Relational benefits of relational aggression: Adaptive and maladaptive associations with adolescent friendship quality. *Developmental Psychology* 47(4): 1153–1166.

Beauvoir S (1970) *La Vieillesse*. Paris: Gallimard.

Behr H and Hearst L (2005) Groups for children and adolescents. In: Behr H and Hearst L (eds) *Group-Analytic Psychotherapy: A Meeting of Minds*. London: Whurr, pp. 203–219.

Bengtson VL and Whittington FJ (2014) From ageism to the longevity revolution: Robert Butler, pioneer. *The Gerontologist* 54(6): 1064–1069. Available at From Ageism to the Longevity Revolution: Robert Butler, Pioneer | The Gerontologist | Oxford Academic (oup.com)

Berger KS (2008) *The Developing Person Through the Life Span*. New York: Worth Publishers

Billow RM (2004) Working relationally with the adolescent in group. *Group Analysis* 37(2): 201–217.

Bion WR (1961) *Experiences in Groups*. London: Tavistock.

Blackwell D (2005) *Counselling and Psychotherapy with Refugees*. London: Jessica Kingsley.

Blumer H (1969) *Symbolic Interactionism*. Upper Saddle River, NJ: Prentice Hall.

Bowlby J (1951) *Maternal Care and Mental Health*. Geneva, Switzerland: World Health Organization.

Bowlby J (1953) *Child Care and the Growth of Love*. Harmondsworth, UK: Penguin Books.

Bowlby J (1958) The nature of the child's tie to his mother. *International Journal of Psychoanalysis* 39: 350–373.

Bowlby J (1969) *Attachment and Loss. Vol 1: Attachment* (1991 edition). London: Penguin Books.

Bowlby J (1973) *Attachment and Loss. Vol 2: Separation, Anxiety and Anger* (1991 edition). London: Penguin Books.

Bowlby J (1980) *Attachment and Loss. Vol 3: Loss, Sadness and Depression* (1991 edition). London: Penguin Books.

Bowlby J (1988a) *A Secure Base: Clinical Applications of Attachment Theory*. London: Routledge.

Bowlby J (1988b) Developmental Psychiatry Comes of Age. *American Journal of Psychiatry* 145: 1–10.

Bowlby J (1991). The role of the psychotherapist's personal resources in the treatment situation. *Bulletin of the British Psychoanalytical Society* 27(11): 26–30.

Bowles S (2006) Group competition, reproductive leveling, and the evolution of human altruism. *Science* 314: 1569–1572.

Bowles S (2009) Did warfare among ancestral hunter-gatherers affect the evolution of human social behaviors? *Science*, 324: 1293–1298.

Brown D and Zinkin L (eds) (1994) *The Psyche and the Social World. Developments in Group-Analytic Theory*. London: Routledge.

Bruggen P (1979) Authority in work with younger adolescents: A personal review. *Journal of Adolescence* 2: 345–354.

Bruggen P (2006) Castaway's Corner. *Clinical Child Psychology and Psychiatry* 11(2): 307–311.

Butler RN (1975) *Why survive? Being old in America*. New York: Harper and Row.

Butler RN (2010) *The longevity prescription: The 8 proven keys to a long, healthy life*. New York: Avery/Penguin Group.

Canete M and Ezquerro A (2012) Bipolar affective disorders and group analysis. *Group Analysis* 45(2): 203–217.

Caparrós N (ed) (2004) *Y El Grupo Creo al Hombre*. Madrid: Biblioteca Nueva.

Cassidy J and Shaver PR (eds) (2008). *Handbook of Attachment: Theory, Research, and Clinical Applications* (second edition). New York: The Guilford Press.

Clulow C (ed) (2001) *Adult Attachment and Couple Psychotherapy: The 'Secure Base' in Practice and Research*. London: Brunner-Routledge.

Cortina M and Liotti G (2010) Attachment is about safety and protection, intersubjectivity is about sharing and social understanding. The relationships between attachment and intersubjectivity. *Psychoanalytic Psychology* 27(4): 410–441.

Csikszentmihalyi M (2021) Adolescence. *Encyclopaedia Britanica*. Available at: https://www.britanica.com/science/sdolescence

Dalal F (2011) *Thought Paralysis: The Virtues of Discrimination (The Exploring Psycho-Social Studies Series)*. London: Karnac.

Denton FT and Spencer BG (2009) What is retirement? A review and assessment of alternative concepts and measures. *Canadian Journal on Aging* 28: 63–76.

Dies KG (2000) Adolescent development and a model of group psychotherapy: Effective leadership in the New Millennium. *Journal of Child and Adolescent Group Therapy* 10: 97–111.

Dwivedi KN (ed) (1998) *Group Work with Children and Adolescents: A Handbook*. London: Jessica Kingsley.

Erikson EH (1959) Identity and the life cycle. New York: International Universities Press.

Erikson EH (ed) (1963). *Youth: Change and Challenge*. New York: Basic Books.

Erikson EH (1966) Eight ages of man. *International Journal of Psychoanalysis* 47: 281–300.

Erikson EH (1971) *Identity: Youth and Crisis*. London: Faber and Faber.

Evans J (1998) *Active Analytic Group Therapy for Adolescents*. London: Jessica Kingsley.

Evans J (2000) Adolescent group therapy and its contribution to the understanding of adult groups. In: Pines M (ed) *The Evolution of Group Analysis*. London: Jessica Kingsley, pp. 98–108.

Ezquerro A (1989) Group psychotherapy with the pre-elderly. *Group Analysis* 22(3): 299–308.

Ezquerro A (1991) *Attachment and Its Circumstances: Does It Relate to Group Analysis?* Theoretical dissertation for membership of the Institute of Group Analysis (IGA). Archives IGA Library, London.

Ezquerro A (1995) Group therapy within the NHS III: Should we invest in group psychotherapy? A personal account. *Group Analysis* 28(4): 453–457.

Ezquerro A (1997) Tradición institucional y cambio. *Boletín Sociedad Española de Psicoterapia y Técnicas de Grupo* 4(11): 183–190.

Ezquerro A (2017) *Encounters with John Bowlby: Tales of Attachment*. London: Routledge.

Ezquerro A (2019a) Sexual abuse: a perversion of attachment? *Group Analysis* 52(1): 100–113.

Ezquerro A (2019b) The power of group work: personal recollections on Peter Bruggen. *Group Analysis* 52(3): 362–374.

Ezquerro A (2019c) The Power of Group Attachment. In: Group Analysis North Open Seminar (8 November), University of Manchester, UK.

Ezquerro A (2020a) Brexit: Who is afraid of group attachment? Part I. Europe: what Europe? *Group Analysis* 53(2): 234–254.

Ezquerro A (2020b) Attachment and survival in the face of Covid-19. *Attachment: New Directions in Psychotherapy and Relational Psychoanalysis* 14: 171–187.

Ezquerro A (2021a) Brexit: Who is afraid of group attachment? Part II. Democracy: what democracy? *Group Analysis* 54(2): 265–283.

Ezquerro A (2021b) Captain Aguilera and filicide: An attachment-based exploration. *Attachment: New Directions in Psychotherapy and Relational Psychoanalysis* 15: 279–297.

Ezquerro A and Canete M (in-press) *The Power of Group Attachment*. London: Routledge.

Farrell M (1984) Group-work with children: the significance of setting and context. *Group Analysis* 17(2): 146–155.

Feldman RS (2018) *Development Across the Life Span*. Harlow, UK: Pearson Education Limited.

Foulkes SH (1964) Therapeutic group analysis. London: Allen & Unwin.

Foulkes SH (1977) Notes on the concept of resonance. In: Wolberg LR and Aronson ML (eds) *Group Therapy: An overview*. New York: Stratton Intercontinental Book Corp., pp. 52–58.

Frankel R (1998) *The Adolescent Psyche. Jungian and Winnicottian Perspectives.* New York: Routledge.

Freud S (1896) The Aetiology of Hysteria. In: *Standard Edition of the Complete Works of Sigmund Freud. Vol 3* (1953 edition). London: Hogarth Press.

Freud S (1905a) Three Essays on the Theory of Sexuality. In: *Standard Edition of the Complete Works of Sigmund Freud, Vol 7* (1953 edition). London: Hogarth Press, pp. 123–246.

Freud S (1905b) On Psychotherapy. In: *Standard Edition of the Complete Works of Sigmund Freud, Vol 7* (1953 edition). London: Hogarth Press, pp. 257–268.

Garland C (ed) (2010) *The Groups Book. Psychoanalytic Group Therapy: Principles and Practice.* London: Karnac.

Gaudilliere JM (2021) *Madness and the Social Link.* New York: Routledge.

Glenn L (1987) Attachment theory and group analysis: The group matrix as a secure base. *Group Analysis* 20(2): 109–126.

Griffin L (2014) Lessons from the new science of adolescence. *Psychology Today.* Available at Lessons from the New Science of Adolescence | Psychology Today

Grunebaum H and Solomon L (1980) Toward a peer theory of group psychotherapy. Part I: On the developmental significance of peers and play. *International Journal of Group Psychotherapy* 30(1): 23–49.

Grunebaum H and Solomon L (1982) Toward a theory of peer relationships. Part II: On the stages of social development and their relationship to group psychotherapy. *International Journal of Group Psychotherapy* 32(3): 283–307.

Haen C and Aronson S (eds) (2017) *Handbook of Child and Adolescent Group Therapy: A Practitioner's Reference.* New York: Routledge.

Hafen CA, Laursen B, Kerr M and Stattin H (2011) Homophily in stable and unstable adolescent friendships: Similarity breeds constancy. *Personality and Individual Differences* 51: 607–613.

Harlow HF (1971) *Learning to Love.* San Francisco, CA: Albion.

Harris JR (1995) Where is the child's environment? A group socialization theory of development. *Psychological Review* 102(3): 458–459.

Harris JR (2009) *The Nurture Assumption: Why Children Turn Out the Way They Do?* New York: Free Press.

Haslam C, Lam BCP, Branscombe NR, Steffens NK, Haslam SA, Cruwys T, Fong P and Ball TC (2018) Adjusting to life in retirement: the protective role of new group memberships and identification as a retiree. *European Journal of Work and Organizational Psychology* 27(6): 822–839.

Haslam C, Steffens NK, Branscombe NR, Haslam SA, Cruwys T, Lam BCP, Pachana NA and Yang J (2019) The importance of social groups for retirement adjustment: Evidence, application and policy implications of the Social Identity Model of Identity Change. *Social Issues and Policy Review* 13(1): 93–124.

Hershenson DB (2016) Reconceptualizing retirement: A status-based approach. *Journal of Aging Studies* 38: 1–5.

Hildebrand P (1995) *Beyond the mid-life crisis.* London: Sheldon Press.

Holmes J (1993) *John Bowlby and Attachment Theory.* London: Routledge.

Hopper E (1996) The social unconscious in clinical work. *Group* 20 (1): 7–42.

Hopper E (2000) From objects and subjects to citizens: Group analysis and the study of maturity. *Group Analysis* 33(1): 29–34.

Hopper E (2003) *The Social Unconscious: Selected Papers.* London: Jessica Kingsley.

Hopper E and Weinberg H (eds) (2016) *The Social Unconscious in Persons, Groups and Societies*. London: Karnac.

Johansson L and Werbart A (2009) Patients' views of therapeutic action in psychoanalytic group psychotherapy. *Group Analysis* 42(2): 120–142.

Karen R (1998) *Becoming Attached: First Relationships and How They Shape Our Capacity to Love*. New York: Oxford University Press.

Latorre JM, Serrano JP, Ricarte J, Bonete B, Ros L and Sitges E (2015) Life review based on remembering specific positive events in active aging. *Journal of Aging and Health* 27: 140–157.

Lanyado M and Horne A (2009) *The Handbook of Child and Adolescent Psychotherapy: Psychoanalytic Approaches*. New York: Routledge.

Liu Z, Yang F, Lou Y, Zhou W and Tong F (2021) The effectiveness of reminiscence therapy on alleviating depressive symptoms in older adults: A systematic review. *Frontiers in Psychology* 12: 1–13.

Ludlam M and Nyberg V (eds) (2007) *Couple Attachments: Theoretical and Clinical Studies*. London: Karnac.

Maldonado CE (ed) (2005) *Complejidad de las Ciencias y Ciencias de la Complejidad*. Bogotá: Universidad Externado de Colombia.

Maratos J (1996) Self through attachment and attachment through self in group therapy. *Group Analysis* 29(2): 191–198.

Marmarosh CL (ed) (2020) *Attachment in Group Psychotherapy*. New York: Routledge.

Marmarosh CL, Forsyth DR, Strauss B and Burlingame GM (2020) The psychology of the COVID-19 pandemic: A group-level perspective. *Group Dynamics: Theory, Research, and Practice* 24(3): 122–138.

Marrone M (1998) *Attachment and Interaction*. London: Jessica Kingsley.

Morgan E (2013) Contemporary issues in sexual orientation and identity development in emerging adulthood. *Emerging Adulthood* 1(1): 52–66.

Moss E (2017) I still want to be relevant: On placing an older person in an analytic therapy group with younger people. In: Friedman R and Doron Y (eds) *Group Analysis in the Land of Milk and Honey*. London: Karnac, pp. 177–190.

Music G (2014) *The Good Life: Wellbeing and the New Science of Altruism, Selfishness and Immorality*. New York: Routledge.

Neugarten BL (1977) Personality and aging. In: Birren JE and Schaie KW (eds) *Handbook for the Psychology of Aging*. New York: Van Nostrand Reinhold.

Nitsun M (1989) Early development: Linking the individual and the group. *Group Analysis* 22: 249–260.

Nitsun M (2006) *The Group as an Object of Desire: Exploring Sexuality in Group Therapy*. New York: Routledge.

Nitsun M (2015) *Beyond the Anti-Group: Survival and Transformation*. New York: Routledge.

Nitzgen D (2008) Development by adaptation: Notes on applied group analysis. *Group Analysis* 41(3): 240–251.

Ormay T (2012) *The Social Nature of Persons: One Person is No Person*. London: Routledge.

Parker V (2020) *A Group-Analytic Exploration of the Sibling Matrix*. London: Routledge.

Parkes CM, Stevenson-Hinde J and Marris P (eds) (1991) *Attachment Across the Life Cycle*. London and New York: Tavistock/Routledge.

Peck RC (1968). Psychological developments in the second half of life. In: BL Neugarten BL (ed) *Middle Age and Aging*. Chicago, CA: University of Chicago Press.

Penberthy JK and Penberthy JM (2020) *Living Mindfully Across the Lifespan: An Intergenerational Guide*. London: Routledge.

Piaget J (1953) *The Origins of Intelligence in the Child*. New York: International Universities Press.

Pigott C (1990) Deep truth, madness and paradox in analytic children's groups. *Group Analysis* 23: 99–111.

Pines M (1998) *Circular Reflections: Selected Papers on Group Analysis and Psychoanalysis*. London: Jessica Kingsley.

Quinodoz D (2009). *Growing Old: A Journey of Self-discovery*. London: Routledge.

Roberts J and Pines M (eds) (1991) *The Practice of Group Analysis*. London: Routledge.

Robinson CC, Anderson GT, Porter CL, Hart CH and Wouden-Miller M (2003) Sequential transition patterns of pre-schoolers' social interactions during child-initiated play: Is parallel-aware play a bidirectional bridge to other play states? *Early Childhood Research Quarterly* 18: 3–21.

Robinson M (1980) Systems theory for the beginning therapist. *Australian Journal of Family Therapy* 1(4): 183–194.

Rubin KH, Coplan R, Chen X, Bowker, JC, McDonald K and Heverly-Fitt S (2015) Peer relationships in childhood. In: Bornstein MH and Lamb ME (eds) *Developmental Science: An Advanced Textbook* (7th edition). New York: Psychology Press, pp. 591–649.

Rutter M (1980) Attachment and the development of social relationships. In Rutter M (ed) *Scientific Foundations of Developmental Psychiatry*. London: Heinemann Medical, pp. 267–279.

Ryalls BO, Gull RE and Ryalls KR (2000) Infant imitation of peer and adult models: Evidence for a peer model advantage. *Merrill-Palmer Quarterly* 46: 188–202.

Samuels A (1993) *The Political Psyche*. London: Routledge.

Saunders R et al. (2021) Older adults respond better to psychological therapy than working-age adults: evidence from a large sample of mental health service attendees. *Journal of Affective Disorders* 294: 85–93.

Schechter M, Herbstman B, Ronningstam E and Goldblatt MJ (2018) Emerging adults, identity development and suicidality: Implications for psychoanalytic psychotherapy. *The Psychoanalytic Study of the Child* 71(1): 20–39.

Schlapobersky JR (2016) *From the Couch to the Circle: Group-Analytic Psychotherapy in Practice*. New York: Routledge.

Shechtman Z (2014) Counseling and Therapy Groups with Children and Adolescents. In: DeLucia-Waack JL, Kalodner CR and Riva MT (eds) *Handbook of Group Counseling and Psychotherapy*. Washington DC: Sage Publications Inc., pp. 1068–1108.

Shechtman Z (2017) *Group Counseling and Psychotherapy with Children and Adolescents*. New York: Routledge.

Slavson SR (1943) *Introduction to Group Psychotherapy*. New York: International Universities Press.

Slavson SR (1978) *Dynamics of Group Psychotherapy*. New York: Jason Aronson.

Sochos A (2015) Attachment: Beyond interpersonal relationships. *The Psychologist* 28(12): 986–989.

Stacey R (2001) Complexity and the group matrix. *Group Analysis* 34(2): 221–239.

Stern DN (1998) *The Interpersonal World of the Infant: A View from Psychoanalysis and Developmental Psychology*. New York: Basic Books.

Stern DN (2006) Some implications of infant research for psychoanalysis. In: Cooper AM (ed) *Contemporary Psychoanalysis in America*. Washington DC, USA: American Psychiatric Publishing Inc., pp. 673-641.

Tasca G (2014) Attachment and group psychotherapy: Introduction to a special section. *Psychotherapy* 51(1): 53–56.

Tasca GA and Maxwell H (2021) Attachment and group psychotherapy: Applications to work groups and teams. In: Parks CD and Tasca GA (eds) *The Psychology of Groups: The Intersection of Social Psychology and Psychotherapy Research*. New York: American Psychological Association, pp. 149–167.

Thornton C (ed) (2019) *The Art and Science of Working Together: Practising Group Analysis in Teams and Organizations*. London: Routledge.

Tomasello M (2009) *Why we cooperate*. Cambridge, MA: Boston Review Book.

Trevarthen C (2005) "Stepping away from the mirror: Pride and shame in adventures in companionship"— Reflections on the nature and emotional needs of infant intersubjectivity. In: Carter L, Ahnert KE, Grossmann SB, Hrdy ME, Lamb SW, Porges W and Sachser N (eds) *Attachment and Bonding. A New Synthesis*. Cambridge MA: MIT Press, pp. 55–84.

Tuckman B (1965) Developmental sequence in small groups. *Psychological Bulletin* 63(6): 384–399.

Vaish A, Carpenter M and Tomasello M (2009) Sympathy through affective perspective taking and its relation to prosocial behavior in toddlers. *Developmental Psychology* 45(2): 534–543.

Vandell DL and Mueller EC (1980) Peer play and friendships during the first two years. In Foot H, Chapman T and Smith J (eds.) *Friendship and Childhood Relationships*. London: Wiley, pp. 181–209.

Van der Horst FCP (2011) *John Bowlby: From Psychoanalysis to Ethology*. Chichester, UK: Wiley-Blackwell.

Vygotsky LS (1978) *Mind in Society: The Development of Higher Psychological Processes*. Cambridge MA: Harvard University Press.

Waddell M (2007) Only connect – the links between early and later life. In: Davenhill R (ed) *Looking into Later Life: A psychoanalytic Approach to Depression and Dementia in Old Age*. London: Karnac, pp. 187–200.

Wallin DJ (2007) *Attachment in Psychotherapy*. New York: The Guilford Press.

Warneken F and Tomasello M (2006) Altruistic helping in human infants and young chimpanzees. *Science* 311: 1301–1304.

Woods J (1993) Limits and structure in child group psychotherapy. *Journal of Child Psychotherapy* 19(1): 63–78.

Zulueta F (1993) *From Pain to Violence: The Traumatic Roots of Destructiveness*. London: Whurr.

ORCID iD: Arturo Ezquerro https://orcid.org/0000-0002-9910-4576

ORCID iD: María Cañete https://orcid.org/0000-0001-7967-1103

2 Early psychosocial development

Can children benefit from group-analytic therapy?

Arturo Ezquerro and María Cañete

Introduction

The London Institute of Psychoanalysis introduced specific training in child analysis in the 1930s, and child psychotherapy became a distinct specialty in the UK in the 1940s, with the pivotal support of John Bowlby (the *father* of attachment theory).

In contrast to that, established in 1971, the Institute of Group Analysis (IGA) has not paid much attention to, let alone incorporated, child group therapy into its training programmes. In the UK, group work with children is largely the property of child psychotherapists. In this respect, the late Jim Bamber left a prophetic warning:

> Unless future group analysts are trained to conduct such groups, they will be left to the less well trained and group analysis will be the more impoverished for neglecting such a potential area for group-analytic application.
>
> Bamber (1988: 102)

The current chapter will critically address this longstanding unfinished business in group analysis. Prior to looking into the growing field of child group psychotherapy, we shall review and evaluate relevant research studies into psychosocial and group development in children.

Indeed, early relationships with primary attachment figures, like parents and other caregivers, provide a basis for and have a profound influence on future psychosocial development.

However, children increasingly spend much time in groups, relating to and interacting with many other important people in their lives. These significant others include secondary caregivers outside the family, teachers, siblings and peers. Relating in groups becomes a key component of the child's integral development.

Sibling and peer relationships deeply influence the character traits that children develop, as well as their capacity for social, cognitive and emotional understanding, for adjustment and for well-being. Siblings and peers might

DOI: 10.4324/9781003167747-3

represent a *potential self* that the child can reflect upon in relation to himself and to future relationships (Ezquerro, 2017).

Until recently, relationships with siblings and peers have been a relatively neglected area in both psychoanalytic and group-analytic literature (Parker, 2020). The main emphasis has been on rivalry, envy and jealousy.

However, the equation has to include other important aspects such as friendliness, loyalty to each other and a sense of belonging, as well as an ability to form a united front in response to an external threat or discomfort. Sibling and peer experiences provide frequent and ongoing opportunities for children to develop a capacity for empathy (Parens, 1988; Sanders, 2004).

Sigmund Freud mainly wrote about the sibling as a displacement in the relationship with the mother. In 1917, he stated:

> A child who has been put into second place by the birth of a brother or a sister, and who is now for the first time almost isolated from his mother, does not easily forgive her for this loss of place.
>
> Freud, quoted in Sanders (2004: 56)

Half a century later, John Bowlby put together a more detailed observation of a young child's reaction to the presence of a new sibling, and linked it to attachment:

> In most young children the mere sight of mother holding another baby in her arms is enough to elicit strong attachment behaviour. The older child insists on remaining close to his mother, or on climbing onto her lap. Often, he behaves as though he were a baby…
>
> The fact that an older child often reacts in this way even when the mother makes a point of being attentive and responsive suggests that more is involved.
>
> Bowlby (1969: 260)

According to Bowlby (1969, 1973), attachment is crucial for physical and emotional survival. Particularly for young children, perceiving that their mother attending to a sibling is not readily accessible or available can generate for them a survival-related anxiety at an unconscious level (Ezquerro, 2017).

Sibling relationships are likely to be the longest standing that any of us has: longer than the relationships with our parents, or with our children, or with our partners.

Dunn (2014) described the sibling relationship as distinctive in its emotional power and intimacy, as well as its qualities of competitiveness, ambivalence and mutual understanding. The child learns who he is (and who he is not) through ongoing comparisons with siblings and peers, selectively imitating, contradicting or avoiding the other, depending on circumstances.

Siblings are prominent figures in many children's early life and may come to constitute the first peer group experience. Sibling relationships in early development are commonly seen as preparations for the kind of relationships children will establish with peers and friends outside the family (Hindle and Sherwin-White, 2014). Initially, the sibling is not really an attachment figure. However,

> as parents are absent either emotionally or physically, the siblings may be forced to reach out for one another.
>
> Bank and Kahn (1997: 123)

There is an ongoing debate about *compensatory* versus *congruent* models of sibling and parent–child relationships. The idea that if one type of relationship is bad (or absent) the other would be good, as a compensatory mechanism, does not always apply.

In fact, there are many situations where it is possible to observe a congruent model. According to this, if relationships with parents are good, relationships with siblings and with other children will also be good, and if parent–child relations are bad, sibling and peer relationships will be bad too.

Whether the link between the two types of relationships is compensatory or congruent may depend on other variables such as the developmental stage of the child, environmental factors and individual differences between children (Sanders, 2004).

The traditional psychoanalytic perspective of the sibling relationship with the mother as mainly a rival-attachment system has been under increasing review; a wider picture, including sibling collaboration and altruism, has been provided in the last forty or so years (for example, Dunn, 1983, 2014; Dunn and Kendrick, 1982; Dunn and McGuire, 1992; Brunori, 1998; Maratos, 1998; Fonagy, 2001; Fonagy and Target, 1996, 2007; Akhtar and Kramer, 1999; Coles, 2003; Sanders, 2004; Rustin, 2009; Kriss, Steele M and Steele H, 2014; Music, 2014; Davies, 2015; Target, 2018; Parker, 2020).

Competitive interactions are undeniable and frequent among siblings, but they represent only one aspect of the wide range of capabilities that children possess. Despite the stress involved with the birth of a younger sibling, this arrival can also be a stimulus for cognitive, emotional and social growth on the part of the older child, as well as on the part of the baby. The mutual efforts to understand each other can form the basis for a loving and enduring attachment bond (Ezquerro, 2017).

Siblings and peers can adopt various relational roles with one another, including acting as comforters and teachers, as devious and manipulative bullies, or as sensitive companions who can enter the play world of the other (Dunn, 2014; Dunn and Kendrick, 1982).

Bowlby made a distinction between attachment figures and playmates. According to him, a child seeks his attachment figure when he is tired, ill or alarmed and, also, when he is uncertain of that figure's whereabouts. By contrast, a child seeks playmates (usually peers) when he is in good spirits and confident and wants to engage in playful interaction. He further elaborated on this:

the roles of attachment-figure and playmate are distinct. Since, however, the two roles are not incompatible, it is possible for any one figure at different times to fill both roles:

> ... an older child who acts mainly as playmate may on occasion act also as a subsidiary attachment figure.

> Bowlby (1969: 307)

Psychosocial and group development in childhood

For the human infant, people constitute the first source of interest and attraction. A number of developmental researchers and clinicians (Rutter, 1980; Stern, 1998; Bowlby, 1969, 1974, 1988; Hrdy, 2005, 2009; Cortina and Liotti, 2010; Music, 2014; Rubin et al., 2015) have reported systematic studies showing that infants are socially responsive from birth onwards.

Babies can recognise the mother's smell within hours and her voice within days. This is facilitated by the familiarity with the mother's voice, gained from the experience of hearing her talking during the last stages of the pregnancy. Babies can also smile and take and keep a firm grasp with their hands within a few weeks.

The smile

These early signs of sociability are enhanced by the emergence of the smile, which may appear as early as four or five weeks after birth, and progressively becomes more prevalent and differentiated in the following weeks and months (Bowlby, 1958, 1969).

At first, the smile is released by high-arousal states, such as in a rapid-eye-movement sleep phase, but by the fourth week of life, the smile is released by seeing a human face or the gestalt of the human face. By the second or third month, the emotion that accompanies the social smile is also transformed from signals of pleasure to definite expressions of joy (Cortina and Liotti, 2010; Sroufe, 1979, 1996; Sroufe et al., 2005).

Initially, the social smile is quite indiscriminate: babies will smile to anybody who smiles at them. Most adults find these smiles and giggles endearing and irresistible. So powerful is smiling that it promotes strong affective sharing and attachment between infants and parents or caregivers (Bowlby, 1958, 1969, 1974; Stern, 1998; Ezquerro, 2017).

This form of emotional engagement ushered in by the social smile is part and parcel of a larger system of intersubjective or interpersonal communication that continues to develop throughout life (Cortina and Liotti, 2010).

In terms of his attachment theory, Bowlby (1958) included smiling within a set of instinctual social releasers together, among others, with crying, sucking, clinging and following, directed at eliciting social responses from the mother (or primary attachment figure) and forming a bond with her.

He emphasised that a baby's smile powerfully attracts the mother unless she is impaired – for instance, by severe trauma or depression. Healthy smiling promotes attachment:

> Can we doubt that the more and better an infant smiles the better is he loved and cared for?
>
> > Bowlby (1958: 366–367)

Una McCluskey elaborated on this:

> eye contact is the greatest source of information and emotional connection between the nonverbal infant and his or her caregiver.
>
> > McCluskey (2002: 138)

Indeed, human faces are equipped with the most sophisticated system of muscles of all living beings. The mutually dependent muscular movements that need coordinating to produce a smile are extremely complex.

Affect attunement

By the age of two or three months, healthy infants show distinct preferential responses to mother and father (Bowlby, 1969).

At about five or six months, the infant shows clear signals of social reciprocity and mutual enjoyment in the interactions with the parents, as well as an incipient awareness of other babies. However, this interest in peers does not appear to be a source of enjoyment until the end of the first year of life (Dunn and Kendrick, 1982; Ezquerro, 2017). More about that later.

The infant's developing communicative system gradually builds into it a motivational component. To begin with, a desire to share feelings and, by the end of the second year of life, a desire to share in more complex interactions such as social games; as well as higher levels of collaboration that are required to construct joint projects (Trevarthen, 1979, 1988, 2005; Tomasello, 2008, 2009; Tomasello and Carpenter, 2005).

There is also a growing affective exchange that operates across different perceptual and expressive modalities. This emotional correspondence, which Stern (1998, 2004, 2006) called *affect attunement*, concerns how inner-feeling states are shared. This affective core provides a sense of continuity that bridges the dramatic changes in social cognition that take place between the first and second years of life.

Pointing

Towards the end of the first year, there is a subtle developmental landmark: the apparently simple gesture of pointing, as a pre-linguistic form of communication. Bates, Camaioni and Volterra (1975) made a key distinction between a pointing that is an instrumental request from the infant to get an object from an adult (imperative pointing) and a pointing that is a request to attend to some interesting external object (declarative pointing).

The first type of pointing usually develops between the age of nine and twelve months, once the infant has developed a capacity to understand goal-directed behaviours and to discover that goals can be reached through different means (Piaget, 1951, 1965; Trevarthen, 1980, 1988).

The second type of pointing involves infants sharing events or objects with caregivers (Bruner, 1977). Infants begin to explore the world with others.

Declarative pointing is brought about by the acquisition of new abilities, such as a capacity to maintain some joint attention towards objects of interest. It involves infant and parent in a meaningful social exchange and marks the appearance of a mutual understanding of goals and intentions; a sense of 'we' begins to emerge (Tomasello et al., 2005; Tomasello, Carpenter and Liszkowski, 2007).

At its simplest, this incipient form of joint attention can be seen when infants begin to follow the gaze of the parent. But this does not necessarily mean that the infant understands that others have intentions similar to its own.

The ability to understand the intentions of others is a necessary step for declarative (rather than imperative) pointing to occur.

Declarative pointing is emblematic of a new form of mutuality that develops during the second year of life. It soon expands to more sophisticated intentional behaviours, such as holding objects up to show them to others and bringing others to specific locations, so they can observe something the infant finds interesting (Trevarthen, 2005; Hobson, 2004).

Mirroring

A more rudimentary form of mutuality may appear as early as six months, since babies start to imitate facial expressions, something that has been described as *imitative mirroring* (Atkins, 1983). Through these interchanges, a capacity to monitor reciprocity begins to develop. Knowing when to trust or not to trust another person is an important evolutionary mechanism, as we will see later when we discuss the figure of the stranger.

Alongside imitative mirroring, the infant gradually develops self-awareness and self-recognition. This happens through stages, roughly, between six and twenty-four months. Although babies can clearly show surprise at their own mirror image by about eight months, it does not mean that they are recognising themselves.

Cherry (2020) referred to a simple experimental technique in which an infant's nose is coloured with the dab of red powder and then is seated in front of a mirror. If the infant touches their nose or attempts to wipe the rouge, this would give evidence that he or she has at least some knowledge of their physical characteristics.

Although some infants as young as twelve months seem startled on seeing the rouge spot on their nose, for most a reaction does not occur until sixteen months and for some it may take as long as twenty-four months.

Interestingly, although there is quite often a stage of joyful recognition and play with the mirror image towards the end of the first year of life, during the second year, children sometimes withdraw from their mirror images, as they become self-conscious. A division between private and public self-awareness appears to begin at this stage, which is one crucial step towards developing self-understanding (Buss, 1980).

It is also during this period that children begin to show some cognisance of their own capabilities. Of course, children's cultural upbringing also impacts the development of self-awareness (Cherry, 2020).

In parallel to the mirror self-recognition, children behave in a typical way towards other children of their own age, who are their *homologues* (Pines, 1998). As well as through imitative mirroring, the child's self-awareness is greatly enhanced through their responses to and interactions with their specular image and the images of their homologues.

Atkins (1983) observed how babies react and respond to the presence of other babies and suggested that the concept of mirroring can be usefully applied to the understanding of these processes. Atkins invoked the gratifying experience of mirroring to explain the fascinating lure that infants have for one another. Watching the play of two eight-month-old babies, he picked up smiles and mutual interest in each other and in the other's activities, as well as some actions directed apparently towards the other.

These interactions can be interpreted in terms of the increasing awareness that infants have of their similarities to each other. This has been described as "*twinship mirroring*" (Pines, 1998: 54).

This phenomenon can be evaluated in phase-specific sensory, sensory-motor and sensory-affective integration components. Infants tend to be attracted by perceptual similarities, sensing that the other is like oneself:

> *Clearly little ones like other little ones (even strangers) even more than they like adults.*
>
> Atkins (1983: 237)

The other is distinct, yet like oneself, and we may infer that the child becomes aware of being himself or herself through this resemblance and differentiation from the other similar person. According to George Herbert:

> *the best mirror is an old friend.*
>
> Herbert, quoted in Pines (1998: 37)

Winnicott (1971) suggested that the very earliest social responses of caregivers to infants can also be viewed as *mirroring* responses at a biological level.

By speaking to infants using high-pitch sounds, repetitive phrases, non-sense utterances and exaggerated facial expressions, parents and caregivers offer emotional states of joy, encouragement, approval or even amused disapproval.

Optimally, this intuitive parenting is delivered through multiple sensory modalities, in adequate amounts, at appropriate times and with respect for the recipient's capacity to process them, which is a basic educational principle.

If the mother looks with love and with tenderness, the baby experiences himself or herself as joyfully alive. However, if the mother is depressed and cannot maintain the reciprocity of looking, the baby experiences herself or himself as joyless and unlively:

> If the mother face is unresponsive then a mirror is a thing to be looked at but not to be looked into.
>
> Winnicott (1971: 113)

In psychoanalysis and group analysis, mirroring is frequently used as a metaphor, with a view to both observing social responses to the developing infant and studying different components of adult relationships:

> Group analysis taught me to make use of mirrors, to find one's self in and through others; not just to retrieve the lost or buried part of the self but to discover some I didn't even know were there; sometimes to bring together elements that had seemed irreconcilable and make them, even momentarily, into a coherent whole.
>
> Garland (1980: 43)

The view of the other

During the second year of life, the emergence of a role-reversal form of imitation (Meltzoff, 2007) and the related ability to identify with the intentions of others (Hobson, 2004) also allow infants to engage in games that involve reciprocal roles; for example, taking turns rolling a ball back and forth with an adult, taking turns in feeding, or more complex games like peek-a-boo.

By the time infants are eighteen months old, a shared form of intentionality and role-reversal imitation set the stage for collaborating in joint plans and shared goals, such as building a tower with blocks, or in tasks like picking up toys together (Moll and Tomasello, 2007; Tomasello and Carpenter, 2005).

The ability to share intentional states with others creates the possibility of taking on the perspective of others. This is already implicit in the ability of eighteen-month-old infants to assume the role of others in social games and to coordinate activities and develop joint plans of action. By eighteen months, infants begin to develop a capacity to see the same thing from their own point of view and from the point of view of others, in an incipient form (Moll and Tomasello, 2007).

After twenty-four months, children's interactions with peers become increasingly complex and multifaceted in nature. In many respects, these developments can be attributed to continued advances in the abilities to understand and appreciate others' thoughts, intentions and emotions (Izard, 2009). Social communicative competence continues to improve with age, and children become more adept at establishing shared meanings with their peers in group situations (Goldstein, Kaczmarek and English, 2002).

The stranger

Before going any further, in ordinary development, it should be pointed out that wariness of strangers usually begins to manifest itself after six months. Typically, people who are perceived as strangers triggering caution or distrust are unfamiliar adults, adolescents and even older children; interestingly, babies are not wary of other, unknown babies but seem to show a positive curiosity about them, as discussed earlier.

The development of guardedness towards strangers happens in parallel with an increase of the intensity of attachment behaviour towards the mother or the main caregiver. The timing of this distinctive proximity-seeking behaviour towards main attachment figures makes sense: the infant is rapidly becoming more aware of its separateness and mobility, and in need of protection from potential dangers (Bowlby, 1969, 1973; Ezquerro, 2017, 2019, 2020).

However, by the end of the first year and rapidly accelerating during the second year, infants learn to use the parent's emotional responses to assess how they should react to unfamiliar situations, a phenomenon described as *social referencing* (Emde, 1992). This has an impact on the infant's perception of strangers.

When the mother or primary attachment figure behaves in a familiar or friendly way with an unknown person, for the infant this stranger no longer means danger. And, from the age of eighteen months, it is possible to consistently observe altruistic gestures toward strangers, as we will later elaborate on.

Language

The acquisition of language is another crucial element in the development of the child's sociability. By ten months, babies can clearly distinguish speech sounds and engage in babbling. As previously mentioned, the earliest form of language learning had, in fact, begun in the utero, as the foetus can recognise the sounds and speech patterns of its mother's voice and differentiate them from other sounds. Typically, children develop receptive language abilities before their verbal or expressive language develops.

During the course of the first year of life, parent-infant dyads respond to each other's nonverbal cues, vocalisations, gestures and emotions. In these proto-conversations, infant cues are matched in timing, form and intensity by their caregivers.

However, strictly speaking, this match is not an exact mirroring response. Even at its best, there are minor cycles of disruption and repair – including situations with parents who are sensitively responsive and attuned to their babies' communications (Beebe and Lachmann, 2002).

In addition, very often, caregivers' responses to infants' cues and vocalisations use a simplified and redundant grammar, a high-pitched voice and exaggerated gestures. This form of child-directed speech is meant to facilitate language development and emotional communication, as well as capturing babies' attention and soothing children's distress (Sroufe, Cooper and DeHart, 1992).

As language takes off in earnest by the second year of life, shared intentionality and perspective-taking abilities make another huge step forward. With language, humans can better understand how others might feel or think from many other nuances and perspectives (Cortina and Liotti, 2010), including the perspectives of siblings and peers.

Older preschool-age children increasingly use in their communication with peers more indirect language (declarative, interrogative and implied requests) than direct (imperative) utterances (Garvey, 1984). Various forms of adulation in children's speeches gradually emerge between the ages of three and six years. Older pre-schoolers learn fast to appropriately employ such flattery comments, in keeping with the familiarity and presence or absence of the intended target in the group (Genyue and Lee, 2007).

Peer group relationships

Vygotsky (1978) placed peer influence in children at a level that is comparable with adult influence, as he defined a 'zone of proximal development' in terms of:

> the distance between a child's optimal developmental level ... and the higher level of potential development ... under adult guidance or in collaboration with more capable peers.
>
> Vygotsky, in Wertsch (1991: 86)

Grunebaum and Solomon (1980, 1982) postulated that, although influenced by the early attachments with parents, sibling and peer relationships can develop quite autonomously following a different pathway of psychosocial development.

In their study of the growing capacity for friendship and group formation, these authors identified at least four stages: toddlerhood (ages one to three years), pre-school child (ages three to six), middle childhood (ages six to nine) and late childhood or pre-adolescence (ages nine to twelve years).

Under normal circumstances, the capacity for meaningful contact with peers grows steadily throughout childhood. Parten (1932) had originally described six sequential categories of developing social participation:

- unoccupied behaviour,
- solitary play,
- onlooker behaviour (observing others but not participating in the activity),
- parallel play (playing alongside but not with other children),
- associative play (playing and sharing with others),
- and cooperative play (social play in which there is a clear division of tasks).

Of course, children become socially more sophisticated with age, but the above sequence is not at all linear and there are significant overlaps. Non-social play does not disappear as children get older and parallel play appears to function as a transitional bridge from solitary to group activities (Robinson, Anderson, Porter, Hart and Wouden-Miller, 2003). Children fluctuate as part of their normal development.

With the rapidly developing ability to speak, the possibilities of social interchanges expand. Piaget (1953) coined the term *collective monologue* for group situations in which children talk enthusiastically but without connection with one another – something that can also be observed in adolescent groups and in adult groups, from time to time.

Typically, a collective monologue involves several children playing in close proximity. They may play different games and might be commenting on them, even taking turns in vocalising, but the context of their speech is not correlated with each other.

From the age of eighteen months, children begin to take complementary roles with one another (e.g., one child throws the ball and the other receives it). By the age of two years, they start to make friends with specific peers and show delight on meeting them. From the age of three onwards, there is a dramatic decrease in solitary play and a corresponding increase in co-operative play.

Playing pretend games begins to emerge during the pre-school phase. At this point, the child also shows awareness of the similarity of other children's feelings to their own – something described as *resonant empathy* (Slavson and Schiffer, 1975).

It is towards the end of the pre-school period that children become clearer in their minds that their peers may have feelings, ideas and expectations *different* from their own (Garvey, 1984). This primitive reflective function of exploring the meaning of actions of others has been more recently linked to the child's ability to recognise and find his or her own experience meaningful (Fonagy and Target, 1996, 2007).

Emotional ambivalence can be an important feature in the child's relationship with his or her peers. Yesterday's best friend will be today's worst enemy and tomorrow will become best friend again (Stringer, 1971).

Friendships typically follow ongoing social interaction and play and can be viewed as a culmination of toddler social skills. The quality of early peer friendship predicts future social competence (Vandell and Mueller, 1980).

At about the age of three or four, and usually up to the age of six, some children have an imaginary companion, often as a psychological mechanism to compensate for absences in their lives. These children can be quite creative, of average intelligence, and frequently have good verbal skills; they tend to co-operate with adults and generally do not have siblings. Imaginary friends can have a positive effect on the child's social and cognitive development (Bettelheim, 1976).

Until the age of five, friends had been selected mainly on the basis of availability. From this age onwards, however, children look for friends with whom they can share common interests and exclude other children who do not enjoy the same activities.

Around the age of eight the foundation of friendships shifts from playing together to an increasing interest in the character traits of one's peers. This is also a time when wanting to be with one's friends becomes an important motive for going to school (Rubin et al., 2015).

As the child gets older, relationships with peers become more imperative for the shaping of a healthy personality. By the age of nine or ten, children have developed their own ideas about what constitutes reciprocity: matching of give-and-take, fairness in exchange for fairness, dependability in exchange for dependability and so on (Stringer, 1971).

These new abilities enable pre-adolescent children to establish some kind of social contracts and resolve some of their earlier ambivalent feelings.

For a number of people friendships during late childhood are erratic, but for others they continue through higher school and even later. With age, friendships tend to be more constant (Smith, 2005).

During the pre-adolescent period, there is also a strong predisposition to make close friends with a particular member of the same sex. At this time, there is a significant shift in the quality of these friendships:

> the child begins to develop a real sensitivity to what matters to another person and this is not in the sense of 'what should I do to get what I want' but instead 'what should I do to contribute to the happiness or support, the prestige and feeling of worthwhile-ness of my chum'...
>
> Nothing remotely like that appears before the age of say eight and a half, sometimes it appears decidedly later.
>
> Sullivan (1953: 245)

In this pre-adolescent phase, there is also a need to be part of gangs and cliques. Gangs tend to be of the same sex, with sexual secrets becoming a source of intergroup curiosity and giggling:

The gang character has the quality of being subversive to adult (parental) standards. The courage to stick to his pal against the parent (no matter how much he loves the parent) is a step forward in the youngster's growth.

Redl (1966: 404)

Children with a history of insecure patterns of attachment may find it more difficult to share friends:

being exposed to the constant dangers of rivalry and loss makes it hard for some children to dare to make any deep relationships at all.

Redl (1966: 448)

Additionally, pre-adolescents need their own space and time for privacy and freedom from group exposure. This has to be negotiated against the background of a powerful drive for intimate group association.

The experience of group lives in pre-adolescence is, more often than not, positive and fulfilling. The developing sense of intimacy, and the capacity of seeing one's self through the eyes of the others, may often foster the validation of one's personal worth, as well as the growth of self-esteem and personal creativity.

On the other hand, there can be damaging group experiences of bullying and scapegoating. Becoming the single-one-out in a group may generate a devastating feeling of isolation. Being left alone and unaided by the other group members can be particularly difficult to handle.

Children who become victims of such destructive forces, and who did not experience satisfactory childhood friendships, would be more vulnerable to enter adolescence with a greater risk of isolation and would be prone to mental health problems (more about that in Chapter 4).

Friendship

In the first century BC, Cicero made a classic statement: *Sine amicitia vitam nullam essem* [without friendship nothing is worth in life]. From an existential perspective, that was a powerful statement.

Friendship in childhood serves several important functions: it provides emotional security and support, self-esteem enhancement and positive self-evaluation, as well as affection and opportunities for intimate disclosure and consensual validation of interests, hopes, and fears (Bagwell and Schmidt, 2011).

Friends can also offer helpful information and instrumental assistance; promote the growth of interpersonal sensitivity; and offer prototypes for later romantic and parental relationships (Sullivan, 1953, 1955).

In attachment terms, friendship can offer children an extra-familial *secure base* from which they may explore the impact of their behaviours on themselves, their peers, and their environments. Friends can be both trusted exploration companions and reliable attachment relationships. And a peer group of friends, as-a-whole, can be perceived and function as an attachment figure (Bowlby, 1969; Ezquerro, 2017).

From a developmental perspective, Parker and Gottman (1989) argued that the functions of friendship for children vary at different points in their development:

- in early childhood, friendship predominantly serves to maximise excitement and amusement levels in play and, more importantly, it also helps organise behaviour in the face of arousal;
- in middle and late childhood, friendships gradually aid children to gain knowledge about behavioural norms and to learn the skills necessary for successful self-presentation and impression management.

These skills become increasingly important, as anxiety about peer relationships develops from middle childhood onward.

A number of recent studies have provided interesting findings. We would highlight the following:

- first, prosocial behaviour is typically associated with peer acceptance and good friendship quality (Rubin et al. 2015);
- second, aggressive behaviour characteristically predicts peer rejection (Vitaro, Pedersen and Brendgen, 2007);
- third, children who are highly aggressive tend to make friends with others much like them and to join groups with aggressive norms, so their aggressive behaviour tends to be reinforced (Dishion and Piehler, 2009);
- fourth, when children's gossip is reinforced by friends, it may be viewed as the sharing of intimate disclosure and actually improve the quality of the friendship (Banny, Ames, Heilbron and Prinstein, 2011).

Peer group difficulties tend to have a negative impact on academic achievement and motivation (Altermatt and Pomerantz, 2003; Bowker and Spencer, 2010; Bowker et al., 2010), as well as on hobbies, interests and creativity (Selfhout, Branje, ter Bogt and Meeus, 2009).

According to a number of clinicians and research studies (Cassidy, Scolton, Kirsh and Parke, 1996; Simpkins and Parke, 2002), friendship is not only a social and positive relational context, but it also provides for the expression and regulation of affect.

Cooperation, altruism and empathy

It is by the age of eighteen to twenty-four months that infants begin to understand that others' behaviours have meaning, and they clearly show a preference for helpful behaviours, a kind of innate morality or consciousness (Cortina and Liotti, 2010).

By the age of two years, infants can demonstrate some rudiment of empathy, as their emotional responses start corresponding to the feelings of another person. At twenty-four months, infants sometimes comfort others or show concern for them. In order to do this, they need to be aware of the emotional states of others.

Cooperative social behaviour is deeply rooted in the make-up of the human species (Axelrod and Hamilton, 1981). Close observation of children reveals that they are not only motivated to reach goals, but also motivated to cooperate for the sake of cooperation (Cortina and Liotti, 2010).

Helping and sharing behaviours with peers can be observed to gradually increase during the preschool years (Eisenberg, Fabes and Spinrad, 2006). This is likely a result of improved social-cognitive and affective perspective-taking abilities.

A more sophisticated understanding of how others think and feel promotes the development of empathy, which may in turn lead to an increase in helping, sharing, and caring behaviours (Vaish, Carpenter and Tomasello, 2009).

An evolutionary explanation for the urge to cooperate among individuals that are not genetically related was originally based on the concept of *reciprocal altruism*, as advanced by Trivers (1971). Literally, this is a sort of tit-for-tat exchange: 'I will cooperate with you if you cooperate with me'.

But conditional strategies do not explain the spontaneous altruistic behaviour that children display from the age of eighteen months toward strangers, without seeking any apparent reward (Warneken and Tomasello, 2006).

An alternative hypothesis to reciprocal altruism has been proposed to explain cooperation and altruism towards non-kin members, based on the concept of *group selection* (Bowles, 2006, 2009; Cortina and Liotti, 2010). This is the group equivalent to natural selection. Simply put, in intergroup competition, groups with more cooperative and altruistic members will outcompete groups that are less cooperative and altruistic.

Other authors (Boyd, 2006; Boehm, 1999) have indicated that group selection requires a system of sanctions and punishment which can spread the high costs of the enforcement of prosocial values to the group-as-a-whole.

Surviving hunter-gatherer groups still perform this function efficiently by the use of *levelling* mechanisms, which function as a *social tax* and permit the high price of implementing altruistic norms (and punishments for violators of these norms) to be spread throughout the whole group, rather than on a few individuals. This levelling function is accomplished through shared cultural norms or values (an egalitarian ethos) enforced through shame, guilt and ostracism, and occasionally even murder (Boehm, 1999, 2012).

Mutatis mutandis, this mechanism can explain why the so-called *level playing field* is so important for the European Union, and why the UK will be punished with tariffs should it deviate from the levelling norms stipulated in the Brexit trade deal agreed on Christmas Eve 2020.

For the growing child, altruism and cooperation gradually become more sophisticated and ambitious. There continue to be age-related increases in altruistic behaviour from early to middle and late childhood (Eisenberg, Fabes and Spinrad, 2006).

By late childhood, social cooperation has become the norm, with children observed to be engaged in dyadic or peer group activities over 90% of the time on average in the schoolyard playground (Rubin et al., 2015).

Group socialisation theory

In parallel with the stages of psychosocial and group development described earlier, other significant findings should be stressed. Rubin et al. (2015) observed that, towards the end of the first year of life, infants can already show evidence of group orientation. Ahlin (1995) reported similar observations, placing the earliest peer groups between eighteen months and three years.

By the toddler period, children are more likely to socially imitate peers than adults (Ryalls, Gull and Ryalls, 2000). Toddler groups are, on the whole, loosely structured and ephemeral.

From then on, children show an increasingly active social group life and begin to organise themselves in more structured group formations at the age of four or five.

These early groups can be short-lived and may serve the purpose of some opposition to adults, as well as a mechanism of group inclusion or exclusion of other children.

By the ages of six and seven, it is possible to see more stable groups in which increasingly advanced forms of sharing and social learning can take place, including a sense of fairness (Rubin et al., 2015).

During late childhood, the need to belong to a peer group is increasingly stronger (Banny et al., 2011). Conflicts may become more apparent between the authority of parents and teachers, on the one hand, and the new principles, norms and culture set by the group, on the other.

Piaget (1954) reported the behaviour of one late-childhood group in which, in order to throw snowballs at one another, the children spent a quarter of an hour in electing a president, fixing the rules of voting, dividing themselves into two teams, deciding upon distances and, finally, framing the sanctions to be applied in case of infringement of the rules.

Harris (1995) put across a *group socialisation* theory, in which she suggested that the peer group plays more significant a role in personality and social development than the parents. Harris based this theorising on her observations that, outside the home, children and adolescents take on the norms and culture prevalent in the peer groups within which they spend most of their time.

Drawing from psychosocial perspectives on the relevance of peer group rules and the need to belong and to fit in, as well as intra-group biases, inter-group hostilities, and other group processes, Harris (2009) further argued that children's personal and group identities develop primarily from their experiences within peer groups.

Additionally, Harris (2009) postulated that developing long-term personality traits away from the home environment must be advantageous from an evolutionarily perspective, because future success is more likely to depend on interactions with peers than interactions with parents.

Moreover, evolutionary success would be enhanced by diversifying personality characteristics away from the already existing genetic similarities with parents.

The evolution of child group psychotherapy

In the last fifty or so years, the field of child group therapy has experienced tremendous growth. Groups for children are now offered in most child mental health services, schools, children's homes, hospitals and additional residential facilities, as well as in other out-patient settings all over the world.

The specialist literature is diverse, but rather scattered. A review of all methods of therapeutic group work with children is beyond the scope of this chapter. However, for the interested reader, we would highlight a number of publications, gathering different professionals and approaches, which have contributed to a more united dialogue within this developing field. For example, Marmarosh (2020), Aichinger and Holl (2017), Dwivedi (1998), Lanyado and Horne (2009), Haen and Aronson (2017) and Shechtman (2014, 2017).

These approaches range from classical (psychoeducational, psychodrama, psychoanalytic, play, activity, art-based, support, and dialectical-behavioural groups) to cutting-edge (attachment-based, mindfulness, mentalisation and sensorimotor groups).

Overall, these authors emphasise the importance for therapists to gain adequate knowledge of child development; and they advocate child group therapy as a beneficial and cost-effective treatment that promotes wellness of children and families, and of society by and large.

In the following passages, we will outline, from a historical perspective, the emergence and development of those group techniques for children that, in our opinion, are more relevant to the group-analytic approach.

The Romanian-born psychiatrist Jacob Moreno is considered an early pioneer of therapeutic group work with children. In 1911, he developed a technique of puppetry and drama in a child guidance clinic in Vienna – which he called *psychodrama* (Moreno, 1946).

His book *Who Shall Survive?* (Moreno, 1934) contains some of the earliest graphical depictions of sociograms (representations of the structure of interpersonal relations in a groups), as well as an ahead-of-his-time explanation of the emergence of runaways at a girls' school in New York.

The Austrian psychiatrist and psychoanalyst Alfred Adler, after having departed from Sigmund Freud's inner circle, undertook his own independent research on human development. In the 1920s, Adler established a number of child guidance clinics in Vienna, where he emphasised that responsibility for the optimal development of the child is not limited to the parents, but rather includes teachers and society more broadly.

In consequence, Adler (1938) argued that teachers, nurses, social workers and other professionals working with children needed training in child education, to complement the work of the family in fostering a democratic character. According to him, when a child does not feel equal and is abused or neglected, he or she is likely to develop inferiority or superiority complexes and various concomitant compensation strategies. These strategies may lead to criminal tendencies or to psychopathology.

Adler and his followers promoted *parent education groups*, in connection with schools. The original procedure took place in the presence of a small group of teachers, parents, and other interested people. Quite often, it was a teacher who presented the problems of particular children.

This was followed by an analysis of the background and possible reasons for the problems. Then the parents were invited to present their side of the story and, after that, the children were encouraged to tell how they felt about the situation.

Following the presentations, the therapists made friendly and, quite often, humorous suggestions to the children for changing their attitudes – something that would usually be reviewed the following week or soon after.

At the review, in a tactful manner, the therapists conveyed the understanding gained so far to the parents and proposed ideas for improvement, rather than criticism. This kind of group procedure was also to serve as a training programme for future therapists.

A similar combination of psychoanalysis and education with children was practised by Fritz Redl, an Austrian-born child analyst.

Redl (1944) was involved with the psychoanalytically-oriented Montessori movement in Vienna, and ran summer camps for disturbed children in the Austrian countryside; he focused on the promotion of healthy socialisation. In 1936, he emigrated to the USA and, inspired by the work of Aichhorn (1922, 1925), became more interested in using milieu therapy with troubled adolescents (see Chapter 3).

A more specific account of early child group therapy is attributed to Samuel Slavson, a Ukrainian-born engineer and school teacher interested in psychoanalysis.

He described some of the small therapy groups that he conducted in the 1930s, consisting of five to eight children between the ages of eight and twelve years (Slavson, 1940). In his view, the group therapist working with children has to show a number of benign qualities, such as being warm, accepting, non-directive and relatively permissive.

In this model, children were allowed to act spontaneously in order to facilitate the expression of feelings, fantasies and conflicts. Slavson suggested a technique in which the activity needs of the children were very much taken into consideration. He sometimes allowed children in the group to have an activity period of their own choosing, followed by a talking period. Older children habitually enjoyed discussing personalities and group relations.

The technique became known as *activity group therapy* (Slavson and Schiffer, 1975), which exploited the natural drive of children for playful action. Encouraging spontaneity sometimes led to the expression of aggressive feelings in both boys and girls. In the more severe cases of aggression, this was linked to past experiences in which the child had been the recipient of aggression, or exposed to witnessing it (Bowlby, 1938, 1939).

Slavson believed in the natural development of *resonant empathy* in children's groups, which is congenial and congruent with group-analytic thinking that incorporates the therapeutic use of *resonance* (Foulkes, 1977). He persevered to overcome difficult situations and became reasonably optimistic about the group's therapeutic potential for working through the children's aggressive feelings and behaviour, in the long term:

> The members of the group work together: they quarrel, fight – and sometimes strike one another; they argue and haggle, but finally come to some... understanding with one another. Sometimes this process takes six months or more, but once it has been established becomes a permanent attitude on the part of the individuals involved.
>
> Slavson (1940: 526)

Slavson (1943) also described how the child gradually becomes attached to the group. Once a reasonably secure attachment to the group is established, the rapidity of the therapeutic progress can sometimes be quite astonishing, over and above the pace of change in adult groups. Slavson conducted groups for children and for adults, separately. He concluded that group psychotherapy with children is

> less difficult, less protracted and the outcomes are more basic and more lasting than with adults ... Because the neurotic engrams have not been as yet crystalised, they can be altered more easily.
>
> Slavson (1978: 559)

In the 1940s, a similar technique called *group play therapy* was developed by the American psychologist Virginia Axline (1947, 1950). This was expanded by the Israeli teacher and child psychologist Haim Ginott (1961) in the following decade and has continued growing until the present time.

These practitioners incorporated some of the strategies of individual child analysis; they used play as a developmentally natural tool for the communication of thoughts, wishes, fears and other feelings in the group, both to the members and the therapists. This is particularly useful a technique, as the child's verbal-expression abilities are not entirely developed yet.

Different forms of group play therapy have been practised since then to the present day, particularly with younger children. James Anthony (a founding member of the Group Analytic Society and distinguished child psychiatrist) described a mixed therapy group for kindergarten children, aged from four to six, in which play and activity *"supplemented language to a large extent"* (Anthony, 1965: 192).

In the mid-1970s, in Mexico, Dupont and Jinich (1993) developed an innovative group psychotherapy programme for children of both sexes, aged six to eleven years, with a broad range of problems, excluding organic brain damage and severe physical or learning disabilities. Minimum stay was normally one year, with an average stay of twenty months. The average group membership was four to six children.

Sessions ran for sixty minutes and were non-directive, although they were structured in three parts:

a   time for action to facilitate the cathartic expression of primary processes,
b   time for thinking about their feelings and actions and
c   time for tidying-up with its symbolic meaning of reparation.

In contrast to other group therapy programmes, toys were excluded to promote a more direct interaction between the children and the therapists.

Initially, the two co-therapists met with the family for a discussion of the project, which included the expectation that the parents would attend a weekly therapy group that was run in parallel for them. The therapy ended with a family review meeting and a follow-up was offered six to ten months later.

The group technique used incorporated and tried to integrate three important influences from some of the pioneers described above: Moreno's modified psychodrama for children, Adler's ideas of community group work with children and parents, and structural elements of Slavson child therapy activity groups.

The project started in the therapists' private consulting rooms. Their enthusiasm, and the improvements reported in children and parents, led to an extension of the project to state-run institutions, voluntary organisations and the wider community. The work generated a huge clinical demand, which contributed to the creation of a teaching programme. A number of professionals working in various settings were trained and ran such groups under supervision in the following decades.

By the age of four, most children have developed a major social interactive tool: the ability to share with other children in groups symbolic meanings through *social pretence* (Howe, Petrakos, Rinaldi and LeFebvre, 2005). Children can spontaneously take on complementary roles; which, other than their symbolic function, have no correspondence with their real-life circumstances and identities. In some children, this remarkable accomplishment can be seen as early as during the third year of life.

Socio-drama group play becomes increasingly common from four to six years of age; it is widely viewed as an indicator of social competence, self-regulation and advanced cognitive and linguistic skills (Smith, 2005). This type of group play can be exploited therapeutically, as it provides a path to a deeper understanding of conflicts and emotional situations of which children are not consciously aware.

In any case, playing is a normal activity through which younger children can have a more rapid access to group formation. Toys such as dolls, puppets, animals and a range of characters, as well as materials such as water, sand or plasticine can be used. Through the play characters, children can create symbolic dialogues. Such materials are particularly attractive to younger children and help them to feel less anxious and to hold on to their interests in the group.

It is generally accepted that, in young children, play can be the therapeutic equivalent of *free association* in adults:

> Gradually, children are able to move from egocentric, solitary, exploratory motor (playground type), oral (cooking, and so forth) and anal (messy) levels of play to more social, representational and constructive play...
>
> Various characters, toys, dolls, animals and so forth become endowed with feelings, intentions and relationships representing those from the world of the child. Social play allows the children to experiment with new ways of relating, with improved ego strength, attitudes and insight gained during the work of the group.
>
> Dwivedi (1998: 118)

Certainly, therapeutic group work can help children to overcome egocentricity, to learn delaying gratification, to manage difficult feelings, to develop symbolic thinking and to explore new values; as well as to develop creativity, empathy, altruism and pro-social behaviour (Dwivedi, 1998; Lanyado and Horne, 2009; Haen and Aronson, 2017; Ezquerro, 2017; Marmarosh, 2020).

Child group psychotherapy is growth engendering and provides a rich experience for children to give and receive support, and to learn from each other. It has proven to be a beneficial and cost-effective form of treatment, at least since the age of four years. The areas of improvement more widely reported are social skills, enhanced self-awareness and empathy and better self-esteem and reality testing (Kymissis, 1996; Rose, 1998; Schaefer, 1999; Haen and Aronson, 2017; Shechtman, 2014, 2017).

A meta-analysis of 111 research studies, published between 1970 and 2003, indicated that the average recipient of group treatment is better off than 72% of untreated controls (Burlingame, Fuhriman and Mosier, 2003). A number of other outcome research studies have demonstrated that group psychotherapy with children can be as effective as individual psychotherapy (Hoag and Burlingame, 1997; McRoberts, Burlingame and Hoag, 1998; Shechtman and Ben-David, 1999; Shechtman, 2014, 2017; Haen and Aronson, 2017).

Salloum and Overstreet (2008) reported on a comparative research study over a ten-week therapeutic intervention with fifty-six children (aged seven to twelve years) suffering from moderate to severe symptoms of posttraumatic stress. The children were randomly assigned to group or individual treatment. Results showed equally significant symptomatic improvement in both treatment modalities. Thus, the study showed that group treatment was as effective as individual treatment for these traumatised children.

Springer, Misurell and Hiller (2012) reported on a piece of research involving 91 children, who had been sexually abused and subsequently received play-based group therapy. The results showed symptomatic improvement, as well as improved behaviour and better safety and social skills, both immediately and at three-month follow-up.

Daigle and Labelle (2012) reported on a pilot study evaluating a group therapy program tailored specifically for bereaved children, after a parent or close relative had committed suicide. Results indicated positive change in basic safety and realistic understanding, as well as amelioration of physical and psychological symptoms, and improved behaviour, self-esteem, personal awareness and social skills.

Craven and Lee (2010) reported on a unique intervention tailored to first-time fostered children, named *transitional group therapy*. The treatment included psychoeducational and play therapy. Results showed a positive change in prosocial behaviour, as well as improved orientation toward peers, family and school.

Psychotherapy groups for children can indeed have a number of advantages. They operate as a peer group and have developmental as well as therapeutic value. Children can overcome feelings of loneliness, whilst in the supportive environment of a therapy group. Belonging to such a group can distinctly help members to develop self-esteem and to become more confident about making friends (Ezquerro, 2017; Shechtman, 2014, 2017).

Many parents (and children) perceive the group as less threatening a format than individual therapy, where the child could be seen as being singled out. Denial of real-life experiences is more difficult in a group, as these are shared by members. In turn, the positive experiences in the group can be applied to other situations outside the group's life, such as home or school (Reid and Kolvin 1993; Ezquerro, 2017).

Apart from clinics and hospitals, groups can be provided in many other settings like children's homes, schools and remand homes. For school-age children, the group situation fits well developmentally into their ordinary lives. In the 1970s, child group therapy became an accepted and well-established form of treatment in the British NHS (Farrell, 1984).

However, despite the clear benefits and growing popularity of group work with children, group analysis paid minimal attention to this form of therapy, in terms of practice, training, lectures and publications, during the first five decades since its inception, as appraised by James Bamber in the late 1980s.

Bamber (1988) pointed out a paradox that, in spite of its therapeutic potential, particularly after James Anthony (1965) had left a blueprint of how group-analytic psychotherapy with children might develop, group analysis was (and still is) overwhelmingly unconcerned with child group development, let alone child group therapy. The child became an excluded stranger in the therapeutic *stranger* group (Hopper, 2009; Nitzgen, 2016).

Out of the forty-five emblematic annual Foulkes lectures in the UK so far, only one has devoted itself to work with children. That speaks for itself. It was delivered by Claude Pigott, a French psychoanalyst travelling from the Continent for the occasion in 1989, maybe, as a result of Bamber (1988)'s complaint. The theme was: *Deep truth, madness and paradox in analytic children's groups* (Pigott, 1990).

Interestingly, at his Foulkes Lecture, Pigott presented a strong case for group-analytic work with children who, with their bodies, were able to express primary thoughts straight-forwardly, giving easier access to underlying themes and causes:

> Children talk with their bodies as well as with speech and have the gift of condensing a whole situation.
>
> Pigott (1990: 99)

Foulkes had been interested in condensation as an important psychological phenomenon in human evolution, which can operate in groups, especially at the primordial level.

> The process by which, since prehistoric times, human beings assimilate images produces condensations ... These can become attached to particular persons ... Hence the belief in devils and gods, angels and evil spirits, witches and so forth.
>
> Foulkes (1990: 282)

This type of phenomena can very much be present in the child's mind but, by and large, group analysts have been uninterested in exploring it further. In the last thirty years, we could only find eight articles specifically dealing with child group therapy published in the journal *Group Analysis* (Ezquerro, 1995; Behr, 1996; Barratt and Segal, 1996; Hamori and Hodi, 1996; Westman, 1996; Woods, 1996; Pinel, 2011; Leal, 2013).

Of these, five articles were part of a special 1996 issue of the journal on group psychotherapy with children and adolescents; which was put together by John Woods in his attempt to follow James Bamber with the task of addressing this big gap in group-analytic theory and practice.

Harold Behr (a child psychiatrist and group analyst) described a children's therapy group of different ages ran in parallel with parents' groups, as part of a creative programme of multiple family group therapy:

The children's group has proved the most taxing and difficult of all the sessions ... The quieter, more articulate children tend to be distracted by one or two boisterous, disruptive children ... it has sometimes proved difficult to sustain attention for the stipulated hour.

Behr (1996: 16).

The technique applied was a combination of play and talking. In order to avoid too much disorganisation in the group, some structuring was introduced at times, such as asking each child to pair up with another child or with a therapist for the more vulnerable children. Other techniques involved encouraging a conversation above good experiences before exploring more difficult situations; going round in turn; suggesting a theme for drawing a picture and then pooling the productions for a free-associative session (Behr, 1996).

Rita Leal (a Portuguese group analyst) followed some of Behr's combined techniques. Play among the children in various forms, as well as between the children and the therapists, was a core element of the therapy, followed by an analysis of the interactions that took place. Children were encouraged to be spontaneous and to take the initiative to choose their own themes (Leal, 2013).

Gill Barratt and Barbara Segal (a psychiatric social worker and a child psychotherapist respectively) used some elements of the socio-drama group play reported earlier, in a weekly group with school-age children, which they ran for one year. They were struck with the way in which the children's issues came alive and how they could be addressed more quickly than in individual therapy. Like with Behr's, a concurrent parents' group was a necessary part of the treatment.

By the end of the group programme, the children had improved at home and at school, and their presenting symptoms had largely disappeared (Barratt and Segal, 1996).

Hamori and Hodi (both child psychotherapists) reported an eighteen-month-long weekly group for pre-adolescent children, successfully ran on group-analytic lines. They stressed to the children that every action that happened in the group would be seen as a communication about themselves and their problems, which would then be analysed with a view to understanding it together (Hamori and Hodi, 1996).

Along these lines, Pinel (2011) also reported that, in the therapy groups he co-conducted for pre-adolescents, it was possible to make use of transference and counter-transference in an analytic fashion.

Alison Westman (a child psychiatrist and group analyst) reported her experience of co-running an analytic group for severely disturbed children between the ages of seven and eleven.

These children presented major difficulties in establishing positive peer relationships and were initially unable to form an attachment to the group.

Instead, they sought a relationship with the therapists in the group, pushing them to do some form of 're-parenting' for about one year. Only after this, did the children become able to relate to one another positively, which coincided with reports from carers and teachers of a significant improvement in their behaviour (Westman, 1996).

John Woods (a group analyst and child psychotherapist) reflected on the challenges and difficulties that violent children presented in his service's therapy groups. That happened at a time when conservative Prime Minister John Major was publicly stating that we should *"understand less and punish more"*!

Despite this anti-therapeutic political climate, Woods persevered. In his experience, when the co-therapists supported each other sufficiently the group was able to weather the storm, until the child no longer needed antisocial behaviour and his or her aggression was contained (Woods, 1996).

The general consensus among this minority of group-analytic practitioners is that, for optimal results, child group therapists must actively provide some structure to the sessions, particularly in the early stages, with the aim of forming relationships, developing a language of feelings, establishing constructive group norms and providing a secure base.

The therapeutic value of the above group-analytic interventions with children is clear. However, the number of group analysts working with children and writing about it pales into insignificance, when compared with the number of group analysts working with adults.

A case study by Arturo Ezquerro: developing a group-analytic culture in a unit for traumatised children

In the late 1980s, I set up a group psychotherapy programme in a special residential unit for children with emotional, behavioural and communication difficulties affecting their learning (Ezquerro, 1995, 1997, 1998, 2017). At the time of my appointment as the child psychiatrist to this Unit, the institution was jointly managed by the National Health Service and the Education Department, as a part of a transitional funding arrangement.

Initially, a hospital for autistic and, so-called, *psychotic* children between the ages of five and eleven, the Unit had opened in the early 1950s and developed a strong individually-oriented therapeutic tradition, based on classical psychoanalytic principles. Individual sessions were considered best from a developmental perspective, because of the implicit nurturing and teaching elements of one-to-one therapy. Group psychotherapy had not been tried.

When I suggested that therapeutic groups could also be beneficial and cost-effective, the staff expressed concerns that I was making such a proposal on economic grounds rather than therapeutic criteria. However, the institution eventually accepted the group idea – with caution.

The Unit offered twenty long-term boarding places as well as additional day places, ad hoc. In his book, *A History of Autism,* Adam Feinstein (2010) presented some helpful descriptions of the early years of the hospital, when the children were particularly challenging and showed major difficulties in forming attachments.

In addition, Golding (2006) provided a vivid account of her own work at the Unit:

> I well remember picking mushrooms in the early hours of the morning – anything rather than have to get up and face those strange children who did not seem to respond to all my lovely, carefully planned activities...
>
> The general ethos was to keep the children calm and not disturb them further so that hopefully with all the therapy (both for them and their parents) they would emerge from their 'psychotic' or 'schizophrenic' state.
>
> Golding, 2006, quoted in Feinstein (2010: 83)

Since the Unit opened, its predominant therapeutic culture consisted of individual psychoanalytic sessions for the children, applied flexibly. Therapy had been strongly linked to feeding, both metaphorically and literally. In view of the gross developmental deficits presented by most of the children, staff considered that trying some supplementary feeding strategies would also be worth it:

> to return the children there to their infancy so that they could restart their development. One technique was to give them baby-feeding bottles to suck from... the children used these to squirt milk at the ceiling.
>
> Feinstein (2010: 83)

I discussed this approach with John Bowlby in our supervision. He was sceptical about its usefulness and provided an attachment-based perspective instead. He encouraged me to give priority to supporting the staff and helping the children, in conjunction with their parents and carers, so they could all perceive the Unit as a secure base (Holmes, 2001) – rather than focussing on feeding.

Besides this, Bowlby conveyed the idea that putting diagnostic labels on the children, such as psychosis or schizophrenia, was unhelpful – since they were still developing a personality structure, which was too tender for adult-like psychopathology. He was adamant that whilst recognising that some children are more vulnerable to future psychosis than others, such an adverse course can be prevented with adequate environmental support.

However, Bowlby (1988) agreed with the diagnosis of childhood autism as a complex neuro-developmental disorder.

Autistic children have great difficulties in using language and abstract concepts, which makes it rather difficult for them to communicate meaningfully and to form relationships with other people. This puts additional demands on parents and carers, which may sometimes stretch the caregiving and attachment systems to breaking point.

When I joined the staff team, the institution was still struggling to come to terms with a major bereavement, following the sudden death of its director – a psychiatrist, psychoanalyst and founding member who had been a charismatic leader and parental-like figure to the team.

Kaplan (1991) postulated that in the condensed imagery of some of the staff, the late director was perceived as a *messianic* type of figure. The loss appeared to be so painful that hardly anybody talked about it.

When I reported this to Bowlby, he suggested that the late director had probably been an attachment figure for the staff and advised me to do some bereavement work with them as an essential part of my job. The rationale for this was to protect the children from the unresolved institutional bereavement and to improve the functioning and effectiveness of the team.

It happened that the institution was also going through important structural changes, from being centrally managed by the regional Health Authority to being locally managed by the Education Department; from being a hospital to becoming a special boarding school. These changes were generating significantly high levels of anxiety among many members of the staff, particularly as there was a threat that the Unit might be closed altogether.

In these circumstances, I set up a weekly staff group. The task was twofold: first, to help staff grieve the loss of their leader; second, to work through the anxieties experienced in connection with the uncertainty about the future of the institution.

Gradually, a group-analytic culture developed, as the institution became structured along various layers of group work for the staff, the children and their parents or carers holding legal responsibility. My aim was to create a therapeutic environment and a healthy collective consciousness in the organisation.

At the Unit, children continued their education. They were allocated to classes on grounds of similarities in development and ability, rather than age. So, prior to the start of the therapy group programme, it was natural for staff to argue for homogeneity of disordered behaviour in the group.

However, after reading Reid and Kolvin (1993), I considered that including an excess of aggressive children could keep the therapists occupied most of the time in preventing disasters. On the other hand, a group of very timid or depressed children might become flat.

Eventually, Alice Byrnes (an art therapist) and I agreed to set up and co-conduct a mixed group of children with heterogeneity of personalities and presenting problems. She and I hoped that this would enhance the therapeutic potential for both identification and differentiation among the children in the group.

As an integral part of the programme, I also arranged regular meetings with the parents (many of whom were foster parents) and the professionals responsible for the care of the children. These meetings, to which the teachers were also invited, were unanimously welcomed and became an effective tool for the evaluation of the therapeutic project and the monitoring of the children's progress.

The Education Department decided to keep the Unit open, which helped the organisation with long-term planning.

Alice and I initially invited two boys and two girls, to start a slow-open group which children joined and left when ready. Maximum membership was six, with an average stay of a year and a half to two years.

After three and a half years, Alice changed jobs and moved out of town. I continued running the group on my own until I left, some eighteen months later. Over the five years, more than twenty children were treated in the group.

Running it on my own was harder for me and, initially, appeared so for the children; but gave them further opportunities to explore their feelings about separation, loss and single parenting.

> **John**, a seven-year-old, became very upset when his parents split up, around the time Alice, the co-therapist, had left. He had a number of aggressive reactions in the group but one day burst into tears, and said that he was very angry with his parents and with me; he added: *"Nobody wants me"*.
>
> **Peter**, an eight-year-old, put his arm around him and said: *"Don't worry John; I'll be your friend"*.

As discussed earlier in the chapter, friends are governed by different sets of rules at different stages of development. Qualities of friendship include trust, loyalty, reciprocity, emotional fulfilment and a validation of each other's identity.

Alice and I had told the children at the outset that there would be a regular meeting of one hour, on the same day and time each week, in the same room, to talk about things that were important to them.

During the early sessions, when the children first discover the opportunity to express themselves, the level of noise was quite considerable at times. Alice and I were not sure if our interpretations were getting through or getting lost within the maelstrom.

Later, at quieter moments, our comments were more distinctively heard. We tried to keep them simple, playful and colloquial.

We learned that what we said rarely went unperceived. We exploited this and tried to ensure that every comment, no matter how trivial or peripheral, contributed to the creation of a therapeutic group environment. Once this was established, the children became more able to think in psychological terms with surprising rapidity.

Our attitude, as therapists, was usually reflective and unobtrusive – unless disrupted by violence. We encouraged contributions consisting of verbal communication and interpretation. The group was not formally structured but carefully planned and thought about.

> **Clare** was five when her single-parent mother, as a result of psychotic breakdown, had a long stay in a psychiatric hospital, during which Clare

was received into care. In the group she broke toys and threw the pieces at other children.

Alice, the co-therapist, held her in a caring but firm way, saying: *"I am doing this because I care for you, Clare, and want to keep you and the other children safe"*.

Clare did not listen but shouted: *"She is going to hurt me; she is going to hurt me!"*

Then, **Jane**, a nine-year-old, said: *"Alice is not hurting you, Clare; she is only trying to keep you safe",* following which Clare stopped shouting and calmed down.

The children were expected to stay in the room, not to damage the furniture, or hurt each other physically, and to keep confidence. The last was clearly important for them. When a child did bring up group matters outside, the others usually reacted angrily in the next meeting, insisting that the group was private and different from the rest of the week.

We, the therapists, did not primarily seek to alter surface behaviour, but to help the children towards a deeper understanding of their feelings and reactions.

All of them had a considerable need to *belong*, particularly those who were *not wanted* in their own lives outside the group. The relationship between group members, including the therapists, was emphasised. For many of the children, this was the first experience of feeling important in the life of a peer group.

The setting was safe and protected for them. This facilitated the creation of learning opportunities for them about how to relate to adults and peers, as well as how to make friends. Interpersonal learning was one of the main therapeutic factors.

Paul, a seven-year-old, had serious difficulties in forming relationships of any kind. He was playing on his own with two dolls, which would kick and punch each other increasingly hard.

Sue, a nine-year-old, was watching him when she picked up two other dolls, making them shake hands and kiss each other, which trapped Paul's attention.

I said that it would be easier for Sue's dolls to make friends.

Then, **Paul** uttered: *"I also want to have a friend but I don't know how"*.

I added that maybe the best way to have friends is to try to be friendly with them.

At that point, **John** nodded and joined the conversation with a smile...

Fostering peer relationships is an important part of group therapy.

The experience of making friends is not only a source of gratification and of learning social skills, but an opportunity to experience a companion who is supportive and can become a supplementary attachment figure at times of adversity.

Friendship is a unique form of pair bonding and one of the most precious human experiences. It is reciprocal, established between equals, and can be fragile or enduring. Friendships, unlike familial bonds, but like group-analytic bonds, are voluntary.

Co-therapy enabled us to offer the best of both worlds. In children's groups, the level of activity is such that it becomes difficult to keep an eye on all the moves, whilst preserving an analytic mode. Flexibly sharing both roles (looking after the safety of the group and creating thinking space) enhanced the therapeutic potential.

For some of the children, this was the first time they had experienced a kind of *parental couple* working together.

When I became a sole therapist, I needed to be more proactive and leader-like at the expense of interpretation. In contrast to adult groups, in children's groups there is far less verbal interpretation anyway.

The majority of parents, carers and teachers were appreciative of the changes observed in the children, particularly an improvement in the quality of relationships with peers and grown-ups, and in school performance.

Staff sensitivity groups continued running weekly; which contributed to the overall success of the project. The institution changed its approach and child group therapy continued after I left.

I also changed through this experience. I learned from Alice and the other staff and, above all, from the children.

Discussion

In therapy groups, children can swiftly see the impact of their behaviour on other people, and the impact of others' behaviour on them, without being as exposed to the consequences as they might be in their own daily lives. Strengths and weaknesses are exposed in the group, in a safe and confidential way.

For most school children, the small therapy group can be a highly attractive setting because of the resemblance to and kinship with the natural peer group. This setting provides them with good opportunities to learn about themselves in relation to other children, as well as in relation to the therapists who represent the adult world.

Although children naturally show a good dose of physical energy and a drive for activity, non-verbal narratives can be interpreted verbally to the child.

In groups with adults, who are compelled to express themselves in words, activity tends to be seen as a form of acting out and inactivity as a potential form of reflection. In contrast to that, in groups with children, activity is part of their ordinary language and inactivity may represent a state of resistance.

Indeed, physical movement is another basic difference between children and adults in groups, which may partly explain why group analysts have largely shied away from running children's groups.

The group-analytic approach focuses on verbal expression, both in children and in adults, as the preferred mode of communication. In this respect, it has been suggested that the main technical problem in child group therapy consists

> not in interpreting activity but in converting it into a speech.
>
> Anthony (1965: 187)

To carry out any sort of therapy with children involves having a capacity to talk to them. Talking to children entails effort and practice. It is more difficult to talk therapeutically to children than to adults, because it requires a radical change in one's normal talking habits. Since most adult communications to children take the form of passing information, giving advice, or dictating prohibition, they are largely one-way channels allowing for minimum feedback.

To establish a two-way communicative process with the child may demand from the adult a change of attitude and behaviour, as well as language. Group therapists working with children must indeed learn to speak the language of the child, which is simple, brief, direct and concrete:

> It has a starkness which defies artful dissimulation and circumlocution. It attempts to say what is means.
>
> Anthony (1965: 189)

The group therapist must become interested in what the child has to say, which may represent an unusual viewpoint of the world, seen through innocent eyes. Sometimes, therapists can become interested because the child reactivates part of their own childhood experiences and opens up a lost world of childhood.

According to Anthony (1965), this may have 'circular' therapeutic value; which resonates with Foulkes's (1964) conception of group analysis as a form of psychotherapy of the group, by the group, including its conductor.

Getting back in touch with one's own childhood could be a gratifying experience on its own right, but it definitely is an essential element in the process of establishing contact with the child and developing empathy. It allows the group therapist to experience what it feels like to be a child of a particular age.

Relating to a child without talking down to him or her is not an easy task for many adults. Successful talking with children, above all, implies reciprocal communication:

> The child will open the door to his magical world of childhood and admit the right sort of adult in.
>
> Anthony (1965: 189)

Age and natural group formation to some extent dictate the therapeutic techniques used with children.

It is vital that therapists make themselves comprehensively conversant with the developmental phases of childhood and the sequential changes that occur in the cognitive, emotional, psychosocial, moral, and linguistic spheres. This demands a fair understanding of developmental child psychology as background knowledge to group therapy with children, which may include a wide range of situations.

Some children do better in heterogeneous diagnostic groups. Other in homogeneous diagnostic categories. There is a tendency to put children together in similar age groups. Overall, group analysts working with children prefer mixed-gender groups and tend to stretch the age range a little to include both younger and older children, with a view to maximising therapeutic potential.

Much of what group analysts know about group work with children is based on adult groups. It would be a huge mistake to generalise information from adult groups to children's groups, because children have unique developmental needs and operate differently from adults. Children perform specific tasks, display certain abilities and have special needs, according to each stage of their development.

Play is another important distinction between adults and children in therapy groups. Playfulness is key to any meaningful therapeutic relationship with children. It may take the form of socio-dramatic play, an enactment of traumatic experiences, or a playful approach to the world of the adult.

Thus, play is a crucial form of communication for the child, particularly when language is insufficient. It is a natural outlet for the expression of fantasies, wishes and fears that constitute a vital part in the child's day-to-day psychosocial life.

Group therapy with children also differs from that of adults in the quality and quantity of *dynamic administration*. This involves setting up the group, arranging the meetings and dealing with boundaries.

In view of the strong tendency towards action, groups for children require even more careful advanced planning than for adults, as well as special attention to boundary activities and incidents that may impinge on the group processes (Behr, 1988; Woods, 1993, 2003; Behr and Hearst, 2005; Lust and Hamori, 1996).

In individual therapy, the huge disparity between the status of the child and that of the therapist is too obvious and can lead to an intense transference. In a therapy group, such transferences tend to become diluted and might be better managed. According to Pigott (1990) and Pinel (2011), there is usually more counter-transference response in child therapy than in adult therapy, and in group therapy as compared with individual therapy.

In doing group therapy with children, therefore, the therapist should expect to experience appreciable amounts of positive and negative counter-transference feelings in quick sequence. Special attention should be paid, so as not to inadvertently project these feelings onto the children.

In well-functioning therapy groups, the group-as-a-whole may represent a secure base for the individual child; something that he or she can use to explore and overcome fears and difficult feelings, rather than act them out. However, therapists must be prepared to provide a more parental-like attachment figure by giving special attention and care to a particular child, when needed.

Conclusion

The conclusion of this chapter is threefold:

First, positive relationships with siblings and peers are precious during childhood for optimal development. Thus, a proper knowledge of the psychosocial and peer group developmental stages of children should be an integral part of the training of any child therapist; *mutatis mutandis*, it would help parents to understand their children better. It would also be of great value in group-analytic training, thinking, writing and working.

Second, child group psychotherapy is a growing, highly beneficial and cost-effective form of treatment, at least since the age of four years. A deep understanding of early psychosocial and peer group development by child psychotherapists, individual and group, is key for best therapeutic interventions and results.

Third, paying more attention to the group-specific developmental characteristics of children and to the evolution of child group psychotherapy might be advantageous for the development of group analysis itself, as a theoretical, scientific and clinical discipline.

References

Adler A (1938) *Social Interest: A Challenge to Mankind*. London: Faber and Faber.

Ahlin G (1995) The interpersonal world of the infant and the foundation matrix for the groups and networks of the person. *Group Analysis* 28(1): 5–20.

Aichhorn A (1922) On education in training schools. In: Fleischmann O, Kramer P and Ross H (eds) (1964) *Delinquency and Child Guidance: Selected Papers*. New York: International Universities Press, pp. 15–48.

Aichhorn A (1925) *Wayward Youth* (1965 edition). New York: Viking Press.

Aichinger A and Holl W (2017) *Group Therapy with Children. Psychodrama with Children*. New York: Springer.

Akhtar S and Kramer S (1999) Beyond the parental orbit: Brothers, sisters and others. In: Akhtar S and Kramer S (eds) *Brothers and Sisters: Developmental, Dynamic, and Technical Aspects of the Sibling Relationship*. North Bergen, NJ: Jason Aronson, pp. 3–24.

Altermatt E and Pomerantz E (2003) The development of competence-related and motivational beliefs: An investigation of similarity and influence among friends. *Journal of Educational Psychology* 95(1): 111–123.

Anthony EJ (1965) Group analytic psychotherapy with children and adolescents. In: Anthony EJ and Foulkes SH (eds) *Group Psychotherapy: The Psychoanalytic Approach*. London: Maresfield, pp. 186–232.

Atkins RN (1983) Peer relatedness in the first year of life: the bird of a new world. *Annual of Psychoanalysis* 11: 227–244.

Axelrod R and Hamilton WD (1981) The evolution of cooperation. *Science* 211(-4489): 1390–1396.

Axline VM (1947) *Play Therapy*. Boston, MA: Houghton Mifflin.

Axline VM (1950) Entering the child's world via play experiences. *Progressive Education* 27: 68–75.

Bagwell CL and Schmidt ME (2011) *Friendships in Childhood and Adolescence*. New York: Guildford Press.

Bamber JH (1988) Group Analysis with Children and Adolescents. *Group Analysis* 21(2): 99–102.

Bank S and Kahn M (1997) *The Sibling Bond*. New York: Basic Books.

Banny AM, Ames A, Heilbron N and Prinstein MJ (2011). Relational benefits of relational aggression: Adaptive and maladaptive associations with adolescent friendship quality. *Developmental Psychology* 47(4): 1153–1166.

Barratt G and Segal B (1996) Rivalry, competition and transference in a children's group. *Group Analysis* 29(1): 23–35.

Bates E, Camaioni L and Volterra E (1975) The acquisition of performatives prior to speech. *Merril-Palmer Quarterly* 21: 205–226.

Beebe B and Lachmann FM (2005) *Infant Research and Adult Treatment: Co-Constructing Interactions*. New York: Routledge.

Behr H (1988) Group analysis with early adolescents: Some clinical issues. *Group Analysis* 21(2): 119–133.

Behr H (1996) Multiple family group therapy: A group-analytic perspective. *Group Analysis* 29(1): 9–22.

Behr H and Hearst L (2005) Groups for children and adolescents. In: Behr H and Hearst L (eds) *Group-Analytic Psychotherapy: A Meeting of Minds*. London: Whurr, pp. 203–219.

Bettelheim B (1976) *The Uses on Enchantment: The Meaning and Importance of Fairy Tales*. New York: Vintage Books.

Boehm C (1999) *Hierarchy in the Forest: The Evolution of Egalitarian Behavior*. Cambridge, MA: Harvard University Press.

Boehm C (2012) *Moral Origins*. New York: Basic Books.

Bowker J, Fredstrom B, Rubin K, Rose-Krasnor L, Booth-LaForce C and Laursen B (2010) Distinguishing those children who form new best friends from those who do not. *Journal of Social and Personal Relationships* 27: 707–725.

Bowker JC and Spencer SV (2010) Friendship and adjustment: A focus on mixed-grade friendships. *Journal of Youth and Adolescence* 39: 1318–1329.

Bowlby J (1938) The abnormally aggressive child. *Human Relations* 19: 230–234.

Bowlby J (1939) Jealous and spiteful children. *Home and School* 4(5): 83–85.

Bowlby J (1958) The nature of the child's tie to his mother. *International Journal of Psychoanalysis* 39: 350–373.

Bowlby J (1969) *Attachment and Loss. Vol 1: Attachment* (1991 edition). London: Penguin Books.

Bowlby J (1973) *Attachment and Loss. Vol 2: Separation, Anxiety and Anger* (1991 edition). London: Penguin Books.

Bowlby J (1974) Problems of marrying research with clinical and social needs. In: Connolly K and Bruner J (eds) *The Growth of Competence*. London: Academic Press, pp. 303–307.

Bowlby J (1988) Developmental psychiatry comes of age. *American Journal of Psychiatry* 145: 1–10.

Bowles S (2006) Group competition, reproductive leveling, and the evolution of human altruism. *Science* 314(5805): 1569–1572.

Bowles S (2009) Did warfare among ancestral hunter-gatherers affect the evolution of human social behaviors? *Science* 324: 1293–1298.

Boyd R (2006) The puzzle of human sociality. *Science* 314: 1555–1556.

Brown D (1998) Fair shares and mutual concern: the roll of sibling relationships. *Group Analysis* 31(3): 315–326.

Bruner J (1977) Early social interaction and language acquisition. In: Schaffer HR (ed.) *Studies in Mother-Infant Interaction*. New York: Norton, pp. 271–289.

Brunori L (1998) Siblings. *Group Analysis* 31(3): 307–314.

Burlingame GM, Fuhriman A and Mosier J (2003) The differential effectiveness of group psychotherapy: A meta-analytic perspective. *Group Dynamics: Theory Research and Practice* 7(1): 3–12.

Buss AH (1980) *Self Consciousness and Social Anxiety*. New York: WH Freeman.

Cassidy J, Scolton KL, Kirsh SJ and Parke RD (1996) Attachment and representations of peer relationships. *Developmental Psychology* 32(5): 892–904.

Cherry K (2020) Self-awareness development and types. *Very Well Mind*. Available at What Is Self-Awareness and How Does It Develop? (verywellmind.com)

Coles P (2003) *The Importance of Sibling Relationships in Psychoanalysis*. London: Karnac.

Cortina M and Liotti G (2010) Attachment is about safety and protection, intersubjectivity is about sharing and social understanding. The relationships between attachment and intersubjectivity. *Psychoanalytic Psychology* 27(4): 410–441.

Craven PA and Lee RE (2010) Transitional group therapy to promote resiliency in first-time foster children: A pilot study. *Journal of Family Psychotherapy* 21(3): 213–224.

Daigle MS and Labelle RJ (2012) Pilot evaluation of a group therapy program for children bereaved by suicide. *Crisis: The Journal of Crisis Intervention and Suicide Prevention* 33(6): 350–357.

Davies K (2015) Siblings, stories and the self: the sociological significance of young people's sibling relationships. *Sociology* 49(4): 679–695.

Dishion TJ and Piehler TF (2009) Deviant by design: Peer contagion in development, interventions and schools. In: Rubin KH, Bukowski W and Laursen B (eds) *Handbook of Peer Interactions, Relationships, and Groups*. New York: Guilford, pp. 589–602.

Dunn J (1983) Sibling relationship in early childhood. *Child Development* 54(4): 787–811.

Dunn J (2014) Sibling relationships across the life-span. In: Hindle D and Sherwin-White S (eds) *Sibling Matters: A Psychoanalytic, Developmental and Systemic Approach*. London: Karnac, pp. 69–81.

Dunn J and Kendrick C (1982) *Siblings: Love, Envy and Understanding*. London: Grant McIntyre.

Dunn J and McGuire S (1992) Sibling and peer relationships in childhood. *Journal of Child Psychology and Psychiatry* 33(1): 67–105.

Dupont MA and Jinich A (1993) *Psicoterapia Grupal para Niños*. Guadalajara, México: Universidad de Guadalajara y Asociación Psicoanalítica Jalisciense.

Dwivedi KN (ed) (1998) *Group Work with Children and Adolescents: A Handbook*. London: Jessica Kingsley.

Eisenberg N, Fabes RA and Spinrad TL (2006) Prosocial development. In: Damon W and Lerner RM (Series eds) and Eisenberg N (Vol. ed) *Handbook of child psychology*.

Vol 3: Social, emotional, and personality development (6th edition). New York: Wiley, pp. 646–718.

Emde RN (1992) Positive emotions for psychoanalytic theory: Surprises from infant research and new directions. *American Psychoanalytic Association* 39: 5–44.

Ezquerro A (1995) Group therapy within the NHS III: Should we invest in group psychotherapy? A personal account. *Group Analysis* 28(4): 453–457.

Ezquerro A (1997) Tradición institucional y cambio. *Boletín Sociedad Española de Psicoterapia y Técnicas de Grupo* 4(11): 183–190.

Ezquerro A (1998) Abuso Sexual Infantil. *Boletín Sociedad Española de Psicoterapia y Técnicas de Grupo*, 4 (13): 139–140.

Ezquerro A (2017) *Encounters with John Bowlby: Tales of Attachment*. London: Routledge.

Ezquerro A (2019) Brexit: Who is afraid of group attachment? *La Revista. The British Spanish Society Magazine* 248: 18–19.

Ezquerro A (2020) Brexit: Who is Afraid of Group Attachment? Part I. Europe: what Europe? *Group Analysis* 53(2): 234–254.

Farrell M (1984) Group-work with children: the significance of setting and context. *Group Analysis* 17(2): 146–155.

Feinstein A (2010) *A History of Autism: Conversations with the Pioneers*. Chichester, UK: Wiley-Blackwell.

Fonagy P (2001) *Attachment Theory and Psychoanalysis*. New York: Other Press.

Fonagy P and Target M (1996) Playing with reality. Part I: Theory of mind and the normal development of psychic reality. *International Journal of Psychoanalysis* 77: 217–233.

Fonagy P and Target M (2007) The rooting of the mind in the body. New links between attachment theory and psychoanalytic thought. *Journal of American the Psychoanalytic Association* 55(2): 411–456.

Foulkes SH (1964) *Therapeutic Group Analysis*. London: George Allen & Unwin.

Foulkes SH (1975) Concerning criticism of inner-object theory. In: Foulkes E (ed) (1990) *S. H. Foulkes Selected Papers: Psychoanalysis and Group Analysis*. London: Karnac, pp.281–284.

Foulkes SH (1977) Notes on the concept of resonance. In: Wolberg LR and Aronson ML (eds) *Group Therapy: An overview*. New York: Stratton Intercontinental Book Corp., pp. 52–58.

Freud A and Dann S (1951) An experiment in group upbringing. *Psychoanalytic Study of the Child* 6: 127–168.

Garland C (1980) Face to face. *Group Analysis* 13(1): 42–43.

Garvey C (1984) *Children's Talk*. Cambridge, MA: Harvard University Press.

Genyue F and Lee K (2007) Social grooming in the kindergarten: The emergence of flattery behaviour. *Developmental Science* 10: 255–265.

Ginott H (1961) *Group Psychotherapy with Children*. New York: McGraw-Hill.

Golding M (2006) The hitch hiker's guide to autism: An educator's unique account of the history of autism and the development of a relevant and empowering curriculum 1959–2005. In: *The Second World Autism Congress*. Cape Town, South Africa (October).

Goldstein H, Kaczmarek LA and English KM (2002) *Promoting Social Communication: Children with Developmental Disabilities from Birth to Adolescence*. Baltimore, MA: Brooks.

Grunebaum H and Solomon L (1980) Toward a peer theory of group psychotherapy. Part I: On the developmental significance of peers and play. *International Journal of Group Psychotherapy* 30(1): 23–49.

Grunebaum H and Solomon L (1982) Toward a theory of peer relationships. Part II: On the stages of social development and their relationship to group psychotherapy. *International Journal of Group Psychotherapy* 32(3): 283–307.

Haen C and Aronson S (eds) (2017) *Handbook of Child and Adolescent Group Therapy: A Practitioner's Reference*. New York: Routledge.

Hamori E and Hodi A (1996) Reflection of family transference in group psychotherapy for preadolescents. *Group Analysis* 29(1): 43–54.

Harris JR (1995) Where is the child's environment? A group socialization theory of development. *Psychological Review* 102(3): 458–459.

Harris JR (2009) *The Nurture Assumption: Why Children Turn Out the Way They Do?* New York: Free Press.

Hindle D and Sherwin-White S (eds) (2014) *Sibling Matters: A Psychoanalytic, Developmental and Systemic Approach*. London: Karnac.

Hoag MJ and Burlingame GM (1997) Evaluating the effectiveness of child and adolescent group treatment: A meta-analytic review. *Journal of Clinical Child Psychology* 26: 234–246.

Hobson R P (2004). *The cradle of thought. Exploring the origins of thinking*. Oxford, UK: Oxford University Press.

Holmes J (2001) *The Search for the Secure Base*. Hove, UK: Brunner-Routledge.

Hopper E (2009) The theory of the basic assumption of incohesion: Aggregation/massification or (BA) I: A/M. *British Journal of Psychotherapy* 25(2): 214–229.

Howe N, Petrakos H, Rinaldi CM and LeFebvre R (2005) "This is a bad dog, you know…" Constructing share meanings during sibling pretend play. *Child Development* 76(4): 783–794.

Hrdy SB (2005) Evolutionary context of human development. In: Carter CS, Ahnert KE, Grossmann SB, Hrdy SB, Lamb SW, Porges W and Sachser N (eds) *Attachment and Bonding: A New Synthesis*. Cambridge, MA: The MIT Press, pp. 9–32.

Hrdy SB (2009) *Mothers and Others: The Evolutionary Origins of Mutual Understanding*. Cambridge, MA: The Belknap Press.

Izard CE (2009) Emotion theory and research: Highlights, unanswered questions and emerging issues. *Annual Review of Psychology* 60: 1–25.

Kaplan T (1991) Death in an institution. *British Journal of Medical Psychology* 64(2): 97–102.

Kriss A, Steele M and Steele H (2014) Sibling relationships: an attachment perspective. In: Hindle D and Sherwin-White S (eds) *Sibling Matters: A Psychoanalytic, Developmental and Systemic Approach*. London: Karnac, pp. 82–95.

Kymissis P (1996) Developmental approach to socialization and group formation. In: Kymissis P and Halperin DA (eds) *Group Therapy with Children and Adolescents*. Washington, DC: American Psychiatric Press, pp. 35–54.

Lanyado M and Horne A (2009) *The Handbook of Child and Adolescent Psychotherapy: Psychoanalytic Approaches*. New York: Routledge.

Leal R (2013) Disturbed development and group psychotherapy with children. *Group Analysis* 46(4 suppl.): 9–20.

Lust I and Hamori E (1996) The dynamics of losing and building boundaries in an adolescent group. *Group Analysis* 29(1): 37–42.

McCluskey U (2002) The dynamics of attachment in systems-centred group. *Psychotherapy, Group Dynamics: Theory, Research and Practice* 6(2): 131–142.

McRoberts C, Burlingame GM and Hoag MJ (1998) Comparative efficacy of individual and group psychotherapy: A meta-analytic perspective. *Group Dynamics: Theory Research and Practice* 2(2): 101–117.

Maratos J (1998) Siblings in ancient and Greek mythology. *Group Analysis* 31(3): 341–349.

Marmarosh CL (ed) (2020) *Attachment in Group Psychotherapy*. New York: Routledge.

Meltzoff AN (2007) "Like me": A foundation for social cognition. *Developmental Science* 19: 126–134.

Moll H and Tomasello M (2007) Cooperation and human cognition: The Vygotskian intelligence hypothesis. *Philosophical Transactions of the Royal Society B: Biological Sciences* 362: 1–10.

Moreno JL (1934) *Who Shall Survive? A new Approach to the Problem of Human Interrelations*. Washington, DC: Nervous and Mental Disease Publishing Co.

Moreno J L (1946) *Psychodrama. Vol 1*. New York: Beacon House.

Music G (2014) *The Good Life: Wellbeing and the New Science of Altruism, Selfishness and Immorality*. New York: Routledge.

Nitzgen D (2016) Reflections on group analysis and philosophy. *Group Analysis* 49(1): 19–36.

Parens H (1988) Siblings in early childhood: some direct observational findings. *Psychoanalytic Enquiry* 8(1): 31–50.

Parker JG and Gottman JM (1989) Social and emotional development in a relational context: Friendship interaction from early childhood to adolescence. In: Berndt TJ and Ladd GW (eds) *Peer Relations in Child Development*. New York: Wiley Interscience Publication, pp. 15–45

Parker V (2020) *A Group-Analytic Exploration of the Sibling Matrix*. London: Routledge.

Parten MB (1932) Social participation among pre-school children. *Journal of Abnormal and Social* Psychology 27: 243–269.

Piaget J (1951) *Play, Dreams and Imitation in Childhood*. New York: Norton.

Piaget J (1953) *The Origins of Intelligence in the Child*. New York: International Universities Press.

Piaget J (1954) *The Child's Construction of Reality*. New York: Basic Books.

Piaget J (1965) *The Moral Judgment of the Child*. New York: The Free Press.

Pigott C (1990) Deep truth, madness and paradox in analytic children's groups. *Group Analysis* 23: 99–111.

Pinel JP (2011) Group analytical work with violent preadolescents: Working through and subjectivation. *Group Analysis* 44(2): 196–207.

Pines M (1998) *Circular Reflections: Selected Papers on Group Analysis and Psychoanalysis*. London: Jessica Kingsley.

Redl F (1944) Diagnostic group work. *American Journal of Orthopsychiatry* 14: 53–67.

Redl F (1966) *When We Deal with Children*. New York: Free Press.

Reid S and Kolvin I (1993) Group Psychotherapy for Children and Adolescents. *Archives of Disease in Childhood* 69: 244–250.

Robinson CC, Anderson GT, Porter CL, Hart CH and Wouden-Miller M (2003) Sequential transition patterns of pre-schoolers' social interactions during child-initiated play: Is parallel-aware play a bidirectional bridge to other play states? *Early Childhood Research Quarterly* 18: 3–21.

Rose SR (1998) *Group Work with Children and Adolescents*. Thousand Oaks, CA: Sage.

Rubin KH, Coplan R, Chen X, Bowker, JC, McDonald K and Heverly-Fitt S (2015) Peer relationships in childhood. In: Bornstein MH and Lamb ME (eds) *Developmental Science: An Advanced Textbook* (7th edition). New York: Psychology Press, pp. 591–649.

Rustin M (2009) Taking account of siblings. In: Lewin V and Sharp B (eds) *Siblings in Development: A Psychoanalytic View*. London: Karnac, pp. 147–168.

Rutter M (1980) Attachment and the development of social relationships. In: Rutter M (ed) *Scientific Foundations of Developmental Psychiatry*. London: Heinemann Medical, pp. 267–279.

Ryalls BO, Gull RE and Ryalls KR (2000) Infant imitation of peer and adult models: Evidence for a peer model advantage. *Merrill-Palmer Quarterly* 46: 188–202.

Salloum A and Overstreet S (2008) Evaluation of individual and group grief and trauma interventions for children post disaster. *Journal of Clinical Child and Adolescent Psychology* 37(3): 495–507.

Sanders R (2004) *Sibling Relationships: Theory and issues for practice*. New York: Palgrave MacMillan.

Schaefer CE (ed.) (1999) *Short-Term Psychotherapy Groups for Children: Adapting Group Processes for Specific Problems*. Northvale, NJ: Aronson.

Selfhout M, Branje S, ter Bogt T and Meeus (2009) The role of music preferences in early adolescents' friendship formation and stability. *Journal of Adolescence* 32: 95–107.

Shechtman Z (2014) Counseling and therapy groups with children and adolescents. In: DeLucia-Waack JL, Kalodner CR and Riva MT (eds) *Handbook of Group Counseling and Psychotherapy*. Washington, DC: Sage Publications Inc., pp. 1068–1108.

Shechtman Z (2017) *Group Counseling and Psychotherapy with Children and Adolescents*. New York: Routledge.

Shechtman Z and Ben-David M (1999) Group and individual treatment of childhood aggression: A comparison of outcome and process. *Group Dynamics: Theory Research and Practice* 3(4), 1–12.

Simpkins S and Parke R (2002) Do friends and non-friends behave differently? A social relations analysis of children's behavior. *Merrill-Palmer Quarterly* 48: 263–283.

Slavson SR (1940) Foundations of group therapy with children. In: Schiffer M (ed) *Dynamics of Group Psychotherapy* (1979 edition). New York: Jason Aronson, pp. 523–537.

Slavson SR (1943) *Introduction to Group Psychotherapy*. New York: International Universities Press.

Slavson SR and Schiffer M (1975) *Group Psychotherapies for Children*. New York: Free Press.

Slavson SR (1978) *Dynamics of Group Psychotherapy*. New York: Jason Aronson.

Smith PK (2005) Play: types and functions in human development. In: Ellis BJ and Bjorklund DF (eds) *Origins of the Social Mind*. New York: Guildford Publications, pp. 271–291.

Springer C, Misurell JR and Hiller A (2012) Game-based cognitive-behavioral therapy (GB-CBT) group program for children who have experienced sexual abuse: A three-month follow-up investigation. *Journal of Child Sexual Abuse* 21(6): 646–664.

Sroufe LA (1979) Socioemotional development. In: Osofsky J (ed) *Handbook of infant development*. New York: John Wiley, pp. 462–515.

Sroufe LA (1996) *Emotional Development: The organization of Emotional Life in the Early Years*. New York: Cambridge University Press.

Sroufe LA, Cooper RG and DeHart GB (1992) *Child development: Its nature and course.* New York: McGraw-Hill.

Sroufe LA, Egeland B, Carlson E and Collins WA (2005) *The Development of the Person. The Minnesota Study of Risk and Adaptation from Birth to Adulthood.* New York: The Guilford Press.

Stern DN (1998) *The Interpersonal World of the Infant: A View from Psychoanalysis and Developmental Psychology.* New York: Basic Books.

Stern DN (2004) *The Present Moment in Psychotherapy and Everyday Life.* New York: Norton.

Stern DN (2006) Some implications of infant research for psychoanalysis. In: Cooper AM (ed) *Contemporary Psychoanalysis in America.* Washington, DC: American Psychiatric Publishing Inc., pp. 673–641.

Stringer L (1971) *The Sense of the Self.* Philadelphia, PA: Temple University Press.

Sullivan HS (1953) *The Collected Works of Harry Stack Sullivan. Vol 1: The Interpersonal Theory of Psychiatry. Conceptions of Modern Psychiatry. The Psychiatric Interview.* New York: Norton.

Sullivan HS (1955) *The interpersonal Theory of Psychiatry.* London: Tavistock.

Target M (2018) Mentalization within intensive analysis with a borderline patient: Mentalization within intensive analysis. *British Journal of Psychotherapy* 32(2): 202–214.

Tomasello M (2008) *Origins of Human Communication.* Cambridge, MA: MIT Press.

Tomasello M (2009) *Why We Cooperate.* Cambridge, MA: Boston Review Book.

Tomasello M and Carpenter M (2005) The emergence of social cognition in three young chimpanzees. *Monographs of the Society for Research in Child Development* 70: 279.

Tomasello M, Carpenter M, Call J, Behne T and Henrike M (2005) Understanding and sharing intentions: The origins of cultural cognition. *Behavioral and Brain Sciences* 28: 675–735.

Tomasello M, Carpenter M and Liszkowski U (2007) A new look at pointing. *Child Development* 78: 705–722.

Trevarthen C (1979) Communication and cooperation in early infancy: A description of primary intersubjectivity. In: Bullowa M (ed) *Before Speech: The Beginning of Human Communication.* London: Cambridge University Press, pp. 321–346.

Trevarthen C (1980) The foundations of intersubjectivity: The social foundations of language and thought. In: Olsen DR (ed) *The Social Foundations of Language and Thought.* New York: Norton, pp. 316–342.

Trevarthen C (1988) Universal cooperative motives. How children begin to know language and skills and culture. In: Jahoda G and Lewis IM (eds) *Acquiring Culture: Cross-cultural Studies in Child Development.* London: Croom Helm, pp. 37–90.

Trevarthen C (2005) "Stepping away from the mirror: Pride and shame in adventures in companionship"— Reflections on the nature and emotional needs of infant intersubjectivity. In: Carter L, Ahnert KE, Grossmann SB, Hrdy ME, Lamb SW, Porges W and Sachser N (eds) *Attachment and Bonding. A New Synthesis.* Cambridge, MA: MIT Press, pp. 55–84.

Trivers RL (1971) The evolution of reciprocal altruism. *Quarterly Review of Biology* 46: 35–37.

Vaish A, Carpenter M and Tomasello M (2009) Sympathy through affective perspective taking and its relation to prosocial behavior in toddlers. *Developmental Psychology* 45(2): 534–543.

Vandell DL and Mueller EC (1980) Peer play and friendships during the first two years. In: Foot H, Chapman T and Smith J (eds) *Friendship and Childhood Relationships*. London: Wiley, pp. 181–209.

Vitaro F, Pedersen S and Brendgen M (2007) Children's disruptiveness, peer rejection, friends' deviancy, and delinquent behaviors: A process-oriented approach. *Development and Psychopathology* 19(2): 433–453.

Vygotsky LS (1978) *Mind in Society: The Development of Higher Psychological Processes*. Cambridge, MA: Harvard University Press.

Warneken F and Tomasello M (2006) Altruistic helping in human infants and young chimpanzees. *Science* 311: 1301–1304.

Wertsch JW (1991) *Voices of the Mind. A Socio-Cultural Approach to Mediated Action*. London: Harvester Wheatsheaf.

Westman A (1996) Cotherapy and 're-parenting' in a group for disturbed children. *Group Analysis* 29(1): 55–68.

Winnicott DW (1971) *Playing and Reality*. London: Tavistock Publications.

Woods J (1993) Limits and structure in child group psychotherapy. *Journal of Child Psychotherapy* 19(1): 63–78.

Woods J (1996) Handling violence in child group therapy. *Group Analysis* 29(1): 81–98.

Woods J (2003) *Boys Who Have Abused*. London: Jessica Kingsley.

ORCID iD: Arturo Ezquerro https://orcid.org/0000-0002-9910-4576

ORCID iD: María Cañete https://orcid.org/0000-0001-7967-1103

3 The power and therapeutic potential of the adolescent peer group

Arturo Ezquerro and María Cañete

Introduction

Adolescence is a distinct and vital developmental stage, involving dramatic multi-dimensional changes: rapid bodily growth, psychosocial shifts, mood swings, emotional conflict and identity confusion, as well as a thriving sense of energy, idealism and creativity. The changes of this period rival those of infancy in speed and drama. However, there is a significant difference: adolescents have heightened self-awareness, while infants' self-awareness is rudimentary.

Abstract reasoning, which Piaget (1951, 1953, 1954) called formal operations, emerges at adolescence from the childhood state of concrete operations. Adolescents have an ability to unhinge the concrete world of what is to create an instant of what might be. This means an increasingly larger and deeper array of the possible.

A number of progressive improvements occur in the adolescent's information processing, which changes the ways adolescents organise their thinking about the world, develop strategies for dealing with new situations, sort facts and achieve advances in memory capacity and perceptual abilities (Wyer and Jing Xu, 2010).

One of the most important reasons for advances in such mental capacities is the growth of *metacognition*; which has been conceptualised as the knowledge people have about their own thinking processes and their ability to monitor their cognitions. Although some primary school-age children can use some metacognitive strategies, adolescents are much more adept at understanding their own mental processes (Feldman, 2018).

In adolescence, there is also an unprecedented upsurge of sexual drives. Sexual thoughts and feelings are central concerns of adolescents; which they need to make sense of, with a view to developing a healthy and fulfilling sexuality.

In addition, there is a stronger social nature in this period of development than in childhood; the peer group becomes essential to the adolescent's identity and wellbeing, more than in any other stage in the life cycle (Griffin, 2014).

DOI: 10.4324/9781003167747-4

Overall, these new qualities expand the natural modes in which adolescents can be engaged therapeutically. For many of the multitude of psychological and social problems of adolescence, group therapy is the treatment of choice (Dies, 2000; Shechtman, 2014, 2017).

However, despite the emergence of abstract reasoning, improved information processing and enhanced metacognition, the conditions prevailing during adolescence are sometimes unfavourable to logical thinking and reasonable problem-solving.

Action is often a keynote, not only in the adolescent but also in those surrounding him or her; particularly those responsible for the care of young people in difficulty. Because of the pressure for action, the provision of group space for thinking and reflection is critical for adolescents, their parents and care professionals.

Authority during this life period is a key issue for parents, for society and for the adolescents themselves. Interestingly, the word authority comes from the Latin *augere*, meaning to increase or to multiply.

From a phenomenological perspective, for most adolescents, a quintessential and valued authority is someone who can existentially enrich their position as a rapidly growing human being (Frankel, 1998), or who can help them develop and exercise a sense of inner authority that they can recognise as their own (Bruggen, 2006).

Adolescents are regularly creating situations where they put themselves in a position of challenging authority and the existing order. Anna Freud expressed it in a rather dramatic fashion:

> Adolescents are accessibly egoistic, regarding themselves as a centre of the universe ... and yet at no time in later life are they capable of so much self-sacrifice and devotion ....
>
> They oscillate between blind submission to some self-chosen leader and defiant rebellion against any and every authority.
>
> Freud (1966: 137–138)

Quite often, when an adolescent oversteps a boundary, he or she may not find an authoritative adult to relate to but rather one who is angry, and authoritarian, expressing moral outrage and external prohibition; which may prevent (or delay) the development of age-appropriate inhibitory mechanisms and self-regulation – a sense of *inner* authority.

The general consensus in the literature is that the ultimate goal of adolescence is the growth into adulthood (Blos, 1962: Erikson, 1971; Winnicott, 1965, 1969; Briggs, 2002, Griffin, 2014; Feldman, 2018). Of course, being an adult can mean different things, at different times and in different cultures. In Western cultures, there is a popular piece of wisdom that says that adolescence begins with *biology* and ends with *society* (see Chapter 4). For this task to be completed successfully, a satisfactory peer group life is essential.

Blos (1962) partly treated early adolescent attempts at political involvement as the lost remnants of childhood. For example, he interpreted black adolescents' idealisation of a political leader, like Malcolm X, as a regressed ego state analogous to early infantile idealisation of parents.

Unfortunately, this limited and speculative interpretation clouds a truly powerful potential in adolescence, which raises a question: how can a political figure carry something that might be valuable for adolescent development? Or, if you like, what was it about the figure of Malcolm X that evoked such a passionate response that many adolescents were pulled into civil-rights political action?

The political consciousness that emerges in adolescence is unique. According to Frankel (1998), adolescents are acutely responsive to matters of economic injustice and human rights:

> they are able to make observations, ask questions, and hypothesise solutions with a great freedom of mind. Their ideals are not tainted by cynicism and, therefore, they are pulled into the political arena with power and fiery energy … The subtleties, sophistications, and fine shadings come later in life.
>
> Frankel (1998: 126)

Indeed, adolescents are vulnerable and easy prey for consumption by destructive group forces. Hitler's mobilisation of Germany's youth into a disciplined future army, enforcing the doctrine of the Third Reich, was a good example. Tragically, Hitler exploited the needs that young people have for identification with collective ideals, for group belonging and for group attachment.

There has been a tendency in traditional psychoanalytic literature to perceive adolescence as a period in which a recapitulation, or a reworking of the dynamics of childhood, becomes necessary after *latency*; the emphasis has been on *regression* to child-like states, like daydreaming, as one of the main psychological-defence mechanisms in adolescence (Miller, 2013; Freud, 1966; Blos, 1962).

Anna Freud went further than that and interpreted that any kind of attachment or close emotional link during adolescence, such as peer-friendships and intense connections with teachers and leaders, should be considered as taking

> *the place of repressed fixations to the love-objects of childhood.*
>
> Freud (1966: 119)

But this view tends to ignore the fact that something unique is given at adolescence – a spirit of ideals, which directly informs the experience of being an adolescent.

Frankel (1998) asserted that something is born or generated in adolescence that was not generated in childhood: a kind of spirit that is hungry for experience and seeks extreme states of being, whether these be emotional, bodily or ideational:

> The manner in which the emerging spirit in youth is received by the surrounding culture has a significant impact on the process of becoming, an impact that has lasting consequences throughout the rest of one's life.
>
> Frankel (1998: 50)

Kegan (1982) proposed an evolutionary model of development which permits one to perceive recurring phenomena of similar colour and tone throughout the lifespan without having at the same time to regard such similarities as regression or recapitulation:

> *These later phenomena, while similar on the surface, are also far more complex and importantly different from their earlier cousins.*
>
> Kegan (1982: 188)

Kegan based his work on a constructive-developmental approach, emphasising the differences between the various stages of development in the life cycle; but emphasising their unity, continuity and, optimally, integration.

Most teenagers really try, above all (and often desperately), to navigate through the processes of self-initiation, shuttering their innocence, building their capacity to endure losses, expressing the purity of their idealistic visions. Adolescents have a profound need to connect with a larger circle of meaning and with a cultural environment.

Winnicott (1991) valued the new and fresh ideas that adolescents can, in fact, bring to the group culture, stemming from the fact that they are freed from having to think through a long-term perspective. Adolescents possess the vision to see the injustices and inequities in society without the burden of having to come up with a solution. For the adult world, this can be a wake-up call:

> … immaturity is a precious part of the adolescent scene. In this is contained the most exciting features of creative thoughts, new and fresh feelings, ideas for new living. Society needs to be shaken by the aspirations of those who are not responsible.
>
> Winnicott (1991: 146)

Staying narrowly confined to a view of adolescence as a recapitulation of childhood or a mere transition to adulthood, would not allow us to perceive who the adolescent is in his or her own right and, in so doing, we may relinquish the opportunity to learn from them. The extremes of adolescence are intrinsic to it and must be understood on their own terms, not through the *lenses* of childhood or adulthood (Frankel, 1998; Griffin, 2014; Csikszentmihalyi, 2021).

Along these lines, with his touch of genius, Friedrich Nietzsche (2000) sensed that daydreaming is not so much a regressive phenomenon, but an ability to try an action out in fantasy; which may allow an adolescent to assimilate in small doses the affective experience towards progressive development:

> They say he is going backwards; indeed, he is, because he is attempting to take a big jump.
>
> Nietzsche (quoted in Blos, 1962: 92)

Is there a remedy for adolescence?

Most authors (classic and contemporary) have come to agree with the notion of *turbulence*, in order to understand and agglutinate adolescent dynamics in the years that follow puberty: a disruption of peaceful and relatively predictable child growth. In Classical Greece, Plato held a view of youth as a time of marked *emotional upheaval*. William Shakespeare portrayed teenagers as spending their time doing little more than *"wronging the ancientry"* (Shakespeare, in Ezquerro, 2017: 125).

The start of a specialist psychological study of adolescence is attributed to Granville Stanley Hall (1846–1924). He borrowed the concept *sturm und drang* (storm and stress) from German literature and applied it to young people.

In Hall's (1904) appraisal, the emotional turmoil and rebelliousness of adolescence are primarily expressed as defiance against authority and establishment thinking. He also believed that the adolescent psyche contains the remnants of, both, an uninhibited childish selfishness and an increasingly idealised altruism, fluctuating between the two.

Bowlby's (1973, 1988a) language towards children and adolescents was friendlier than Hall's. He thought that childhood is not a period of selfishness, with its negative connotations; and reframed it with an understanding of the underlying reasons for proximity-seeking versus exploration, and other vicissitudes of attachment. In his view, attachment serves physical and emotional survival; which explains why attachment behaviour in children is activated more often and in more intense a fashion than in adolescents or adults.

Attachment (and group-attachment) needs are present throughout the whole life cycle, from cradle to grave; although they manifest themselves differently, according to the specific developmental stage and to environmental circumstances.

In adolescence, Bowlby (1969, 1988b) considered that the excursions from attachment figures become longer in time and space and that new attachment figures are likely to be sought – such as attachment to the group. According to him, these adolescent excursions are a form of exploration; which is a key component of the attachment system that tends to be neglected as a concept in the literature and, sometimes, in the consulting room.

Quite a few adults (and indeed some health professionals) come to regard adolescence itself as psychologically abnormal, owing to the strong feelings aroused in them by young people. Ordinary adolescent explorations tend to be seen as destructive and reprimandable experimentation. Adolescence itself is often "pathologised".

Anna Freud, who was a model of care and concern in her work as an eminent child psychotherapist, became rough, at times, in her conception of adolescence:

> Ego transformations at puberty are distinct from any other phase of life … aggressive impulses are intensified to the point of complete unruliness, hunger becomes voracity, and the naughtiness of the latency period turns into the criminal behaviour of adolescence.
>
> Freud (1966: 146)

Lifton (1979) put the emphasis, not so much on criminality, but on the quieter periods of adolescence. He described the concept of adolescent *stasis*, as the feeling of being stuck or dead inside, which can alternate with an opposite sense of brimming over with energy and vitality. Winnicott (1969) had previously referred to this quiet, but powerful, emotion as *the doldrums*: feeling mentally dead or numb.

It is typical for adolescents to submerge themselves into the doldrums by sleeping a lot, watching hours upon hours of Netflix, holing up in their own room for days on end. The fluctuation between stasis, the cessation of activity, and its counterpart, movement and vitality, can be a prominent element in adolescent development and can play an integral role in the process of adolescent psychotherapy (Frankel, 1998; Fonagy et al., 2002; Fonagy, 2003; Ezquerro, 2017, 2019).

Working with teenagers requires a deep-enough knowledge of their development, as well as a reflective question: are we sometimes trying to cure the adolescents of their own adolescence?

In this respect, Winnicott suggested we keep an eye on counter-transference, as working with adolescents may bring forth feelings of jealousy, envy and resentment over the possible obstructions that may have prevented parents, and therapists, from living out their own adolescence:

> The big threat from the adolescent is the threat to the bit of ourselves that has not really had its adolescence. This bit of ourselves makes us resent those people being able to have their phases of the doldrums and makes us want to find a solution for them.
>
> Winnicott (1990: 155)

Winnicott (1965, 1969, 1990, 1991), time and again, evoked the adolescent's experience of stasis. He concluded that there is no cure for adolescence and that the cure can only belong to the passage of time and the maturation process. In his view, the moments of immobility are a natural part of growing up, and adolescent progression is largely a social phenomenon that takes time and cannot be hurried along.

Having said that, it is necessary to point out that, more than anything else, teenagers have a remarkable built-in capacity for resilience. This can be observed in their exceptional ability to overcome crises and find something positive in negative events. Some studies (Marmarosh et al., 2020; Csikszent-mihalyi, 2021) have found that teens fully recover from bad moods in about half the time it takes adults to do so, of course, with all the pros and cons inherent in that.

Griffin (2014) referred to other studies showing that adolescence is the second period of heightened brain plasticity, similar to the first three years of life. This makes adolescence not only a time of resilience and opportunity, but also a really vulnerable time, because the brain can be damaged by harmful experiences or by drug taking. Teenagers need distinct protection from harm as a few things can go wrong, such as significant personality problems and mental illness, including psychosis.

Sinason (2011) pointed out that, in adolescence, there is an increasing liability to dissociative disorders, particularly amongst adolescents with a history of child sexual abuse. However, multiplicity of identity in adolescents should not be confused with multiple personality disorder, manic-depressive psychosis or schizophrenia.

These serious illnesses may have an early onset in adolescence; but we need to be aware that adolescent personal identity is in a flux anyway, because it is not yet integrated, let alone consolidated. Mental health professionals ought to be mindful not to put too heavy a diagnostic burden on young people prematurely.

Fordham (1994) made an important distinction between *disintegration* and *deintegration* in adolescence. For him, disintegration is a state of being where the ego is completely overwhelmed and things may fall apart beyond repair; it can block natural recovery and prevent further maturation. On the other hand, deintegration corresponds to a process of closing down and opening up of the self that allows for psychological maturation. The state of being *deintegrated* may cause confusion, but it is necessary for progressive development.

Erikson (1971) regarded adolescence as a normative process and not an affliction, a time of discomfort rather than disturbance. According to him, the trails by which a young person may traverse this phase show broad individual variations. The adolescent journey seems to take a long time and yet it tends to be remembered as a short time.

Some parents, who may have kept difficult memories about their own teen years, could think of adolescence as a problem waiting to happen. As a result, they may have too low an expectation, for their kids just to survive these years without anything terrible happening to them.

These parents will typically be aware that the plasticity of the adolescent brain cuts both ways but, possibly in connection with their own histories, they could be too preoccupied about vulnerability and overlook opportunity.

Protection is important, but *overprotection* or excessive parental anxiety is counterproductive. Consequently, anxious parents may need to be reminded that, as the adolescent brain is decidedly malleable, their adolescent children are definitely susceptible to positive influences, not just harmful ones.

It is important to go beyond a mentality of just surviving adolescence (Bruggen and O'Brian, 1986, 1987). And it is crucial that parents continue to be available and accessible, as reliable and consistent attachment figures, to encourage their kids to explore and to thrive.

Of course, in their day-to-day life, adolescents are influenced considerably more by peers than by adults. Teenagers are highly susceptible to the influence of their peers in ways that are more powerful than what we usually think of as peer-group pressure (Griffin, 2014).

However, recent research indicates that those adolescents who have the opportunity to develop a relationship with an adult role model (parental or otherwise) are more successful than their peers in coping with the challenges and stresses of life (Csikszentmihalyi, 2021).

Unlike children, adolescents are wordy and worldly enough to perceive with exacting precision the inconsistencies between what adults say they think and how they act. Ambivalence towards adults is not an unusual feature in the adolescent mind.

Frankel (1998) pointed the finger at a number of common scenarios, in which adults severely interdict adolescents from engaging in certain behaviours in one context, yet these are concurrently fostered and promoted in another.

For instance, many adults tell adolescents that street drugs are undeniably bad, but they use prescription drugs massively to control mood, attention and anxiety, and regard them as unquestionably beneficial. Adolescents are also told never to resolve conflicts through the use of physical aggression, whilst the reigning culture captivates them with violence in films, video games and real life. They are cautioned to restrain their sexual impulses but, at the same time, they are urged to freely partake as developing consumers in society's abundant sexual imagery. And so forth.

We may then need to formulate a legitimate question: what is the impact on the adolescent psyche of this constant bombardment with loud, inconsistent and conflicting messages from adults?

Historically, many traditional and tribal societies instituted formal ways for adults to help young people take their place in the community. Initiations, and other coming-of-age ceremonies or rites of passage, helped boys and girls make the transition from childhood to adulthood.

These rites and ceremonies were highly valued in traditional societies as significant religious rights. The sacred nature of the ritual passage into adulthood was celebrated for the benefit of the entire culture; the ceremony was understood as a form of group regeneration (Eliade, 1958; Lifton, 1979). At the end, the initiates were invited to a reunion with the group, now as "adults", whether or not they were emotionally prepared for it.

Frankel (1998) considered that, in modern societies, rites of passage have taken on newer and disguised forms of expression. Some of these rituals create group connection and a shared sense of identity, which are basic needs in adolescent development.

Today, unfortunately, our youth often reach out to grasp adulthood in rather dangerous ways: by participating in city street gangs or religious cults, by the abuse of increasingly more harmful drugs, by running away from home, by self-starvation, self-mutilation or other forms of parasuicidal behaviour and, in extreme cases, by killing themselves.

In Chapter 2, we pointed out that, from an early age, children are attracted to and choose friends who are like themselves in observable characteristics (Parker and Gottman, 1989; Simpkins and Parke, 2002).

Moving beyond gender, age and ethnicity, it is also the case that children are attracted to peers whose behavioural tendencies are comparable to their own, as well as to similar peer-group functioning (Selfhout et al., 2009).

These tendencies continue during the adolescent phase of development, in which greater behavioural similarities exist between friends than non-friends. Teenagers share friendships with other teenagers who resemble themselves in terms of, both, prosocial and antisocial or delinquent behaviours (Hafen et al., 2011).

A vivid example of adolescent delinquent-group behaviour can be traced back to the fourth century. In his *Confessions*, Augustine of Hyppo wrote an unprecedented piece of self-analysis, in which he bares his soul without reservation. Augustine confessed that he stole when he was sixteen years old, displaying remarkable insight into the motivations for stealing and, even, for the psychology of kleptomania and the influence of the peer group:

> Yet I lusted to thieve, and did it, compelled by no hunger, nor poverty ... For I stole that of which I had enough, and much better. Nor cared I to enjoy what I stole, but joyed in the theft and sin itself. A pear tree there was near our vineyard, laden with fruit, tempting neither for colour nor taste. To shake and rob this, some lewd young fellows of us went and took huge loads, not for our eating, but to fling to the very hogs.
> Augustine (in Alexander and Selesnick, 1995: 57–58)

Augustine did not stop at recognising the lure of the forbidden fruit. He went further in his search for secret motivations, demonstrating an understanding of the psychology of adolescent gangs, with his discovery that committing a crime in the company of others further enhances the gratification derived from it:

> I loved then in it also the company of the accomplices, with whom I did it ... For had I then loved the pears I stole and wished to enjoy them I might have done it alone, had the bear commission of the theft sufficed to attain my pleasure; nor needed I have inflamed the itching of my desires by the excitement of accomplices. But since my pleasure was not

in those pears, it was in the offence itself, which the company of fellow-sinners occasioned.

Augustine (in Alexander and Selesnick, 1995: 58)

In *Confessions*, group psychology becomes real; in contrast to the abstract descriptions of Plato and Aristotle, it assumes flesh and blood (Alexander and Selesnick, 1995). Augustine tells about the feelings, conflicts and anguish he experienced in a peer-group context, with great sincerity and introspective power. He can be rightly considered an early forerunner of psychoanalysis, and of group analysis!

Seventeen centuries after Augustine's insights, Harris (1995, 2009) convincingly argued that, in adolescence, the peer group plays even more significant a role than in childhood. She further argued that adolescent identities develop, to a large extent, from experiences with friends and peers.

According to Bagwell and Schmidt (2011), friends are particularly important, as they provide emotional security and support, self-esteem enhancement and positive self-evaluation, as well as affection, opportunities for intimacy and validation of interests, hopes, and fears.

Above all, friendships offer young people an extra-familial base of security from which they may explore the effects of their behaviours on themselves, their peers and their environments. Friendship is not only a social and positive relational context, but it also provides for the expression and regulation of affect (Mehta and Strough, 2009). The psychic strengthening that comes from the establishment of secure friendship is undeniable.

The force and strength of teenage friendships are rooted in a rapidly developing capacity to connect to a peer group in dramatic, adventurous and playful ways, something that is not often repeated in adult friendship. Loyalty and faithfulness within an adolescent peer group is a remarkable phenomenon (Frankel, 1998).

Peer-group attachment is a basic need of adolescent development. Teenagers protect and shelter each other; they allow themselves to be taken care of by their friends and display genuine warmth and nurturance when they are in the role of care-giver. As intimacy needs are no longer exclusively met by the family, closeness and attachment are transferred over to friends and to the peer group (Kymissis, 1996; Pines, 1996; Altermatt and Pomerantz, 2003; Bowker and Spencer, 2010; Bowker et al., 2010; Banny et al., 2011; Rubin et al., 2015).

Adolescence is often a difficult time for family relationships. Conflict rises, as teenagers press for more autonomy while parents continue to feel responsible for protecting them from potential harm. Physical closeness within the family declines, as teenagers begin to have experiences, especially involving sexuality, that they feel uncomfortable discussing with their parents and would much rather discuss with their friends.

Some parents tend to blame their adolescent-children's peers for causing all the problems. However, by seeing the peer group as a negative and corrupting influence, these parents may avoid coming to terms with the fact that a transformation is happening within their own children's mental life, and that they can no longer rely upon previous familiar patterns of relating and communicating:

> Blaming the peer group is one of the primary defences that parents utilise to avoid facing the 'otherness' that presents itself in adolescence.
>
> Frankel (1998: 2)

In some cases, parents may see this otherness (represented by the adolescent's change) as a disease and they turn to doctors, psychiatrists, psychologists or psychotherapists to find a remedy for it. And therapists, who are themselves adults, may potentially take for granted *adult* ways of perceiving the world, whilst misunderstanding the world of the adolescent. Thus, let us try to explore this world further.

Adolescent ages and stages

Etymologically, the word adolescent comes from the Latin verb *adolescere,* meaning to grow, to blossom and to develop.

Interestingly, the word adult has the same origin. However, adolescent comes from the present participle *adolescentem,* meaning "it is growing"; while adult comes from the past participle *adultum* meaning "it has grown".

The Latin noun *adolescens* or *adulescens* was used in ancient Rome to designate a young person until approximately twenty-five years of age. After this, the person was called *iuvenis* until about the age of forty. Indeed, some of us will remember, with fondness, singing *Gaudeamus igitur juvenis dum sumus,* together with our peers, at our university graduation ceremonies.

In the second century BCE, the Roman writer Marco Terencio Varrón recognised that *adulescentes ab alescendo sic nominatos* (adolescents are called this because they are growing). In the Romance European languages, the terms *adolescent* and *adolescence* appeared for the first time in French in the thirteenth century and in Spanish soon after, as *adolescente* and *adolescencia* (Ezquerro, 2017).

The word *adolescent* appeared in English in 1482, well before the first written record of the word *adult*, which appeared in 1531. According to the Oxford English Dictionary, the original 1482 definition of adolescence referred to a period between childhood and adulthood, which extended between the ages of fourteen and twenty-five in boys and between twelve and twenty-one in girls (Perry, 2009).

In the twenty-first century, there is no worldwide agreement with regard to the time boundaries for adolescence. Nearly every culture recognises adolescence as a distinct developmental phase in the life cycle, but the duration and experiences of adolescence vary greatly across different cultures.

The most widely accepted view is to understand adolescence in broad terms that encompass emotional, cognitive, psychosocial and moral terrains, as well as the strictly physical aspects of maturation.

The United Nations Population Fund and the World Health Organization define adolescents as being between the ages of ten and nineteen. However, the World Bank, the International Labour Organization and the World Programme of Action for Youth refer to adolescents as those who are between the ages of fifteen and twenty-four. Other agencies define adolescence differently, according to cultural beliefs and practices.

In most countries, adolescence is broadly seen as a transition between childhood and adulthood, from dependence on family to autonomy. According to this conception, particularly in the current context of psychosocial and financial crises, adolescence could terminate in one's late twenties, thirties or even later – or the individual may never land at the airport of adulthood, as with Peter Pan and, sadly, Michael Jackson!

Although physical development is largely completed by the age of nineteen, in the third decade of life the body continues developing and the brain continues maturing, working faster and more efficiently. Young people are increasingly undergoing longer higher education and training, as well as delaying long-term personal and work commitments. These new realities have changed popular perceptions about when adulthood begins.

Briggs (2002) argued that a prolonged phase of adolescence might be needed to prepare for the demands of adulthood, in the context of our increasingly turbulent society.

Jacobsson (2005) was unhappy with the idea of extending adolescence indefinitely and postulated that *young* or early adulthood may have to be considered as a separate and distinct developmental stage in the life cycle.

Arnett (2015) took this idea further and proposed the concept of *emerging* adulthood, to describe a broad developmental period from eighteen or nineteen to twenty-five, sometimes extending to thirty years of age. According to him, young persons within this age range are not quite adolescents any longer, nor are they fully responsible adults; they have their own developmental needs and deserve their own space.

But that is another story, which requires a separate book chapter in its own right (see Chapter 4). Giving space for a separate developmental period, for emerging adults, can liberate adolescents from the pressure of *having to* become full adults, and they can feel freer to enjoy being adolescents in their own right.

A number of authors (for example, Blos, 1962; Miller, 1974; Steinberg, 1983; O'Connell, 1979; Coleman, 1985; Frankel, 1998; Griffin, 2014; Feldman, 2018) have suggested that it is useful to differentiate several sub-phases during adolescent development, such as early, middle and late adolescence.

We shall now summarise some of the main features of each of these adolescent periods. However, these should only be seen as a rough guidance, as there are many individual and cultural variations. Our description will have the limitation of being predominantly based on Western cultures.

The age of puberty keeps dropping, whilst it is taking increasingly longer for young people to become full adults. In addition, the tasks and behavioural patterns of these periods overlap and inter-mingle significantly, particularly those of early and middle adolescence, as well as those of late adolescence and early (or emerging) adulthood.

Early adolescence

Starting with puberty, this sub-phase is characterised by intense turmoil, due to hormonal changes and the rapid spurt of physical growth, including sexual organs; which brings with it an inability to accurately estimate the new body space and self-image. Quite often, emotional growth cannot keep pace with the rapid bodily changes.

This early adolescent process reminds us of the experience of jet lag, after long flights – something that was reframed by Gabriel García Márquez, a Nobel Prize-winner for Literature. He suggested that, when we travel by plane across the continents, the body arrives first, while the mind is still wandering for a day or two until it can re-join the body.

In the early teens, at least initially, the physical and sexual changes are not matched by a psychological equivalent. A thirteen-year-old girl spontaneously said in an outpatient therapy group for early adolescents:

I feel my body is ahead of my brain.

We would not have been able to put it more clearly.

This often generates a sense of inner turmoil and a sharp increase of aggressive drives. The young person dealing with these urges may feel bewildered – at times able to control them and, at other times, at their mercy.

In some adolescents, there can be a rollercoaster of ups and downs. The same person is by turn assertive and submissive; industrious and lazy; charming and offensive, cynical and idealistic, arrogant and self-effacing; cruel and considerate; elated and downcast (Ezquerro, 2017).

In the same early adolescent group, a fourteen-year-old boy confessed:

One minute I am on top of the world; next minute I am the most miserable person in the entire universe.

Self-esteem fluctuates greatly in early adolescence, and there are some gender differences. Girls' self-esteem tends to be lower and more exposed than that of boys. One reason for this difference is that, compared to boys, girls tend to be more concerned about physical appearance and social success, in addition to academic achievement. Although boys are also concerned about these things, their attitudes are often more casual (Feldman, 2018).

However, boys do have vulnerabilities of their own. For example, society's stereotypical gender expectations may lead boys to feel that they should be confident, tough, and fearless all the time. Boys facing difficulties, such as not making a sports team, are likely to feel not only miserable about the defeat they face but also incompetent because they don't measure up to the stereotype (Pollack, Shuster and Trelease, 2001).

The increase in sexual and aggressive drives at this time, in addition to colouring the struggle for incipient autonomy from their parents, may often lead to the rejection of previously internalised attitudes. Parental values and standards can then be experienced as harsh, controlling and punitive; parents can be felt as less loved and less loving. The early adolescent often turns to a special friend who acquires an important significance for both boys and girls (Jenkins and Demaray, 2015).

During this sub-phase, the young person may experience emotional pain, as well as a sense of loss or inner emptiness and impoverishment. This may lead to a retreat to familiar positions, from which to make some plea for help from a parent or other authority figure to control the turmoil. Alternatively, the young person may withdraw into a self-centred world or seek refuge in drug-taking.

Early adolescents can be pressed into sexual intercourse before they are emotionally ready for it – as if they were trying to get rid of the *sexual problem*. For adolescents, quite often, sexual initiation is not a joy but an irrepressible relief.

Middle adolescence

During this sub-phase, in addition to continuing their struggle to adapt to the impact of their changing bodies and increased instinctual impulses, young people are moving towards establishing their individual identities and exploring ways of becoming emotionally more autonomous. This includes sexual identities, orientation and choices.

In order to achieve a sense of individual uniqueness, the young person has to give up their unquestioned childhood acceptance of parental attitudes about the world, morals and society, and forge for themselves their own viewpoints. The loosening of the bond to their parents usually comes together with an increased contact with peers. Particularly in middle adolescence, more than in any other life stage, the need for and influence of the peer group are critical.

Acceptance by their peers is a powerful antidote to the sense of loneliness and isolation experienced by many mid-adolescents. Failure to achieve membership of a peer group (maybe due to personal inadequacy, emotional insecurity and fear of rejection) can drive the adolescent back to their parents. This might be experienced as a humiliating surrender. Parents would need to be understanding and sympathetic in order to help the adolescent save face.

Giving in to child-like demands for immediate gratification can be counterproductive at this stage: it can reinforce feelings of powerlessness and humiliation in the adolescent. In turn, this may trigger anger and aggressiveness towards the parents (Griffin, 2014).

Sometimes the middle-aged adolescent feels trapped in a vicious cycle of anxiety, hostility and depression, as he or she tries to renegotiate the terms in the relationship with their parents. In a short-term therapy group for middle-aged adolescents, a fifteen-year-old girl made the following reflection:

> I am nervous about making my own decisions and my mum tells me what to do. I don't know why I say to her: no, I won't do it, no fucking way! Then, I feel bad with myself, because I know my mum is trying to help me. But I can't help it … I feel stuck and I think about harming myself.

It is especially important for parents to understand their mid-adolescent-children's needs to regulate the emotional distance, to make their own decisions and to explore relationships with their peer group. For these young people to develop in a balanced and harmonious manner, it would have to be done in the company of their peers. This may involve friendship or rivalry; collaboration or competition. It can be comforting and reassuring for the mid-adolescent to turn to others with similar uncertainties to their own.

Peer-group closeness is for mutual support, for exploration of related conflicts, for comparison and validation of sexual identity and choice and for experimentation with social roles. Differing identities are tried out. Sometimes, the basis of identification comes from significant adults or role models other than the parents, like teachers, footballers, pop stars or other celebrities.

These models of identification may sometimes possess features that resemble parental characteristics. At other times, they may well be oppositional and contradict parental values.

In this sub-phase, the views on oneself become more sophisticated. It is usually possible to distinguish others' views from self-perceptions, as described by a sixteen-year-old boy in the same mid-adolescent group:

> People look at me as if I were a relaxed, easy-going and confident person; but, quite often, I am really nervous and emotional inside.

This broader assessment of themselves is one aspect of mid-adolescents' increasing understanding of who they are. They can see various aspects of the self simultaneously, and this perception of the self becomes more organised and coherent.

Although adolescents become increasingly accurate in understanding who they are (self-concept), this knowledge does not guarantee that they like themselves any better (self-esteem). In fact, their increasing accuracy in understanding themselves permits them to see themselves fully (warts and all). It's what they do with these perceptions that leads them to regulate their self-esteem (Feldman, 2018).

The same cognitive sophistication that allows adolescents to differentiate various aspects of the self also leads them to evaluate those aspects in different ways (Griffin, 2014). For instance, an adolescent may have high self-esteem in terms of academic performance but lower self-esteem in terms of relationships with others, or vice versa. Indeed, a gradual movement towards intimacy commonly sets in at this stage, involving partners of the opposite or same sex.

Late adolescence

In this sub-phase physical growth is largely completed, but the late adolescent is still facing the task of consolidating personal identity in the multi-relational context of an increasingly complex world. Society expects that some of their personality structure and mature cognitive abilities can now be reasonably established.

Peer-group life continues to be essential. Comparing themselves to their peers helps late adolescents to clarify and consolidate their own identities, as well as to appraise their talents and performance.

Indeed, late adolescents show significant improvements in the specific mental capabilities that underlie intelligence. Memory capacity grows; verbal, mathematical, and spatial abilities increase, making them quicker with a comeback, as well as impressive sources of information. They become more adept at the executive function, effectively dividing their attention across more than one stimulus at a time. And, indeed, some become accomplished athletes (Perry, 2009; Feldman, 2018).

Optimally, late adolescents would have achieved some consistency in their sense of identity, as well as some constancy with regard to self-esteem, personal interests and relationships. These achievements will help them navigate through the stresses of everyday life.

At this point, however, there might be a resurfacing of those conflicts that were not properly worked through during the previous stages. This may generate problems with personal choices, friendships and love relationships – perhaps leading to a difficulty in coping with the increasing academic, social and, in some cases, work demands.

This *closing* sub-phase of adolescence is a testing one, throwing a heavy load on the integrative capacity of the young person. Important life decisions have to be made about examinations, career choice, sexual relationships, living arrangements and social roles. Previous tenuously held adaptations will no longer suffice.

As we said earlier, settling into adulthood may take a good number of years. It is not unusual to retreat into psychological defences that were previously useful but are no longer effective. This dynamic was originally described by Erikson (1971) as a *developmental moratorium*.

There is a significant overlap between late adolescence and early adulthood. We shall explore this further in Chapter 4, in which we will mainly concentrate on the period eighteen to twenty-five years of age. Most countries confer full citizen rights, including a right to vote, at age of eighteen. However, being legally a full adult does not necessarily mean having fully developed a capacity for exercising all the responsibilities that are expected from adult citizens.

Group-analytic interventions with adolescents

James Bamber (1988) pointed out the lack of publications on group work with children and adolescents, in the first three decades of the journal *Group Analysis*. His admonition had little impact on the work with children (see Chapter 2). However, in the last three decades, the journal has regularly published clinical papers on group therapy with adolescents.

A review of all methods of therapeutic group work with adolescents is beyond the scope of this chapter. However, for the interested reader, we would highlight a number of publications, gathering different professionals and approaches, which have contributed to a more united dialogue within this developing field. For example, Aichinger and Holl (2017), Reid and Kolvin (1993), Berkovitz (1995), Hoag and Burlingame (1997), Dwivedi (1998), Rose (1998), Woods (1993, 2003, 2014), Lanyado and Horne (2009), Harris (2011), Haen and Aronson (2017), Malberg and Midgley (2017), Shechtman (2014, 2017) and Marmarosh (2020).

Although adolescents appear to be best equipped for group work, they may also present a big challenge for group therapists. In their attempts to achieve greater autonomy, teenagers are often resistant to authority. In their struggle for identity formation, sometimes they are inflexible and intolerant. Therapists, particularly with early adolescents, may have to introduce some structure to the sessions whilst allowing for freedom of expression (Goldstein, 2001).

In this section, we will focus on a thorough review of the group-analytic literature, stressing those contributions that we consider more influential and relevant to the development of group-analytic approaches and interventions with adolescents.

Milieu group therapy with juvenile delinquents was pioneered by the Austrian-born psychoanalyst August Aichhorn (1925, 1964a, 1964b), in the 1920s. He criticised the punitive methods that were common practice in the traditional reformatories of his time and tried to understand the anti-social nature of troubled adolescents from the perspective of faults or disruptions in their psychosocial development. He made an important distinction between manifest and latent delinquency, and influenced several generations of practitioners.

After World War II, a small group of residential institutions, infused with psychoanalytic thinking, were established to treat adolescents with a range of severe psychological disturbances. From the onset, these were heavily influenced by Aichhorn's work.

Fritz Redl built the Pioneer House in Detroit, Michigan, based on Aich-horn's theories about the origin of aggression and delinquency, as a conse-quence of problems in psychosocial development (Redl and Wineman, 1952).

In England, the Peper Harow therapeutic community for disturbed ado-lescents opened in 1970 and operated over three decades, offering long-term milieu therapy. A number of group analysts worked in this unit. The resi-dents and staff, together, took responsibility for the daily maintenance of the community, and all contributed to cooking and cleaning. The young people were considered to be partners in the therapeutic venture and there was an expectation that everyone would attend the daily community meetings.

In the milieu therapy tradition, Fairall and Glerson (2007) co-conducted a group for offending adolescents, in which they aimed to engage with de-linquent mental processes (described as "absence" of thinking, "hole" in the mind and "concrete" level of symbolic functioning) and transform them into thinking and development. They emphasised that the community's response to these young offenders varied from bewildered indifference to demands for correction and retribution, but without engagement with the meaning of delinquent behaviour; which may contribute to re-enactment, creating a vicious circle.

According to Fairall and Glerson (2007), a custodial and punitive approach in some way mirrors aspects of the delinquent mentality itself and promotes splitting rather than integration in its management of detainees. In contrast to that, they tried to create a therapeutic community environment that cul-tivates engagement, emotional containment and holding together in the ser-vice of integration.

Roth (2014a) described a group of eight boys and three girls, aged fifteen and sixteen, in a residential unit. They all were victims of various degrees of domestic violence and sexual abuse and had a delinquent background. He de-scribed some of the difficulties in the early stages, which sometimes bordered on disturbing emotional cruelty, displayed by some members towards other members, as an expression of unresolved trauma.

Roth (2014b) further elaborated on what he considered ramifications of adolescent processes, later in life. For example, he perceived the interplay between the small and large group in a group-analytic training situation as a re-staging of some adolescent conflicts and dilemmas, particularly regarding norms and the *civilising* process.

John Evans (1998) developed a modified group-analytic approach for ad-olescents, which he termed "active-analytic" group therapy. He argued that the kind of purely reflective stance considered appropriate for adult groups is simply not workable for adolescents, who are neither as articulate nor as intellectually defensive as the adults. His central thesis is a pragmatic one: ad-olescents have to be engaged with tactics that recognise their developmental level and match their active social behaviour.

Evans (1998) maintained that a purely non-directive approach can some-times lead to a kind of aimless, manic distractibility, even a breakdown of group function. According to him, the group conductor must be prepared to support the youngsters, mirroring them actively and affirming them promptly. He profiled such a conductor as a supple, responsive person; someone who has to be prepared to change tack at a moment's notice in order to set limits, anticipate impulsive acts or join with an isolated youngster.

Evans gave special attention to the use of appropriate language with this population, particularly early adolescents. According to him, a common language needs to be developed between conductor and members so that the gap stemming from different personal backgrounds, culture and age is bridged by trust. Then, communication becomes more effective. An expeditious apology might be necessary when the conductor contributes to miscommunications.

Using words with several layers of meanings can create confusion, distraction or may increase tension and not lead to reflection. For example, a lack of awareness of the members having ambivalence (mixed feelings in their own language) by ignoring a dimension that is important to a youngster may simply cause misunderstanding or resistance. And attempting to link the here-and-now with the patient's past in only one go, not realising that it may be too complex for the adolescent to grasp the connection, could make an accurate interpretation useless or counterproductive (Evans, 1998, 2000).

We agree with Evans that interventions are better to be made in a tentative way: "*I wonder whether...*" or "*It seems to me...*" In adolescent groups, checking with members if a comment makes sense, and welcoming their corrections or clarifications, is a good way of creating a culture where dialogue and mutual understanding become an intrinsic part of the therapeutic process.

Recognition on the part of the therapist that it is not possible to get it right all the time, and the acceptance that an interpretation or intervention may be either wrong or misunderstood, can allow for a rapid repair of the rupture and a re-connection. Such recognition prevents the false conclusion that the recipient's response is resistance or merely bloody-mindedness.

Anthony (1965), Behr (1988), Lucas (1988), Woods (1993), Behr and Hearst (2005), Tijhuis (1997) and Pinel (2011) reported on group-analytic therapy with early teens showing a strong tendency towards action; which required more careful planning than for adult groups, as well as special attention to boundary activities and incidents.

Spilling over of the group into the waiting room before or after the sessions and, also, anywhere inside or outside the building was not uncommon. Themes of conversation often changed rapidly, jumping from topic to topic. Moods were usually volatile with, predominantly, non-verbal expressions. Emotional group-holding was an important part of the therapy.

These clinicians prioritised the developmental needs of their early adolescent patients, who were often eager for someone to honestly engage with them in a real conversation where they were not lectured. They also held a common view that interpretations can be delivered in different ways. A group therapist's respectful silence, or brief appreciative acknowledgement in the face of an angry adolescent's verbal challenge, may be a powerful interpretation. Conversely, verbal formulations may rightly be valued for their effort and concern, as much as for their acuity and depth.

Ghiraldelli (2001) reported on a therapy group with early adolescents and suggested that they sometimes behaved as if they did not want to be understood by the therapist, perhaps in an attempt to be separate and different from the adults. The adolescents brought strange objects, displayed odd non-verbal language and kept deliberately silent at times; which required high doses of stamina, patience and containment on the part of the therapist.

This material resonates with some of Winnicott's observations that there can be a quality of concealment in adolescents and that they do not assign the same kind of meanings to what they are experiencing as adults do. He formulated a question about this:

> Do adolescent boys and girls wish to be understood? The answer I think is no. In fact, adults should hide among themselves what they come to understand of adolescence.
>
> Winnicott (1990: 145)

Lust and Hamori (1996) reported on a mix group for adolescents aged fifteen to eighteen with educational and social problems. Initially, the patients idealised the therapists as a perfect couple and the group as an ideal family. However, they soon exposed their anxieties about an uncertain sense of identity, which was mainly expressed through challenging behaviour and boundary problems. That pushed the therapists to use their authority to set limits. Eventually, the adolescents were able to put their anger into words rather than acting it out.

Gianni Nagliero (1996) reported on a mixed therapy group with late adolescents, which he ran in Italy. He highlighted the importance of providing a stable group setting and of keeping an eye on his countertransference, as some of the patients projected onto him their ambivalence towards their parents, who seemed to have exhibited negative parental attitudes that prevented growth in the adolescent.

In connection with that, Racker (1968) had coined the term *complementary countertransference*, to refer to clinical situations in which the therapist perceives the adolescent similarly to how he or she is perceived by the parents.

Leo Tijhuis (1998) reported on a group therapy programme for adolescents in Holland, running over fifteen years. He paid special attention to some adolescents with weak egos or shyness, who perceived the peer group as threatening. Tijhuis provided a model in which he encouraged peer-relating in a safe group environment. This resulted in a therapeutic process in which peers played the role of *guardian angels* of each other's ego development and individuation.

David Wood (1999) reported on the group work at an eating-disorders unit for adolescents, in which anorexic patients frequently viewed therapy as they viewed food; that is, something feared and to be avoided, as intolerable intrusiveness:

> They respond in the same way that they do to the offer of food; they shut their mouth.
>
> Wood (1999: 54)

However, the therapists found creative ways of dealing with silent patients, such as communicating through shared drawing, and a seventeen-year-old girl was allowed to bring a friend to her therapy group; which was a game-changer.

Ben Davidson (1999) reported on another eating-disorders unit, in which a thirteen-year-old boy regularly made a mess by vomiting in his therapy group, which generated anger and a great desire of punishment amongst his peers, as well as a split in the therapists. It happened that the boy had been bullied at school and his mother had died, after which his father became an alcoholic; which led to a damaging role reversal in the parent-child relationship.

Only when his father accepted treatment for his alcohol dependency, was the boy able to stop being sick and to gain enough weight to be discharged from the unit to his aunt's care. A supervision group for the staff was crucial, to be able to stay with the experience of pain from this patient and other patients' stories.

Degli Stefani and Cibin (2000) described two psychotherapy groups for drug-addicted adolescents, as they were having conflicts with their parents and struggling in their search for identity. The therapists used straightforward and simple language to address defensive attitudes. And gaining a sense of peer-group positive norms and stability was crucial for favourable outcomes.

Schwartz and Melzak (2005) reported on the development of story-telling as an aid in their therapy groups with adolescents, survivors of political violence and seeking asylum in the UK. Most of these young people had witnessed violent death and experienced violation and brutality, both to close family members and to themselves. The story-telling ritual helped these survivors deal with the overwhelming nature of their cumulative trauma at their own pace, and to reconnect with a sense of creative imagination and of personal and group development.

Millar (2006) set up a heterogeneous mixed group for adolescents, aged fourteen to seventeen years, presenting a broad range of problems. The group was described as a place to meet and talk in order to learn more about themselves and each other.

There were powerful shifting transferences towards the therapist who, in the eyes of the adolescents, fluctuated from being *"a sad, impotent git"* to some sort of *"super stud"*. He seemed to stand in for a variety of external and internal figures in their lives, both, real and fantasised. And he interpreted that they were trying to give him, in quite an overt and forceful manner, their own experiences of being on the extreme fringes of ordinary life.

Billow (2004) emphasised the holding and containing functions of the group-analytic conductor, in the handling of a therapy group for adolescents showing poor communication skills and anti-social tendencies. He avoided being oracular or too definite and used a conversational style to deliver group-as-a-whole interventions.

For example, Billow may address the group by commenting that everyone seemed jumpy and then might ask, "*what's up?*" Or he may confront them with an idea that, when they talk about parents "*not getting it*" and about giving up on adults, perhaps they are being "*a different kind of adult*" in the way they talk about them.

A comment or interpretation directed to the group may not be experienced as applying to all the members, and no therapist can be certain that the interpretation does apply to all, or reaches members equally or in the same spirit:

> An interpretation does not become a group interpretation because it is given in the form 'we', 'all of us', 'the group this' or 'the group that'. Neither does it become an individual interpretation because it is directed to and concerned with any particular individual.
>
> Foulkes (1964: 163)

Billow integrated some of the basic principles of Bion's (1961) theorising with Foulkesian group-analytic interventions. He explored how multiple aspects of relational experience enter into adolescent group therapy, often at once. He employed a number of technical interventions to try to attend mentally to all levels, such as interpretation, confrontation, holding, mirroring, limit-setting and containment, delivering his messages to individual members and to the entire group.

According to Billow (2004), the therapist must engage the adolescent and the group at different relational levels, such as the symbolic and the bonding level. If successful, this allows for the progressive construction of a secure base and the gradual formation of group attachment (Bowlby, 1969).

Ezquerro (2017, 2019) described a therapeutic group-work programme with adolescents, aged twelve to sixteen, in the context of a regional inpatient unit, near London, with a catchment area of over four million; which was run by the late Peter Bruggen (2006), on modified therapeutic community principles.

Due to its short-stay nature, group attachment was not actively promoted inside this unit; but a powerful experience of peer-group therapeutic interventions was offered, which the adolescents could later apply in their own lives outside the unit. Authority was democratically negotiated and exercised by, both, the staff and the adolescents, as further examined in the following case study.

A case study by Arturo Ezquerro: a therapeutic community for adolescents

In the 1980s and 1990s, I worked with the late Peter Bruggen. He has been one of the great influences on adolescent mental health and, from my perspective, on innovative group-analytic psychotherapy.

Inspired by the work and ideas of Donal Winnicott (1965, 1969), Derek Miller (1974), Tom Main (1946) and Foulkes (1946), in the late 1960s, Bruggen created an in-patient adolescent unit for troubled and troubling adolescents on the outskirts of London, with a catchment area of over four million. At the Unit, all therapeutic work took place in groups. It was run on a modified *therapeutic community* model.

The Unit primarily provided ongoing specialist consultation and support to families and professionals in the community, as well as short-term group treatment for adolescents up to the age of sixteen. Bruggen was indeed the consultant "in charge": a charismatic, unconventional and democratic leader.

Peter Bruggen had trained at the Tavistock Clinic, in the mid-1960s, and subsequently worked there as a consultant alongside his clinical and managerial role at the Unit. Derek Miller (director of the Adolescent Department) was his tutor at the Tavistock, while Winnicott was the supervisor for his training in adult psychoanalysis, which led to his membership of the Independent Group of the British Psychoanalytical Society.

Bruggen (1979, 2006) was strongly influenced by both, who encouraged him to make a therapeutic use of *authority* in his work with young people, and this concept became one of the foundations for his therapeutic philosophy at the in-patient adolescent unit.

Many parents sought professional help for their adolescent children when they were no longer able to contain their transgressions and challenging behaviour. They may have given up any attempt to set limits, which resulted in real fear for their children' safety. A similar breakdown can sometimes exist in society where responses to teenage delinquent behaviour are either vindictive and retaliatory or completely absent.

At the Unit, an important distinction between prohibitory and inhibitory forces was established. A prohibition is a negative command, usually a forbidding by someone in a position of power. An inhibition is the action of hindering, restraining, checking, and preventing, coming from inside a person. A prohibition requires an external authority. An inhibition, on the other hand, can be conceived as native to, and as part of, a mental capacity for self-regulation (Hillman, 1975; Cousteau, 1987).

A purely prohibitive approach is bound to fail because an outside authority cannot always be there to monitor an adolescent's behaviour. In this sense, the Unit supported the authority of the parents and, also, the developing authority of the adolescents to help them develop a sense of inner authority which they could recognise as their own.

Perceiving the inhibition as originating from personal insights (as opposed to an external prohibition) is a psychological experience that has a tremendous therapeutic import.

On referral to the Unit, the adolescents would never be seen on their own but together with parents or those holding legal authority. These young people were assessed with their family or the professionals caring for them.

Bruggen's initial question inevitably was: "*Who is in charge?*" This would sometimes be followed by another question: "*Who wants what?*", as originally employed by Bowlby (1949) in his ground-breaking work: *The study and reduction of group tensions in the family* – a pioneering publication on family therapy, inspired by some of the group work projects at Northfield Hospital during the Second World War (Bion and Rickman, 1943).

During my work at the Unit, in the mid- and late-1980s, I found these probes powerful and insightful: therapeutic shortcuts that invited everyone both in the family and in the staff team to think together as a group, and to try to understand other members' motives and expectations.

There were powerful group dynamics around the process of deciding whether a young person would be admitted to the Unit. Many parents expected the professionals to decide for them. In fact, in a good number of the families referred, the parents had abdicated their authority and responsibility for the care of the adolescent. A crisis had inevitably followed, leading sometimes to the adolescent getting into trouble with the law.

In the circumstances, Bruggen and the team seriously valued the opportunity to support, rather than take over, the authority of the parents or those with parental responsibilities.

The staff group clearly emphasised that a decision to admit would always have to be made not by the doctors but by the parents, or those holding legal authority, as part of a planned return to the family or to children's home (Bruggen, 1979).

The primary task of the initial assessment was to work with the family's resources and to support the authority of parents and professionals, with a view to keeping the young person living in the community. Bruggen literally meant this, even when it might not be politically correct. He and the team were so successful with this proposition that a number of the Unit's thirty beds remained empty.

The achievement was not properly understood by the Department of Health's advisors who soon recommended that he be removed from the job. But Peter Bruggen was a good fighter and managed to persuade the Health Authority to see merit in the *empty beds*. He reframed these as promoting care in the community (Bruggen et al., 1973; Bruggen and O'Brian, 1986, 1987).

Additionally, Bruggen thought, having enough empty beds would be of help in case of a sudden increase of illness, like in epidemics or the current Covid pandemic. In spite of strong opposition, he kept his job during the four decades until his retirement in 1994. And he provided a good role model for those of us who worked with him.

The Unit developed an ethos through which it became possible to integrate authority, parental care and self-care. Almost always, the parents' decision-making on in-patient admission was based on their ability, or otherwise, to cope with their adolescent-children's difficult behaviour.

As a matter of course, staff encouraged parents to explore whether there might be anything else they or the adolescent could do differently, a *minimum change* (Kaplan and Racussen, 2012), in order for the parents or carers to cope with the adolescent at home – and so to prevent the in-patient admission. That was sorted out at the initial family consultation, or at a follow-up meeting. The benefits of such consultations seemed more obvious when the families or professionals seeking help were close to despair (Bruggen and O'Brian, 1987).

Family work at the Unit was inspired by the Palo Alto Mental Research Institute (MRI), in California. Opened in 1958, MRI was one of the founding institutions of brief and family therapy. MRI gradually became one of the foremost sources of ideas in the area of interactional and systemic studies, applied to clinical work with individuals, families and groups. Many MRI members became leading figures in the field. Among them, Don Jackson, Jay Haley, Paul Watzlawick, Richard Fish, Irvin Yalom, Virginia Satir and Salvador Minuchin were prominent.

Bruggen and his team were also influenced by the systemic family therapists of the Milan Group. In one of their books *Paradox and Counter-Paradox* (Palazzoli et al., 1978), it was possible to understand apparently contradictory messages in families: coming to therapy for help to change whilst also showing a resistance to change. In order to find a way forward, family relationships and interactions were not seen as *linear*, but as complementary and linked to one another: a system of somewhat *circular* feedback loops.

The symptoms of the adolescent were no longer seen as being caused by, or causing problems to, another family member – but as a form of communication. The therapist's task was to tackle the family system differently; for example, to respond with the counter-paradox of *positive connotation*.

In the family interventions at the Unit, the parents' ability to cope with the problems presented with their adolescent-children was explored and strongly supported throughout. The team's availability for further consultations and guidance, more often than not, helped parents and carers to rediscover and develop their own capacity to manage the adolescent at home or at the institution where the young person lived.

Once authority in the family was no longer disputed, anxiety went down and family members could start thinking, collaborating with each other, and even feeling the affection that was previously lacking (Bruggen and O'Brian, 1987).

Another important part of the therapeutic process was to help parents reclaim some of the memories and emotions that occurred for them as adolescents. It produced a shift in how they perceived and related to their adolescent-children; it increased their capacity for empathy.

At that moment, the parental lectures and threats gave way to a more meaningful engagement, through which parents became able to express their concerns in a way their kids were more capable of listening to.

At the Unit, peer-group support, analysis and sanction proved to be sensitive and effective. The Unit's young patients learned fast and took over from the staff the role of chairing the community meeting, as well as other adult-like roles, as we shall now see.

The authority of the adolescent peer group

As outlined earlier, a flexibly designed and unorthodox group-analytic approach was the backbone of the adolescent unit. The entire therapy programme took place in family group or peer-group sessions, based on a *therapeutic community* model, adapted to adolescence. Like most of the early therapeutic communities, the Unit developed a policy in which the use of medication was reduced to a strict minimum – so the development of the young people's internal resources would be maximised.

Adolescents can indeed grow in peer-group therapy and in individual therapy, but one-to-one therapy sessions were not available at the Unit. So, what happened when an adolescent became very distressed and felt in need of individual support?

The answer was this: the adolescent was offered the possibility of calling a group meeting. This would be attended by all (staff and patients) available at that particular moment. Allowing adolescents to exercise their own authority flexibly, to expose their vulnerability within an unambiguous boundary structure, paid off. At the *ad hoc* therapeutic group meetings, there were moving episodes of open communication among the adolescents who became more able to empower one another.

I have described elsewhere some of the processes through which the adolescents exercised their authority, in their therapeutic group work at the Unit (Ezquerro, 2017, 2019). A sense of belonging to a peer group played a crucial part in the positive therapeutic outcomes.

When the Unit opened, the handover from the morning shift of nurses to the afternoon shift took place behind the closed door of the nurses' office. After that, the daily community meeting took place; staff felt that it was important for them to be in control of the potentially out-of-control adolescents.

The meeting was followed by a staff discussion group, in which propositions were gradually made about opening up communications and making them as transparent as possible. As a result, a resolution was agreed neither to talk about colleagues in their absence nor to have secrets or gossip about work; which was quite an advanced type of work on confidentiality (Bruggen, Brilliant and Ide, 1982).

In addition, staff decided that the handover process itself (until then kept private) should be brought into the existing community meeting. The rationale was that, in order to become a true therapeutic community, this change would be necessary for reasons of professional responsibility and common-sense management. The staff handover acquired a new dimension that was easily understandable to all concerned: each person in the meeting had a role in exploring the meaning of what had been said and of what had happened.

The next suggestion came from the adolescents: one of them suggested that they themselves should give the handover. Staff met the proposal with a certain degree of suspicion and concerns about the pace of change. At the staff meetings, some expressed anxieties that the adolescents might be too punitive, may not be objective, would exploit the opportunity to manipulate each other, disrupt the work or split the staff. Was that counter-transference?

Indeed, one important responsibility of the therapeutic team was to protect the residents from how they may sometimes treat each other badly or unreasonably. However, the majority in the staff group opted for giving the adolescents a try and,

> when at last they were allowed to take over this role, the boys and girls were, of course, more fluent, more flexible, more imaginative and less punitive than the staff had ever managed to be.
>
> Bruggen and O'Brian (1987: 138)

The next natural step came when the adolescents suggested that they should take over the role of chairing the community meeting too. Again, their handling of this piece of delegated authority was far more creative than the staff had ever achieved. With these two changes, the daily community meeting became, for boys and girls, the most valuable experience of their brief stay at the Unit – four to six weeks on average.

The factual information, feelings, dreams, wishes and fears shared at the meeting acquired new meaning; ideas and suggestions for further work or focus would arise spontaneously, as in the following clinical vignette (Ezquerro, 2019):

School work ran alongside therapy work at the Unit, in order to keep up continuity of education. At the end of a school day, **Roger** (a fifteen-year-old boy) called a meeting because **Angela** (a thirteen-year-old girl) was looking very depressed and withdrawn. At the community meeting, earlier in the day, staff had attempted to support her to explore her feelings about her father's recent death. Some had asked her to talk about it but to no avail. At the extra therapy meeting, the boy said that he was feeling sorry for her, while the girl looked at the floor silently.

> I invited Angela to talk about good memories of her father. The rationale was that, in identifying the good parts of the parent, she would be in a better position to mourn the loss of his goodness. This, in turn, might enable her to face the not so good side of her father and also express her feelings about it.

Suddenly, **Angela** shouted: *"My father is dead! Why does everyone go on talking about him?"* I was surprised by her painful exclamation and thought of saying that anger was part of a normal bereavement – an idea that I had learned from Bowlby (1980).

However, in the circumstances, such a comment would have been an expression of intellectual defensiveness rather than a helpful expression of sympathy to Angela. The idea was correct; the timing wrong.

Fortunately, **Roger** reacted more quickly than anybody else in the room: *"They talk about your father because you don't, but I think you need to"*. This time, she listened to him intently and was able to accept his words – to my relief and that of my colleagues.

In the next few days and weeks, **Angela** talked about how she was desperately missing her father who had usually been caring and supportive of her. Later, she also expressed anger about him who, at times, had not been emotionally available, due to his excessive drinking. This problem contributed to the cirrhosis that killed him. Angela was angry with his father who, in dying, had abandoned her.

At the Unit, it was possible to see quite a remarkable transformation in psychological functioning in most of the adolescents, when they experienced a sense of belonging to a supportive and caring peer group; which demonstrates the necessity of group life as a central part of adolescent development.

Although some adolescents may be timid and frightened about becoming intimate (indeed, as many adults are), they are willing to explore intimacy. In therapy groups, they take risks to become intimate with their peers and with the therapists; which enhances the possibility of healing and growth.

Adolescents at the Unit were very much encouraged to think about attachments in their own lives. The quality of attachment in adolescence depends on, both, the young people and the parents' capacity to redefine their relationship with one another. Co-constructing such relationships is a key element in achieving a secure-enough attachment during this complex and rapidly changing developmental stage.

Most adolescents experience a need for an increasing distance from the parents. Physical proximity and spending time together are less necessary to ensure protection, comfort, and confident exploration (Ezquerro, 2017). However, it is still reassuring for these young people to know that their parents will be readily available, especially during stressful periods.

For a majority of adolescents, it is easier to develop healthily when there is a safe structure around which they can experiment, play, comply or rebel against:

the structure of standards of behaviour, of ideas, of times, of places and of limits.
Bruggen and Pitt-Aikens (1975: 154).

In attachment terms, they need a secure-enough base without which the task of growing is harder.

At the Unit, most of the adolescents became able to project their incipient and fragile sense of personal authority onto their peer group, which became a secure base. This therapeutic group investment proved to be an effective way for them to develop their own views and status.

For these youngsters, it was easier to recognise in their peers the parts of themselves that they had projected onto them. The authority of the peer group was helping them become assertive, rather than aggressive, and regulate the distance from (and to) the authority of parents and other adults.

Experiencing a sense of community and peer-group belonging provided young people at the Unit with opportunities to reflect upon and re-negotiate the relationships with their primary attachment figures, as well as exploring new attachment relationships with peers and other adults in their lives.

Staff often worked with the youngsters on what it was that they did to make it so difficult for their parents and, sometimes, for the staff. This provided a main focus of work and helped most adolescents take charge of their own life. This put them in a better position to accept the imperfect authority of the parents and to develop their own authority.

In view of the far-reaching consequences of the changes introduced by the adolescents, staff had to rethink their own attitudes and prejudices.

The staff meeting developed a deeper self-reflective function, where it was possible to ventilate feelings and mentally tidy up. In turn, each member of the team was invited to comment on the running and handling of the community meeting, and on the quality of their interventions, as part of our ongoing reflective group work.

Indeed, we (the staff) retained the responsibility of exercising the authority that we had delegated, as and when this might be required. But this only happened rarely. Staff later introduced other therapeutic functions in the community meeting such as greeting new people, making important decisions and saying farewell.

Bruggen designed a *leaving* exercise through which, in the last part of the community meeting, everyone in the group circle would give a positive memory or anecdote as a genuine appreciation of the good aspects of the adolescent.

In my view, this was a moving and therapeutic way of saying goodbye to the adolescents leaving the Unit, as well as an encouragement for them to say hello, more confidently, to the next chapter in their lives.

Conclusion

Adolescents have a profound necessity to connect with a larger circle of meaning and with a cultural environment. Peer group relationships and group attachment play an essential role in the life of adolescents, more than in any other stage in the life cycle, particularly in their search for identity and autonomy and in their explorations of intimacy. Peers represent an important source of information, support and modelling. Friendship in adolescence is not only a social and positive relational context, but it also provides for the expression and regulation of affect.

Adolescence varies significantly, according to ages, stages and cultures, and it is useful to divide it into early, middle and late adolescent sub-phases. Most teenagers navigate through the growing pains and adaptations of adolescence without necessitating psychiatric treatment or psychotherapy. But others require specialist help, as they become emotionally vulnerable or get into trouble with the law and struggle to come to terms with traumatic experiences or with mood fluctuations and self-doubts, regarding their sexuality, their conflictive relationships and the multiple versions they may have of themselves.

In these cases, group therapy frequently is the treatment of choice. Such groups operate at the formative peer group level, have an integrative developmental function, contribute to the process of identity construction, and enable adolescents to reflect, feel understood and supported and to learn from others like themselves. Beside this, in therapy groups, adolescents can develop and exercise a sense of inner authority that they recognise as their own.

Group therapists and other professionals working with adolescents need to be accommodating and fully conversant with adolescent developmental processes, and to understand their counter-transference reactions in order to disentangle what belongs to them and what to the adolescent. They have to learn to make therapeutic use of their authority, being authoritative but not authoritarian. Some of this applies to parents as well.

Working with adolescents in groups can be challenging, but also a rewarding, fulfilling and therapeutic experience, both, for the adolescents and the therapists.

References

Aichhorn A (1925) *Wayward Youth* (1965 edition). New York: Viking Press.

Aichhorn A (1964a) On education in training schools. In: Fleischmann O, Kramer P and Ross H (eds) *Delinquency and Child Guidance: Selected Papers.* New York: International Universities Press, pp. 15–48.

Aichhorn A (1964b) On the technique of child guidance: The process of transference. In: Fleischmann O, Kramer P and Ross H (eds) *Delinquency and Child Guidance: Selected Papers.* New York: International Universities Press, pp. 101–192.

Aichinger A and Holl W (2017) *Group Psychotherapy with Children: Psychodrama with Children.* Wiesbaden, Germany: Springer.

Alexander FG and Selesnick ST (1995) *The History of Psychiatry: An Evaluation of Psychiatric Thought and Practice from Prehistoric Times to the Present.* Northvale, NJ: Jason Aronson.

Altermatt E and Pomerantz E (2003) The development of competence-related and motivational beliefs: An investigation of similarity and influence among friends. *Journal of Educational Psychology* 95(1): 111–123.

Anthony EJ (1965) Group analytic psychotherapy with children and adolescents. In: Anthony EJ and Foulkes SH (eds) *Group Psychotherapy: The Psychoanalytic Approach.* London: Maresfield, pp. 186–232.

Arnett JJ (2015) *Oxford Handbook of Emerging Adulthood.* New York: Oxford University Press.

Bagwell CL and Schmidt ME (2011) *Friendships in Childhood and Adolescence.* New York: Guildford Press.

Bamber JH (1988) Group analysis with children and adolescents. *Group Analysis* 21(2): 99–102.

Banny AM, Ames A, Heilbron N and Prinstein MJ (2011). Relational benefits of relational aggression: adaptive and maladaptive associations with adolescent friendship quality. *Developmental Psychology* 47(4): 1153–1166.

Behr H (1988) Group analysis with early adolescents: Some clinical issues. *Group Analysis* 21(2): 119–133.

Behr H and Hearst L (2005) Groups for children and adolescents. In Behr H and Hearst L (eds) *Group-Analytic Psychotherapy: A Meeting of Minds.* London: Whurr, pp. 203–219.

Berkovitz IH (ed) (1995) *Adolescents Grow in Groups. Experiences in Adolescent Group Psychotherapy.* New York: Jason Aronson.

Billow RM (2004) Working relationally with the adolescent in group. *Group Analysis* 37(2): 201–217.

Bion WR (1961) *Experiences in Groups.* London: Tavistock.

Bion WR and Rickman J (1943) Intra-group tensions in therapy. *The Lancet* 242(6274): 678–681.

Blos P (1962) *On Adolescence: A Psychoanalytic Interpretation.* New York: The Free Press of Glencoe.

Bowker JC, Fredstrom B, Rubin KH, Rose-Krasnor L, Booth-LaForce C and Laursen B (2010) Distinguishing those children who form new best friends from those who do not. *Journal of Social and Personal Relationships* 27: 707–725.

Bowker JC and Spencer SV (2010) Friendship and adjustment: A focus on mixed-grade friendships. *Journal of Youth and Adolescence* 39: 1318–1329.

Bowlby J (1949) The study and reduction of group tensions in the family. *Human Relations* 2: 123–128.

Bowlby J (1969) *Attachment and Loss. Vol 1: Attachment* (1991 edition). London: Penguin Books.

Bowlby J (1973) *Attachment and Loss. Vol 2: Separation, Anxiety and Anger* (1991 edition). London: Penguin Books.

Bowlby J (1980) *Attachment and Loss. Vol 3: Loss, Sadness and Depression* (1991 edition). London: Penguin Books.

Bowlby J (1988a). *A Secure Base: Clinical Applications of Attachment Theory.* London: Routledge.

Bowlby J (1988b) Developmental psychiatry comes of age. *American Journal of Psychiatry* 145: 1–10.

Briggs S (2002) *Working with Adolescents: A Contemporary Psychodynamic Approach.* New York: Palgrave MacMillan.

Bruggen P (1979) Authority in work with younger adolescents: A personal review. *Journal of Adolescence* 2: 345–354.

Bruggen P (1997) *Who Cares? True Stories of the NHS Reforms.* Charlbury, UK: John Carpenter.

Bruggen P (2006) Castaway's corner. *Clinical Child Psychology and Psychiatry* 11(2): 307–311.

Bruggen P, Brilliant B and Ide S (1982) Secrets and gossip: staff communication. *Bulletin of the Royal College of Psychiatrists* 6 (7): 117–119.

Bruggen P, Byng-Hall J and Pitt-Aikens T (1973) The reason for admission as a focus of work for an Adolescent Unit. *British Journal of Psychiatry* 122(568): 319–329.

Bruggen P and O'Brian C (1986) *Surviving Adolescence: A Handbook for Adolescents and Their Parents.* London: Faber and Faber.

Bruggen P and O'Brian C (1987) *Helping Families: Systems, Residential and Agency Responsibility.* London: Faber and Faber.

Bruggen P and Pitt-Aikens T (1975) Authority as a key factor in adolescent disturbance. *British Journal of Medical Psychology* 48(2): 153–159.

Coleman JC (1985) *Psicología de la Adolescencia.* Madrid: Morata.

Cousteau V (1987) How to swim with sharks: A primer. *Perspectives in Biology and Medicine* 30(4): 486–489.

Csikszentmihalyi M (2021) Adolescence. *Encyclopaedia Britanica.* Available at: https://www.britanica.com/science/sdolescence

Davidson B (1999) Writing as a tool of reflective practice: sketches and reflections from inside the split milieu of an eating disorders unit. *Group Analysis* 32(1): 109–124.

Degli Stefani M and Cibin M (2000) Institutional experiences in psychotherapy with drug-addicted patients and their families: Substance, drug and group in the opiate-dependence dynamic. *Group Analysis* 33(2): 289–294.

Dies KG (2000) Adolescent development and a model of group psychotherapy: Effective leadership in the New Millennium. *Journal of Child and Adolescent Group Therapy* 10: 97–111.

Dwivedi K N (ed) (1998) *Group Work with Children and Adolescents: A Handbook.* London: Jessica Kingsley.

Eliade M (1958) *Rites and Symbols of Initiation: The Mysteries of Birth and Rebirth.* New York: Harper and Row.

Erikson EH (1971) *Identity: Youth and Crisis.* London: Faber and Faber.

Evans J (1998) *Active Analytic Group Therapy for Adolescents.* London: Jessica Kingsley.

Evans J (2000) Adolescent group therapy and its contribution to the understanding of adult groups. In: Pines M (ed) *The Evolution of Group Analysis.* London: Jessica Kingsley, pp. 98–108.

Ezquerro A (2017) Authority and attachment in adolescence. In: *Encounters with John Bowlby: Tales of Attachment.* London and New York: Routledge, pp. 121–141.

Ezquerro A (2019) The power of group work: personal recollections on Peter Bruggen. *Group Analysis* 52(3): 362–374.

Fairall C and Glerson A (2007) Daring to engage: Psychoanalysis for young offenders in a unit-based therapy programme. *Group Analysis* 40(1): 43–58.

Feldman RS (2018) *Adolescence Social Development.* Harlow, UK: Pearson Education Limited.

Fonagy P (2003) Towards a developmental understanding of violence. *The British Journal of Psychiatry* 183(3): 190–192.

Fonagy P, Gergely G, Jurist E and Target M (2002). *Affect Regulation, Mentalization and the development of self.* New York: Other Press.

Fordham M (1994) *Children as Individuals.* London: Free Association Books.

Foulkes SH (1946) Group analysis in a military neurosis centre. *Lancet* 247(6392): 303–313.

Foulkes SH (1964) *Therapeutic Group Analysis*. London: George Allen & Unwin.

Frankel R (1998) *The Adolescent Psyche. Jungian and Winnicottian Perspectives*. London: Routledge.

Freud A (1966) *The Writings of Anna Freud. Vol 2: The Ego and the Mechanism of Defence*. New York: International Universities Press.

Ghirardelli R (2001) Silence and the use of objects brought to the session as a resistance in a group with adolescents. *Group Analysis* 34(4): 531–537.

Goldstein N (2001) The Essence of effective leadership with adolescent groups: Regression in the service of the ego. *Journal of Child and Adolescent Group Therapy* 11: 13–17.

Griffin L (2014) Lessons from the new science of adolescence. *Psychology Today*. Available at Lessons from the New Science of Adolescence | Psychology Today

Haen C and Aronson S (2017) *Handbook of Child and Adolescent Group Therapy: A Practitioner's Guide*. New York: Routledge.

Hafen CA, Laursen B, Kerr M and Stattin H (2011) Homophily in stable and unstable adolescent friendships: Similarity breeds constancy. *Personality and Individual Differences* 51: 607–613.

Hall GS (1904) *Adolescence*. New York: Appleton and Company.

Harris B (2011) *Working with Distressed Young People*. Exeter, UK: Learning Matters.

Harris JR (1995) Where is the child's environment? A group socialization theory of development. *Psychological Review* 102(3): 458–459.

Harris JR (2009) *The Nurture Assumption: Why Children Turn Out the Way They Do?* New York: Free Press.

Hillman J (1975) *Loose Ends*. Dallas, TX: Spring Publications.

Hoag MJ and Burlingame GM (1997) Evaluating the effectiveness of child and adolescent group treatment: A meta-analytic review. *Journal of Clinical Child Psychology* 26: 234–246.

Jacobsson G (2005) *On the Threshold of Adulthood: Recurrent Phenomena and Developmental Tasks During the Period of Young Adulthood* [Doctoral Thesis Monograph]. Stockholm, Sweden: Pedagogiska Institutionen.

Jenkins LN and Demaray MK (2015) Indirect effects in the peer victimization-academic achievement relation: the role of academic self-concept and gender. *Psychology in the Schools* 52(3): 235–247.

Kaplan T and Racussen L (2012) A crisis recovery model for adolescents with severe mental health problems. *Clinical Child Psychology and Psychiatry* 18(2): 246–259.

Kegan R (1982) *The Evolving Self: Problem and Process in Human Development*. Cambridge, MA: Harward University Press.

Kymissis P (1996) Developmental approach to socialization and group formation. In: Kymissis P and Halperin DA (eds) *Group Therapy with Children and Adolescents*. Washington, DC: American Psychiatric Press, pp. 35–54.

Lanyado M and Horne A (eds) (2010) *Handbook of child and adolescent psychotherapy. Psychoanalytic approaches*. Monica, East Sussex, UK: Taylor & Francis.

Lifton RJ (1979) *The Broken Connection*. New York: Simon and Schuster.

Lucas T (1988) Holding and holding-on: Using Winnicott's ideas in group psychotherapy with twelve-to-thirteen-year-olds. *Group Analysis* 21(2): 135–151.

Lust I and Hamori E (1996) The dynamics of losing and building boundaries in an adolescent group. *Group Analysis* 29(1): 37–42.

Main T (1946) The hospital as a therapeutic institution. *Bulletin of the Menninger Clinic* 10(3): 66–70.

Malberg N and Midgley N (2017) A mentalization-based approach to working with adolescents in groups (MBTG-A) In: Haen C and Aronson S (eds) *Handbook of Child and Adolescent Group Therapy – A Practitioner's Guide*. New York: Routledge.

Marmarosh CL (ed) (2020) *Attachment in Group Psychotherapy*. New York: Routledge.

Marmarosh CL, Forsyth DR, Strauss B and Burlingame GM (2020) The psychology of the COVID-19 pandemic: A group-level perspective. *Group Dynamics: Theory, Research, and Practice* 24(3): 122–138.

Mehta CM and Strough J (2009) Sex segregation in friendships and normative contexts across the life span. *Developmental Review* 29: 201–220.

Millar D (2006) The adolescent experience: From omnipotence to delinquency. *Group Analysis* 39(1): 37–49.

Miller D (1974) *Adolescence: Psychology, Psychopathology and Psychotherapy*. New York: Jacob Aronson.

Miller JM (2013) Developmental psychoanalysis and developmental objects. *Psychanalytic enquiry* 33(4): 312–322

Nagliero G (1996) Countertransference in adolescent psychotherapy. *Group Analysis* 29(1): 69–79.

Nietzsche F (2000) *Basic Writings of Nietzsche*. New York: Random House Inc.

O'Connell BA (1979) Normal adolescence. *Journal of the Irish Medical Association* 72(-9): 359–365.

Palazzoli M, Boscolo L, Cecchin G and Prata G (1978) *Paradox and Counterparadox*. London: Jason Aronson.

Parker JG and Gottman JM (1989) Social and emotional development in a relational context: Friendship interaction from early childhood to adolescence. In: Berndt TJ and Ladd GW (eds) *Peer Relations in Child Development*. New York: Wiley Interscience Publication, pp. 15–45.

Perry A (ed) (2009) *Teenagers and Attachment: Helping Adolescents Engage with Life and Learning*. London: Worth Publishing.

Piaget J (1951) *Play, Dreams and Imitation in Childhood*. New York: Norton.

Piaget J (1953) *The Origins of Intelligence in the Child*. New York: International Universities Press.

Piaget J (1954) *The Child's Construction of Reality*. New York: Basic Books.

Pinel JP (2011) Group analytical work with violent preadolescents: Working through and subjectivation. *Group Analysis* 44(2): 196–207.

Pines M (1996) Dialogue and selfhood: Discovering connections. *Group Analysis* 29(3): 327–341.

Pollack WS, Shuster T and Trelease J (2001) *Real Boys' Voices*. New York: Penguin Books.

Racker H (1968) *Transference and Countertransference*. New York: International Universities Press.

Redl F and Wineman D (1952) *Controls from Within: Techniques for the Treatment of the Aggressive Child*. New York: Free Press.

Reid S and Kolvin I (1993) Group psychotherapy for children and adolescents. *Archives of Disease in Childhood* 69, 244–250.

Rose SR (1998) *Group Work with Children and Adolescents*. Thousand Oaks, CA: Sage.

Roth WM (2014a) The birth of group analysis from the spirit of the theatre. *Group Analysis* 47(3): 293–311.

Roth WM (2014b) Adolescences: Adolescence re-staged. The interplay between small groups and the large group in a group analytic training situation. *Group Analysis* 47(4): 436–455.

Rubin KH, Coplan R, Chen X, Bowker, JC, McDonald K and Heverly-Fitt S (2015) Peer relationships in childhood. In: Bornstein MH and Lamb ME (eds) *Developmental Science: An Advanced Textbook*. New York: Psychology Press, pp. 591–649.

Schwartz S and Melzak S (2005) Using story telling in psychotherapeutic group with young refugees. *Group Analysis* 38(2): 293–306.

Selfhout M, Branje S, ter Bogt T and Meeus (2009) The role of music preferences in early adolescents' friendship formation and stability. *Journal of Adolescence* 32: 95–107.

Shechtman Z (2014) Counseling and therapy groups with children and adolescents. In: DeLucia-Waack JL, Kalodner CR and Riva MT (eds) *Handbook of Group Counseling and Psychotherapy*. Washington, DC: Sage Publications Inc., pp. 1068–1108.

Shechtman Z (2017) *Group Counseling and Psychotherapy with Children and Adolescents*. London and New York: Routledge.

Simpkins S and Parke R (2002) Do friends and non-friends behave differently? A social relations analysis of children's behavior. *Merrill-Palmer Quarterly* 48: 263–283.

Sinason V (ed) (2011). *Attachment, Trauma and Multiplicity: Working with Dissociative Identity Disorder*. London: Routledge.

Steinberg D (1983) *The Clinical Psychiatry of Adolescence*. Chichester, UK: John Wiley.

Tijhuis L (1997) Transition and conflict in the development of individuals and the group in group psychotherapy with adolescents. *International Journal of Adolescent Medicine and Health* 9(2): 135–149.

Tijhuis L (1998) Peers as the guardian angels of individuation in the therapy group: Ego supportive group therapy for children and adolescents. *Group Analysis* 31(4): 547–563.

Winnicott DW (1965). *The Maturational Processes and the Facilitating Environment: Studies in the Theory of Emotional Development*. London: The Hogarth Press and The Institute of Psychoanalysis.

Winnicott DW (1969) Adolescent process and the need for personal confrontation. *Paediatrics* 44: 752–756.

Winnicott DW (1990) *Deprivation and Delinquency*. London: Routledge.

Winnicott DW (1991) *Playing and Reality*. London: Routledge.

Wood D (1999) From silent scream to share sadness. *Group Analysis* 32(1): 53–70.

Woods J (1993) Limits and structure in child group psychotherapy. *Journal of Child Psychotherapy* 19(1): 63–78.

Woods J (2003) *Boys Who Have Abused: Psychoanalytic Psychotherapy with Young Victims/Perpetrators of Sexual Abuse*. London: Jessica Kingsley.

Woods J (2014) Principles of forensic psychotherapy. In: Woods J and Williams A (eds) *Forensic Group Psychotherapy: The Portman Clinic Approach*. London: Karnac, pp. 3–31.

Wyer RS and Jing Xu A (2010) The role of behavioral mind-sets in goal-directed activity: Conceptual underpinnings and empirical evidence. *Journal of Consumer Psychology* 20(2): 107–125.

ORCID iD: Arturo Ezquerro https://orcid.org/0000-0002-9910-4576

ORCID iD: María Cañete https://orcid.org/0000-0001-7967-1103

4 Young adults' group lives

An increasingly long-winded road to adulthood?

Arturo Ezquerro and María Cañete

Introduction

Having travelled through childhood and adolescence, in previous chapters, we may think that we are now ready to face adulthood; but are we? Indeed, the quality and nature of earlier attachment relationships, as well as former experiences with peers and peer groups and other social interactions, play a crucial part in the workings of *young* adulthood.

Most adolescents complete their developmental tasks successfully (see Chapter 3) but it is not uncommon that many issues, which are either re-solved or unresolved in adolescence, have reverberations throughout adult life; particularly during the period that has been mainly described as young, early or emerging adulthood (three terms that we shall use almost inter-changeably in the current chapter).

Young adults may need to come to terms with a range of different expe-riences: making or breaking affectional bonds, being rejected or rejecting, being accepted or accepting, and so on. Society and its wider context be-come increasingly relevant to this age group: digital media, violence, war, the Brexit restrictions on freedom of movement, global warming, global or local financial crises and dramatic changes in the nature of work will necessarily have an impact on emerging adults, and on their chances of making their own lives.

Recent generations of young adults have increasingly needed to stay in the parental home for longer. And they may seek psychological help to grow out of this.

In contrast to psychotherapy groups with full grown-ups, in groups for young adults, the conductor must accept a transitional position as a leader, extending their leadership role beyond the early phases of group develop-ment. This role can be modified later on, from being a leader *of* the group to being a leader *in* the group. As the group matures, through reliance on its own strength, it replaces the authority of the leader with the authority of the group (Ezquerro, 1996).

Optimally, emerging adults become confident enough to exercise their own authority and to recognise it as an integral part of themselves.

DOI: 10.4324/9781003167747-5

Sexuality and love come from the perspective of consenting but, perhaps, still insecure adults. Meaningful and enduring sexual encounters usually have a powerful influence on the way people relate to others. Much of the challenging excitability and offensive language of adolescents are left behind. A balance between desire and acting on it, between sexual identity and generative capabilities, is often achieved during this period.

Young adults tend to progressively explore deeper and more stable relationships, which may eventually lead to parenthood and new family life. Gradually, they develop stronger commitments to enduring roles and group affiliations in society (Feldman, 2018).

Patients going through this developmental stage may bring to the group (and to the individual consulting room) a powerful, attractive, even seductive, sexual transference. This requires that psychotherapists, working with young adults, examine carefully their counter-transference reactions (Ezquerro, 2019).

Erik Erikson (1963, 1971) dealt thoroughly with this age group. In his theory, as they try to achieve a stable sense of personal identity, many young adults experience a sort of dichotomy: intimacy versus isolation. For him, this may result in a crisis that arises from the powerful desire to share one's personal life with other people. Without intimacy, adults may suffer from loneliness and isolation. He put it this way:

> The young adult, emerging from the search for and the insistence on identity, is eager and willing to fuse his identity with others. He is ready for intimacy, that is, the capacity to commit himself to concrete affiliations and partnerships and to develop the ethical strength to abide by such commitments, even though they call for significant sacrifices and compromises.
>
> Erikson (1963: 263)

According to more recent theories, an important aspect of close human connections is "self-expansion": the idea that each of us enlarges our understanding, our experiences and our resources, through the development of intimacy with friends, lovers and family (Aron et al., 2005). Intimacy and self-expansion are desirable parts of the human psyche; which each person may seek, to some extent, differently.

All intimate relationships have much in common – not only in the psychic needs they satisfy but also in the behaviours they require (Reis and Collins, 2004). Intimacy progresses from attraction to close connection to ongoing commitment. Each relationship demands some personal sacrifice and may lead to a sense of ego loss. This usually brings deeper self-understanding and shatters the isolation caused by too much self-focus or self-protection.

However, this process may also expose the individual's vulnerability. Erikson had in fact suggested that, in order to establish intimacy, the young person must:

face the fear of ego loss in situations which call for self-abandon: in the solidarity of close affiliations [and] sexual unions, in close friendship…, in experiences of inspiration by teachers and of intuition from the recesses of the self. The avoidance of such experiences… may lead to a deep sense of isolation and consequent self-absorption.

Erikson (1963: 163–164)

We decided earlier to use the term "generative capabilities" in a broad sense to refer, not only to reproduction, but also to the development of productivity and creativity. The notion of generative capabilities is related to but distinct from the concept of "generativity". The latter was coined by Erikson (1971) and refers to a concern for people besides self and family that usually develops during middle or late-middle adulthood (see Chapter 6); generativity is a mature need to nurture and guide younger people and so contributes to the well-being of the next generation.

No doubt, emerging adults rapidly absorb both the caring values and the carelessness of previous generations. But it does not mean that they will have to follow suit; in fact, they can generate new ideals that passionately engage the moral, social and political imagination. Emerging adulthood is a fascinating time to tune into what has been described in the literature as the political development of the person (Samuels, 1993), and as the birth of a political self (Gaudilliere, 2021).

Politics leads to a discovery of one's own take on the world; what moves the psyche finds expression in political choices. There is a growing interest during young adulthood in large-group and global-group dynamics, which can be seen as a search for meaning in the political and social events occurring around the world. Although young adults tend to be self-absorbed, they can also be remarkably attuned to world events and, in fact, they are more awake to the environmental problems currently swiping across the world than older generations.

Settled adults with "fully" developed brains may respond defensively and arm themselves with an "I know better" type of cynicism, and justify it as a way of protecting young people from getting too carried away. However, if we destroy the ideals of the youth, society may stagnate or may burn away, both symbolically and literally.

Has the brain of young adults completed its development? Research indicates that it actually has not, as it continues developing until the late-twenties and, even after that, some plasticity remains. Rather than being fully grown, the young adult's brain continues to grow new neural connections and to prune away unused pathways. This is generally a good thing – it means that young adults' brains are still malleable and adaptive to new experiences. For example, learning a new language, musical instrument or job skill is easier for young adults than it is for older adults (Whiting et al., 2011).

One part of the brain in particular, the prefrontal cortex, does not mature until well into the last part of young adulthood. This region is responsible for higher-order mental functions such as planning, decision making and impulse control. It is little wonder, then, that the greatest risks to health and well-being in this stage of life mainly involve poor judgment: motor vehicle accidents, violence, drug abuse and excessive drinking chief among them. But it is also a time of opportunity, when young adults can instil highly beneficial traits such as resilience, self-control and self-regulation (Raznahan et al., 2011; Giedd, 2012; Steinberg, 2014).

In most countries, people have full-citizen rights at the age of eighteen, including the right to vote. At this age, they can also have a driving licence, but they cannot rent a car or have car insurance, without heavy surcharges, until their twenty-sixth birthday or even later. Furthermore, some travel and health insurers allow cover, on their parents' policies, for people up to the age of thirty. Interestingly, parents have no access to their children's college records if the pupil is over eighteen; but parents' income is taken into account when the student applies for financial aid up to age twenty-six, and so forth.

Certainly, emerging adults have increasing responsibilities, clearer identities and deeper explorations than they had in adolescence; but they are not yet constrained by definite adult-role requirements in society (Arnett, Žukauskienė and Sugimura, 2014). Consequently, there is no definite agreement about when someone is old enough to take on full adult responsibilities. We shall now explore this further.

Early or emerging adulthood: a transition or a developmental stage?

The psychosocial, educational, economic and cultural *elongation* of adolescence in recent decades has gradually shaped a rather distinct period in the life cycle, comprising roughly the eighteen to twenty-nine age group. Several terms have been used to describe these years, which are sometimes seen as a process or transition and, at other times, as a developmental stage in its own right.

Some of the terms employed to describe this period include "developmental moratorium" (Erikson, 1971), "young adulthood" (Shanahan, 2000), "emerging adulthood" (Arnett, 2000), "threshold of adulthood" (Jacobsson, 2005), "arrested adulthood" (Côté, 2006), "passage to adulthood" (Zarrett and Eccles, 2006), "twenty-somethings" (Henig, 2010), "delayed adulthood" (Johnson, Crosnoe, Elder and Glen, 2011), "extended adolescence" and "youthhood" (Engelberg, 2013), "half-baked cake" (Henig and Henig, 2013), "transition-age youth" (Sheidow, McCart and Davis, 2016), "feeling in-between" (Shulman et al., 2017), "early adulthood" (Currin, 2018), "neither-nor" (Lowrey, 2020), and so on and so forth. Even some neologisms, such as "twixter years" and "adultolescence", have been used in the media.

Henig (2010) also referred to the expression "boomerang kids", a term coined to designate young adults moving back in with their parents. This author precisely recalled a young man hanging up his second PhD in his old boyhood bedroom, being officially overqualified for ordinary jobs and leaving his parents perplexed. Situations like this are happening all over, in all sorts of families. And it is something that predates the 2008 global financial crisis.

There is a 2006 film, *Failure to Launch* (directed by Tom Dey), which portrays a handsome yacht salesman (Tripp) who still lives with his parents, at age thirty-five, and has problems committing himself to just one of the many beautiful women who want to sleep with him. His mother contributes to perpetuating the situation by often having a run-in with anyone who tries to get close to him.

This film is no more than a superficial comedy, but it also generates a poignant feeling: in real life, there are many "failure-to-launch" young adults who, unlike Tripp, are financially dependent on their parents and live a socially limited existence. This often leads to mental health problems, whilst their parents wonder if they will ever be able to enjoy retirement in peace, being criticised and, ultimately, feeling failures themselves.

Of all the above terms, *emerging adulthood* seems to have become the most popular for sociologists, psychologists and government agencies in the Western world.

In the USA, a network on transitions to adulthood was constituted in 1999, and the Society for the Study of Emerging Adulthood (SSEA) was created in 2003. There are some ongoing programmes, like City Year, in which young people aged eighteen to twenty-five, from diverse backgrounds, can spend a year mentoring inner-city children in exchange for a stipend, health insurance or the like.

Around the same time, a European Group for Integrated Social Research into misleading trajectories and transition dilemmas of young adults was set up (EGRIS, 2001).

Arnett (2000, 2007, 2013, 2015) has been particularly keen on expanding the concept of emerging adulthood and has devoted the last two decades to studying the period from the late teens to the late twenties.

According to him, this phase is not simply an extended adolescence, as people in this age group display more independent explorations and are much freer from parental control than adolescents. It is not early adulthood either, since this term implies that an early sub-phase of adulthood has been reached, whereas many people in their twenties have not fully taken up the obligations and responsibilities inherent in adult status.

As a concept, emerging adulthood is not universal and manifests itself differently in different countries and cultures. It primarily describes people living in developed countries, but it is increasingly encompassing young people in the urban areas of less developed countries. The term mainly describes young adults who do not have children, do not live in their own home and do not have sufficient income to be fully independent (Arnett, 2015).

Emerging adults have increasing responsibilities, clearer identities and deeper explorations than adolescents; but they are not yet constrained by definite adult-role requirements in society (Arnett, Žukauskienė and Sugimura, 2014).

There are cultural differences in how young adults themselves experience these years. For instance, in a sample of college and non-college participants, aged between eighteen and twenty-six years, in India, the idea of "accepting responsibility for your actions" was found to rank high as a criterion for adulthood, which coincided with Western studies. However, in the Indian sample "learning to have good control over your emotions" and "being capable of keeping a family physically safe" scored higher than in Western countries as markers of adulthood (Seiter and Nelson, 2011; Douglass, 2005, 2007).

To quite a significant extent, some of the socio-political and cultural roots of emerging adulthood can be traced back to a number of vast changes that have taken place in modern societies over several decades, including the sexual revolution, the women's liberation movement, the digital revolution and the global financial crises.

The sexual revolution spread widely in the 1960s and 1970s with the hippie culture (sex, drugs and rock'n'roll) and was boosted by the development of more effective methods of contraception. This contributed to postponing marriage and parenthood a few years. Interestingly, the slogan "don't trust anyone over thirty" (attributed to New Left activist Jack Weinberg) became popular at the time.

The women's liberation movement during that period, which coincided with (and was recognised as part of) the second wave of feminism, also contributed to the development of emerging adulthood. Women in their twenties increasingly pursued careers and higher education rather than starting families (Roseneil, 2020; Roseneil et al., 2020).

Remarkable advances in technologies have dramatically changed our way of life. With the digital revolution, longer, more technical and more sophisticated education has been required for employment and career success, all things considered. This has partly prompted younger adults to spend more time studying and training, rather than working full time or starting families. Emerging adults, old enough to master the technologies and young enough to welcome their novelty, are at the forefront of this digital revolution.

However, some voices have alerted us to the danger that modern media technologies may create an illusion of intimacy. Sherri Turkle (2011) and Linda Cundy (2015) have suggested that people are increasingly expecting more from technology and less from each other.

Turkle's critique is especially notable because she was one of the first scholars to focus on the Internet's positive potential for enhancing social connections. She is now concerned that new media have become too intrusive in our social lives, to the point of drawing us away from being entirely present with each other and making us be "alone together".

Looking back, in the early 1960s, the average age at which young adults were marrying was twenty years for women and twenty-three years for men. In particular, these young women settled quickly into full-time mothers' roles, whereas fathers established themselves in their working careers. In the 1970s, the average age for childbirth started to increase; by 2010, it rose to twenty-six years for women and twenty-eight for men (Henig and Henig, 2013).

The current UK's birth rate is at a record low, with fertility rates for women under thirty at their lowest levels since records began in 1938. There are many factors that have contributed to this, including the fact that, apart from those who struggle with infertility, an increasingly large number of people make a positive personal choice not to have children, and others decide against having offspring because of the uncertainties and peril of the climate crisis (John, 2021). In addition, global and local financial crises and the rising costs of living are a persistent and growing issues.

Also in the UK, the Office for National Statistics shows that the number of people who have never married, and do not live as a couple, is rising in every age range under seventy. In the period from 2002 to 2018, the percentage of never-married singletons in their forties doubled. Amongst heterosexual couples, the average age at marriage has never been later: thirty-one for women and thirty-three for men. Interestingly, the singles "market" is at its most crowded between the ages of thirty-five and forty-seven (John, 2021).

To some authors, the new realities are a transient epiphenomenon, the by-product of cultural and economic forces. To others, the longer road to adulthood signifies something deeper, more durable and maybe better-suited to our neurological hard-wiring. What we are seeing, they insist, is the dawning of a new developmental stage in the life cycle, a stage that all of us need to adjust to (Henig, 2010).

In previous generations, attaining the stability of a secure job, marriage, home and children seemed like a great achievement. These markers were considered milestones of adulthood and treated as evidence of having settled down.

In contrast to that, today's young people tend to approach adulthood and its obligations in quite a different light. Many of them see marriage and children not as achievements to be pursued, but as perils to be avoided. However, most do not reject the prospect of going down that road eventually; so, it is a "not yet" rather than "never". By the age of thirty, the majority see themselves as adults, regardless of marital status. This is based on the belief that they have achieved self-responsibility, financial autonomy and independence in decision-making (Arnett and Tanner, 2006).

Adulthood and its commitments usually offer security and stability, but also represent some closing of doors: the end of a sense of unobstructed freedom and of wide-open possibility. Young adults today are potentially freer than those in previous generations, whose choices were constricted by cultural norms that prevented them from exploring future paths more openly.

In contrast to traditional societies, by and large, modern societies tend to give emerging adults additional time to move into full adult responsibilities, so they can go at their own pace. However, people's experience of this period varies considerably across national, cultural, socio-economic, personal and political contexts (Shanahan and Longest, 2009).

Half a century ago, Erikson (1971) had already pointed out that, in Western societies, it was increasingly common to offer young people a moratorium in their psychosocial development, during which the emerging adult, through free-role experimentation, may find a place in some section of society.

In the early part of the twenty-first century, a number of authors (Shulman and Ben-Artzi, 2003; Henig and Henig, 2013; Shulman and Connolly, 2013) suggested that the transition to adulthood calls for some degree of reckoning with issues of educational and occupational achievement, financial and residential independence, freedom from parental influence and the establishment of romantic relationships in rapidly changing contexts.

Along those lines, Côté and Bynner (2008) and Côté (2006) referred to diminished normative structures governing young or emerging adulthood and to changes in education-to-work transition, by virtue of which many people are now required to postpone aspects of their identity formation. According to these authors, it has become necessary to go beyond the conventional view that most identity formation occurs primarily during adolescence, particularly considering that the young adult has to deal with new contexts where key identity issues have to be resolved.

Arnett (2014, 2015) argued that emerging adulthood has five discrete characteristics: instability, self-focus, feeling-in-between, explorations for a more solid sense of identity and the discovery of new possibilities. These features are not unique to emerging adulthood (as they can also be experienced in other life stages), but they are more distinctive, prevalent and prominent during this period. We shall now examine them further:

Explorations for a deeper and more solid sense of identity

An active process of identity formation clearly shows in adolescence (see Chapter 3) and intensifies in early adulthood, as emerging adults try to clarify their sense of who they are and what they want out of life. They do it in different ways, in different places and at different times.

In terms of relationships, emerging adults tend to look for the qualities that are most important to them in another person, distinguishing more clearly than in previous developmental stages the characteristics that attract them from those they dislike. They also perceive more clearly how they are evaluated by others who come to know them well, and learn what others may find attractive or distasteful in them (Arnett, 2014; Shulman and Connolly, 2013).

In contrast to adolescent love, which tends to be tentative and transient, love in young adulthood involves a deeper level of intimacy and is identity focused. Emerging adults increasingly ask themselves about the type of person that may suit them best as a partner through life.

In terms of work experiences, emerging adults become increasingly focused on laying the ground for adult occupation. In testing out various educational paths and occupational options, young adults are preparing themselves for a fulfilling working life, as well as exploring professional and group identity issues. They tend to look for the type of job that they are good at and that would satisfy them in the long term (Arnett et al., 2001).

This is often a two-way process. As emerging adults try out a new job, they learn about their abilities and interests, on the one hand, and about what they are less good at or do not want to do, on the other. In turn, this enables them to make better decisions regarding future jobs.

Young adults' approach to work is in sharp contrast with adolescents', who either do not work or get part-time, low-skill service jobs that are un-related to the occupation they expect to engage with in adulthood. Teen-agers tend to view their jobs not as occupational preparation but as a way of obtaining the money that will support an active leisure life, such as concert tickets, meals, clothes, travel, etc., without giving a thought to how any current job might lead to long-term prospects. On the contrary, for young adults, work gradually becomes identity-based and a central part of life (Arnett, 2015).

Of course, failures and disappointments are an integral part of the process of learning from experience and improving self-understanding, both in ad-olescents and young adults. However, the latter are better equipped to learn from their mistakes, as well as from their accomplishments. Bearing in mind the human propensity to repeat mistakes, vicarious learning, from other people's mistakes and successes, is an importance source of knowledge that young adults increasingly take into account in their own decision-making processes.

In emerging adulthood, many explorations are playful and casual and can be seen as a way of gaining a wide range of experiences before settling down (Arnett, 2014). The common parental surveillance typical of ado-lescence has been left behind, which gives emerging adults unprecedented levels of freedom. They may not be free in the same way again, due to the more stable and enduring commitments inherent in full adult life, and to the restrictions and decline associated with the last stages in the life cycle, particularly old age.

Instability

After leaving the parental home, young adults change residence quite fre-quently. They may also change subjects of study, partners and jobs. All this moving around makes emerging adulthood a rather unstable time. The inse-curities of adolescence diminish, but unsteadiness can still be a source of dis-ruption and anxiety (Arnett 2015). And disruptions can be more prominent in at-risk populations.

In this respect, Greeson (2013) used a life course perspective to better understand young adults who age out of foster care and advocated natural mentoring to aid them in the process of becoming full adults.

Although the unpredictability and uncertainty experienced in young adulthood can give a sense of instability, the variability and volatility of adolescence have diminished considerably. Ideals are still high, but more pointed, and plans more realistic and regularly revised; which makes this life stage remarkably lively and intense.

A constellation of multiple-group configurations becomes prominent in young adults: college groups, friends and other social groups, work groups, political groups, religious groups, sport groups, etc. As children and adolescents, they had been predominantly involved in a school-based peer-group culture and, indeed, many emerging adults are involved in university-based peer-group culture.

However, a large proportion of them explore a wider and deeper range of group connections, with work and institutions, which go beyond the peer-group experience. The importance of coordinating this diversity of group lives with romantic relationships and life plans has been emphasised (Shulman and Connolly, 2013).

In addition, Altermatt and Pomerantz (2003) and Morgan (2013) pointed out that, although individual work on sexual orientation and sexual identity becomes prominent in adolescence, it continues unfolding well into the late teens and through the twenties, when sexuality becomes more definite and certain in terms of choices and commitments.

Self-focus

According to Arnett (2015), there is no time in human life that is more self-focused than emerging adulthood. Of course, children and adolescents are self-focused in their own way, but they have adults, like parents and teachers, to whom they have to answer to on a daily basis. Although adolescents have greater autonomy than when they were children, they remain part of the family and there are household rules and standards to follow. In addition, nearly all of them attend schools, where teachers set standards and monitor their behaviour and performance.

To be self-focused is not necessarily to be selfish; for emerging adults, in fact, it can be quite healthy. By focusing on themselves, they learn daily living skills, gain a better understanding of themselves and their expectations, and begin to build a foundation for their adult lives. Their objectives include learning how to fend for themselves and to do their own thing, whilst standing alone as a self-sufficient person, which is usually a key step before involving themselves in enduring relationships and other long-term commitments (Twenge, 2013).

Young adults have to make many decisions, frequently on their own. These include choices about university or work, or a combination of the two, as well as about residencies, flatmates, friends, partners, group memberships and so on. No one else can really make decisions for them.

Feeling-in-between

When Arnett (2014, 2015) interviewed a large sample of American people in the age group eighteen to twenty-five, he received responses which indicated that most emerging adults feel they are on their way to adulthood but not there yet. "Are you an adult?" A typical response was "yes and no" or "in some respects yes, in some respects no". They felt they had completed adolescence, but not yet entered full adulthood. So, they considered themselves to be somewhere in-between, neither adolescents nor adults.

When they commit themselves to doing something, most emerging adults do it. They are responsible with their studies, their jobs and their money, but they do not really feel like an adult. The main three criteria they mentioned to consider themselves adults were: making independent decisions, becoming financially autonomous and accepting responsibility for themselves. And they considered that these goals have to be achieved gradually and incrementally rather than all at once.

Arnett (2015) and Currin (2018) also referred to an "age-thirty deadline". These authors highlighted that most emerging adults do not feel they have reached adulthood, whilst most people in their thirties do; most emerging adults are still in the process of seeking out the education, training and job experiences that will prepare them for a long-term occupation, whilst most people in their thirties have settled into a more stable occupational path; most emerging adults are not yet married, whilst most people in their thirties are married; most emerging adults have not had a child, whilst most people in their thirties do have at least one child.

The discovery of new possibilities

Early or emerging adulthood is fundamentally an age of possibilities, when many different futures remain real options, when little about a person's direction in life has been decided for certain. It can be an age of high hopes and expectations (Arnett, 2015). Emerging adults are not yet fully committed to a new network of relationships and obligations; despite their uncertainties, instability and vulnerabilities, and partly as a result of these, they have a wide range of possibilities for changing drastically directions in their lives.

This is especially important for young people who have grown up in difficult or unfavourable environments: a new opportunity begins for them to change the life course. On the other hand, young people coming from stable backgrounds can transform themselves, so they are not merely made in their parents' images but decide what kind of person they wish to be. They now have a wide scope for making their own decisions. They are aware that, eventually, they will have to enter long-term commitments and obligations, which will probably set them on paths that resist drastic changes in trajectory. This is in contrast to adolescence, in which dramatic fluctuations are a hallmark (see Chapter 3).

Indeed, emerging adults carry their family influences with them when they leave home, and the extent to which they are able to change the personality traits they had shaped by the end of adolescence becomes increasingly limited (Becht et al., 2021). However, the potential of young adults is still huge and their range of choices about how to live, work and love is greater than it has ever been before and possibly greater than it will ever be again.

Group-analytic psychotherapy with young adults

By the age of twenty-five, usually earlier, young adults have reached full physical, hormonal and sexual maturity; but many brain connections continue growing with all the pros and cons, as we outlined earlier. There is an increasingly greater processing of emotions, cognitions and psychosocial information.

These changes result in improved self-control, cautiousness, intentionality, life planning, reflectivity and sophisticated thinking; cognition becomes more complex but its development is mediated by the level of education (Griffin, 2014). Young adults are less susceptible to physical disease than they were in childhood and adolescence, but remain vulnerable to mental health problems (Kessler et al., 2007; Arnett, Kloep, Hendry and Tanner, 2011).

In recent decades, there has been a disturbingly increasing level of psychological distress among young adults (Galambos and Krahn, 2008; Galambos et al., 2020). In terms of the DSM-IV classification of mental disorders, about 75% of any lifetime anxiety, mood, impulse-control and substance abuse problems begin before age twenty-five (Regier et al., 1998; Kessler et al., 2007). And half of the young adults between the ages of eighteen and twenty-five experience at least one mental health problem at some point (Kessler et al., 2005).

Symptoms of depression are higher in people in their twenties compared to older generations, except older adults in their eighties (Arnett et al., 2011). However, after the age of twenty-eight, the chance of developing a psychiatric disorder decreases significantly (Kessler et al., 2005; Tanner, 2010).

It is striking that, despite the huge developmental relevance of early or emerging adulthood, and the significant emotional vulnerability during this period, group analysts have paid relatively little specific attention to this age group. We could only find three clinical articles on group-analytic psychotherapy for young adults, published in the journal *Group Analysis* (Gargiulo and Tenerini, 2020; Geyer, 2017; Shulman et al., 2017), and a brief report (Johansson and Werbart, 2009) on a semi-structured interview with twenty-eight young adults after a period of analytically oriented group psychotherapy.

The main findings of this interview (Johansson and Werbart, 2009) were that most patients had increased self-knowledge about their identities and roles, and an improved and more mature handling of emotions in their own lives outside the group. Patients also referred to the experience of needing increasingly less leadership from the group therapist, although those with greater negative experiences stated that they needed a more active involvement of the therapist in the group sessions.

With regard to the clinical papers, Gargiulo and Tenerini (2020) reported on the first year in the life of a weekly outpatient psychotherapy group that they co-conducted. The group consisted of three women and four men in their early- and mid-twenties, with an average age of twenty-two. All of them were experiencing difficulties in the relationship with their parents, and struggling with the process of developing a separate adult identity.

As is customary in group-analytic psychotherapy, these young people were meant not to socialise in-between therapy sessions. However, at the end of each session, they all walked down the street together as a group; which became a pattern.

The therapists did not challenge this boundary issue, as they would have done in an adult group, but invited members to reflect on its meaning in the context of their developmental process. The patients were able to make a therapeutic use of this incident. These authors concluded that the outside-group walking ritual was a symbolic transitional phase that helped young adults connect and separate.

Geyer (2017) reported on some of the unconscious processes that became apparent in a weekly, slow-open, mentalisation-informed psychotherapy group for young adults, aged eighteen to twenty-five, in a secondary care NHS setting. The group consisted of three women and two men of mixed ethnic, social and cultural backgrounds, which reflected the demographics of their local catchment area. All members had complex needs and incomplete educational trajectories; they felt stigmatised by their mental health problems and were at risk of social marginalisation.

The group developed a culture of regular attendance and good participation, which helped members work through dynamics of acceptance and rejection and, in turn, develop a sense of identity, self-worth and group belonging that was previously lacking in their lives. The complexity of the material was elaborated taking into account Earl Hopper's notion of the social unconscious, defined as:

> the existence and constraints of social, cultural, and communicational arrangements of which people are unaware, in so far as these arrangements are not perceived (not 'known'), and if perceived, not acknowledged ('denied'), and if acknowledged, not taken as problematic ('given'), and if taken as problematic, not considered with an optimal degree of detachment and objectivity
>
> Hopper (1996: 9).

According to Geyer, in their struggle to become independent, young adults are particularly vulnerable to destructive social-unconscious dynamics.

However, the benign and inclusive atmosphere of a therapy group conducted on group-analytic lines can be a good antidote against such destructive forces.

Shulman et al. (2017) compared young adults on a waiting list with those undergoing group psychotherapy. Thirty-one patients (eighteen women and thirteen men) ranging in age from twenty-one to thirty years, with an average age of twenty-six, were treated at an outpatient clinic in Israel. Each of the therapy groups consisted of six to eight patients and was co-conducted by two therapists for ninety-minutes weekly over five months.

Members were encouraged to share their own stories, conflicts and difficulties with the group. The study was primarily meant to evaluate changes in the young adults' capacity for mastering age-related developmental tasks, such as work and love.

When compared with people on the waiting list, the group participants showed a significant decrease in psychological distress, as well as a significant increase in adaptive goal pursuits and independent functioning. The group was particularly successful in enhancing career and romantic goal pursuits. Comparison of pre- and post-treatment levels showed a significant increase in goal elaborateness, sense of goal progress and goal controllability. Members also reported an increased level of independent decision-making.

The above results speak in favour of the importance of incorporating a developmental perspective in therapeutic group interventions, in order to enhance young adults' competence in handling age-related tasks and improving their well-being. These findings are consistent with previous research studies (Shulman et al., 2006; Sneed et al., 2007; Shulman et al, 2009; Heckhausen et al., 2010; Jacobsson et al., 2011; Walker, 2015).

Outside group analysis, a number of practitioners have increasingly advocated group psychotherapy for young adults (Maar and Sloth, 2008; McEneaney and Gross, 2009; Johnson 2009; Bleiberg, 2014; Melton et al., 2017; López-i-Martín, et al., 2019). But it is beyond the scope of this chapter to review the literature of non-analytic approaches to therapeutic group work with this population.

We are aware that a few other group analysts have conducted groups for early adults but have not written about their clinical findings. A group-analytic trainee (Dhillon, 2016) wrote about a special interest group he conducted for young adults, between the ages of eighteen and twenty-six, as part of his training at the Institute of Group Analysis, in London.

He identified a number of common themes, as all the patients were struggling to work through some recurrent issues in their lives. These included conflicts with their parents, ambivalence about leaving home, difficulties in making and sustaining relationships, feelings of hurt and anger, finding work and a loving partner, and learning to become an authentic adult.

It is clear that the road to adulthood has become increasingly convoluted in recent decades, affecting the mental health of a large proportion of young or emerging adults. In the circumstances, we would like to suggest that new group-analytic thinking is warranted, with a view to exploring further the benefits of group-analytic psychotherapy with this population. And we would encourage group analysts to get their clinical case experiences with young adults into print.

A clinical case study by María Cañete

The following clinical material refers to a weekly therapy group for patients within the age range nineteen to twenty-nine years, which I ran at an NHS out-patient psychotherapy service, in an inner-London district, from the mid-2000s to the mid-2010s. The service did not have specific provision for this age group and young adults were usually seen in standard adult groups. However, through the psychotherapy assessment process, I realised that some young-adult patients were struggling with developmental issues and decided to set up an age-homogeneous group for them.

For this new group, I selected seven patients (three women and four men), whose names and ages were as follows: Cristina (twenty-two), Victoria (twenty-four), Sophie (twenty-five), Bob (nineteen), Roger (twenty-one), Freddy (twenty-three) and Derek (twenty-nine). The group was slow-open; when ready, members left and were replaced by newcomers. I asked for a minimum time commitment of one year; average length of membership was three years. For the purpose of illustrating some of the developmental and clinical issues outlined earlier in this chapter, I will not go through the whole history of the group. Instead, I shall concentrate on the trajectories of these seven founding members.

In terms of national and cultural backgrounds, the group had substantial diversity. Cristina's parents had migrated to England from Argentina when she was a baby. Victoria was Italian-born and came to London in her late-teens to study interior design. Sophie, the eldest of six siblings, was born in London but her parents were Moroccan. Roger was Afro-Caribbean; Freddy and Derek were English; Bob was Scottish.

At the time of the initial assessment, three of the patients were living at home with their parents; one was at a university hall of residence; another shared a flat with other young people of roughly the same age; the remaining two lived independently in rented accommodation. Only one member was married and had a child; the other six members were not committed to a long-term relationship. In terms of education and work, four members had university degrees, whilst two were still at college; only two people had substantial jobs; the remaining members worked on and off, whilst one of them was on a disability allowance.

All seven patients were experiencing a general dissatisfaction with their life. Most had various degrees of depression and anxiety. Three had a diagnosis of personality disorder. Three were survivors of child sexual abuse. Two had needed in-patient psychiatric admissions in the past. One was considered a suicide risk, after having seriously attempted to take his life.

The group beginnings

At the first session, following the initial introductions, there was a brief silence. **Freddy** took his shoes off and put his feet on the chair; he held his knees tightly, with his arms around them, and adopted an almost foetal position. His body language was a distinct-enough form of communication, but I did not say anything about; at that early stage, he may have been made to feel too exposed.

Roger, who had a leg in plaster and was making a noticeable noise with his chewing gum, said that he had recently completed one year of weekly individual psychotherapy. He explained that, at the end of it, his therapist recommended group therapy. However, Roger had doubts about its value. He added that there were times when he felt so disturbed and distressed after a therapy session that he found it difficult to wait for a whole week to see his therapist again.

Sophie commented that she was not as nervous in the group as she had anticipated. She was aware that she carried a can of worms with her, but was unsure about whether she should open it.

Derek said that it had taken him many years to accept that he needed therapy and that he had now realised he should not continue brushing his problems under the carpet, pretending they did not exist.

Roger then remarked that it was fine to talk to psychotherapists because they are professionally trained, but he was unsure about sharing intimate things with a group of strangers. He added that, when he met strangers, he usually talked at a superficial level or not at all.

Sophie nodded and commented:

> Yes, when you ask somebody: 'How are you?', you don't actually expect people to say anything other than I am very well, thank you!

Victoria then recalled that, the previous week, the postman had asked her the same question and her response was:

> I am fine; what about you?

To which the postman replied:

> Not as well as you.

She took it as an invitation to ask him why, but did not say anything because she was afraid that, if the postman started talking about his problems, she would not have anything helpful to say to him.

At that point, I suggested that they seemed to be negotiating the level of intimacy in their exchanges in the group, as they were still strangers to one another.

Sophie, who had got married at seventeen when she was pregnant with her son, responded quickly:

> I've joined the group because I want to do something about my problems; but my husband doesn't accept that he also needs help, which is causing difficulties in our marriage.

Cristina acknowledged that she had problems too, as she kept repeating the same troubling patterns in her relationships. She wanted to learn how to change that and, also, how to get on better with her divorced mother, with whom she lived.

Roger then said that he also had problems in the relationship with both his parents, particularly his mother. He explained that they had neglected him as a child, as they had chronic drug-addiction problems. As an adolescent, he left home and stopped talking to his parents. Many years later, with the help of his individual therapy, he felt able to talk to his father again, but not to his mother. He elaborated on that:

> I was able to forgive my father because I never felt closely attached to him. What I find really difficult is to forgive my mother. As a small child, I was very attached to her and I loved her very much. But, after my parents separated, she left me unprotected and some of her boyfriends abused me sexually. She is still abusing drugs and almost brainless. I know drug addiction is an illness, but I cannot feel any sympathy for her.

After a brief pause, **Roger** added:

> I started using drugs in my early teens and became street wise. My parents were not there for me. Drugs and raving gave me a boost and made me feel connected. But I got bored of it after a while. I was lucky not to have got hooked into it but to find my way back to school. I realised that I was good with digital technology and became an IT technician. I started earning good money and, at last, I had plenty of food in the fridge – something my parents had never managed. However, after a while, I got bored and felt IT was not the career I wanted to pursue. I decided to seek psychological help in order to work out who I was and what I wanted out of life. I am currently studying sociology at Open University.

The group listened to Roger with interest. **Bob** said he could identify with the raving and drug culture to escape from boredom, and added that he was still going to wild parties from time to time.

Victoria remarked that she did not like raving and explained that, on one occasion, she joined a raving party but did not belong in there and felt she was the odd one out. After going home, she wrote a bleak poem about her experience.

Derek then said that he could recognise the feeling of excitement and the boost, not so much from drugs but from alcohol. He used to be a discotheque regular and also enjoyed the Soho bars' gay atmosphere which, he said, was very exciting in the late 1990s.

Roger looked surprised and commented that Derek seemed to belong to a different generation.

Derek responded that he would be thirty in two weeks and, looking around the room, added:

I am probably the oldest member of this group.

Roger did not make any comment on Derek's becoming thirty soon but said that, the week after he had ended his individual therapy, he had a nasty cycling accident from which he had not recovered. He explained he sustained multiple fractures and had so many complications that he needed to spend several months in hospital, and one of his legs was nearly amputated. He was now stuck at home, facing a real prospect of becoming a disabled person for life. He felt the accident had restricted many of the possible choices he had as a young adult.

Derek expressed sympathy towards Roger and added that he had also spent several months in hospital after seriously hurting himself, when he attempted to commit suicide, jumping from the top of a building. He survived miraculously.

Cristina asked him if he was sober when he jumped.

Derek replied that he could not remember what happened before or after the jump.

Sophie commented that she could not understand why someone so young may want to kill himself. She added that, for her, life was precious, particularly since she had suffered from a serious illness and nearly died. She had to fight for her survival.

Victoria said that one has to feel overwhelmingly desperate and hopeless to contemplate suicide. She added that she was depressed but not to the point of wanting to kill herself.

I said that I was wondering about the impact of this conversation on the quiet members.

Bob then talked about a crisis he had gone through twelve months previously, after having failed to get a work placement; he felt so disappointed and stuck that he could not see the light at the end of the tunnel. Literally, he locked himself out of the house by throwing the keys to the river. Then, he walked to a nearby forest with the idea of starving himself and dying slowly. He spent three days and two nights homeless, on a hunger strike, hiding himself from everybody; eventually, he did not have the courage to kill himself and called a locksmith to re-enter to his home.

Freddy, who had not yet said anything but had listened intently, commented that he felt out of place in the group because his difficulties were more trivial than other people's problems. He wondered if he was a bit selfish, as he was taking a therapy place that could be occupied by a more deserving patient.

It was nearly the end of the initial group session. Several members made reassuring comments to Freddy and encouraged him to come back to the group the following week and talk about himself.

Everybody arrived on time for the second group session. Members started commenting on some of their feelings and thoughts about the previous session.

Victoria intimated to the group that she had ruminated over Bob and Derek's suicide attempts. She added she felt very sad and wanted to make both of them think of the suffering they would cause to their families and to other people close to them, if they killed themselves.

Bob responded that he did not really want to kill himself but to just run away from his pain.

Derek said that his suicide attempt was a momentary lapse of madness and that he had joined the group with a view to sorting things out in his life.

In a later part of the session, **Sophie** said she had also thought about Freddy's comment of the previous week that he did not deserve a place in the group. She added that she could identify with his feeling and invited him to talk about himself.

Freddy then said that his parents had often told him that he should be a happy person because he had a privileged upbringing, full of choices and opportunities, in contrast to other people of his age who had to work much harder. He added that he was an only child, and his parents were comfortably off and proud of the fact that he obtained a good degree at Oxford University and a well-paid job in the financial sector.

Nevertheless, he hated his job because he felt it was not his choice but his parents'. Most of the time he was unhappy, often depressed, and emotionally unable to leave the parental home, despite the poor communication and difficult relationship he had with his parents.

Bob then asked Freddy what he would like to get out of the group. **Freddy** responded that he would like to become confident enough to separate from his parents, to develop his own identity and lifestyle, and to find his own path without disappointing them. At the moment, he said, he was feeling lost and did not know what he really wanted from life.

The first couple of sessions struck me as having elements of the casualness and spontaneity of adolescent groups, whilst also showing a deeper level of sharing and disclosure. I felt members brought a mixed sense of both cautiousness and urgency in engaging with intimacy. Difficulties in the relationship with their parents and in finding a sense of direction and identity in their lives appeared to be common themes from the outset. They were quite self-focused in the way they reported their stories, but they were also showing an incipient caring concern for one another.

Developing group attachment for deeper explorations

Attendance was regular. Several members commented that they were feeling attached to the group and very much looked forward to the weekly sessions. Some remarked that the group had become a safe haven for them.

Three months after the group had started, **Victoria** came to a session dressed in a man's suit and had her head completely shaven. She said she wanted to know how she would feel if she were a boy and how people would react to it; she felt safe enough to explore it in the group. She added that, although she had a clear heterosexual orientation, she had sometimes felt confused about her gender identity. Every now and then, she did not know who she really was and wanted to try different versions of herself.

Cristina commented that she could understand where Victoria was coming from because she herself felt sometimes utterly confused about who she was and could not find a clear direction in her life. In those moments, she experienced a sense of failure and felt deeply depressed.

Bob said that, although he had no doubts about his gender identity, he was uncertain about the choice of his university studies and anxious about his sexual orientation. This made him feel that his life was unstable and, in many ways, on hold. He was afraid of getting involved in a romantic relationship because he did not know whether he was gay or straight. He also struggled to motivate himself at university, where he felt lonely.

Victoria then said that, following the recent break-up of her relationship with a boyfriend, she was afraid of feeling lonely but had decided not to get involved in another relationship until she could sort herself out.

Cristina commented that she did not want to have any long-term commitments either, until she could understand why she got involved in abusive relationships

Sophie joined the conversation at this point to say that she wondered if she had chosen the wrong person, for the wrong reasons. She explained that, at seventeen, she was desperate to leave the parental home and became involved with a man from a different cultural and religious background; she wanted to break away from her family's norms and traditions. Her parents opposed her marriage and were absent at the wedding. She added she now realised that she and her husband were worlds apart and felt pessimistic about their future as a couple.

Roger related to Sophie's story and said that, from a young age, he had also wanted to break away from his parents who did not protect him adequately. After leaving home, he did not feel confident enough to trust somebody and to establish an intimate relationship. He could hang around with his mates, but did not really feel close to anybody.

Derek then talked about his own experience and said that, for many years, he had felt intimately connected to the gay community. He had a number of reasonably satisfactory, short-term relationships. However, losing his job as a model and the traumatic end of a love relationship led to his suicide attempt. This left physical and emotional scars, which made him feel unattractive and unable to face the challenges ahead.

New themes, such as their ambivalence and difficulties in their relationships, were emerging in the group. And earlier themes around their identity were acquiring new dimensions. They felt safe enough to explore their dilemmas and confusion. In doing so, there was some dramatising that resembled adolescent-like behaviour; it helped them express internal conflict and doubts about gender identity and sexual orientation. They related actively and identified with one another, as part of a process of forming a peer group. Mutual trust and group attachment developed gradually. However, they also brought a sense of instability and lack of integration in their lives.

A half-baked cake?

At the beginning of a session, as we were approaching the first year into the life of the group, **Victoria** shared a dream she had dreamt the previous night. In her dream, all group members (including me) were actively involved in making a cake. However, when the cake came out of the oven, it was only half-baked and the ingredients were not properly mixed. She woke up with a sense of frustration and disappointment.

I asked her to free associate. **Victoria** linked the dream with the therapeutic group process and said she was feeling a bit impatient because things were not changing for her as quickly as she was hoping for. She was still feeling confused, not getting guidance and not seeing the course clearly in her career and in her life. She added that it was also frustrating to share her flat with other young people who had a laid-back attitude, almost lazy, did not mix well with her and did not pull their weight in household duties. The flat was often untidy and she hated having to take her flatmates to task.

I then said that I wondered if Victoria was also seeing me as being laid-back, not giving guidance for her and other group members to see their course more clearly.

Victoria looked surprised and, before she could respond, **Cristina** said that she actually appreciated my reflective attitude, not putting pressure on group members to perform any particular task, but enabling them to go at their own pace.

Sophie agreed with Cristina and said she did not want to feel under any additional pressure in the group, as she already had enough pressure in her own life, from work and family.

Roger then commented that he found Victoria's dream more interesting than the dreams he brought to his individual psychotherapy sessions because it was a group dream. In his view, the different ingredients of the cake could symbolically represent group members who, in fact, were all different from each other and had diverse problems and personalities. He added that it can be difficult to accept and integrate differences and that achieving long-term goals can take time.

I thought the half-baked cake with its not-fully mixed ingredients could be a metaphor for how they perceived themselves during this life stage. Different aspects of their identities and personalities were not yet fully integrated into a coherent adult self. In addition, within their age homogeneity, they had different life situations and goals, as well as different measures of individual and group attachment security.

In some way, this session was a turning point in the development of the group and of members empowerment and differentiation; they showed an enhanced capacity for both self-knowledge and group awareness. Not long after the session, members started to negotiate their specific individual processes with a view to separating from the therapy group and getting on with their own lives in a new light. Those members who stayed in the group took care of new members, which boosted their confidence in growing and undertaking adult responsibilities.

Developmental snapshots

A total of twenty-eight patients were treated over the ten-year history of the group. However, this is a qualitative rather than quantitative study and I will stay only with the seven founding members, giving a brief summary of their trajectory and other relevant aspects that showed in connection with their group departure. The following summary, together with the previous clinical material provided, might be deemed sufficient for the purpose of illustrating some of the main issues that tend to concern young adults more explicitly, when compared with people going through other stages in the life cycle (see Chapters 2, 3, 5, 6 and 7).

Bob, the youngest member, was the first to leave the group, after one year. During this time, he mainly focused on his developing identity, his sexual orientation, his difficulties in becoming emotionally autonomous and his inability to tolerate disappointment. All these issues combined led to his wish to live no longer. He recovered his appetite for life, became able to affirm his homosexuality and decided to continue with his studies.

Interestingly, he arranged a transfer to a university closer to his parents. After being brought up in a small and protective rural community, coming to London had been a big leap for him. He now wanted to be somewhere in-between, to gradually learn to regulate the distance and re-negotiate the attachment relationship with his parents.

Derek, the oldest member, left the group after eighteen months. He was popular in the gay community and, for a number of years, had enjoyed working as a model. His crisis was largely related to his inability to cope with the pressure of sustaining the lifestyle required to keep his body and mind in shape for optimal job performance, in a very competitive trade.

In the group, he sometimes found it difficult to go beyond the surface and, although he no longer had suicidal ideation, we were left with a feeling that he may need further therapeutic work after leaving the group. It was reassuring to know that he was not oblivious to it and that he seemed to be reasonably satisfied with his change of career, having obtained a managerial job in the entertainment industry.

Freddy attended the group for three years. After his initial reticence and shyness, he became less self-absorbed and more communicative, with more forward-looking body language. He noticeably developed his assertiveness both in the group and with his parents. He started a romantic relationship and left the parental home to move in with his girlfriend.

Like his father, he had a highly profitable job in the financial sector but found it uninspiring. He decided to go back to university to study anthropology. He developed a new identity, different from his father's, and their relationship and mutual acceptance improved.

Victoria attended the group for four years. She was an enthusiastic and intuitive character, who often acted as a catalyst in group discussions, prompting other members to embark on deeper explorations. She herself brought some unresolved adolescent dilemmas about her own self-image and gender identity. She gradually developed a reasonably solid sense of confidence, even power, as a woman.

Eventually, she obtained a secure and satisfying-enough job which enabled her to get a mortgage and buy a flat. She also decided to settle into a relationship with a new boyfriend. She gave a one-year notice of her departure, as she wanted to work through the uncertainties associated with her new status before separating from the group. For the good-bye session, she made a beautiful cake representing members in the group circle. And it was fully baked!

Roger stayed in the group for five and a half years. However, he had a couple of breaks from the group due to surgical interventions on his leg. During those periods, he was in touch through emails and telephone messages. Realising that the group and I kept him in mind through his absences was a therapeutic experience for him, during an uncertain and emotionally taxing time.

He had a background of insecure-attachment relationships with his parents, who had serious problems of drug addiction and often kept him out of their minds. He developed enough psychological and physical resilience to walk again without orthopaedic aids. He completed his studies at Open University and met a girlfriend; they decided to move together to a warmer, southern European country.

Sophie attended the group for six years. Both her parents had mental health problems and wanted an arranged marriage for her. She could not wait to leave home and, deliberately, became pregnant and married someone from a different cultural and religious background, without her parents' consent.

She acknowledged that she had attempted to gain adult status prematurely, at a time when she was experiencing significant identity problems and not yet able to integrate her family background with her personal choices. The group empowered her to catch up with her unresolved developmental tasks, to re-establish the communication with her parents, to persuade her husband to have marital therapy, and to continue her personal growth.

Cristina attended for the whole of the ten-year history of the group. An only child, she was two years old when her parents separated. She was brought up in two conflictive and boundary-less households. She constantly received contradictory messages, which confused her. She was sexually abused in her early teens, developed a promiscuous sexual life, and sought refuge in drugs and alcohol.

The group became a sort of replacement family for Cristina, but she remained largely unsettled and unable to care for herself for a long while, surviving on unsatisfactory odd jobs and on her parents' savings. I encouraged her to attend both Alcoholics Anonymous and Narcotics Anonymous' meetings, alongside the group. The turning point for her was when she was invited to act as a mentor for other young drug users. Through learning to care for other people, she eventually developed enough consistency to look after herself.

Discussion

The seven patients in this clinical case study were able to gain, in different ways and at different times, a reasonably solid footing in the group. In turn, this empowered them to take hold of their lives and to make the choices that would build the kind of commitments and lifestyle they wanted for themselves as adults in the longer term.

At the point of starting the group, all seven patients showed significant anxieties and uncertainties about their identities, prospects and relationships, particularly unfinished business with their parents and ambivalent feelings about love relationships. They were quite self-focused, brought a sense of inner instability and lacked a clear direction in their lives.

However, being self-focused did not mean that they were selfish or self-absorbed. In fact, they soon developed a capacity to show consideration and caring concern for other group members. This therapeutic experience helped them take responsibility for themselves, whilst having the well-being of others in mind and becoming more aware of the responsibilities they had towards other people in their own lives outside the group.

At different strides, all seven patients eventually developed a capacity to shape the future according to their goals. It seemed clear that these young adults needed to work towards personal developmental goals more specifically than what is normally expected in other age groups or stages. They were in-between adolescence and adulthood, struggling to clarify and consolidate their identities, longing for stability but also wanting to explore new ventures, keeping their options open without feeling confused and overwhelmed.

For all of them, the therapy group became a secure-enough base from which to explore many shameful and negative aspects of their past; which, for some, included pathological family situations and abusive experiences. Having greater cognitive ability for self-knowledge and self-understanding than in adolescence helped them consolidate their inner authority, and they became more capable of assessing what they needed to change in their lives.

The clinical material that emerged in the group, and which is presented in this case study, is consistent with the extended contemporary view that there is a distinct phase in the life cycle, after adolescence but before settling into adulthood. This in-between stage is characterised by intense identity exploration, formation and consolidation, with specific developmental, intrapsychic and psychosocial challenges (Arnett, 2015; Knight, 2017; Knight and Miller, 2017; Miller, 2017; Stambler, 2017; Schechter et al., 2018). Part of it already starts in adolescence but, in young adults, it gradually takes on new depth and urgency.

Nowadays, a majority of young or emerging adults have not passed the milestones that traditionally structured adult life during most of the twentieth century, such as completing their education, leaving home, finding a stable job, marrying and becoming parents, which are no longer the main criteria used in determining adulthood.

However, as stated by Henig and Henig (2013), emerging adulthood is the life period with the least demographical consistency. Young adults have hugely diverse educational, working and living circumstances. Some twenty-five-year-olds are married homeowners with good jobs and children; others are still living with their parents and working at transient jobs, or not working at all.

According to data from the United States Census Bureau, in 1960, 77% of women and 65% percent of men had passed all five markers, by the time they reached thirty. In 2000, among thirty-year-olds, fewer than half of women and one-third of men had done so. Those traditional indicators imply a lockstep march towards adulthood that is increasingly rare and, as such, it can now be deemed an anachronism (Henig, 2010).

Does that mean that society should extend some of the protections and special status of adolescence to all people in their twenties? Only to some of them? If so, to whom? Questions like these are important because failing to protect and support vulnerable emerging adults can lead them down a wrong path at a critical moment, conditioning subsequent trajectories. But over-protecting and over-supporting them can sometimes make matters worse. Young people do not march in unison on the path to adulthood – but they do so at an uneven, highly individual, pace. Furthermore, not every young person goes through a distinct period of emerging adulthood. The heterogeneity of the concept and its existence in some cultures but not in others (even in some people but not in their neighbours or friends) is what prevents some scholars from giving to it the unequivocal *status* of a new developmental stage in the life cycle. However, Arnett (2014) argued that people who *skip* the developmental tasks of emerging adulthood might have to face them at a later time, maybe as a midlife crisis.

Griffin (2014) suggested that *delaying* adulthood is not necessarily a bad thing and that, in some respects, it may even be beneficial. This author based her opinion on contemporary neurobiology studies that indicate that brain plasticity begins to close when we stop exposing ourselves to novel and challenging experiences and immerse in the routine and repetitive activities that are typical of many adult-work environments.

Moreover, Henig and Henig (2013) considered that young adulthood is a stem cell of human development, a pluripotent moment when any of several outcomes is possible. Decisions and actions during this time have lasting ramifications. This stage is when most people accumulate almost all of their formal education; when most people meet their future partners and the friends they will keep; when most people start on the careers that they will stay with for many years. It is also a period when adventures, experiments, travels and relationships are embarked on with an abandon that probably will not happen again.

Some group attachment implications

Why is it, then, so important to think about the developmental implications of going through an extended period of emerging adulthood or otherwise? For a number of experts (Currin, 2018; Arnett, 2015; Henig and Henig, 2013), it is vital because if the delay in achieving adulthood is just a temporary aberration caused by passing social mores and economic gloom, it would be something to struggle through for now, maybe just supporting the young people who had the misfortune to come of age in a recession.

But if this period were an unequivocal life stage, it would be necessary to review systems of education, social supports and health care, including psychotherapy, in order to take it more fully into account.

Only when society recognised that the educational, medical, mental-health and social-service needs of adolescence proved to be unique were developmentally appropriate institutions created and such an investment paid off in the long run. From a group-attachment perspective, many young or emerging adults deserve that society grants them a better measure of security, acknowledging they have developmental tasks to focus on.

Ultimately, they need a measure of group attachment through which they can perceive society as a secure-enough base. And it is in the interests of society to look after young adults, so they become productive contributing members, making the most of their abilities for the benefit of themselves and others.

Henig and Henig (2013) appreciated both pros and cons in letting the twenty-somethings meander before they settle down. On the one hand, if young adults have more space to choose their long-term commitments and their careers, they could make fewer mistakes and live happier lives. But, on the other hand, things may get precarious for their parents paying bills they never counted on paying, and for social institutions missing out on young people's contributions to productivity and growth.

They suggested taking a middle course that can allow emerging adults to have some timeout from fixed adult routines and responsibilities, whilst developing skills for daily living, gaining a better understanding of who they are and what they want from life, and building a foundation for their full adult lives. In this way, a longer road to adulthood can lead to healthier self-regulation, deeper insight and better choices. Self-regulation, or self-governance if you like, has always been crucial for young adults' success and well-being; but it has become even more so in our increasingly complex and diverse societies.

Traditionally, developmental psychology and psychoanalysis (Wood, 1975; Miller, 1999; Lanyado and Horne, 2010) put an emphasis on autonomy and separation from parents for the young adult to become a self-sufficient person; but there has been less attention to the importance of attachment and other meaningful interpersonal and group connections in adult life, for balanced identity and healthy development (Ezquerro, 2017).

In Chapter 3, we argued that, for adolescent development, the peer group is more essential than in any other life stage. For young adults, the peer group continues to be prominent; but they also need to explore and negotiate membership of more complex group structures, as they engage with the uncertainty and changes of emerging adulthood, and become vulnerable to anxieties related to personal, social, professional and group identities.

According to Hogg (2015), particularly in the face of uncertainty and change, people seek to be included in, and accepted by, the group they want to belong to and identify with. This usually provides social support and identity validation from which to build trust, commitment and attachment. However, whilst a measure of group attachment is a *sine qua non* for optimal development, for young adults involved in a love relationship, the partner is usually the main confidant and attachment figure.

Indeed, any person acting as a primary attachment figure has their own necessity for wider group belongingness. This need to belong to, identify with and become attached to a group is a fundamental human motivation, as it serves survival. In many ways, psychopathology is the result of insecurity and sheer purposelessness when one's needs for belongingness and group attachment go unmet. According to Schechter et al. (2018), what is essential is not simply belonging to one or more groups, but the experience of genuine connection to and secure attachment with others.

Conclusion

The road to adulthood has become increasingly complex, stressful and long-winded in recent decades, particularly in developed countries, due to changes in society that can be traced back to the 1960s. Nowadays, more and more people in their twenties consider themselves to be neither adolescents nor adults, and the concept of emerging adulthood as a distinct developmental stage has been proposed.

This may have implications for institutional structures, social supports and healthcare services, including psychotherapy and group analysis. However, the characteristics of this period are neither uniform nor universal. There are different emerging adulthoods with a broad range of possible trajectories that vary significantly, depending on cultural, socioeconomic, personal and political context.

The specialist literature has shown that young or emerging adults can be particularly vulnerable to mental health problems and may require special attention as an age group, despite the fact that there is no demographical consistency due to the huge variability of educational, working and living situations during this life period. Traditional milestones of adulthood, such as obtaining a stable job, getting married and having children, have become less defining and the development of a capacity to experience oneself as a coherent, whole person within diverse interpersonal and group contexts has been emphasised as a new marker of adult status.

Paradoxically, group analysis has paid little specific attention to early or emerging adulthood, both theoretically and clinically. This chapter shows that there is merit in new thinking about this crucial stage in the life cycle; it should not be studied as a mere transition because this may narrow our perception and our understanding of who these young people really are. The chapter advocates a middle-of-the-road approach, through which age-homogeneous therapy groups might be particularly indicated for some young adults struggling with developmental tasks, whilst other people of the same age may fit in better within standard adult groups.

The clinical case study presented supports previous research that includes a developmental perspective in therapeutic group interventions, in order to enhance young adults' competence in handling age-related tasks. Further group-analytic thinking, as well as qualitative and quantitative research, is required for the benefit of young adults and of society as a whole.

References

Altermatt E and Pomerantz E (2003) The development of competence-related and motivational beliefs: An investigation of similarity and influence among friends. *Journal of Educational Psychology* 95(1): 111–123.

Arnett JJ (2000) Emerging adulthood: A theory of development from the late teens through the twenties. *American Psychologist* 55(5): 469–480.

Arnett JJ (2007) Emerging adulthood: What is it, and what is it good for? *Child Development Perspectives* 1(2): 68–73.

Arnett JJ (2013) The evidence of generation we and against generation me. *Emerging Adulthood* 1(1): 5–10.

Arnett JJ (2014) *Emerging Adulthood: The Winding Road from the Late Teens through the Twenties.* New York: Oxford University Press.

Arnett JJ (2015) *Oxford Handbook of Emerging Adulthood.* New York: Oxford University Press.

Arnett JJ, Kloep M, Hendry LA and Tanner JL (2011) *Debating Emerging Adulthood: Stage or Process?* New York: Oxford University Press.

Arnett JJ, Ramos KD and Jensen LA (2001) Ideologies in emerging adulthood: Balancing the ethics of autonomy and community. *Journal of Adult Development* 8: 69–79.

Arnett JJ and Tanner JL (eds) (2006) *Emerging Adults in America: Coming of Age in the 21st Century.* Washington, DC: American Psychological Association Books.

Arnett JJ, Žukauskienė R and Sugimura K (2014) The new life stage of emerging adulthood at ages 18–29 years: implications for mental health. *The Lancet Psychiatry* 1(7): 569–576.

Aron A, Fisher H, Mashek DJ, Strong G, Li H, Brown LL (2005) Reward, motivation, and emotion systems associated with early-stage intense romantic love. *Journal of Neurophysiology* 94(1): 327–337.

Becht AI, Nelemans SA, Branje SJT, Vollebergh WAM, Meeus WHJ (2021) Daily identity dynamics in adolescence shaping identity in emerging adulthood: An 11-year longitudinal study on continuity in development. *Journal of Youth and Adolescence* 50(8): 1616–1633.

Bleiberg JR (2014) A model of leadership: Therapy groups for ambivalent emerging adults. *Group* 38(4): 301–316.

Côté JE (2006) Emerging adulthood as an institutionalized moratorium: Risks and benefits to identity formation. In Arnett JJ and Tanner JL (eds) *Emerging Adults in America: Coming of Age in the 21st Century*. Washington, DC: American Psychological Association Books, pp. 85–116.

Côté JE and Bynner J (2008) Changes in the transition to adulthood in the UK and Canada: The role of structure and agency in emerging adulthood. *Journal of Youth Studies* 11: 251–268.

Cundy L (ed) (2015) *Love in the Age of the Internet: Attachment in the Digital Era*. London: Karnac.

Currin D (2018) Early adulthood: Changes and challenges. *Psychology in Action*. Available at Early Adulthood: Changes and Challenges — Psychology in Action.

Dhillon HS (2016) *Group analysis with a group of young adults* [Institute of Group Analysis (IGA) Qualifying Course Clinical Paper, unpublished]. Archives IGA Library, London.

Douglass CB (2005) *Barren States: The population "implosion" in Europe*. New York: Berg.

Douglass CB (2007) From duty to desire: Emerging adulthood in Europe and its consequences. *Child Development Perspectives* 1: 101–108.

Engelberg A (2013) Religious Zionist singles and late-modern youth culture. *Israel Studies Review* 28(2): 1–17.

Erikson EH (ed) (1963). *Youth: Change and Challenge*. New York: Basic Books.

Erikson EH (1971) *Identity: Youth and Crisis*. London: Faber and Faber.

European Group for Integrated Social Research [EGRIS] (2001) Misleading trajectories: Transition dilemmas of Young Adults in Europe. *Journal of Youth Studies* 4: 1011–1018.

Ezquerro A (1996) The Tavistock and group-analytic approaches to group psychotherapy: A trainee's perspective. *Psychoanalytic Psychotherapy* 10(2): 155–170.

Ezquerro A (2019) Sexual abuse: A perversion of attachment? *Group Analysis* 52(1): 100–113.

Feldman RS (2018) *Development Across the Life Span*. Harlow, UK: Pearson Education Limited.

Galambos NL and Krahn HJ (2008) Depression and anger trajectories during the transition to adulthood. *Journal of Marriage and Family* 70(1): 15–27.

Galambos NL, Krahn HJ, Johnson MD and Lachman ME (2020) The U shape of happiness across the life course: Expanding the discussion. *Perspectives on Psychological Science* 15(4): 898–912.

Gargiulo A and Tenerini A (2020) Understanding the group process in the first year of psychotherapy: the walk, the basic assumptions and the challenges of young adults. *Group Analysis* 53(1): 3–19.

Gaudilliere JM (2021) *Madness and the Social Link*. New York: Routledge.

Geyer C (2017) The social unconscious in action: Linking theory to group work with young adults. *Group Analysis* 50(2): 203–216.

Giedd JN (2012) The digital revolution and adolescent brain evolution. *Journal of Adolescent Health* 51(2): 101–105.

Greeson J (2013) Foster youth and the transition to adulthood: The theoretical and conceptual basis for natural mentoring. *Emerging Adulthood* 1(1): 40–51.

Griffin L (2014) Lessons from the new science of adolescence. *Psychology Today.* Available at Lessons from the New Science of Adolescence | Psychology Today

Heckhausen J, Wrosch C and Schulz R (2010) A motivational theory of lifespan development. *Psychological Review* 117: 32–60.

Henig RM (2010) What is it about the twenty-somethings. *The Times* (18 August). Available at What Is It About 20-Somethings? - The New York Times (nytimes.com)

Henig RM and Henig S (2013) *Twentysomething: Why Do Young Adults Seem Stuck?* New York: Plume.

Hopper E (1996) The social unconscious in clinical work. *Group* 20 (1): 7–42.

Jacobsson G (2005) *On the Threshold of Adulthood: Recurrent Phenomena and Developmental Tasks during the Period of Young Adulthood* [Doctoral Thesis Monograph]. Stockholm, Sweden: Pedagogiska Institutionen.

Jacobsson G, Tysklind F and Werbart A (2011) Young adults talk about their problems. *Scandinavian Journal of Psychology* 3: 282–289.

Johansson L and Werbart A (2009) Patients' views of therapeutic action in psychoanalytic group psychotherapy. *Group Analysis* 42(2): 120–142.

John E (2021) Why are increasing number of women choosing to be single? *The Guardian*, 17 January. Available at Why are increasing numbers of women choosing to be single? | Women | The Guardian

Johnson CV (2009) A process-oriented group model for university students: A semi-structured approach. *International Journal of Group Psychotherapy* 59(4): 511–528.

Johnson MK, Crosnoe, R, Elder J and Glen H (2011) Insights on Adolescence from a Life Course Perspective. *Journal of Research on Adolescence*, 21(1): 273–280.

Kessler RC, Berglund P, Demler O, Jin R, Merikangas KR and Walters EE (2005) Lifetime prevalence and age-of-onset distributions of DSM-IV disorders in the national comorbidity survey replication. *Archives of General Psychiatry* 62(6): 593–602.

Kessler RC, Amminger GP, Aguilar-Gaxiola S, Alonso J, Lee S and Ustun TB (2007) Age of onset of mental disorders: A review of recent literature. *Current Opinion in Psychiatry* 20(4): 359–364.

Knight R (2017) Emerging adulthood and nonlinear dynamic systems theory. *The Psychoanalytic Study of the Child* 70(1): 74–81.

Knight R and Miller JM (2017) Emerging adulthood: A developmental phase. *The Psychoanalytic Study of the Child* 70(1): 5–7.

Lanyado M and Horne A (eds) (2010) *Handbook of child and adolescent psychotherapy. Psychoanalytic approaches.* East Sussex, UK: Taylor & Francis.

López-i-Martín X, Castillo-Garayo JA and Cabré-Segarra V (2019) Group psychotherapy with young adults: Exploring change using the Core Conflictual Relationship Theme method. *The Arts in Psychotherapy* 63: 46–50.

Lowrey A (2020) Millennials don't stand a chance. They're facing a second once-in-a-lifetime downturn at a crucial moment. *The Atlantic.* Available at Millennials Are the New Lost Generation - The Atlantic

Maar V and Sloth HR (2008) Unge voksnes oplevelse og udbytte af gruppeanalytisk psykoterapi, fortalt med de unges egne ord [Young adults' experiences and gains from group analytic psychotherapy, as told by the young persons themselves]. *Matrix: Nordisk Tidsskrift for Psykoterapi* 25(1): 4–44.

McEneaney AMS and Gross JM (2009) Introduction to the Special Issue: Group interventions in college counseling centers. *International Journal of Group Psychotherapy* 59(4): 455–460.

Melton L, Brewer B, Kolva E, Joshi T and Bunch M (2017) Increasing access to care for young adults with cancer: Results of a quality-improvement project using a novel telemedicine approach to supportive group psychotherapy. *Palliative and Supportive Care* 15(2): 176–180.

Miller JM (2017) Young or emerging adulthood: A psychoanalytic view. *The Psychoanalytic Study of the Child* 70(1): 8–21.

Miller L (1999) The transition from late adolescence to young adulthood Oedipal themes. In: Hindle D and Vaciago Smith M (eds) *Personality Development a Psychoanalytic Perspective*. London: Routledge, pp. 138–57.

Morgan E (2013) Contemporary issues in sexual orientation and identity development in emerging adulthood. *Emerging Adulthood* 1(1): 52–66.

Raznahan A, Shaw P, Lalonde F, Stockman M, Wallace GL, Greenstein D, Clasen L, Gogtay N and Giedd JN (2011) How does your cortex grow? *Journal of Neuroscience* 31(19): 7174–77.

Regier DA., Rae DS, Narrow WE, Kaelber CT and Schatzberg AF (1998) Prevalence of anxiety disorders and their comorbidity with mood and addictive disorders. *The British Journal of Psychiatry* 173(34): 24–8.

Reis HT and Collins WA (2004) Relationships, human behavior, and psychological science. *Current Directions in Psychological Science* 13(6): 233–237.

Roseneil S (2020) It's time to end the tyranny of coupledom. *The Guardian*, 14 November. Available at It's time to end the tyranny of coupledom | Relationships | The Guardian

Roseneil S, Crowhurst I, Hellesund T, Santos AC and Stoilova M (2020) *The Tenacity of the Couple-Norm: Intimate citizenship regimes in a changing Europe*. London: UCL Press.

Samuels A (1993) *The Political Psyche*. London: Routledge.

Schechter M, Herbstman B, Ronningstam E and Goldblatt MJ (2018) Emerging adults, identity development and suicidality: Implications for psychoanalytic psychotherapy. *The Psychoanalytic Study of the Child* 71(1): 20–39.

Seiter L and Nelson LJ (2011) An examination of emerging adulthood in college students and nonstudents in India. *Journal of Adolescent Research* 26(4): 506–536.

Shanahan MJ (2000) Pathways to Adulthood in Changing Societies: Variability and Mechanisms in Life Course Perspective. *Annual Review of Sociology* 26: 667–692.

Shanahan MJ and Longest K (2009) Toward useful theories of the transition to Adulthood. In: Schoon I and Silbereisen RK (eds) *Transitions from School to Work*. Cambridge, UK: Cambridge University Press, pp. 30–41.

Sheidow AJ, McCart MR and Davis M (2016) Multisystemic therapy for emerging adults with serious mental illness and justice involvement. *Cognitive and Behavioral Practice* 23(3): 356–367.

Shulman S and Ben-Artzi E (2003) The Transition from adolescence to adulthood and links with family relationships. *Journal of Adult Development* 10: 217–226.

Shulman S, Blatt SJ and Feldman B (2006) Vicissitudes of the impetus for growth and change among emerging adults. *Psychoanalytic Psychology* 23: 159–180.

Shulman S and Connolly J (2013) The challenge of romantic relationships in emerging adulthood: Reconceptualization of the field. *Emerging Adulthood* 1(1): 27–39.

Shulman S, Kalnitzki E and Shahar G (2009) Meeting developmental challenges during emerging adulthood: The role of personality and social resources. *Journal of Adolescent Research* 24(2): 242–267.

Shulman S, Rozen-Zvi R, Almog Z, Fennig S and Shavit-Pesach T (2017) Effects of group psychotherapy on young adults' romantic and career functioning. *Group Analysis* 50(1): 70–90.

Sneed JR, Hamagami F, McArdle JJ, Cohen P and Chen H (2007) The dynamic interdependence of developmental domains across emerging adulthood. *Journal of Youth and Adolescence* 36: 351–356.

Stambler MJL (2017) 100 Years of Adolescence and its Prehistory from Cave to Computer. *The Psychoanalytic Study of the Child*, 70(1): 22–39.

Steinberg L (2014) *Age of Opportunity: Lessons from the New Science of Adolescence.* Boston, MA: Houghton Mifflin Harcourt.

Tanner JL (2010) *Mental Health in Emerging Adulthood. The Changing Spirituality of Emerging Adults' Project.* Washington, DC: The Catholic University of America.

Turkle S (2011) *Alone Together: Why We Expect More from Technology and Less from Each Other?* New York: Basic Books.

Twenge J (2013). The evidence for Generation Me and against Generation We. *Emerging Adulthood*, 1(1): 11–16.

Walker JS (2015) A theory of change for positive developmental approaches to improving outcomes among emerging adults with serious mental health conditions. *The Journal of Behavioral Health Services and Research*, 4(2): 131–149.

Whiting E, Chenery HJ and Copland DA (2011) Effect of aging on learning new names and descriptions for objects. *Aging, Neuropsychology and Cognition* 18(5): 594–619.

Wood MM (1975) *Developmental Therapy.* Baltimore, MD: University Park Press.

Zarrett N and Eccles J (2006) The passage to adulthood: Challenges of late adolescence. *New Directions for Youth Development* 111: 13–28.

ORCID iD: Arturo Ezquerro https://orcid.org/0000-0002-9910-4576

ORCID iD: María Cañete https://orcid.org/0000-0001-7967-1103

5 Adult life in its prime

Integrating differences and complex group configurations

Arturo Ezquerro

Introduction

The process of personal growth in adulthood has been described as a journey in search of authenticity and the development of a truthful self (Feldman, 2018). This task is open-ended and adult individuals have to pursue it on an ongoing basis. It is a dynamic process resulting from the continuous interaction with an ever-evolving environment, within which interpersonal relationships, intimacy and group identity and attachment play a crucial part.

A balanced relationship between interpersonal and group attachment development in this life period enhances the chance of freeing the mind from a troubled past, coming to terms with it and moving on. This is especially relevant to people whose attachments and other relationships (in the family, at work or in other group configurations) had been disturbed by repetitive or pervasive difficulties and conflicts.

Adults come to serve multiple roles in a myriad of relationships, in diverse and complex group contexts, typically more than in any other stage in the life cycle. The multiplicity of situations and statuses involved in being an adult in today's world can be an exhausting experience.

Our society demands that adults be competent and reliable professionals, exemplary parents, responsible and caring adult-children to their own parents, loyal friends, loving partners and so forth. Furthermore, adults are being asked to perform these roles with good will, empathy and *mentalising*, as well as being creative and obtaining great satisfaction in the process. Who can live up to these expectations?

Within this context of challenging developmental adult tasks, people sometimes forget to take care of themselves and may deny their own needs for secure attachment relationships. They could breakdown and require psychotherapy or another form of mental health treatment.

At this point, like in previous chapters, I would like to emphasise that attachment needs are not just a matter of babies needing their mothers, or of young children and adolescents needing their parents and their peer group; attachment (like food and sexuality) is a basic and integral part of our existence all the way from cradle to grave.

DOI: 10.4324/9781003167747-6

Adults have to face and navigate through a striking diversity of beliefs, values, knowledge, opinions and situations. In the modern (or post-modern) world, if there is a unifying developmental theme and a key developmental task in adulthood, these might have to consist of dealing with diversity in its most comprehensive sense.

Nowadays, people's expectations clash with social changes; but in our diversity comes fulfilment. According to Berger (2008), diversity is the hallmark of contemporary adult life:

> Adults vary widely in maturity, family, work, and lifestyle. For emerging adults who are less restricted by family or culture, the choices for education, work, friends and partners are mind-boggling. For other young adults, especially in poorer nations or earlier times, adulthood options are (or were) quite limited. The patterns described soon in friendship, love and psychological health are relevant to all, but diversity is particularly dramatic for the current generation.
>
> Berger (2008: 499)

According to Earl Hopper (2000), adult maturity must also include the development of the willingness and ability to take the role and status of citizen:

> Inevitably, this will also be a group phenomenon in that people cannot take such roles if they have not ensured that citizenship is available, which is a political process.
>
> Hopper (2000: 32)

Chapter 4 offered a detailed analysis of the increasingly deeper exploration of interpersonal and group intimacy which, according to Erikson (1963), is particularly prominent during emerging or young adulthood. Full grown-ups take intimacy one step further into what Blumer (1969) conceptualised as *intimate citizenship*; he put it this way:

> Intimate citizenship includes a plurality of public discourses and stories about how to live interpersonal and group lives in an increasingly complex world where we are confronted by an escalating series of choices and difficulties around intimacies.
>
> Blumer (1969: 148)

Drawing from various traditions of citizenship studies, Blumer further examined the development of rights, obligations, recognitions and respect around those most intimate spheres of life: who to live with, how to raise children, how to handle one's body, how to relate as gendered beings and how such arrangements are bound up with membership of different and complex groups and communities, bringing their own inevitable tensions and splits. Thus, conflict is ubiquitous and the mature citizen has to learn creative ways for dealing with it.

Respecting others' opinions is part of a larger attitude of respect. Adults are expected to develop respect for the whole person. Respect for opinions is not an easy art; it requires self-esteem, self-control, sensitivity, tolerance, fairness and generosity. This applies both to stated opinions and to views that are *unspoken*, but it does not mean being untrue to one's own (Ezquerro, 2019, 2020, 2021).

It simply requires people to recognise that others are entitled to look at the world differently and that, when they share their views, they can expect a fair hearing. As part of their development, adults must be increasingly prepared to allow that, if they knew more, their opinion might change.

However, irrespective of any diagnosis or issues that adults face, a common pathway is that they must tap into and identify some passions, experience the joy that comes with expressing them and have opportunities to share this joy with others. There must be a conscious effort to cultivate and integrate not just the logics of the mind, but also the desires of the heart. This is what ultimately leads to a sense of balance and satisfaction in life, a developmental goal that takes a full dimension in adulthood.

There is an extensive view that most people achieve adulthood by their mid- to late-twenties (see Chapter 4). According to Freud (1905), love and work are the cornerstones of adulthood. Healthy adults must have developed a capacity for intimacy, responsibility and autonomy, as well as an ability for making one's own decisions, for tolerating uncertainty and not knowing and for continuing further development as social beings (Garland, 2010).

Having said that, in adulthood, it is also important not to lose some of the fluidity and developmental strengths of childhood, adolescence and emerging adulthood: the curiosity to engage with the world and a sense of playfulness linked to the aptitude of being creative with new ideas (Lanyado and Horne, 2009).

To some extent, the structure of this chapter is a departure from that of previous and subsequent chapters. Although it focuses on adults and their key developmental characteristics and tasks, these are mainly explored through a qualitative piece of research into group psychotherapy with adult patients. The study provides opportunities to reflect on the vicissitudes of interpersonal and group attachment relationships in this life period, and their connections with earlier experiences.

The clinical and applied group-analytic literature on adulthood is vast and exponentially larger than that on all the other periods in the life cycle, put together. It is beyond the scope of this chapter to review such literature, which is widely available in Schlapobersky (2016), Barwick and Weegman (2018), Thornton (2019) and Parker (2020).

Instead, I will concentrate on the specific literature that deals with differences, similarities and overlaps between the Bionian and Foulkesian approaches to group psychotherapy, which have been largely considered antagonistic and incompatible.

Furthermore, in the case study below, I will reflect on my own adult development as well as interpersonal and group attachment relationships in adults, in the context of an out-patient group with members aged twenty-five to fifty-five, which I conducted weekly over three years during my early to mid-thirties, in the early 1990s.

Conducting this group was an integral component of my training at the Institute of Group Analysis (IGA), although the group met at the Tavistock Clinic ("next door"). I had previously trained for four years in child and adolescent psychiatry at the Tavistock, which helped me negotiate this unusual set-up with the Clinic's management. In an unplanned fashion, I came to be the Institute's first trainee to conduct such a group at the Tavistock.

I had two supervisors simultaneously, one from each institution; hence there was constant tension between the two theories throughout the history of the group. Dr Sandy Bourne (the Tavistock's supervisor) played an active part in the early stages, especially during the process of setting up the group; his role progressively changed to that of overseeing the work. On the other hand, supervision at the IGA was ninety minutes weekly for three years, in a small group of four trainees, led by Dr Harold Behr.

In contrast to traditional group-analytic practice, on the advice of Dr Bourne at the Tavistock, I invited eleven patients to join the group without meeting me, the conductor, beforehand. In contrast to usual Tavistock practice, on the advice of Dr Behr at the IGA, I saw one member of the group for individual psychotherapy.

Being caught in the middle, I was stretched to breaking point; however, I survived and every one of the eleven members survived with me.

Preparing for an adult group training

A vivid example of attachment in adults, especially in terms of group attachment, can be found in Nelson Mandela's (1994) autobiographical book *Long Road to Freedom*.

Here, Mandela confessed that he could not have survived twenty-seven years in prison if he had not belonged to a group of comrades fighting together against *apartheid*. The group made him stronger and more determined to continue fighting for survival and freedom. For a single person, it would have been extremely difficult, if not impossible, to resist the political and personal suppression to which they were being subjected.

Despite appalling prison conditions and depressing circumstances, members of Mandela's group supported each other; they shared every item of news, every concern and every discovery. Although not all had the same capacity for resilience, in this group the strongest took care of the weakest. Group attachment was key to everyone's survival.

Some members of the IGA had actively supported the campaign *Free Nelson Mandela*, which was a recurrent theme during the time I was a student at the IGA's Foundation Course, in the academic year 1987–1988. Mandela was released from jail in February 1990, the month after I had begun my training group for the IGA Qualifying Course at the Tavistock Clinic.

I had applied to start this course in 1988 and went through a thorough selection process. The Chair of the IGA's admissions panel told me that I came
across as a talented professional and enthusiastic young adult (I can recall
talking to them passionately about life and work). However, he added, the
panel advised that I should wait for one academic year, as they felt that my
approach was *"too Spanish!"*.

Oh…, whatever the panel meant, that was an interesting remark in its own
right. Nonetheless, being forced to wait for a year came to be a blessing in
disguise.

Towards the end of the Autumn 1988, my father was diagnosed with terminal cancer. He survived for just under one year. Every month, I travelled
from London to Spain to support him through his surgery and chemotherapy,
and to prepare for our good-bye. It was painful and hugely sad.

At the time, I was still training and working as a child psychiatrist in the
NHS. It would have been very difficult for me to cope with the additional
demands of the IGA's full training.

I started this training in September 1989. My father died in December,
only a few weeks before the training group I had to conduct was due to start,
in January 1990.

I was in pain but, with the support of my training analyst and, above all,
my partner, I decided to go ahead. Understandably, in my therapy group, I
developed a strong filial transference to my analyst. He became a father figure
in my life. I became attached to him.

My group attachment to the Institute was indeed mediated by the attachment relationship I had with my group analyst. I gradually developed an
attachment to my peer group of trainees and, eventually, to the institution.
But that is a different story.

In October 1989, I told Dr Behr and my fellow trainees at the IGA that
I intended to conduct the training group at the Tavistock Clinic. I was met
with disbelief and comments that the Tavistock (Bionian) and group-analytic
(Foulkesian) approaches were so different from each other that they should be
considered mutually exclusive and incompatible.

To make things worse, one of my trusted colleagues at the Tavistock
exclaimed:

Oh no, you are not training 'next door', are you?

Whilst I struggled in my mind with an uncertainty about how it might
be possible, or otherwise, to reconcile two models of group work that
were deemed to be antagonistic to one another, I was comforted by hearing a powerful message from South Africa – with plain words, full of
humanity:

Differences are not intended to separate, to alienate. We are different
precisely in order to realize our need of one another ….

The fundamental law of human beings is interdependence. A person is
a person through other persons.

Tutu (1989)

All in all, I decided to go ahead with a rather complex and unusual group
training exploration … Looking back, such an experience pushed me to the
limit. When I completed my IGA training, I needed to talk about it:

Different elements of the work were presented at a number of scientific
meetings in London, at the Tavistock Clinic in November 1994 and at the
IGA in November 1995; in Buenos Aires, at the Twelfth World Congress of
Group Psychotherapy in August 1995; in Copenhagen, at the Tenth European
Symposium of the Group Analytic Society in August 1996; in Santander, at
the Forty-Fourth Symposium of the Spanish Society of Group Psychotherapy
in April 1997; in Asturias, at an International Psychoanalytic Congress on
The Group: An Inevitable Encounter in October 2004.

Overall, the work came to be considered a model for the tasks of engaging patients with therapeutic group processes and promoting healthy group
attachment, as well as achieving an integration of the approaches of Bion,
Foulkes and Bowlby and of the various requirements in the training of group
analysts (theoretical seminars, clinical work and supervision, and personal
therapy).

Key components of the therapeutic and organisational processes involved
were published in *Psychoanalytic Psychotherapy* in the UK (Ezquerro, 1996a),
and in group-analytic journals in Spain (Ezquerro, 1996b, 1997, 1998a) and
in Italy (Ezquerro, 1998b).

The first group meeting

A storm from Continental Europe swept across the South East of England, on
the very day my IGA training group was due to start.

It happened to be the worst storm seen in the UK for decades, killing
forty-seven people and causing £3billion damage (Yeatman, 2022). Trees
fell down, roads closed; seven patients were missing at the beginning of the
first meeting. On reflection, this probably was serendipity; difficulties about
joining could easily be projected onto the external elements.

For this first session, I collected two men and two women from the waiting
room and led them, through long corridors, to a surprisingly shabby group
room in an internationally renowned National Health Service institution.

In contrast to other therapy groups that I had conducted previously in
which I introduced myself as Dr Ezquerro, this time I gave my full name,
Arturo Ezquerro, without using my title or making any additional comments. I then asked members to introduce themselves. They all gave their
first names plainly: **Abraham, Kelly, Cathy and Charles**. This was followed by a two-minute silence, during which people in the room avoided
eye contact.

I wondered how to make contact and remembered my own anxiously defensive introduction when, a couple of years earlier, I had joined my own therapy group.

Then and there, my analyst invited me to introduce myself. I responded that I was a psychiatrist, which seemed to slightly irritate some of my fellow group members who interpreted that I was resisting the role of being just a patient.

I speculated in my mind with the possibility that entertaining such memory during the silence of the Tavistock group could be a distraction or a form of mental *acting out* on my part. Just in case, I decided to return to the here and now in the room and *take the bull by the horns*.

I thought that I was already learning from Abraham, Kelly, Cathy and Charles and their ability to simply declare themselves patients – something I had not managed myself previously.

I felt free to add that I had also invited seven more people to join the group and decided to list their first names. I had not met any of them but managed to hold all of them in my mind, a process upon which I will later elaborate. Fortunately, my unconscious did not play a trick on me and I was able to remember all of them: **Elizabeth, Neil, Anabel, Raj, Rita, Leon and Laura**.

I paused and realised that four people in the room were looking at me intently. I then said:

I am sorry this may have come across as if I had delivered a list of casualties.

Shy smiles appeared on their faces, but they remained silent. I felt somewhat guilty and wondered if, perhaps, I was paying more attention to the absent members than to the present ones. This thought prompted me to say:

I gather that today you are the survivors.

This time, they responded more engagingly; all of them showed a unanimous smile. After that, they began to discuss how they had managed to survive the storm and get to the Clinic.

People were particularly struck by **Charles,** who said that the storm had not been a major problem for him, as he lived around the corner. **Abraham** commented:

You are lucky.

But **Charles** replied:

I would not have come due to my fear of going out, my agoraphobia, if my Japanese girlfriend had not given me a lift.

To the amusement of the other members, he added that his girlfriend was, in fact, waiting downstairs to take him back home.

At this point, **Anabel** knocked gently at the door, apologised for the interruption, said she was looking for Dr Ezquerro's group and asked if she was in the right place. I invited her in and asked members to introduce themselves to her, which they did willingly. Anabel, who had sat on one of the empty chairs next to me, quietly moved her chair three or four feet backwards.

The safe circular group configuration that I had in my mind felt threatened. A number of interpretations occurred to me but, instead, I decided to tell her that she was welcome and that moving her chair forward might help her feel part of the group.

Anabel gave me an uncertain *thank you* and blushed, whilst she moved her chair back to its original position.

Abraham then said to Anabel:

> Dr Ezquerro suggested earlier that we were a group of survivors. You are also a survivor, welcome!

Anabel replied:

> It has been very hard for me to get here because of the storm and, when I arrived, I wasn't sure whether I should join or go back home. I am still uncertain but, for the moment, I think I can stay.

Well…, they and I had survived the first session.

The Bion-versus-Foulkes tension in the group literature

Experiences in Groups (Bion 1961) became a major contribution to the world of group psychoanalytic psychotherapy; the book brings together Bion's studies of groups during and after the Second World War. His ideas were vigorously taken up by many of his colleagues and followers at the Tavistock Clinic, and at the AK Rice Institute in the USA. He also became most influential in the study of group dynamics and organisations (Banet, 1976; Obholzer and Roberts, 1994).

During the war, Bion made his mark with his leaderless selection groups. His explorations came to fulfilment in the creation of a therapeutic community, for the first time really conceived as such, at Northfield Military Hospital in England.

After the war, he was put in charge of group psychotherapy at the Tavistock Clinic. Like most of his colleagues there, he qualified as a psychoanalyst in the post-war years and was strongly influenced by Melanie Klein.

The exponential increase of patient referrals after the war pushed the Tavistock's management to develop therapeutic methods that would help the institution meet such a demand (see Chapter 6). With the arrival of the National Health Service in 1948, the Clinic was under pressure to maintain a patient load sufficiently large, as to satisfy the new NHS authorities that out-patient psychotherapy would be cost-effective.

War-time experience suggested that the best prospect would lie with group psychotherapy and Bion was asked to set this up. In order to attract patients for the groups, he offered two options: to wait one year for individual treat-ment or to start group treatment immediately (Ezquerro, 2017).

In fact, by the time the Clinic entered the NHS, many of the senior staff were already running patients' groups under Bion's headship. He also con-ducted groups for industrial managers and professionals from the educational world.

In the early days, Bion was very enthusiastic about injecting his group ideas into the Tavistock's post-war culture. Neurosis started to be perceived as a problem of personal relationships and, therefore, it had to be treated as a group phenomenon rather than as a purely individual one (Bion and Rick-man, 1943; Bion, 1946). Group therapy was a most timely development at a key moment when war survivors needed to learn to help one another, and themselves.

Bion's work had wider implications, as it laid the basis of a model focus-ing on the study of the group itself and the tensions within it. His corpus of intellectual axioms describing conscious and, especially, unconscious group dynamics has been a major influence in the field until the present day. His ideas have contributed to the understanding of institutions and to the practice of organisational consultancy across the world.

Bion's model influenced Bowlby (1949), who was appointed as Chair of the Tavistock's Children and Parents Department and found his own way of applying group methods. Bowlby laid the foundations of family therapy in the UK, by seeing all members of the family together. He also started a weekly therapy group for mothers and their babies or young children, which he called the *Well-Baby Clinic*.

Bowlby spent one afternoon every week on this group therapy project and conducted it during the course of three decades. Group membership, of course, changed when some mothers improved and were replaced by others. He created a therapeutic group dynamic and culture in which he was

> trying to help the less experienced learn from those who knew more.
>
> Bowlby (1991: 29)

Despite the huge contributions of Bion and Bowlby to the development of the Tavistock Clinic, the institution went through a great deal of discom-fort and guilt over the departure of those of the pre-war staff who did not meet the criteria for inclusion in the post-war team. An abdication crisis ensued. Tension and confusion invaded the whole Clinic (Dicks, 1970; Trist, 1992).

Some degree of *confusion* had already been present, from the outset, when Bion introduced group psychotherapy at the Tavistock, as described by Eric Trist who was a participant observer in the very first patient group that Bion conducted at the Clinic:

> For weeks on end I remained completely at sea about what he was doing ... He was following a pattern unintelligible to me and using a map I did not know.
>
> Trist (1992: 31)

As a result, Bion did not wish to serve in the NHS any longer. He resigned as chairman of the technical executive committee and restricted himself to the roles of social therapist and consultant to staff groups within the organisation – in order to work through these conflicting feelings and issues.

In addition to the institutional crisis, Bion delegated his leadership responsibility in the Tavistock's group psychotherapy programme for NHS patients to Henry Ezriel (1950a), with whom I came to have a *special* relationship as I inherited his group culture, including one of his former patients, as I will show below.

To a large extent, Bion's (1961) group concepts were also borrowed from his ideas on individual psychopathology. This had a bearing on the Tavistock model of group psychotherapy, in which the emphasis is on the analyst's perception of the group-as-a-whole, as if it were a single patient.

The application of Bion's ideas as a method of group treatment was thoroughly described by Ezriel (1950b, 1952, 1959) and Sutherland (1952, 1990). They both favoured a technique whereby nothing but rigorous group-as-a-whole, here-and-now transference interpretations need to be used. Ezriel particularly considered that these interpretations had to be delivered in the same manner as in individual psychoanalytic sessions. In this approach, the group becomes a *quasi-individual*.

Foulkes (1946, 1948, 1964, 1975) took into account other levels of group life, such as its intrinsic sociability, together with conscious and unconscious understandings that people in the group-analytic *matrix* demonstrate to each other. Like Bion (1946, 1961, 1962, 1967), he conceived man as a social animal whose fulfilment can only achieve completeness in a group. However, Foulkes's therapeutic attitude comprised more distinct holding and containing qualities, towards both the group itself and the different individuals within it.

In contrast to Bion, Foulkes believed that the therapist or conductor must give *security* and *immunity* for as long as the group is in need of them. Whilst Bion was largely influenced by Klein, Foulkes's primary influence was Freud (1921) who himself had concluded that the psychology of the group is the oldest human psychology.

Foulkes and Anthony (1957) also considered that group analysts have to develop *free-floating attention* in the group, in order to respond to *pressures* and *temperatures* as sensitively as a barometric or thermometric gauge. While similarly analytical, the images themselves are more environmental and homeostatic, but less mathematical, than Bionian conceptions of the *group mentality* – such as the *common group tension* or the *common group denominator*.

Bion and Foulkes were on common ground in their clinical and theoretical psychoanalytic orientation. Both aimed primarily at intrapsychic change, rather than only symptomatic relief. And they recognised an unconscious mind, with transference defence mechanisms in the individual and in the group.

Having said that, Foulkes became freer to include the actions, reactions and interactions of the therapeutic group situation, denied to the individual patient on the couch. He gave himself permission to become a *member* of the group and introduced a new frame of reference, in which the transference develops in a different way due to its multi-personal distribution.

Some group analysts attempted to connect both approaches. Pines (1991, 1992, 1998, 2000) provided engaging and coherent links between Bionian and Foulkesian theories, as part of an ongoing dialogue between group-as-whole approaches. Brown's (1992) chapter, *Bion and Foulkes: Basic Assumptions and Beyond*, is also illuminating and well worth reading. But these attempts at working towards a rapprochement of both theories were an exception to the norm.

The reality is that neither Bion nor Foulkes appeared to influence each other, although they have much in common and approached group psychotherapy from the perspective of the group-as-a-whole. In fact,

> they seemed to establish a mutual disregard to which their respective followers had remained loyal.
>
> Hinshelwood (1999: 469)

According to Hinshelwood (2007), it is likely that both, Bion and Foulkes, were influenced by the gestalt psychology of perception, as applied to social psychology. However, they look at the group in different ways. Foulkes was interested in the group as a gestalt, the individual being a foreground pattern of relationships within a whole matrix that forms the background. Bion instead saw the group as a field, rather than a matrix, and highlighted it as the site of the neurosis, giving therapeutic focus to the group's neurosis.

Furthermore, by the time Foulkes came to group psychotherapy, he was an experienced psychoanalyst and saw the group as a set of individuals whose interactions became his focus. In contrast to that, when Bion approached group therapy, his experience was in a large organisation (the British Army) and he focused on the group as an entity in itself. Hence,

> Foulkes applied individual psychology to groups; Bion applied organisational psychology to groups.
>
> Hinshelwood (2007: 353)

In fact, Bion's technique gave rise to a flourishing method of understanding organisations and group relations, the basis of the Tavistock Institute of Human Relations and the Leicester Conference.

On the other hand, Foulkes highlighted the role of the conductor as a *dynamic administrator* who supplies and maintains the setting throughout the life of the group (Behr and Hearst, 2005). Foulkesian group-analytic metaphors often emphasised the sensitive and responsive environment required, both, in early human development and in early group development (Ezquerro, 1996a, 1997).

Bion's more stringent approach led to a sharp decline and nearly extinction of his group therapy method at the Tavistock Clinic. However, with some modifications, such method was beginning to pick up at the time I started my training at the Tavistock in 1984. Caroline Garland (2010) played a large part in the process of re-engaging the institution with a revised, stronger and more effective philosophy of psychoanalytic group therapy.

Surviving primitive integration

I learned from John Bowlby, my mentor, that some psychoanalytic literature tends to use terms such as immaturity, unintegration and the like in a pejorative sense, or even worse, to describe children.

An example of this can be found in Edward Glover, a distinguished British psychoanalyst who was Chairman of the Medical Section of the British Psychological Society and co-founder of the British Society of Criminology and of the Portman Clinic. He wrote:

> The perfectly normal infant is almost completely egocentric, greedy, dirty, violent in temper, destructive in habit, profoundly sexual in purpose, aggrandizing in attitude, devoid of all but the most primitive reality sense, without conscience of moral feeling, whose attitude to society (as represented by the family) is opportunist, inconsiderate, domineering and sadistic. In fact, judged by adult social standards, the normal baby is for all intents and purpose a born criminal.
>
> Glover (1960: 8)

Bowlby strongly disagreed with this attitude of pathologising children or young people. He told me that maturity and integration should be seeing through the lenses of an age-appropriate and developmental perspective. Thus, a five-year-old child should be considered mature if his developmental characteristics correspond to those which are expected from a child of his or her age.

Similarly, Bowlby disagreed with formulations that considered that children are unintegrated *per se*. In his view, there are different levels of integration depending on particular stages of the life cycle. Even an infant, or a new-born baby, show some degree of integration, which might be considered rudimentary but which can be entirely *mature* and appropriate to their developmental stage.

Certainly, it is unhelpful to *judge* children from the perspective of the levels of integration that are expected from adults.

Bearing that in mind, I hesitated at the time of choosing the title for this section. I thought about using the term rudimentary integration but, instead, decided to use primitive integration (I quite like the evolutionary connotation inherent in it) to express an idea that, in the early stages, members had not yet achieved sufficient integration with each other to be considered a group in a group-analytic sense.

These people were indeed a meaningful collection of adult individuals, with their own differing histories and levels of past and current integration; they were trying to constitute a therapy group to help themselves.

As described earlier, I had invited the eleven adult patients on the Tavistock's waiting list, all at once, to attend the first group meeting; their age range was twenty-five to fifty-five; their details and reasons for referral could be summarised as follows:

Cathy, a twenty-five-year-old English librarian, presented herself with problems of identity, low self-esteem and social inadequacy.

Elizabeth, a twenty-nine-year-old Austrian civil servant, had a history of refractory self-harm and a diagnosis of borderline personality disorder.

Leon, a thirty-five-year-old Portuguese university professor, was struggling with a complex adjustment reaction following a recent bereavement.

Rita, a thirty-seven-year-old Argentinian psychologist, was assessed as a controlling, intrusive and obsessional personality.

Raj, a thirty-eight-year-old Pakistani graphic designer, was assessed as an emotionally underdeveloped personality suffering from multiple psychosomatic complaints.

Laura, a forty-year-old English artist, with a history of childhood deprivation, had a diagnosis of bipolar affective disorder.

Anabel, a forty-two-year-old Canadian writer, had a long-standing history of recurrent and disabling depression.

Charles, a forty-five-year-old English teacher, suffered from incapacitating agoraphobia and had made several suicide attempts.

Neil, a forty-nine-year-old Scottish politician, had a long record of psychotic breakdowns which required in-patient psychiatric admissions.

Abraham, a fifty-year-old Israeli barrister, had a history of intermittent anti-social behaviour and disabling hypochondriasis.

Kelly, a fifty-four-year-old South African catering manager, behaved as a compulsive caregiver and suffered from incapacitating acute anxiety states.

Whilst setting up the group, I thought a great deal about its composition. I had doubts as to how possible or realistic it would be to hold together this wide range of different backgrounds, personalities and mental health problems. I was aware that such a diversity would be a challenge, but also hoped that it could maximise the group's potential for healing and growth.

My Tavistock supervisor, Dr Bourne, was an experienced consultant psychiatrist and Kleinian psychoanalyst who developed a Bion-based group therapy programme at the Clinic in the 1980s, following the decline of Bion's technique in the previous decades. He allowed trainees to observe his groups behind a one-way screen.

I told Dr Bourne that I had been advised at the Institute to offer eight separate appointments to eight adult patients to see them individually, with a view to assessing their suitability for my training group. I explained to him that achieving a balanced composition of the group was an important objective from the perspective of the IGA.

Dr Bourne smiled and advised me to invite all eleven patients on the Tavistock's waiting list to attend the first group session, without meeting each individually beforehand.

I then told him that such a practice was undesirable to the IGA's training group analysts at the time. In fact, in *The Practice of Group Analysis*, a blueprint of orthodox group-analytic psychotherapy, the message about the waiting list was clear:

> A therapy group is best composed of people whose personalities, age, sexual orientation and personal difficulties allow the development of an optimally cohesive and therapeutically provocative environment ...
>
> Such a group can only rarely be achieved by taking the first eight patients off the waiting list.
>
> Roberts (1991: 4)

Dr Bourne seemed unconcerned. He explained that the patients had all been assessed by staff at the Clinic, which is a renowned specialist psychotherapy resource within the National Health Service. They had been on the waiting list for periods ranging from six months to three years.

During this time, he had periodically written to them, giving information about prospective vacancies for treatment and enquiring about time availability. In supervision, he predicted that inviting eleven people would result in getting a group of seven or eight members.

In the circumstances, I asked Dr Bourne's secretary to write to the eleven patients offering them an initial group meeting. In the letter, I described the analytic nature of the treatment. This included a commitment to respect the confidentiality and boundaries of the group: members should not discuss group material or meet each other outside the group sessions. Dr Bourne was pleased that we had cleared off the Tavistock's group waiting list.

When I reported this sequence of events to my small supervision group at the Institute, the other three IGA trainees said that they were unhappy with it, as they considered that not seeing the patients individually, before the first group session, was a group-analytic *anomaly*.

One of them was really angry with me and said that I should have waited one week before writing to the patients in order to consult with this supervision group. She looked at Dr Harold Behr and added:

> I think Arturo should write to the patients to cancel the group meeting, and to offer them eleven individual assessments separately!

I responded to my colleague:

> I think that would be confusing for the patients and Dr Bourne, as the consultant-in-charge, would not allow it anyway.

At this point, Dr Behr decided to do some group role-play. He pretended to telephone Dr Foulkes, who had died twenty-four years previously, to consult with him as the main group-analytic authority.

Dr Behr reported that the advice of the founder of group analysis was for me to carry on with the group meeting because, sooner or later, some of the patients would drop out of treatment and, then, I should see future patients on a one-to-one basis, before inviting them to join the group.

During Dr Behr's pretend telephone call, I had thought that, maybe, the group dynamic I was facing was one of *sibling* rivalry. But I did not dare to say anything; after all, I was the *new boy* in the group.

The other trainees were in the second and third years of their training. Paradoxically, sibling and peer development was a neglected area in group-analytic literature at the time; to some extent, it still is (Parker, 2020).

Anyhow, I was relieved by the outcome that I could get on with the training group and pleased that Dr Behr was more flexible and open-minded a person than some of my peers.

But, at that stage, no one in the room (including myself) could suspect that the eleven patients would decide to continue their treatment with me, during the whole three years of my training at the Institute.

Following the *stormy* initial group session, I was reassured to learn that, remarkably, every one of the prospective members absent from that first meeting had telephoned the Clinic during its course, leaving messages in which they naturally blamed the storm and asked if the group was still on.

I thought there was a clear link between the fact that all the patients made contact with the Clinic, and the *dynamic administration* function that Dr Bourne's efforts had served. I wrote to each of them, appreciating their messages and confirming that the group was to continue.

Everybody attended the second session. Those who had come the previous week were initially more active, **Abraham** particularly so. He said that, twenty-five years earlier, he had attended a group at the same Clinic, run by Dr Ezriel. He remembered very little about the group, and could not explain how it was helpful. Abraham then recalled that, when people had asked Dr Ezriel a question, he had always replied:

What do you think?

People in the room listened with interest to Abraham's account, although some of them seemed puzzled and looked towards me inquiringly, as if they wanted to know if I was planning to do the same as Dr Ezriel did.

Abraham continued and explained that he had attended that group for several years, but had got to know very little about other people in it. He stated:

Group membership was constantly changing and unpredictable, as there were lots of comings-and-goings.

At that point, some people's faces showed an expression of confusion or apprehension. I said that there seemed to be anxieties in the room about the unfamiliarity of the situation, contributing to Abraham's need to talk about something known or familiar, like Dr Ezriel's group, in the face of our new group of strangers, particularly today, with the newcomers.

Elizabeth then said that she had felt very anxious about coming to the group; she was afraid of talking to strangers. She added that she had a problem about losing her physical balance, and thought that she would not be able to come to the group, even if she wished to.

Neil and **Kelly** showed sympathy and described how they each had injured their necks in a car accident in the past, which led to a very unpleasant loss of their physical equilibrium.

Charles joined the conversation and said that, although he had never lost his physical balance, he often lost his confidence and, sometimes, he lost his marbles.

I appreciated Charles' sense of humour, and commented that there might be a link between what Abraham was telling us about comings-and-goings, Elizabeth's fear of losing her physical balance, and Charles' fear of losing his emotional balance. I added that these three members could be voicing, in different ways, a fear of losing or not achieving a group balance.

Charles replied that what I had said was a strange way of looking at things, but an original and valuable one.

Elizabeth then explained how, after many physical investigations, she had been told that her problem was psychological. She was now thinking that, after all, it could be a good idea to make an effort to attend the group and get herself sorted out.

I said I had the impression that Neil and Kelly had played a part in Elizabeth's change of heart, as they had sympathised with her and understood how unpleasant it was to lose one's physical equilibrium.

Elizabeth nodded and said that she thought they had understood how she was feeling, as they knew what it was like.

Abraham then said that other people's understanding was all right, but he did not think it could help that much. For him, the only real help would come from Dr Ezquerro.

Laura then said:

Abraham, you don't seem interested in other people at all, do you?.

Abraham replied:

Why are you attacking me?

Leon then intervened:

She's not attacking you; it is you who are feeling attacked by her.

Raj commented:

Attack is a strong word; but I think Laura has been over-critical.

I was afraid of early hostile anxieties and destructive polarisation, but chose to listen, as a powerful and lively interaction was taking place. I thought that I should trust them; to keep the communication going was a priority, in order to establish a group. But I felt that they needed a lead in being able to communicate safely. My anxiety about beginning with too fierce an argument was relieved by the group itself.

Anabel, whilst looking at me, said:

I am feeling uncomfortable. This reminds me of how unhappy I was as a child because my parents kept arguing all the time.

Then **Cathy** asked her:

Where do you come from?

Anabel replied:

From Montreal, but I have lived in England for more than twenty years. What about you?

Cathy responded:

I was born in London, and my parents also had terrible arguments. After a brief pause, she enquired: "May I ask why you need therapy?"

Charles then intervened:

Good question. What are we doing here?

Anabel replied that she had been unhappy and depressed for many years, particularly since her divorce two years previously. Her GP and her psychiatrist put her on antidepressants but, she said, as she did not get better, she was referred for psychotherapy.

Prematurely independent? Holding by the group, including its conductor

In the following meetings, I played a reasonably active role at the risk of promoting a culture of group *dependency* on my leadership. I was pleased to see all members attending regularly. They idealised me and the group, possibly as a psychological defence against anxiety. At the same time, I was reassured to see that they were engaging with one another and gradually forming an attachment to the group-as-a-whole.

This group dynamic stimulated me although, whilst I was also cautious about it. I considered that, maybe, it was a transitional and legitimate form of omnipotence, which helped me with the safely holding and handling of this early group.

Members sometimes started the session by recalling memories of our previous meetings, which provided a sense of continuity. However, during my previous training at the Tavistock Clinic, I had learnt about Bion's (1967) idea of facing the therapy sessions *without memory or desire* …

My understanding of this *attitude* was twofold: first, it helped therapists to avoid imposing their own theoretical bias upon their patients; second, it was an honest and intriguing way of trusting the unconscious. Because of my loyalty to the Tavistock's thinking, I initially tried to restrain my desire to cure or to influence the group members. In the circumstances, I was vigilant about their active remembering of previous sessions.

On the other hand, at the IGA, I was learning from Malcolm Pines (a founder IGA member) that one needs to remember and to *re-member* in order to become a member. I understood that his playing with words referred to both conscious and unconscious memories.

This new *contest* – excuse me, I mean *context*! – was becoming a problem for me: as I was working on the *content*, I felt caught up in the middle of a *conflict*.

We were approaching the first-holiday break. **Charles, Abraham, Raj** and **Elizabeth** had met socially outside the group on a couple of Sundays. They were even planning to organise group meetings during the break, which became a group issue.

This happened at a time when political scandals within the Conservative Party were being debated in the media, and there was talk from the Prime Minister John Major and his Government about "*going back to basics*".

I began again to read papers on psychotherapeutic technique, and the relation of the past to the present. I found myself attempting to go back to basic Freudian theory, from which I had originally learned that remembering is needed to avoid repeating and become ready for *working through*.

In classical psychoanalytic theory, repetition is a transference of the forgotten – the compulsion to repeat replaces the impulsion to remember. When patients do not remember the *repressed*, they reproduce it – not as memory but as an action. They repeat it, of course, without knowing that they are repeating it.

In those circumstances, maybe as a reaction to my announcement of the first-holiday break, it appeared that some of the group members had *forgotten* the initial instruction about our therapeutic-group boundary of not meeting outside.

Part of me considered that I must allow them to take time to become more conversant with their resistance, to work through it, to overcome it. Another part of me was inclined to be more aggressive and, in defiance of such a resistance, to continue the psychotherapeutic work according to the fundamental rules of analysis and interpretation.

Since the *extra* meetings were becoming regular activity, the working through of resistances was, in practice, turning out to be an arduous task for the patients, and a trial of patience for me. I was becoming concerned about the potentially destructive forces that might be operating in the group, as a result.

I mentally speculated about the meaning of this new group behaviour, and wondered if it could be understood as a move from Bion's basic assumption of *dependency* to one of *fight and flight*. It seemed to me that they were perceiving the forthcoming break as a no-group available to satisfy their needs, or an absent-group inside.

I concluded that they might be trying to evade, the frustration or pain about a temporary loss of the group. Then I said to them they could be showing, through the *weekend group*, a difficulty in tolerating the possible frustration of having no therapy group during the break, especially those who felt that they needed it.

Raj reacted quickly:

> I disagree. The weekend meetings have nothing to do with the break, or with our capacity to tolerate frustration.

Abraham and **Elizabeth** nodded in support, whilst a few of the other group members smiled with a sense of complicity.

Charles said that going out with his fellow group members was helping him to feel more confident and independent. After a pause, he added that, at last, he was beginning to hope that he would be cured of his long-standing and disabling agoraphobia, which had previously led him to several suicide attempts.

On the one hand, I thought there was a mutually collusive quality in this "acting-out"; on the other, I felt I should play a safe card. I must confess that I struggled to offer a progressive explanation.

I commented that perhaps the outside contacts were a possible expression of a new developmental stage in the group, a kind of adolescent rebelliousness. I added that, maybe, they were trying to overcome the more child-like anxieties and dependent attitudes of the early stages.

Abraham exclaimed that my comment was "*laughable*".

I realised that he had taken it quite literally. I made an effort to hold myself back; I tried to reflect on a probable angry or offensive quality that I had inadvertently attached to my comment, regardless of its accuracy or lack of it. I was also aware of my background in child and adolescent psychiatry.

To my frustration, the extra-meeting contact carried on. After one of the tricky group sessions, I recalled that, like Bion, Foulkes had also considered that in times of crisis it is important to give the group an interpretation of its total behaviour.

So, I kept trying and interpreted:

In challenging boundaries again, the group continues resisting separation.

But they appeared uninterested.

I discussed the problem in supervision. Dr Harold Behr said that he valued my previous knowledge and experience in Bionian psychoanalytic group therapy; but he added that a more Foulkesian intervention would be required in the circumstances.

After a pause, Dr Behr commented that the group was both challenging and needing my authority more explicitly. His advice was:

Remind them that the meeting outside the group does not belong in this type of treatment.

At the next session, **Kelly** was angry with me. She said that she did not want to meet other members socially and strongly disapproved of it. She added that it was my responsibility to "*tell them off*".

Raj complained:

It is up to us to meet or not to meet outside; we are not children, but grown-ups.

Then, I intervened to give them a clear reminder of my initial instruction:

I am sorry, that's not permissible in this kind of therapy.

Abraham tried to justify the weekend meetings:

We are only trying to support each other…

But **Leon** interrupted him:

Dr Ezquerro has said it's not on, and that's it.

After a tense pause, **Abraham** exclaimed angrily:

He is not my father; he is younger than me!

To which **Leon** responded:

> You are treating him like a father-figure in your mind!

I thought that Abraham was not the only one searching for *authority*. Like him, Leon had recently lost his father. And I suggested this to them in later development. At that point, however, I felt it was important that they exercised their own authority within the group boundaries.

Rita and **Anabel** both reported that they had been approached by Charles and Abraham about the possibility of group meetings during the break, but they did not want to join such an activity.

Elizabeth then commented that, before the discussion started, she thought of saying she was no longer interested in meeting outside the group. The extra meetings stopped.

This change, I think, contributed to alter the course of events in the group. I learned from it and conceptualised the process as *learning from experience*, in the sense that Bion (1962) employed. Certainly, I could testify that, in different ways, I was learning from the experience of conducting this group as much as from the experience of listening to my two supervisors.

Bion himself related learning from experience to the development of the capacity to tolerate frustration, which he linked to the relationship and experience that the infant has of the mother. If the mother is able to contain the projected or evacuated elements in this process, these un-integrated parts can be re-experienced and re-integrated. And a capacity for thinking grows.

Unconscious libidinal ties in holding the group together

The room was often untidy and dirty, due to the carelessness of colleagues using it for seminars, which I found frustrating – to put it mildly.

I considered the provision of an optimal environment should go hand in hand with the therapeutic task. I took extra time to tidy up and clean the room myself before the sessions. Of course, that was not part of my job description; but I felt deeply responsible for looking after the setting.

I talked to those colleagues who were using the room at other times and also negotiated a favourable change in the cleaning rota with the Clinic's administrator. To my great pleasure, presentable curtains and a new carpet were fitted a few weeks later. The environment was used by the group as a screen to project internal conflict; it was also internalised – a two-way process.

A few sessions after the break, **Abraham** talked of his wish to leave the group. He was thinking of either seeing a therapist individually or attending the synagogue to which his father had taken him as a child.

Laura asked him: "*Why?*"

Abraham replied that in recent weeks he had been experiencing stormy feelings and wanted to go to his father's grave and smash his bones. He added that he had always stood in awe of his charismatic but punitive father.

After a brief pause, **Abraham** continued saying that he had been able to talk about his angry feelings towards his father in the group he had attended twenty-five years earlier because Dr Ezriel was older than he was and represented a father figure; but he could not see Dr Ezquerro in the same way.

I thought Abraham was bringing up issues of an unresolved bereavement. There were clear unresolved hostile feelings in his *transference* to me.

In contrast to the usual Bionian way of working, based on interpretations to the group-as-a-whole, I decided to relate directly to him and said:

Excuse a silly question, Abraham. How do I compare with your father?

Initially, **Abraham** looked very surprised. But, a few seconds later, he responded:

I do not think it is a silly question; there is always an underlying reason for your questions.

After a thoughtful pause, he added:

You are much kinder and more sophisticated than my father was.

When Abraham attended Dr Ezriel's group, he was having serious problems with boundaries; he was involved in delinquent activities and physical fights. His recent *attacks* on the group's boundaries had a less destructive quality than his previous out-of-control behaviour.

I decided to share with him my thoughts that he was kinder and more sophisticated than at the time he attended Dr Ezriel's group, to which **Abraham** responded spontaneously:

Thank you for saying that; it is much appreciated!

Over time, the group gradually stabilised; dreams played an important part in the therapeutic process.

Elizabeth dreamt she was coming to the group by bus, but inadvertently passed the bus stop outside the Clinic. She felt frustrated, but relieved; although she thought of going back home, she decided to attend the group. As she was walking to the Clinic, she woke up.

Kelly dreamt of the village where she was brought up. She had not been there for nearly thirty years. Her parents asked her to help with her next baby brother; but, when she arrived, she was shocked to find that her parents had disappeared and a black man was holding the baby in his arms. She was puzzled because there had never been a black person in the village before. As she was trying to talk to him, she woke up.

I thought individual dreams were gradually becoming the property of the group. As dreams reflected concerns of the group as a whole, they also became group dreams.

Raj, the only black member, dreamt of a group session in which everybody was black but himself, who was white. He tried to escape but found himself lying on the floor, in the middle of the room, with everyone else around shouting at him; until Dr Ezquerro picked him up, held his hand, and put him back on his chair. He was surprised to realise that he and I were the same colour. Then he woke up.

Abraham dreamt of a group meeting in which all members were present and sat around a square table rather than in a circle. He brought some of his best drawings, but was frightened that people would be critical of them. He could not believe it when his drawings were highly valued in the group.

Unlike real group sessions, in his dream there was an interval, at which members went out of the room. But he could not move and was left alone with Dr Ezquerro, in the room. At that point, he woke up.

Dreams were well received and allowed for a more spontaneous communication. Members gave themselves permission to relate to each other in depth, which involved powerful affects.

In the early stages, **Rita** had received quite a shock when she realised that I was working on a different system from the one she had been exposed to in her five-times-weekly individual psychoanalysis. She now very often brought dreams whose content was overtly sexual and seductive. She asked me to analyse her dreams.

I wondered if she was again trying to obtain a private interview within the group session by offering tempting material. I needed to explore in my own therapy and in supervision a possible unconscious wish to be seduced. Only after I thought I had overcome my countertransference impulse to *retaliate*, did I say to her:

Rita, perhaps you want to have individual analysis in public.

Rita blushed and looked down for several seconds. I wondered if I had gone too far with my comment and looked around the group circle. (Looking back, I think my comment was a little outrageous; I do not think I would have said it now, but I am thirty-two years older than I was then. Anyhow, I got away with it).

Leon said that, if he had been in Rita's shoes, he would have felt offended. Yet, he realised that the group was not about taking turns but about how members related to one another. He did not know exactly what was going on, but was feeling intrigued by it.

Rita replied that she was unable to put her feelings into words, but felt grateful that Leon had translated things for her.

Two weeks later, **Rita** brought another dream in which she was in the group talking about her parents and everyone was listening to her. At that point in her dream, she said:

Dr Ezquerro became a woman but with a penis.

She added that this image was confusing for her, as she was the only person in the group to be aware of it. She was feeling both disturbed and excited by it and woke up.

Several members offered a number of associative interpretations. Most of them pointed out that Rita was expressing a wish for somebody who could be, both, a man and a woman, maternal and paternal, sexual and caring.

Anabel emphasised that, like herself, Rita may have a need to be understood, as a woman, by a man therapist. After that comment, people looked at me enquiringly. I said to Rita:

> I think the woman with the penis could be expressing something about yourself.

Rita replied that she had not looked at the dream in that way. After a few thoughtful seconds, she added that during her early teens she had wanted to be a boy and got frequently involved in boyish activities, and in physical fights with her brothers because she wanted to have the power and privileges that she felt they had.

Anabel identified with Rita. Unlike her, she had not wanted to be a boy but, like her, she was born soon after the death of a brother and often thought that her parents wanted her to be a replacement for him. She wondered if her very active, almost promiscuous, sexual life was an affirmation of her need to feel wanted as a woman in her own right.

Rita responded:

> What you are saying makes a lot of sense.

And almost everyone in the room nodded.

With this conversation, **Neal** became alive. So far, he had talked profusely in the group about his symptoms, but very little about himself as a person. This time, he said that Rita's story was a relief for him and gave him permission to share his secret with the group. He in fact said:

> Since the age of four, when my sister was born, I had wanted to be a girl.

Cathy said that something similar had happened to her brother, four years her senior, when she was born. She added that it was quite natural to feel envious and jealous of a younger sibling.

Then, **Neil** anxiously replied:

> For me, it has been much more than that … Since the age of twenty, I have been collecting sexy stockings and suspenders that are now the basic essentials in my wardrobe.

The initial group reaction was one of amusement and disbelief. **Abraham** asked:

Are you being serious?

Neil replied that he was feeling angry at the question, but he continued:

I first became fascinated by cross-dressing when I read about the female fashion on the Parisian Can-Can stages of the 1890s. Thinking about the power of how the sight of long-legged girls flashing their black stockings and suspenders wowed audiences at the Moulin Rouge became an obsession for me.

Abraham then said:

Oh no! you are not a pervert, are you?

To which **Raj** responded:

Shut up Abraham, nobody complains about you often running to the Clinic, coming to the group in shorts and showing your legs! Carry on Neil.

Raj's intervention was supported by the group.

Neil then said that he had always kept his cross-dressing activity private at home because he did not want to be the subject of bawdy jokes and sexual innuendo. He added that he did not think he was a pervert, as male stockings and garters were part of men's dressing in the sixteenth and seventeenth centuries, while women legs were still firmly under wraps.

I must confess that I struggled with the fascination that Neil's predicament had produced in the group (an *audience*).

It crossed my mind that, to some extent, transvestism may provide a key for double meaning and for metaphor itself, but did not dare to say anything. I felt there was something exciting, but disturbing, in Neil (a man who desired to be seen as a woman) and in the whole group.

Eventually, I commented:

Neil, maybe, in 'undressing' yourself, you are giving us, like Rita did earlier with her dream, an opportunity to consider our unconscious wishes to live out the fantasy of having it all.

The following week, **Elizabeth** said that she had talked about Neil's predicament to some women friends, who laughed about it. I intervened straightaway to remind her of the expectation that the confidentiality of others was to be respected at all times, and details not disclosed outside the group. I also appreciated her sincerity in bringing her breach of confidentiality back to the group.

After this, **Elizabeth** apologised to **Neil** and he accepted her apology.

The clinical material of the previous sessions indicated that, as well as similarities, members had significant differences between them. They were facing the challenge of integrating these

The group was shaping and re-shaping itself, from a more primitive and cohesive form into a more complex and integrated coherent entity – from *cohesion* through dialogue to *coherency*, a more advanced form of group development (Pines, 1985; Ezquerro, 2010).

Each member was becoming a recipient of caring concern, but also a supporter and a vital link in the group structure. This reciprocity of giving and receiving played an increasing part in holding the group together. Members were interacting more fully with one another and deepening their inner explorations.

Separation-individuation

More than a year later, when the group had been running for over two years, I announced that it would come to an end in ten months' time. The majority of group members seemed satisfied that the termination date was reasonable. However, **Abraham, Neil** and **Elizabeth** felt anxious that they might need further help.

Laura commented that she had initially found the group helpful, but now she felt she was no longer getting better, and wanted to leave. In the early stages, it had been reassuring for her to learn that she was not the only one who had serious problems. However, in recent sessions, she had been feeling badly affected by other people's problems. She could only experience pain, and could not disentangle what belonged to others and what to her.

Meanwhile, at home, Diana (Laura's fourteen-year-old daughter) had become verbally abusive and, at times, was physically aggressive towards her mother. One day Diana walked out, slamming the door, to move in with her biological father.

I thought that prior wounds and failures in Laura's holding environments were surfacing. When she was four, her father committed suicide, and her mother developed a psychotic affective illness. Laura was received into care and had to live in children's homes, on and off, for ten years. She was sexually abused by one of her carers at the age of twelve.

I wondered if Laura's intensely undifferentiated affects could be an internal re-enactment of her abusive and traumatic institutional life, in which she did not experience any secure attachment relationships. It appeared that her transference to the group and to me contained some of her terror swings, between her fear of being abandoned and her fear of being abusively penetrated. As a child, she had experienced a state of intrapsychic catastrophe and deep depression.

At one point in the following group meeting, **Laura** unexpectedly shouted at **Raj**, who had been playing with a watch for a while. She looked agitated and cried out:

Raj, stop looking at your watch like that; it makes me angry!.

Following this, there was a tense silence in the group.

I opted for a direct interpretation and said:

Laura, perhaps you have good reasons to be angry with me because I set up the time-limits to the group.

Laura replied:

"No, I am not angry with you, but with him", pointing at Raj, who turned his eyes away from her.

She then said: "*I can't take this!*" And rapidly got up and walked towards the door.

Charles made a move as if he were going to restrain her, but did not follow her. Whilst she was opening the door, I said:

Laura, I hope you can stay.

She hesitated for one or two seconds, but left.

At the next session, **Abraham** commented that he was pleased to see Laura back. However, he added that he did not like the way in which she had walked out of the room the previous week. In his view, Laura's argument with Raj was a storm in a tea cup.

Laura got angry with Abraham and said that he was insensitive and out of touch, as he had not realised how aggressive Raj had been in ignoring her.

Raj replied that, although he did not think he had done anything wrong, he had felt a bit guilty afterwards and intended to apologise to her. However, he changed his mind because Laura was again unreasonably angry with him.

I then said that Laura was, in a way, showing us how painfully infuriating rejection could be.

Laura looked tense, but sad, and asked to see me for an individual appointment. **Rita** then commented that Laura's request was a bit selfish and that she was feeling uncomfortable about it.

Elizabeth intervened and said that she had also felt a need for a one-to-one session. She then looked at Laura sympathetically and added:

I think last week you were running away from pain, something I am familiar with myself. I felt like following you.

Charles asked her:

> Did you want to follow Laura to bring her back or to run away with her?.

Elizabeth clarified that she had felt like running away with Laura.

I considered that Laura was perhaps trying to run away *to* a more basic and nurturing type of relationship, in which her primitive fears could be contained and digested. However, I was anxious about a potentially destructive element in her anger and invited her to stay in the group. She replied that she would try but added that she really wanted to leave the group.

Laura came to the Clinic the following week and, although she hesitated, eventually left before the beginning of the session. That very day, she wrote to apologise for feeling unable to return to the group. In the letter, she also sent her best regards to the other group members and asked me again to see her for individual psychotherapy.

I read her letter out in the group and subsequently polled the members to ensure that they could all bring their feelings out into the open.

I have to admit that I was afraid that Laura's leaving could have an epidemic effect in the group, particularly should I decide to see her individually. On the other hand, she appeared to be the most vulnerable patient in the group and indicated that she may need a more, maternal-like, one-to-one nurturing relationship.

I also wondered if, at a less conscious level, she might have needed to treat the group in a way similar to how she was being treated by her daughter Diana at home.

In supervision at the Institute, Dr Behr helped me pick up a healthy element in **Laura**'s anger: an expression of her need for separation–individuation. In the circumstances, it seemed that she could individuate only by *attacking* and the intactness of the group, in order to experience it as separate from herself. He encouraged me to see **Laura** on her own.

I had to ask the Tavistock's supervisor for permission to see Laura individually. Dr Bourne responded:

> We do not offer individual appointments to our group patients in that way; but, if you decided to see her for individual psychotherapy, I would turn a blind eye.

And, so, I was able to offer **Laura** individual treatment for two further years, during which she became more able to work through her unresolved feelings of anger, rejection, abandonment and despair, especially those about the abrupt quality of her father's departure (he had committed suicide when she was four years old) and the hostile nature of her recent divorce.

In the last stage of her individual psychotherapy, **Laura** was able to make sense of and to overcome her overwhelming anger and, in turn, managed to get in touch with her sadness and to cry when her therapy came to an end.

When the group, itself, overcame the anger and anxieties about Laura's departure, members were more able to reflect on their contradictions, discrepancies, and complementary relations. These *bi-polar* themes were amplified by resonance, which extended analysis and mutual translation among the members about the issues that were important for them.

The last group stages

Not long after Laura's departure, at the start of the session (on a General Election Day), five months before our ending, I was taken by surprise: several members spoke highly of their group therapy experience. They commented that they perceived me as a reliable person and someone they could trust, and the group as a secure base. **Rita**, **Charles** and **Anabel** added that it would be excellent if we could have an extension of the group.

I was pleased to hear that the group-as-a-whole had become an important attachment figure in their lives, a secure-enough base for them from which to explore at a deeper level troubling aspects of themselves, including long-standing inner conflicts, through participation in the psychic lives of other members.

Almost unanimously, they wanted to extend the group treatment. This was a compliment; but also made me think that, perhaps, I had not provided the psychological conditions required to negotiate successfully the forthcoming ending of the group – which meant separation and loss.

They were looking at me inquiringly. A large part of me would have liked to continue working with them for longer; I really loved this group! Another part of me knew that endings are part of life and an important element of the therapeutic process.

As I hesitated, being very much aware of the context of the day, I tried to refer to their positive comments about the group in this light and said:

> In the context of today's General Elections, I wonder if your vote is for group psychotherapy.

Most members laughed cheerfully, although **Kelly** remarked:

> Can we please have a moratorium on cleverness and humour?.

I said to her that I could accept this *reprimand* (I thought I deserved it). After a pause, I added:

> Forgive me if I share what I learnt from my predecessor, Dr Ezriel. He thought that group psychotherapy is successful when every member changes but the therapist.

That was an extended idea among Bionian group practitioners. But I had other ideas in mind and so, after a brief pause, I added:

> I feel in this group that you have also changed me.

Without hesitation, **Charles** uttered:

> I love that!

Group members nodded unanimously, in agreement. And **Raj** commented that for several weeks he had had a recurrent thought in his mind. Looking at me, he added:

> Dr Ezquerro, you have become a trusted companion and a member of the group.

I thought that, in adult life, a reliable attachment figure often has the quality of being a trusted companion, but did not make any comment, **Rita** then said:

> I am with you, Raj. I also feel that Dr Ezquerro is a member of the group, but a special one.

To which **Cathy** argued:

> Rita, you keep trying, don't you?

Cathy's comment put a smile on everyone's face.

Leon then asked her how she was getting on, as she had been fairly quiet for several weeks. **Cathy** said that, in the early stages, it had been difficult for her to open up and talk in the group. She particularly remembered how she would censor and leave things out because most memories about her family were fuelled by anger. She added that her feelings had changed and commented:

> I don't know how it happened but I'm not so angry anymore; and when I am, I catch myself. That makes it easier for me to talk here.

Leon responded:

> You are important here. I identify with you because I am also someone who is predominantly a listener. I feel I have benefited a great deal from being in the group, by listening to and learning from others and about them, through which I have also learned a lot about myself.

Kelly then said that she was now feeling more relaxed and able to understand other group members better and to care about them, not as the duty she had felt forced to perform in her family of origin from a young age, but as a personal choice. This made her feel freer and emotionally stronger.

She elaborated on this and considered that she had never been able to express any anger at her parents. They pushed her, the eldest daughter in a family of fifteen children, to assume maternal-like responsibilities from about the age of seven. Thereby, she developed a care-taking identity whilst her own needs were neglected. In the group, Kelly gave herself permission to be angry with me and to talk about it rather than acting on it.

This meaningful session was followed, for several weeks, by a storm of protests and complaints. Some members went back to talk about the symptoms, anxieties and problems which had brought them to the group in the first place. My task was, once more, to ride out of the storm and help them make sense of the reactivation of their anger and concerns.

I suggested that their feelings about the forthcoming termination of the group could be getting mixed up with previous experiences of separation and loss in their lives. This insight made sense to them. For a while, it was possible to move on and explore new challenges ahead; but not quite.

In one of the sessions, as she was talking of her anxieties about the future, **Elizabeth** looked around the group circle and said:

> This group has become a secure base for me, in which I can refuel every week.

After a brief pause, Elizabeth added that she was going to miss the group enormously and felt anxious that she would not be able to cope without it; sometimes, she was worried that she may harm herself again.

At this very moment, **Anabel** stood up unexpectedly and said that she felt compelled to leave.

Raj jumped next to her and gently held her arm whilst saying:

> Please, stay.

Anabel replied:

> I am sorry, I don't want to stay.

She then looked at me and asked:

> Dr Ezquerro, do you want me to stay?

I was mindful that Anabel's action had occurred in the context of Elizabeth's talk about self-harming, but did not comment on that. Instead, I followed my trained intuition and responded:

> Yes.

I think my internal group-analytic supervisor had given me permission to be myself.

Anabel replied straightway:

Thank you.

She then returned to her chair and sat down, looking more relaxed and relieved.

Abraham complained about Raj's action because, he said, the physical contact between him and Anabel had been too intimate, almost sexual.

Raj said that he felt very offended by Abraham's comment. He then stood up whilst saying that he was leaving the group.

Elizabeth followed him and held him as he had just started to open the door. For a couple of seconds, they looked at each other whilst the group looked at them. Then, Elizabeth gave Raj a hug, and both went back to their chairs.

Cathy said to Abraham that he had been a bit brutal with Raj, and added that sometimes there is a need for warm physical touch that is not sexual. Almost everyone in the room nodded.

Abraham appeared to be wanting to respond to Cathy directly but hesitated and, instead, turned his head towards me and asked:

Dr Ezquerro, what do you think?

At this point, a memory came to my mind about the anecdote that Abraham had shared in the second session of the group:

"What do you think?" was the recurrent response that he had *inevitably* received from Dr Ezriel, twenty-five years previously, each and every time he asked him a question.

Bearing that in mind, I chose to respond:

Sometimes you need to be held in order to be healed.

Abraham smiled and nodded in acceptance, whilst **Charles** said that this reflection on the therapeutic value of holding touched him deeply.

Members experienced the session as dramatic, pleasurable and moving, but without losing out in the sphere of mental intelligibility and emotional understanding.

In a later development, I invited **Anabel** to think about her special need for feeling wanted and accepted.

She commented that she was born immediately after the death of her two-year-old brother Sean and that she had never been sure if her parents really wanted her for herself or as a *replacement* for her dead brother. She felt that she was born to an emotionally depressed family and, at times, was anxious that she might become depressed again when the group would no longer be available.

I said that I could imagine her mother struggling with overwhelming pain and sadness, and possibly becoming depressed, after Sean's death.

Anabel then talked about memories of her childhood which were coloured by contradictory feelings: she sometimes felt rejected and abandoned by her mother and, at other times, felt that her mother was intensely happy and cheerful with her.

I asked Anabel if she had ever thought about the possibility that her mother may have sometimes needed her as an *antidepressant*, to cope with a complex bereavement that contained contradictory elements: for her mother and other members of the family, death and birth poignantly came together at the same point in time.

Anabel replied that she was surprised but painfully relieved by my question. She added that it gave her permission to separate that which belonged to her from that of her mother.

Rita then commented:

> Anabel, as it happened to me, I feel there is something within you which you might have internalised from your mother.

Anabel nodded and said:

> I realise that I will need to do further emotional work after the group. Despite my anxieties about our ending, I feel reasonably confident that I might be able to get on with it.

Rita then said that, initially, she had felt her previous psychoanalysis and the group were incompatible. She added that, over the months, things came together for her and she now felt the group had, in fact, built upon her individual analysis. She also said that she had gained a new perspective of her life and felt more settled than ever before.

Charles, who was listening to this dialogue intently, commented:

> Anabel, I hope that the memories of your good relationships in our group will give you better chances to be protected from depression in the future.

He added that, with some ups and downs, he was also feeling reasonably optimistic about his capacity to help himself and face new challenges ahead.

As the end came into sight, the pace quickened. Group members were looking ahead and anticipating future personal issues that could either activate old ways of being or be opportunities for developing some of the new ways begun in the group. Many different themes were coming together.

A few meetings before the end, **Rita** talked about her own therapeutic struggle in the early stages of the group. For quite a long time, she had felt that her previous psychoanalysis and the group were incompatible. She now felt that things were coming together for her and that the group had built upon her individual analysis. She added that her life was probably becoming more stable than ever before.

Charles was listening to Rita with empathy and commented that, with some ups-and-downs, he was also reasonably optimistic about his capacity to help himself after the group had ended.

At the very last session, **Abraham** asked a question out of the blue: Dr Ezquerro, what do you think of me?

I smiled thoughtfully and, unlike Dr Ezriel, who never answered his questions in the past, gave him a full response:

> Abraham, I think you have shown in the group a quality of being reliable and resilient, which I hope you can now use to stay at the coping level.

Abraham was moved and I continued talking to him:

> Carry on being a good father, a good husband, a good barrister, and a good runner. I will miss you.

Abraham, the only member who had not cried in the three years of the life of the group, became intensely emotional and had a good cry.

Members (including me) were touched by it. **Neil** moved to the middle of the group circle to pick up the box of tissues, which he handed to Abraham, whilst holding his arm for a good powerful minute.

Anabel recalled a verse from Oscar Wilde's *Ballad of Reading Gaol*:

> … and only tears can heal.

Personal and group reflections

Funerals, commemorations, celebrations and other rituals facilitate the expression of feelings about death, endings, anniversaries or arrivals.

The last session was about dealing with separation and good-byes at an emotional level, after three years working together and developing group intimacy and group attachment. Interpretations were surrendered to accomplish a sense of newly found emotion, even uniqueness, which went beyond any attempt at descriptive technicalities. A reasonable feeling of completion was achieved, one of the variables being that every member got in touch with sadness.

As a preparation for our ending ritual, in the last stages of the therapy, I tried to help members reflect on their contributions and on the impact that the group had on them. It was part of a process of separation–differentiation–individuation, whilst keeping the group experience inside as an influential and integrated part of themselves. Some members were more ready than others.

The group, in its initial stage, was not a cohesive or coherent entity. Its level of integration was in a rudimentary form. It was a collection of individuals who had no relationship with each other or with me, other than the common task of forming a group. The newness of the situation generated considerable anxiety, particularly due to the unstructured nature of the meetings, with no guidelines as to how to establish the group or participate in it.

I had an intuitive desire to protect and unify the early group, whose attitude towards me was one of emotional proximity-seeking. As they struggled with previously unmet attachment needs, I became an idealised figure with parental-like qualities.

I had to remind myself that I was not there to lead the group or to heal its members, but to trust them (perhaps with a *safety net*) and jointly create the conditions where healing and development could take place. Beside their psychological problems and anxieties, they brought a distinct groping for meaningful communication, attachment and intimacy, as adults.

As a psychological defence, idealisation restricted the therapeutic movement of the group. However, it had a protective function as it allowed members to deal with the initial anxieties, whilst gradually becoming a cohesive unit. This function was vital and realistic at the start, and at critical points when the threat to the integrity and survival of the group became an issue.

The group achieved a more solid sense of unity and coherency at having survived the initial period. This was perceived by members with a sense of relief, in which I could share. The group was then more able to settle down and explore personal and interpersonal issues more deeply.

Every now and then, the balance of the group was threatened by potentially destructive anger; at other times, the group's equilibrium was challenged by boundary problems, linked to issues of confidentiality and trust. Sympathetic but firm handling was required, occasionally in the form of reminding members to respect each other and honour their adult commitments.

This was part of my role as *dynamic administrator*, which sometimes involved specific boundary regulation: managing and maintaining the group's structural norms and integrity. It also contained a protective and emotionally holding function – something that is expected from a reliable attachment figure.

I worked hard to help members rectify previous unsatisfactory holding experiences: holding out, withholding, failure to hold, inability to be held, and so on. From my mentorship experience with John Bowlby, I had learned that faulty holding and the lack of secure attachment may produce extreme anxiety in the infant and young child, sometimes leading to a fear of going to pieces and a subsequent difficulty in relating to the external world. This fear can also manifest in other life stages.

In his book *Clinical Applications of Attachment Theory*, Bowlby (1988) stated that the concept of *secure base* is close to Winnicott (1986)'s idea of *holding* and of Bion (1962)'s notion of *containment*. The latter primarily refers to a parental ability to take in, understand and adequately respond to those needs which an infant predominantly expresses through distress.

Containing involves two parties: the container and that which is contained. Originally, the mother's capacity (container) to receive primitive elements of experience (contained) and to make them available for the infant in a modified and more digestible form, which can be taken back.

Like good parental holding, therapeutic group holding grows the capacity for tolerating frustration. This is crucial for the development of creative thinking, particularly in the face of discomfort and pain. The mind becomes a container of thoughts, whilst language expands as a container of experience that can be transmitted from one group member to another.

Pines (1985) suggested that group members, including the therapist, share a common space: the powerful universal symbol of the circle, which has been a setting for the development of human relatedness through our evolution as a species.

I can imagine our distant ancestors sitting in a circle around a comforting fire, after a long day, sharing true stories and fantasies, forming a natural (therapeutic) group and growing in their group attachment.

Ettin (1992) referred to the healing properties of the group circle, about which he described a number of poetic metaphors. In some religious traditions, circular motion has symbolised the sweeping, spinning and stirring process of creation. Indeed, in primitive communities, dancing a round was thought to animate the still forces of nature. Roundness became a sacred shape and evolved into a universal symbol of wholeness, a major goal in adulthood.

The circle was also associated with healing, given its inherent potentials for mixing, arranging and enveloping disordered and polarised multiplicities. Jung (1969) suggested that in a circular configuration, pointed edges can be smooth, relationships circumscribed, splits conjoint and chaos contained.

Other authors (Hearst, 1981; Hawkins, 1986) likened the group to the good-enough environmental mother and equated the group's reliable felt presence with an internally held comforting mother image: an archetype representing the holder of life.

In this case study, members had not had a relationship with me beforehand and the push for group attachment was readily present from the outset. This was in contrast to other dynamics in which group attachment is more clearly mediated by the therapist. As members felt safe enough, they brought a combination of attachment and sexual elements, which were present in conscious and unconscious fantasies, including dreams. They pervaded every part of group members' thinking, including mine.

I had to make an additional effort to recognise counter-transference, in order to remain involved in the group but sufficiently separate to continue providing a safe attachment space, for them to integrate their attachment and sexual needs into their own lives as adults, outside the group.

Survival anxieties re-emerged at different points in the group's development, particularly when Laura left. The holding and attachment function was again important in order to maintain the integrity and hope of the group. I needed to be held at this water-shed time.

Much as a parent depends on a support system of close relationships (partner, grandparents, relatives, friends and community), I was strengthened in my caring and analytic role by my personal therapy, supervision, seminars and peer group attachment.

The ending required, yet again, careful and sensitive handling. It was pleasant but difficult when I realised that I was sometimes perceived in an idealised fashion – the group seemed to need this old perception as a psychological defence against re-activated anxieties about the forthcoming separation and loss.

This time, I was more reluctant to go along with their urge for gratification. An appropriate hostile anxiety emerged, which eventually gave way to a more mature depressive anxiety. A moving feeling of happy sadness evolved during the final good-bye session.

I also cried, alone, when the group had ended.

Further integration: moving on up

At the end of the treatment, I wrote individual clinical reports on the outcomes and sent them to the patients' referrers and to their general practitioners, leaving an open door for a re-referral if needed. I also sent a copy of their particular individual report to each patient, a rather unusual practice at the time; it was the year 1993.

I thought it would only be fair to allow them to see what I wrote in their medical files; it was consistent with the ethos of open communication employed during the three years of the life of the group. In addition, they could make corrections in case I had got things wrong.

All the patients wrote back to me; each expressed gratitude; none made any corrections to their reports. Seven years later, I asked the Clinic for an update and there had been no re-referrals.

Soon after this, whilst I was working as an NHS consultant psychiatrist and head of psychotherapy services elsewhere in London, I received a message from the Tavistock that Laura wanted a consultation with me. The structure of public health services in England did not allow for this type of referral outside the catchment area; thus, it was not possible to offer her an appointment at my new NHS service, but I decided to use my discretion to talk to her on the telephone.

Laura asked me to see her privately. I explained to her that, for ethical reasons, I did not see former NHS patients privately. She then asked me to recommend a colleague for private psychotherapy, which I did. My colleague saw her for a brief-therapy intervention (ten sessions), which seemed to suffice.

Looking back, this group experience itself was unusual, a hybrid piece of work navigating through and working towards the integration of two distinctly different cultures and approaches to group treatment, those of Bion and Foulkes. I was fortunate to be exposed to and learn from both, as I endeavoured to get the best of both worlds. Conducting the group was a challenge; but, also, a therapeutic and mutually enjoyable learning experience.

As I strived to flexibly combine both models, I learned that therapeutic group work should be more than an intellectual analytic exercise of rigorous verbal interpretations; it has to be done with the mind, heart and gut. Optimally, it becomes an integration in its own right.

Through the experience of running this group and my subsequent practice to the present day, it has become clear to me that Bion (1962)'s concept of *learning from experience* (from trial and error, from making mistakes) is not foreign to Foulkes (1964)'s view of *integration*. That is to say, integrity and understanding can only be gained little-by-little, as we come to be ready and able to metabolise experience.

This cannot happen in isolation. Experience is always co-constructed through diverse relationships and contexts; it is inevitably a group phenomenon.

Prior to the first meeting of my IGA training group, as I had not met any of the eleven patients on a one-to-one basis, I felt it was especially important to look deeply into the files of each of them. I was privileged that I could discuss them at length with John Bowlby. It happened just a few months before he died. He had been my mentor for more than five years. This was an independent arrangement outside my statutory supervision.

Bowlby helped me understand the relevance of their interpersonal and group attachment experiences, particularly during their formative years. He advised me that reflecting on their backgrounds and their interpersonal and group attachment histories would help with the task of preparing my mind for the first group encounter.

He also reminded me that my main task should be to provide a secure base for the patients, in order to promote favourable conditions for them to explore and heal themselves. In his opinion, the well-being of patients should be prioritised over and above any therapeutic technique.

I gained a feeling of having *met* them all before the first group session. Having said that, I also tried to deploy a phenomenological stance, putting aside my preliminary knowledge and working hypotheses, so as to relate to them with an open mind, keeping my prejudices to a minimum and experiencing both the anxiety and beauty of a new human encounter.

John Bowlby died on 2 September 1990. I felt hugely sad, but also felt that he had given me a gentle push to continue growing as a professional and a person. I inherited from him an ethos of professional commitment to the patients under my care. In the three years I conducted this group, I managed to be there for every single session. And, in the thirty years I worked for the NHS, I was immensely fortunate that I did not need to take any sick leave.

Reflecting back on my group-analytic training, I think my enthusiasm was contagious at the time. I was eager to explore, learn and encourage people to re-discover how to look after themselves. I was physically in my prime, establishing a young family, and co-constructing the basis for a successful career. I knew what I wanted; I could see the course clearly.

I did not have the experience I have today (I had not made that many mistakes yet) but my work commitment, curiosity and energy levels were considerable. Of course, I might be idealising the past a little bit right now. But I am not denying the dark side, including my own vulnerabilities and shortcomings. Rivalry, disagreements and other issues with colleagues and managers were difficult every now and then; there was pain and I struggled at times.

Yet, it was such a wonderful, productive and fulfilling time that, having now reached late middle-age, I sometimes experience a deep sense of loss. I need to work through this as one of my new developmental tasks. Including those previous experiences and contributions as an integral part of my life is an important element in the process of achieving my own ego-integrity (see Chapters 6 and 7).

Although Foulkes did not write about life-span development, the essence of Foulkesian group analysis is very much developmental. It proposes that any human being is part of a group from birth – or even earlier, if we consider the mother–baby dyad in the womb as already forming a group seed, whose characteristics have been shaped through our evolution as a species. Gradually, the father, siblings and an increasingly more complex series of overlapping family and social groups have to be accommodated in the child's developing brain and mind (see Chapter 2).

According to Gladwell (2012), groups have been essential for our survival as a species and have also played a significant part in the growth of our brains. Looking at any primate species, the larger the neocortex is, the larger the average size of the groups they live with. It is widely accepted today that one of the evolutionary pressures that contributed to the development of the human brain was the need to handle the complexities of increasingly larger and more sophisticated social groups.

Groups co-exist in external reality and in the internal world of the developing individual; the experience of a balanced group life is fundamental for healthy personal development and the fulfilment of a person's mental life. Bion (1961) and Foulkes (1964) strongly agreed on this; the core differences between them are not so much in the theory as such but in their therapeutic *attitude* and *technique*.

A warmer and more relational attitude towards individual patients is a distinct component of the Foulkesian approach, in contrast to a more detached Bionian attitude.

Bion's stance seems to suggest that the therapist has to be guarded against negative group dynamics, in which patients unconsciously split off and project unwanted and destructive elements of themselves. These fragments are collected anonymously into a pool that he described as the *group mentality*, which mainly consists of the patients' disowned or disavowed responses that are hostile to treatment objectives.

In contrast, Foulkes' attitude promotes the process of forming and arranging a *group matrix*, which encompasses the empathic understandings (both conscious and unconscious) as well as the unacknowledged discarded aspects of the experience that members share with one another.

I have suggested elsewhere (Ezquerro, 1996a, 1998b) that Bion's traumatic experiences during the two world wars and his difficult group attachment history contributed to his conception of the individual as a group animal who is at war with his "groupishness" – an assumption which he did not revise and which, in many ways, became deified and dogmatised.

Foulkes also had to endure trauma, but he was able to establish more secure group attachments. His group-analytic mentality, the *matrix*, is not at war with the individual. According to him, the broad range of negative and positive responses generated in a well-functioning group enhances, both, the person's individuality and groupality.

This *group matrix*, with its emphasis on a deepening of group members' capacity for personal insight and mutual understanding through their own contributions, as well as those of the conductor, adds a more horizontal therapeutic dimension or group culture that is lacking in the *group mentality* that Bion had originally described. In terms of attachment theory, the group matrix has been described as a secure base (Glenn, 1987; Ezquerro, 2017; Marmarosh, 2020; Tasca and Maxwell, 2021).

In its purest form, Bion's technique provokes frustration, which is not necessarily a bad thing; after all, learning to tolerate frustration without resorting to destructive anger and aggression is an important developmental task, which has to be consolidated in adulthood. However, too much frustration and disappointment can generate unbearable levels of anxiety and dysfunctional, even aggressive, group mentalities – particularly in more vulnerable patients.

Foulkes gathered that, as well as repressed hostility, patients bring a feel for group connections, collaboration and meaningful and intimate social relatedness. These elements combined can contribute to the formation of *group attachment*, as conceptualised by Bowlby (1969).

Group members present with many different symptoms and problems, but also carry with them a wealth of experience and a capacity for supporting one another, as well as other strengths that can be used therapeutically in the group situation.

In the Bionian model, the analyst is paradoxically the sole (*leaderless*) group leader and becomes the *only* source of higher-level functioning, interpretation and knowledge. In the Foulkesian model, the conductor is *not* the sole group leader, but takes the lead in enabling members to eventually form a *group of co-therapists*.

A group-analytic conductor is meant to foster not so much frustration, but tolerance and appreciation of individual differences. This encourages members to participate actively in their own therapeutic process. Such a conductor sometimes, but by no means always, allows the group to cast him or her in the role of *leader*.

As the group matures through reliance on its own strength, the therapist's role evolves from being a leader *of* the group to becoming a leader *in* the group: the authority of the conductor is integrated into the authority of the group.

Group analysis is not psychoanalysis of the group as if it were a *quasi-individual* (Bion and Rickman, 1943; Ezriel, 1950b, 1959) or individual analysis in the group (Burrow, 1958), but therapy of the group, by itself, including its members and conductor (Foulkes, 1964).

For Foulkes, one of the primary tasks of group analysts is that of deepening and widening communication. He equated this with the therapeutic process itself and described four levels of group communication: current adult relationships; transference relationships from previous stages; unconscious projections and fantasies; archetypal universal symbols.

These levels range from the more conscious everyday relationships to the more unconscious fantasies; from more to less clearly differentiated phenomena. Interpersonal and attachment problems are located in this group matrix, where different individuals can negotiate their boundaries and re-negotiate their unique personal and group identities. If these processes are successfully worked through, old distortions are corrected and a healthy group culture develops.

Bion concentrated very much on the use of his countertransference, as the raw data from which he could draw his hypothesis. The somewhat detached psychoanalytic nature of his technique became an important tool in the study of group dynamics and organisations, but did not allow for the holding qualities that some vulnerable group patients require.

I found Bion's contributions to be sharply provocative, deeply insightful and intellectually very stimulating; he puts us on the alert, to have our eyes wide open to the hostility of the real world. Foulkes's contributions add a dimension of human engagement, compassion and therapeutic effectiveness.

In my experience, the two models that Bion and Foulkes developed for group therapy with adult patients do not need to be antagonistic; in fact, they can complement each other.

Conclusion

Adults have distinct developmental challenges and tasks which require more advanced levels of integration than in previous life stages: dealing with diversity and differences, long-term love and work commitments, complex group configurations, conflict and intimate citizenship, as well as striving to achieve a sense of wholeness, balance and life satisfaction. Although some of these challenges and tasks are present in other developmental stages, they acquire a full dimension in adulthood.

The life-long fundamental human need for belonging to, identifying with and becoming attached to groups unfolds in a distinctly characteristic way in adults. They are expected to make significant contributions to society through multiple roles, often being in the middle of having to care for both new and older generations as well as looking after themselves. Psychopathology can be the result of a failure to meet these expectations, or a consequence of their needs for belongingness and group attachment going unmet.

This case study shows that the experience of open communication, genuine connection and emotional holding and translation of anxieties promotes the development of a well-functioning therapy group. This can help adults deal with and overcome both their phase-specific difficulties and the resurfacing of their unfinished business from previous developmental stages. Therapists have to be prepared to reflect on their own developmental issues and integrate the inevitable differences and discordant elements they will encounter into their training and work.

The present study demonstrates that apparently antagonistic approaches, such as those of Bion and Foulkes, can be integrated and complement each other for the benefit of adult patients. Group attachment can enhance the group's therapeutic potential and, as members gradually perceive the group itself as a secure base, they become more able to explore confidently and to grow.

References

Banet AG (1976) Bion interview. *Group and Organization Studies* 1(3): 268–285.

Barwick N and Weegman M (2018) *Group Therapy: A Group-Analytic Approach*. London: Routledge.

Behr H and Hearst L (eds) (2005) *Group-Analytic Psychotherapy: A Meeting of Minds*. London: Whurr.

Berger KS (2008) *The Developing Person Through the Life Span*. New York: Worth Publishers.

Bion WR (1946) The leaderless group project. *Bulletin of the Menninger Clinic* 10: 77–81.

Bion WR (1961) *Experiences in Groups*. London: Tavistock.

Bion WR (1962) *Learning from Experience*. London: Heinemann.

Bion WR (1967) Notes on memory and desire. *Psychoanalytic Forum* 2: 271–280.

Bion WR and Rickman J (1943) Intra-group tensions in therapy. *The Lancet* 242(6274): 678–682.

Blumer H (1969) *Symbolic Interactionism*. Hoboken, NJ: Prentice Hall.

Bowlby J (1949) The study and reduction of group tensions in the family. *Human Relations* 2: 123–128.

Bowlby J (1969) *Attachment and Loss. Vol 1: Attachment* (1991 edition). London: Penguin Books.

Bowlby J (1988) *A Secure Base: Clinical Applications of Attachment Theory*. London: Routledge.

Bowlby J (1991) The role of the psychotherapist's personal resources in the treatment situation. *Bulletin of the British Psychoanalytical Society* 27(11): 26–30.

Brown D (1992) Bion and Foulkes: basic assumptions and beyond. In: Pines M (ed) *Bion and Group Therapy*. London: Routledge, pp. 192–219.

Burrow T (1958) *A Search for Man's Sanity: Selected Letters with Biographical Notes*. New York: Oxford University Press.

Dicks HV (1970) *Fifty Years of the Tavistock Clinic*. London: Routledge & Kegan Paul.

Erikson EH (ed) (1963). *Youth: Change and Challenge*. New York: Basic Books.

Ettin MF (1992) *Foundations and Applications of Group Psychotherapy: A Sphere of Influence*. Boston, MA: Allyn and Bacon.

Ezquerro A (1996a). The Tavistock and group-analytic approaches to group psychotherapy: A trainee's perspective. *Psychoanalytic Psychotherapy* 10(2): 155–170.

Ezquerro A (1996b) Bion y Foulkes: Una narrativa grupo-analítica en los albores de un Nuevo Siglo y Milenio. *Boletín Sociedad Española de Psicoterapia y Técnicas de Grupo* 4(10): 73–84.

Ezquerro A (1997) Texto y contexto en dos instituciones terapéuticas. *Boletín Sociedad Española de Psicoterapia y Técnicas de Grupo* 4(12): 147–153.

Ezquerro A (1998a) Los modelos Tavistock y grupo-analítico: ¿antagonistas o complementarios? *Clínica y Análisis Grupal* 20(1): 39–62.

Ezquerro A (1998b) Gli approcci Tavistock e gruppoanalitico alla psicoterapia di gruppo. *Rivista Italiana di Gruppoanalisi* 13(1): 41–57.

Ezquerro A (2010) Cohesion and coherency in group analysis. *Group Analysis* 43(4): 496–504.

Ezquerro A (2017) *Encounters with John Bowlby: Tales of Attachment*. London: Routledge.

Ezquerro A (2019) Brexit: Who is afraid of group attachment? *La Revista. The British Spanish Society Magazine* 248: 18–19

Ezquerro A (2020) Brexit: Who is afraid of group attachment? Part I. Europe: what Europe? *Group Analysis* 53(2): 234–254.

Ezquerro A (2021) Brexit: Who is afraid of group attachment? Part II. Democracy: what democracy? *Group Analysis* 54(2): 265–283.

Ezriel HA (1950a) A psychoanalytic approach to group treatment. *British Journal of Medical Psychology* 23: 59–74.

Ezriel HA (1950b) A psychoanalytic approach to the treatment of patients in groups. *Journal of Mental Science* 96: 774–779.

Ezriel HA (1952) Notes on psychoanalytic group therapy. *Psychiatry* 15: 119–126.

Ezriel HA (1959) The role of transference in psychoanalytic and other approaches to group treatment. *Acta Psychotherapy* 7(suppl.): 101–116.

Feldman RS (2018) *Development Across the Life Span*. Harlow, UK: Pearson Education Limited.

Foulkes SH (1946) Group analysis in a military neurosis centre. *Lancet* 247(6392): 303–306.

Foulkes SH (1948) *Introduction to Group Analytic Psychotherapy*. London: Heinemann.

Foulkes SH (1964) *Therapeutic Group Analysis*. London: George Allen & Unwin.

Foulkes SH (1975) *Group Analytic Psychotherapy: Method and Principles*. London: Gordon & Breach.

Foulkes SH and Anthony EJ (1957) *Group Psychotherapy: The Psychoanalytic Approach* (1965 edition). Harmondsworth: Penguin.

Freud S (1905) On Psychotherapy. In: *Standard Edition of the Complete Works of Sigmund Freud, Vol 7* (1953 edition). London: Hogarth Press, pp. 257–268.

Freud S (1921) *Group Psychology and the Analysis of the Ego* (1940 edition). London: Hogarth Press.

Garland C (ed) (2010) *The Groups Book. Psychoanalytic Group Therapy: Principles and Practice*. London: Karnac.

Gladwell M (2012) *The Tipping Point: How Little Things Make a Bit Difference*. London: Abacus.

Glenn L (1987) Attachment theory and group analysis: The group matrix as a secure base. *Group Analysis* 20(2): 109–126.

Glover E (1960) *The Roots of Crime*. London: Imago.

Hawkins D (1986) Understanding reactions to group instability in psychotherapy. *International Journal of Group Psychotherapy* 36(2): 241–260.

Hearst L (1981) The emergence of the mother in the group. *Group Analysis* 14(1): 25–32.

Hinshelwood RD (1999) How Foulkesian was Bion? *Group Analysis* 32(4): 469–488.

Hinshelwood RD (2007) Bion and Foulkes: The group-as-a-whole. *Group Analysis* 40(3): 344–356.

Hopper E (2000) From objects and subjects to citizens: Group analysis and the study of maturity. *Group Analysis* 33(1): 29–34.

Jung C (1969) *Collected Works, Vol 9*. Princeton, NJ: Princeton University Press.

Lanyado M and Horne A (2009) *The Handbook of Child and Adolescent Psychotherapy: Psychoanalytic Approaches*. New York: Routledge.

Mandela N (1994) *Long Walk to Freedom: The Autobiography of Nelson Mandela*. London: Little Brown and Company.

Marmarosh CL (ed) (2020) *Attachment in Group Psychotherapy*. New York: Routledge.

Obholzer A and Roberts VZ (eds) (1994) *The Unconscious at Work: Individual and Organizational Stress in the Human Services*. London: Routledge.

Parker V (2020) *A Group-Analytic Exploration of the Sibling Matrix*. London: Routledge.

Pines M (1985) Psychic development and the group-analytic situation. *Group* 9(1): 60–73.

Pines M (1991) A history of psychodynamic psychiatry in Britain. In: Holmes J (ed) *Textbook of Psychotherapy in Psychiatric Practice*. Edinburgh, UK: Churchill Livingston, pp. 282–311.

Pines M (ed) (1992) *Bion and Group Psychotherapy*. London: Routledge.

Pines M (1998) *Circular Reflections: Selected Papers on Group Analysis and Psychoanalysis*. London: Jessica Kingsley.

Pines M (2000) Reflections of a group analyst. In Shay JJ and Wheelis J (eds) *Odysseys in Psychotherapy*. New York: Ardent Media, pp. 282–311.

Roberts J (1991) A view of the current state of the Practice. In: Roberts J and Pines M (eds) *The Practice of Group Analysis*. London: Routledge, pp. 3–17.

Schlapobersky JR (2016) *From the Couch to the Circle: Group-Analytic Psychotherapy in Practice*. New York: Routledge.

Sutherland J (1952) Notes on psychodynamic group therapy. *Psychiatry* 15: 111–117.

Sutherland J (1990) John Bowlby: Some personal reminiscences. *The Tavistock Gazette* 29: 13–16.

Tasca GA and Maxwell H (2021) Attachment and group psychotherapy: Applications to work groups and teams. In: Parks CD and Tasca GA (eds) *The Psychology of Groups: The Intersection of Social Psychology and Psychotherapy Research*. New York: American Psychological Association, pp. 149–167.

Thornton C (ed) (2019) *The Art and Science of Working Together: Practising Group Analysis in Teams and Organizations*. London: Routledge.

Trist E (1992) Working with Bion in the 1940s: The Group Decade. In Pines M (ed) *Bion and Group Psychotherapy*. London: Routledge, pp. 1–46.

Tutu D (1989) The Words of Desmond Tutu. Available at Desmond Tutu Quotes (Author of The Book of Forgiving) (goodreads.com)

Winnicott DW (1986) *Holding and Interpretation: Fragment of an Analysis*. New York: Grove Press.

Yeatman D (2022) Red Alert. *Metro* (18 February): 1.

ORCID iD: Arturo Ezquerro https://orcid.org/0000-0002-9910-4576

6   Late-middle age

Searching for a new group identity?

Arturo Ezquerro

Introduction

Please allow me to indulge myself. I have a story to tell:

In 1984, aged twenty-seven, I joined the four-year senior registrars' training programme in child and adolescent psychiatry at the Tavistock Clinic, in Hampstead, a rather exclusive area of London, known for its intellectual, liberal, artistic and literary association. I had just completed my four-year training in general psychiatry in Spain, during which adult patients often told me stories about the difficulties they had experienced in their childhood and adolescence.

I became curious and decided to take on a second medical specialty; I believed this might enable me to understand adult patients better. John Bowlby, the *father* of attachment theory, was my mentor from 1984 to 1990; he suggested that, at a less conscious level, I must also have had a curiosity about my own childhood and adolescence.

I also wanted to read psychoanalysis. So, being the largest European institution on psychodynamic approaches to mental health, particularly psychoanalytic psychotherapy, the Tavistock Clinic was an attractive choice for me. Anton Obholzer (my clinical tutor) persuaded me to join a group relations event at the Tavistock.

That was fascinating; I discovered that I loved groups (I still do) and that learning about how to survive them is an open-ended task. Peter Bruggen (my research tutor) taught me that a good way of surviving the difficulties inherent in our work is to write about them and, optimally, put the result into print.

In 1985, it became clear to me that I wanted to run a psychotherapy group for adolescents, but there was no existing or prospective group at the Tavistock's Adolescent Department. There was a group therapy workshop, which I joined, with only one patient on the group waiting list. As a trainee, I was asked by the chair of the workshop to wait until he and his colleagues, assessing adolescents for their suitability, recruited more group candidates.

Interestingly, by the time a new adolescent was recruited, the existing one had decided not to pursue treatment any longer – a dynamic that repeated

DOI: 10.4324/9781003167747-7

itself a few times and became a pattern. As a result, the group waiting list kept reverting to just one patient for several more months.

I had a distinct impression that the culture of the department was strongly oriented towards individual psychotherapy; group psychotherapy was considered second best, or not considered at all.

I tried to learn from the institution's history and read Dicks (1970)'s awe-inspiring book, *Fifty Years of the Tavistock Clinic.* I learned that Wilfred Bion (1946, 1961), who had a god-like status at the Tavistock, had set up the Clinic's group psychotherapy programme in 1946, based on his conception of man as a *political animal.* That is to say:

> an animal whose fulfilment can only approach completeness in a group.
> Bion, in Dicks (1970: 144)

In addition, Bion considered neurosis as a phenomenon of disturbed or disturbing interpersonal relationships and, as such,

> sought to treat neurosis as a group phenomenon rather than as a purely individual one
> Bion, in Dicks (1970: 145)

However, Bion's viewpoint was not fully understood. According to Dicks, the development of group therapy at the Tavistock had to be seen as part of the *second birth* of the institution, struggling to cope with the huge increase in the number of patient referrals, immediately after the Second World War. Thus:

> The theoretical framework characteristic of the Tavistock Clinic's approach to group therapy had been laid down by W. R. Bion and the late John Rickman originally for the purposes of economy in manpower.
> Dicks (1970: 7)

Furthermore, Dicks pointed out that the new Tavistock's professional committee knew pretty well what the views of most colleagues on the old staff were:

> disapproval of group therapy; there was difficulty in understanding that a community view of psychiatric disorders did not imply disrespect for the sanctity of the individual therapeutic relationship.
> Dicks (1970: 154)

In order to attract patients for the new group therapy programme, Bion offered two options: either to wait at least one year for individual treatment or to start group treatment immediately.

The strategy worked and, initially, there was strength in numbers. By the time the Tavistock joined the newly created National Health Service (NHS) in 1948, a number of the senior staff were already running therapy groups under Bion's headship (Dicks, 1970; Trist, 1985).

Bion (1946, 1961) was a hugely influential and charismatic figure, but perhaps employed too radical an approach: he seemed to be treating only the group-as-a-whole, as if it were an individual, rather than treating the individual group members (see Chapter 5). Many patients deserted or dropped out of group treatment.

Bion might have been disappointed with the therapeutic results or unhappy with the sceptical culture towards groups within the institution, or both. In any case, by 1952, he gave up and stopped running groups for patients at the Clinic or elsewhere (Trist, 1985). However, he delegated his leadership of the Tavistock's group therapy programme to Henry Ezriel (1950, 1952).

For several decades, the overall mood in the institution was that therapy groups did not work. In the mid-1970s, David Malan led a comprehensive piece of research: forty-two randomly selected patients were interviewed two to fourteen years after the termination of psychoanalytic group therapy at the Tavistock. The findings were staggering.

Comparison of psychodynamic changes in patients who stayed less than six months with those who stayed more than two years gave a null result. The majority of patients were highly dissatisfied with their group experiences. However, there was a strong positive correlation between favourable outcomes and previous individual psychotherapy. These results cast doubts on the appropriateness of transferring to group treatment the strictly individual psychoanalytic approach (Malan, Balfour, Hood and Shooter, 1976).

I also read a paper that Sigmund Freud (1905) wrote on the patient's suitability for individual psychoanalytic psychotherapy:

> The age of patients has this much importance in determining their fitness for psychoanalytic treatment, that, on the one hand, near or above the age of fifty the elasticity of the mental processes, on which the treatment depends, is as a rule lacking – old people are no longer educable – and, on the other hand, the mass of material to be dealt with would prolong the duration of the treatment indefinitely.
>
> Freud (1905: 264)

Interestingly, Freud was aged forty-nine, and struggling with his own self-analysis, at the time he produced such views. Countertransference? How I long to know!

In any case, considering the highly dynamic intellectual world in which he worked, Freud's dictum was paradoxical and inaccurate. He was, indeed, in contact with many intelligent and elastic older minds.

According to Peter Hildebrand (1982), Freud's pronouncement could have been due to his seeing disorders of sexual life as uniquely pathogenic for neurosis. Hence, he took perhaps the easy but mistaken step of identifying mental activity with sexual activity:

If, in terms of sexual life, a gradual slowing down of gonadal activity led to menopause in women and loss of sexual potency in men, Freud might have inferred that mental activity would become rigid and inelastic after the age of fifty. To others, remarkably, Freud showed great creativity and educability, himself, until his death in 1939 (aged eighty-three).

However, he did not revise his assumption on age and aging which, to a large extent, became deified and dogmatised. As a consequence, the entire old-age field within psychoanalysis was mostly ignored for far too long, which had a knock-on effect on group analysis. In the European context, during the first three-quarters of the twentieth century, less than a handful of clinical papers on the individual psychoanalytic treatment of older patients had been published (Abraham, 1919; Segal, 1958; King, 1974), whilst there was none on *Group Analysis*.

Fortunately, American psychoanalysts were more open-minded about older patients' suitability for psychoanalytic treatment than their European colleagues. However, only a small minority of practitioners explored psychodynamic psychotherapy for this age group before the mid-1970s (Jelliffe, 1925; Wayne, 1953; Goldfarb, 1955; Grotjahn, 1955, 1971; Meerloo, 1955; Berezin and Cath, 1965; Berezin, 1972).

It is quite extraordinary that, until the 1980s, the Tavistock Clinic was routinely rejecting patients over forty-five, and the Institute of Psychoanalysis (the outward face of the British Psychoanalytical Society) was refusing to accept training patients over the age of forty! (King, 1980; Hildebrand, 1982).

Against this background, and as an impatient young man, I was not prepared to wait *in aeternum* until my colleagues in the Tavistock's Adolescent Department, who did not appear to believe in group therapy, got their act together and managed to put enough adolescents on the group waiting list.

I contacted Caroline Garland, a passionate group analyst (Garland, 1980, 1982) and thriving consultant psychotherapist in the Adult Department, to seek her advice. I had met her at the Tavistock's group relations, induction event, the previous year. We were fond of each other and, I felt, she was the right person for me to approach, in the circumstances.

Having completed her training *next door*, at the Institute of Group Analysis (IGA), Caroline Garland was hoping for

> the start of more traffic between the IGA and the Tavistock Clinic.
>
> Garland (personal communication to the author)

She also told me that Peter Hildebrand (1982) had recently pioneered the setting up of a Tavistock workshop on individual psychotherapy for older adults, aged over fifty-five, which had generated a waiting list of nine patients. Caroline Garland suggested that we could offer these patients the possibility of weekly group psychotherapy for one year, not as holding therapy, but as an alternative full treatment in its own right.

Her creative idea was discussed in the Adult Department and the late Naomi Stern, a senior psychotherapist in her mid-fifties, who had recently arrived in London from South Africa, offered to co-run the group and started looking for a co-conductor.

However, several weeks later, no colleague had come forward in the Adult Department for the co-therapist role, despite a number of internal memoranda within the department. Staff were sceptical enough about group therapy in general, let alone group therapy with older adults.

It happened that, whilst waiting for a co-therapist, Naomi Stern interviewed the nine patients and they all agreed to join the group project, which was due to start in January 1986. Time was running out; to my surprise, Caroline Garland offered me, under her supervision, the job of co-conducting this group with Naomi Stern. The three of us arranged a meeting at the beginning of December 1985 and we closed the deal. The patients gave written consent for the weekly group sessions to be video-recorded for qualitative research purposes.

Isn't it ironic that after having waited for months to start an adolescent group, as a trainee in child psychiatry, I suddenly ended up *co-parenting* a new group for older adults?

In fact, this was the first time in the history of the Tavistock Clinic that a psychoanalytic therapy group for older adults took place. The group project was co-constructed as a result of the unlikely combination of Caroline Garland's creativity, Naomi Stern's courage and Peter Hildebrand's groundwork.

The three of them believed in the capacity of older adults to make good use of psychoanalytic psychotherapy and to be capable of forming group attachments. Looking back, I think I contributed with my enthusiasm (or recklessness?) and with my strong willingness to learn.

Thirty-six years later, I am still grateful to my mentor (John Bowlby), my two tutors (Anton Obholzer and Peter Bruggen), my three colleagues (Caroline Garland, Naomi Stern and Peter Hildebrand) and our nine group patients for providing a timeless experience, as reported in the case study below.

The group ran weekly for ninety minutes, from January to December 1986; we held a group review in June 1987; I wrote about it in 1988; the article was published straightaway in the Tavistock's clinical paper series under the title *Late-middle age and group psychotherapy: a fruitful link?* (Ezquerro, 1988).

Another version of this piece of work became the first clinical article on group-analytic treatment for older adults, published by *Group Analysis: The International Journal of Group-Analytic Psychotherapy*, under the title *Group psychotherapy with the pre-elderly* (Ezquerro, 1989). In the wider specialist literature, the paper has been referred to and quoted profusely in a number of languages across the world.

A Spanish version was published by *Clínica y Análisis Grupal,* under the title *An attachment matrix for a group of patients dealing with retirement* (Ezquerro, 2000). For the interested reader, the core of this clinical experience is reproduced in this chapter below, with updated research and additional reflections. After all, I am now 65, so within the age range of the group back then: a new twist to my countertransference?

But let us look first into some of the old and recent specialist literature, prior to reporting the Tavistock group.

The literature

A large part of the group literature with the late-middle-aged has concentrated on retirement as a major life event (Guillemard, 1972; Paradis, 1973; Baillargeon, 1982; Salvendy, 1989; Nobler, 1992; Payne and Marcus, 2008; Hershenson 2016; Haslam, Lam et al., 2018; Mangione and Forti, 2018; Haslam, Steffens et al., 2019). However, different people work through this transition and its aftermath in different ways, at different times and at different paces.

When the late Trevor Dadson (professor of Hispanic studies at Queen Mary, University of London) was interviewed by Ignacio Peyró about his experience of retirement, he produced some interesting reflections:

> The clear and obvious advantage of being emeritus is that you no longer have to fight with the university administration. And let us not deceive ourselves, the difficulty in university life has more to do with colleagues than with the situations themselves.
>
> Anyway, I have more time for myself than before. But I'm still really working at the same pace. I happen to love to investigate. Right now, one of the things I've noticed is that it's easier to say yes, that you can give a presentation, or you can contribute to an article they ask for. And, besides, as you get older, your friends and colleagues are also getting older and retiring.
>
> Dadson, in Peyró (2021)

Indeed, retirement has a constellation of different meanings and can be understood in a variety of ways. It is part of a foremost developmental process that usually occurs in late-middle age; it is also a form of loss that requires grieving and working through (Shultz and Wang, 2011). The concept and the trajectory of retirement are rapidly evolving, particularly in the context of an exponential rise in life expectancy:

> In the beginning, there was no retirement. There were no old people. In the Stone Age, everyone was fully employed until age 20, by which time nearly everyone was dead.
>
> Weisman (1999: 1)

Hershenson (2016) pointed out that, over the course of the past 10,000 years, more and more people have been living further and further, eventually

growing numerous enough for the late-middle-aged to form a distinct population cohort. In the past 150 years, individuals in this age group, have come
to be labelled senior citizens or *retirees*. Not surprisingly for a concept of such
recent origin and widespread use, there is little agreement on its meaning. It
has been stated that:

> The designation of retirement status is famously ambiguous because
> there are multiple overlapping criteria by which someone might be called
> retired, including career cessation, reduced work effort, pension receipt,
> or self-report.
>
> Ekerdt (2010: 70)

It has also been noted that this broad, confusing array of definitions reflects
the practical problem that underlies the concept of retirement:

> It is essentially a negative notion, a notion of what people are not doing –
> namely, that they are not working.
>
> Denton and Spencer (2009: 63)

However, this negative criterion must be put into question. Indeed, the meaning of retirement is multifaceted, has changed over time and can no longer be
defined as a single, one-time event. Furthermore, in recent decades, retirement has increasingly been seen as an opportunity for life review and change,
for new beginnings and identities, including group identity (Davenhill, 2007;
Ezquerro, 2017; Haslam, Lam et al., 2018; Haslam, Steffens et al., 2019).

Since there is no generally accepted definition of the term *retirement*, a
plethora of competing models of the stages of being retired has been generated, which makes research rather complex. To cut this Gordian knot,
Hershenson (2016) proposed the concept of statuses which, unlike stages,
are not necessarily mutually exclusive or sequential; thus, truer to real life.
According to him, statuses better reflect observed human behaviour and are
more open to the multicultural application; hence, facilitating research and
clinical practice.

Hershenson (2016) advanced six statuses, which form the acronym
RETIRE and can exist in any combination or sequence: retrenchment, exploration, trying-out, involvement, reconsideration and exiting. This concept
of statuses relates closely to approaches that pay more attention to developmental tasks than to chronological age.

Within its variability and complexity, research on retirement has been
huge. It is beyond the scope of this chapter to review all the theoretical, empirical and clinical literature on the subject. In fact, the chapter has a more
distinct objective; it aims for a wider perspective on late-middle age, as a
phase-specific period in the life cycle.

Therefore, I shall concentrate on those studies that, in my view, give a
clearer indication of the wide range of themes, tasks and situations or statuses

at stake during this life period; I will then refer to the specialist group literature.

Beehr (1986) studied the fields of gerontology and of social, clinical and developmental psychology on the causes of employees' decisions to retire early in late-middle age, and the effects of retirement on the lives of retirees and on the employing organisation. The main findings included the following:

- first, individuals' activities after retirement tend to be consistent with their pre-retirement leisure activities;
- second, their mental health after retirement is similar to that prior to retirement, but this relationship is moderated by factors such as planning, occupational goal attainment and expectations;
- third, organisations with high rates of retirement have more unstable organisational climates but more motivated new employees;
- fourth, employees are more likely to retire if their jobs have undesirable characteristics and their skills have been superseded.

Post et al. (2013) explored factors contributing to retirement intentions at different career stages. They found that employees' relationships to retirement decisions and the age at which they expect to retire are likely to change as their careers unfold. For instance, in the sample they studied, mid-career professionals planned to retire three years earlier than those in late career (age sixty-two versus age sixty-five).

Work centrality was associated with intentions to retire later, whilst positive retirement attitudes and higher income were associated with intentions to retire earlier. Additionally, the expected retirement age is more sensitive to income at mid-career (than at late career), but more sensitive to work centrality at late career (than at mid-career).

Hallberg, Johansson and Josephson (2015) studied the consequences on the health of military officers within the age range fifty-six to seventy years, following an early retirement offer by the Swedish Ministry of Defence. Before the offer was implemented, the normal retirement age was sixty.

They found a reduction in both mortality and in-patient care as a consequence of taking on the early retirement offer. This result implies that increasing the mandatory retirement age may have, not only positive government income effects, but also negative effects such as poor health and the concomitant increase in healthcare expenditures.

Müller and Shaikh (2018) presented a piece of their research on both spousal and own retirement status, across nineteen European countries. They found significant increases in the frequency and intensity of alcohol consumption combined with a significant decrease in physical activities, as a response to partner's retirement.

In contrast to that, they also found that own retirement had significant positive effects. Overall, on the evidence of their sample, they concluded that health was negatively affected by spousal retirement and positively by own retirement.

In the early days of analytic group therapy with the late-middle-aged, Salvendy (1989) advocated a method of brief group psychotherapy, focusing on mental preparation for retirement and its psychological after-effects. This period in the life-span was perceived by this clinician as a developmental transition, and the therapeutic focus was on overall well-being and adjustment to overcome the stressors associated with retirement.

This study corroborated previous research (Paradis, 1973) on the effectiveness of brief group psychotherapy with older patients in the treatment of age-related problems.

Nobler (1992) argued that it is never too late to change and reported on the first year in the life of a psychotherapy group for older adults, with four women and three men, aged from their mid-fifties to their late sixties. Some distinct themes emerged, including loss, isolation, adapting to a new body image and changing political views. In this particular group, the women appeared to be more sensitive to these themes and better able to make good use of the therapy than the men, especially in terms of self-integration, self-worth and the overcoming of isolation.

Payne and Marcus (2008) examined the effectiveness of group psychotherapy for older adults, above the age of fifty-five, reviewing 44 studies with pre- and post-therapy designs and 27 controlled studies. They found that group psychotherapy was significantly more beneficial than no therapy and that there were significant benefits in the patients after group therapy when compared with how they were before the therapy.

In addition, they also found that age was a significant factor: the younger the patients, the more they benefited from group psychotherapy. This means that late-middle-aged patients around retirement age benefited more from the therapy than the so-called *old-old*.

Mangione and Forti (2018) reported on a short-term psychotherapy group for late-middle-aged women facing retirement. There was a life-review component in the therapeutic work, as members discussed the main changes and transitions that they had previously experienced, including health, relationships, career choices and spirituality.

Moreover, members worked through their anxieties about the future. These included fears of increasing vulnerability to illness and of losing attachment figures and other important people, as well as losing a meaningful role in life, feeling useless and becoming isolated. Time was perceived as moving faster than before.

Haslam, Lam et al. (2018) and Haslam, Steffens et al. (2019) have done significant work on group identity perspectives with the late-middle-aged. They amalgamated evidence showing that social group networks are beneficial for adjustment to significant life changes and transitions, such as those of the late-middle-aged, including retirement.

They developed programmes of therapeutic group interventions, based on a social identity model of identity change (SIMIC). This argues that, in the context of major life transitions, well-being and adjustment are enhanced to the extent that people are able to maintain pre-existing social group memberships that are important to them or, else, acquire new ones. These authors concluded that the SIMIC approach is particularly relevant to the late-middle-aged, particularly regarding the big transition of retiring from work.

In addition, Haslam, Steffens et al. (2019) suggested that, when it comes to preparing for, going through, and recovering from retirement, it is essential to attend to the state of group memberships, attachments and relationships. To date, relevant stakeholders (like management and human resources departments) have had minimal regard for the importance of group identity planning.

From a SIMIC perspective, in order to extend our understanding of how people manage the retirement transition, it is imperative to look into group-identity and group-attachment processes that underpin successful adjustment. These authors highlighted four points:

1   multiple group memberships are important psychological resources for late-middle-aged people to achieve a successful adjustment to retirement;
2   maintaining some existing group memberships supports a sense of self-continuity during life changes, such as retirement;
3   having a platform of group memberships extends one's networks and promotes relations with new meaningful groups;
4   optimally, group memberships and group identities require compatibility and coherency.

According to Haslam, Steffens et al. (2019), SIMIC provides a clear roadmap for the development of psychosocial resources during the late-middle-aged transition. This programme explains not only why it is so important to invest in the development and strengthening of group-identity and group-attachment capital, but also offers a basis for theoretically derived interventions in retirement and its adaptation.

These interventions were agglutinated under the umbrella of *groups for health*. SIMIC programmes ultimately aim to help practitioners, policy makers and retirees themselves better harness the power of group-based resources during the process of adjusting to life after work.

Haslam, Lam et al. (2018) highlighted that, among the many factors that influence retirement adjustment, there is increasing recognition of the role played by groups, including group identity, group belongingness and group attachment. They embarked on two studies that pointed to the benefits that joining new groups can have for people's well-being when they experience a major life change, like retiring from work.

The first study, involving 302 at-random retirees, demonstrated that joining new groups in retirement and developing a stronger sense of group identification can predict life satisfaction. The second study examined the extent to which multiple group memberships support retirement adjustment and well-being. It included a cross-sectional sample of 90 retired academics and a general sample of 121 recent retirees.

Findings from both samples pointed to the importance of gaining new group identity and attachment during late-middle age for retirement adjustment.

Emma Beddington (2021), a well-known Guardian columnist, praised the usefulness of group psychotherapy as an aid to accommodating the challenges of late-middle age. She reported that, after group therapy, she can now love getting older and referred to some of the positive (though infuriating) sides of being late-middle-aged; for instance, less arguing, less fighting, less social anxiety and less bluffing:

> I don't do this sweaty, dishonest dance any more, the scrabbling, uneasy pretending to understand something when I don't. I haven't acquired wisdom, but I have accepted my own stupidity: on many topics … I am as dumb as a rock and happy to admit it.
>
> Beddington (2021)

Interestingly, Beddington added that she also enjoys the fact that the chances of having a vaguely uncomfortable time, walking on her own, have vastly diminished: no more street harassment and grisly attempts at flirting, which for her is a newly found glorious freedom.

She is increasingly thrilled by tiny things, and she hopes that old age can be a creative and colourful wonderland of delight, as long as the *Voltarol* [a pain relief, anti-inflammatory drug available at pharmacies over the counter] keeps flowing!

Let us now look in detail at the material brought up by the group of nine patients that I co-conducted at the Tavistock Clinic, as delineated in this chapter's introduction.

A clinical case study

A year-long, weekly out-patient group for late-middle-aged patients produced familiar themes and raised fresh issues, giving the therapists new sadness but enthusiasm.

Ten minutes after the start of the first session, a sixty-five-year-old polled the group asking:

> What do you think we should be doing here?

A sixty-year-old replied:

> We are facing a new opportunity to grow.

This group, which met in the mid-1980s, when group psychotherapy with this population was neglected, happened to be the first to be conducted at the Tavistock Clinic, for older adults over fifty-five.

At the time, the media was paying increased attention to retirement, and pre-retirement courses were run. Geriatrics had become a specialty in its own right within medicine, and psycho-geriatrics within psychiatry.

There had been a significant growth in the literature both about group psychotherapy and about development in older adults but, to a large extent, separately (Ezquerro, 1989). Trying to bring the two fields closer together seemed worthwhile.

Back then, the number of those expected to live to over sixty-five in developed countries was forecast to rise by yet another 25% by the turn of the century; but predictions proved short (Ezquerro, 2000).

A recent report by the United Nations Department of Economic and Social Affairs showed that the increase in average life expectancy across the world has been dramatic, since the beginning of the twentieth century (UN, 2019).

According to this report, life expectancy in the Neolithic Period was twenty years; in 1900 it was thirty-one; in 1950 it was forty-five; in 2019 (just before the Covid-19 pandemic) it was seventy-three, indeed, ranging from fifty-four in the Central African Republic to eighty-five in Hong Kong.

We were trying not to get distracted by ages but to concentrate on stages, as well as on therapy and developmental tasks. Ideas that Naomi Stern (the co-therapist) and I found helpful in preparing the group included the conception of therapy as a *"third area of human living"* (Winnicott, 1971: 38). This appeared to be particularly relevant to group-analytic psychotherapy, described as some space where the individual can negotiate change,

> as well as ex-change between the inner world and outer realities, within himself, between himself and the group and between the group and the out-side world.
>
> Garland (1982: 14)

We hoped that the group would eventually become a *"group of co-therapists"* (Pines, 1987: 261).

We expected to face specific developmental issues:

> envy of the younger therapist can be more safely explored in the group setting … [and] in on-going groups with elderly patients, denial of age becomes impossible.
>
> Van der Kolk (1983: 101–102)

We faced some sense of immediacy with our group's time limit (one year), reflecting perhaps the group members' more limited remaining life-span; so, we appreciated Kalson's comment that, in work with older adults, we cannot be as open-ended in time as with the young.

Kalson (1982: 79)

We had read that "*it is sometimes necessary to give patients a session on their own*" (Pines, 1980: 174). We also found it helpful to read some encouraging developments about combining both individual and group therapies with borderline patients (Cohn, 1986; Durkin, 1983; Filippi, 1983; Kulawik, 1982; Lofton et al., 1983; Slavinska-Holy, 1983).

A group for the late-middle-aged

The age range of this group was fifty-five to sixty-seven years (Naomi Stern was in her mid-fifties and I was twenty-nine). We offered forty-two sessions of one and a half hours over twelve months, from January to December 1986, with short breaks during the annual holidays.

Sessions were video-recorded and we (the therapists) were supervised together by Caroline Garland, a senior group analyst and psychoanalyst.

Nine people, four men and five women, came to the first session. Each had a wide range of problems and increasing difficulties coping with everyday life. Most felt on the brink of a breakdown. Some had suicidal thoughts. Two had received individual psychotherapy previously. One had a diagnosis of borderline personality disorder.

Each of the nine patients had been referred to the Clinic for assessment and had been put on the waiting list for individual psychotherapy. Caroline Garland suggested that they were offered a weekly psychotherapy group instead.

Naomi Stern volunteered to co-conduct such a group and I joined her. Each person was interviewed by her and was offered a place; each was told how we would run and video-record the group; each chose to join.

Early anxieties, splitting and denial of age

The first stage was characterised by a high level of anxiety. Group members felt prone to fears of non-acceptance and rejection, which mounted particularly towards the end of each session. Negative and aggressive feelings rapidly emerged, particularly towards me, the male co-therapist.

The life-long nature of the oedipal theme was apparent, especially after the individual interviews with the female co-therapist. Also, as it became obvious that I was significantly younger than all of them, perhaps, I was perceived as a *threat*: most of them were facing retirement or displacement by younger people.

> **John**, a fifty-nine-year-old bank manager contemplating retirement, started the fourth session by talking about the frustration he had felt a few minutes earlier, as he walked to the Clinic and was overtaken by a younger person. He said that he had felt half aggressive, half depressed.

David, a sixty-year-old headteacher due to retire in a few months, responded promptly: "*It doesn't matter, you can use your brain and go as fast as you want to*".

Diana, a fifty-eight-year-old nurse, intervened to say that she felt as fit as her husband, fifteen years her junior.

We thought that denial of age was an issue, but our interpretation evoked anxieties and defensive attitudes, until the realisation arrived, in one member's words:

We are all in the same boat!

After a general discussion about trust, confidentiality and the use they and we could make of the video:

Ann, a fifty-six-year-old divorced secretary, commented that she felt I was professionally correct, but cold, mechanical and unapproachable; she also felt that Naomi Stern was warm and caring, but vulnerable. In a further development, Ann decided that she had been dividing things up, and projecting onto us aspects of her own personality and her fear of not coping.

Most of the group members, finding that there were no rules about when they could speak, struggled for control. This was expressed mainly through male rivalry and competition for leadership.

When **Anthony**, a sixty-five-year-old retired company director, tried to *chair* some meetings by getting everyone to take turns, **Tom**, a fifty-eight-year-old dentist, confronted him with an ironic: "*Thank you, Mr Chairman!*"

The first break (after ten sessions) brought some fears of fragmentation, uncertainties about the future and the first drop out.

John left, expressing his anger in a letter. Previously, he had spoken about losing his mastery when his subordinates were no longer dependent on him. He found this thought intolerable.

John was the only one of the nine patients who left prematurely, in an unplanned fashion. He seemed unable, as he put it, to accept, grieve and work through the loss of his mastery, one of the key developmental tasks in late-middle age.

Struggles for group cohesion and coherency

In the second stage, when the group overcame the anger and anxieties about the break and about John's leaving, several members started to exchange more intimate feelings.

Anthony talked about his sexual impoverishment and his fear of being abandoned by his demanding wife.

Ann, who tried to be both sympathetic and understanding, said: "*You are not the young Anthony any longer, but your wife will appreciate your tenderness*".

David shared with the group his anxieties about retirement and his feelings about his almost obsessive reading of books on the subject. He was also attending a pre-retirement course.

Elizabeth, a fifty-five-year-old librarian, contributed with a reflection: "*Books can be helpful, but just for a time. Then you have to get back to living and find a genuine relationship*".

David felt grateful. He had divorced and was in two minds about his relationship with a new partner.

Group members were trying to be mutually supportive and to build some sort of group cohesiveness and coherency. The initial anxieties and hostility were gradually giving way to some identification with me, the young *idealised* therapist.

David at one point commented: "*Look at him, he is a machine recording and processing our conversations*".

This comment, also linked with the presence of the video recorder, opened a way to examine envy of the younger therapist, who, besides, had a partner present in the co-therapist.

One month before the summer break, half-way into the life of the group, three spoke of leaving (a sort of group-mid-life crisis?):

Elizabeth, whose husband had been killed in a car crash two years previously, was feeling better, and the relationship with her new partner was settling down. Although we told her that she might be avoiding the possibility of further exploration, Elizabeth left in her planned fashion.

Tom said that he was also feeling better, but decided to stay until the end of the group.

Another member, **Agnes**, an isolated sixty-two-year-old woman and survivor of the Holocaust, announced her intention to come no more.

She had arrived in London, as a refuge, when she was still an adolescent. Both her parents and all her family had been exterminated in the gas chambers, and she survived miraculously. To our concern, she did not attend the group for a few weeks after the summer break.

Becoming therapists to each other: A powerful sense of group attachment

The group missed Elizabeth, but not without some anger and feelings of being rejected. She, the youngest member, was at the coping level and felt that some of the issues discussed by other members, particularly retirement, were not that relevant to her. When sessions resumed after the summer holiday, group exchanges were lively; everyone participated actively:

> **Jenny**, a sixty-seven-year-old retired civil servant, divorced twice and separated twice, expressed with pain how she was hurt by Elizabeth's departure; she also felt rejected by young people in general and by her own daughter in particular.
>
> **Anthony** considered that there was some discrimination against the elderly in our society, but felt self-rejection was more serious. He commented that he would have liked Elizabeth to stay, but understood her reasons for leaving.
>
> He added that he was still struggling with Ann's comment of a previous session: "*I am not the young Anthony any longer*". However, he concluded that he was beginning to feel something new growing inside: "*I think I am becoming a young-old*".

Several members also expressed feelings of concern about **Agnes** not being in the group meetings. Due to her background, she represented the figure of a *survivor* – and, potentially, a victim.

> **David** had been thinking that a part of him did not like Agnes' complaining continuously and rubbishing the therapists, but he was now feeling a bit guilty about having rejected her inside himself.
>
> **Tom** felt unable to understand Agnes' extreme anxieties and her demanding needs. He added: "*I would not like to be in the therapists' shoes*".
>
> After that **Ann** said: "*I am worried about Agnes: she has nobody and could try to kill herself*". After a brief pause, she added: "*Perhaps we were killing her off by not allowing enough space for her in the group*".

Naomi Stern and I had jointly written to Agnes, the previous week, inviting her to re-join the group, but she did not reply. Then, we decided to offer her an individual session with both of us. She was able to come to see us and, after this, returned to the group meetings.

We thought that creating extra space for her in the group and in our own minds was fundamental for her psychological survival. Although we did not formally offer to combine individual and group therapies for her, Agnes seemed to settle better in her group therapy after the individual session. The group intuitively understood her special need for this.

> In the only session that Agnes missed after her return, **Anthony** pointed out: "*Although we all are in the same boat, I think we are different from her*". He then took a deep breath and added: "*She needs help most, but we need her*".

We thought that **Agnes** was helping other group members work through feelings of sadness, which had started from the appreciation of the similarities in their ages and their life stage. We also felt that Agnes was enabling them to review and re-negotiate, more precisely, their individual and group identities.

It was clear that Agnes was becoming attached to the group, where she was being looked after and sustained; group members were also becoming attached to her and to each other; there was a powerful sense of group attachment.

Death became a major issue when **Ann**'s mother was diagnosed as having leukaemia. This painful event gave group members new opportunities to develop care and concern and to further work on separation and loss. The group began to differentiate the fear of approaching death from more specific and immediate fears about the future, including the progressive self-restriction brought about by bodily changes and new realities.

> **David** elaborated on his pain, remembering the death of his own father the previous year. It had happened a few days before he became a grandfather, "*a joy in the middle of suffering*", as he put it. The grandchild being born gave him more strength to cope with his father's death; but he also had a feeling of being displaced.
>
> David added that both events had heightened his vulnerability to feeling abandoned and being alone, as well as his growing sense of loss and uselessness.

The group was functioning better since all its members were now appreciating the valuable help that they could provide for one another. However, it was only a few sessions before the end when Anthony felt safe enough to talk about his progressive bilateral hearing loss.

> **Jenny** advised him to accept the idea of having to use hearing aids. But **Tom** went further: "*Perhaps Anthony's hearing impairment represents not only his difficulty in listening, but a difficulty the group has had in taking things in*".

The group was becoming a *group of co-therapists*. They now seemed to be more ready to cope with the inevitable life-course changes that accompany the ageing process.

In our discussion after that session, Naomi Stern and I thought that we could understand Tom's remark as a turning point from projective to introjective processes; or, if you like, from acoustic phonetics (sound between mouth and ear) to auditory phonetics (sound between ear and brain).

At the next session, we suggested that the group was also losing the *hearing* they had been having from the two therapists. The group was facing its own end, and we invited members to explore the issue of termination.

The work on termination

The end of the group was difficult, but therapeutically satisfying. We, the therapists, had talked between ourselves about how we were beginning to feel sad. Some of the patients talked about feeling apprehensive and more vulnerable. Some spoke of re-experiencing the very anxiety of breaking down that brought them to ask for help in the first place.

> **Diana** said that she feared her younger husband might leave her; she was also anxious about failing work performance. She had thought she may need further therapy, and commented: "*The group has not helped me enough; I may need individual therapy*".
>
> **David** responded to Diana: "*you are acting as if past achievement didn't score*". He added that he had also thought of requesting individual psychotherapy, but that he had decided to help himself after the group.

Life is limited and the group was limited. We asked members to discriminate between how much of their anxiety had to do with our ending and how much had to do with the work not done. We also tried to help them elaborate how much anger and disappointment were about some of the age-specific matters.

For some, it was particularly hard to accept the end of the group. The members who struggled with the termination of the group could recognise that they were also finding it hard to accept life as it had been lived; they were in touch with needing to do post-therapeutic work.

Follow-up session

In the last meeting, we offered a follow-up group session as a review, to take place half a year after the termination of the group. All members welcomed the offer, some particularly so, although one suggested its value lay simply in letting us know how they were progressing.

> In the six months between the last meeting and the follow-up, **Ann**'s mother died. She felt on the point of phoning us, for the loss was very painful, but said that the group experience had given her strength to cope with her mother's death and work through her bereavement.
>
> She also felt that the group had helped her change and she could relate more openly and harmoniously with her brother, facing new important family issues.
>
> In common with other group members **Diana** voiced sympathy towards Ann, and appreciated the way she was coping with her bereavement.
>
> **Anthony** felt that he had not changed that much. Some days he felt depressed, and thought he would always struggle, one way or another, to accept limitations and minimise his vulnerability. He added that he was not alone; he was in fact trying to re-discover his relationship with his

wife: "*I don't think it will be easy, but our mutual understanding has improved; now I don't think she is going to leave me*".

We thought that Anthony was starting to raise an issue that belonged more specifically to the next developmental stage in the life cycle, that of old age or being *elderly*: in connection with the incipient fear of death, the fear of his wife's dying first and, in dying, leaving him.

David said that the group did not provide all the things he expected. His life was quite difficult and he was still living on his own, but becoming more interested in re-decorating his house.

Agnes complained that she had not improved. She felt her neighbours hated her and ran away from her. Questions from group members revealed that she had, in fact, started to use some community resources and, occasionally, she went shopping with one of her neighbours, a widow.

Jenny said that she had felt uncomfortable about the video at the beginning of the group. Now she had no doubt that she could trust the therapists, and felt the video had helped her to feel useful. She added:

> New generations will be able to learn more about human problems and to understand people of our age better.

The patients made good use of the review and provided evidence that some improvement had taken place. Initial anxieties had been reduced. Anger, denial and idealisation were used less often to cope with loss. Overall, anxieties about mourning and separation no longer seemed to prevent our group members from relating to the external world. At the ultimate goodbye:

> **Anthony** said he had a strange mixture of sadness and happiness. He had missed the weekly group meetings, but also felt that something, derived from the group, was growing inside him. It was something he was trying to look after and develop.

All seven members had attended the last five meetings of the group and only one, **Tom**, did not attend the review. He had to visit a relative who was dying in another part of the country, but he wrote a letter, which I read out in the group:

> I am feeling less inhibited and more able to enjoy the good things of life ... The awareness of my own mortality is more painful, but less frightening.

After the group

At the point of ending, none had requested further therapy. After the review, Naomi Stern and I wrote to Agnes, congratulating her for her work in the group and leaving an open door for her to contact the Tavistock Clinic again.

We also wrote to all the referrers to inform them about the outcome of the group. To our great pleasure, two wrote back expressing gratitude about change in their patients, quoting: *"remarkable improvement"* and *"consistent way of coping"*.

Twelve months later, one member asked to be seen individually.

For us, the therapists, ending brought more sadness that we were used to at the completion of a therapeutic piece of work: counter-transference? In supervision, we were able to tease out some of this. Writing about it helped too.

Discussion

I have always learned from my patients. But there was something special about what I learned from this psychotherapy group of late-middle-aged people. In different ways, each of them was eager to pass on to me a wealth of experience and wisdom: generativity? More about this later.

In this group case study, late-middle-aged members operated within a chronological time scale, but also worked within unconscious processes which are timeless. They started by perceiving me as an intruder or stranger and, so, they tried to get rid of me, as if I were a foreign body. It happened that, apart from being some thirty years younger than them, on average, I had a strong foreign accent at the time. Perhaps, I represented a challenging difference, as well as a symbolic threat, as many of them were feeling displaced by younger people.

Gradually, their attitude changed and they treated me with as if I were one of their children, with both idealised and denigrated feelings and comments. I became the repository of hopes and fears, shames and delights, guilt and integrity, not only in terms of the past but also the future. In some way, I became a guarantor of their permanence by *handing over* to future generations some aspects of themselves that they wanted to be preserved. This links up with Erikson's (1959, 1966) concept of generativity (see Chapter 4). As one of the patients put it:

> New generations will be able to learn more about human problems and to understand people of our age better.

Eventually, they invested in me as a significant adult attachment figure in their lives, caring for them and encouraging them to get on with their developmental tasks. On the other hand, transference and countertransference tended to be more straightforward in respect of my co-therapist, Naomi Stern, who was their contemporary.

This therapy group showed that, in late-middle age, there should be time and space for grieving and working through a number of losses, both past and anticipated, as well as mourning for that which has not been achieved during the mastery of adulthood.

This process of taking up and working through one's own deficiencies and difficulties is a necessary developmental task, which promotes a gradual achievement of balance in order to make a successful adjustment to old age (see Chapter 7). Unless such a process is initiated and carried out, despair may turn against the self in later life. In addition, it is necessary to renegotiate and sort out hopes, expectations and goals for the new challenges ahead.

Overall, the clinical material of this case study supports the view that late-middle age has phase-specific issues and developmental tasks. This is consistent with some of the findings in the post-Freudian psychoanalytic literature. In her landmark *Notes on the Psychoanalysis of Older Patients*, King (1974) identified some of the developmental pressures that operate as sources of concern, anxiety and depression during late-middle age. I would summarise these pressures, as follows:

1 The fear of diminution or loss of sexual potency and the impact this would have on relationships.
2 The threat of redundancy or displacement in work roles by younger people.
3 The uncertainty about the effectiveness of their professional skills, linked with a fear of being unable to cope with their retirement and with their loss of identity and worth, when they no longer have a professional role.
4 Feelings of grief when adult children leave home (empty nest syndrome), which may unmask latent problems in the marital relationship.
5 The awareness of an increasing vulnerability to illness and the inevitability of their own death, with the realisation that they may not be able to achieve the goals they had set for themselves.

There comes a time, in late-middle age, when the establishment of a personal sense of safety and of secure attachment is more important than the fulfilment of sexual drives and wishes, no matter how dominant and motivating these may have been in earlier years (Ezquerro, 2010).

Of course, for the great majority of older adults, sexual function may continue until the very end, but manifests itself differently from previous developmental stages. In this late-middle-aged therapy group, members talked about sexuality in less physical and passionate a fashion than in groups with younger adults; but there were more expressions of tenderness, affection and loyalty, and they continued their search for sensual growth and experience.

In his classical piece of work, *Death and the mid-life crisis*, Elliot Jacques (1965) suggested that such a crisis is often a reaction to the realisation of our mortality.

However, in my clinical experience, working with patients throughout the whole life cycle, preoccupation about death in existential terms (apart from bereavement and suicide) is not a prominent issue until late-middle age.

During this developmental stage, patients bring with them an increasing awareness of their own mortality and a greater exposure to the deaths of those close to them: parents, partners, friends, siblings and peers. For some, this generates an anxiety about gradually losing their peer group and becoming isolated as a result.

In *Beyond the mid-life crisis*, Hildebrand (1995) argued that psychoanalytic theorists had far too uncritically, and for far too long, accepted a hypothesis of continuous psychic and somatic development, with a rapid curve of growth from birth to young adulthood, a long refractory period and, then, a terminal stage of psychic deficit and social withdrawal preliminary to dying and to death itself.

According to him, this conception was not only oversimplified but also detached from reality, since psychosocial and psychosomatic development in the second half of life is far more complex and less regular than had been supposed by Freud and his followers, whose basic developmental scheme largely ended with young adulthood.

Early group analysis was not immune to these misconceptions. It is quite remarkable that, having developed group-analytic psychotherapy from the early 1940s, Foulkes and his followers neglected work with older adults until the late 1980s.

This oversight was so apparent that Martin Grotjahn (1978, 1989), a German-born American psychoanalyst had to raise his concerns in the journal *Group Analysis*:

> It is surprising to me how little space has been given in Group Analysis to the discussion of group therapy for senior citizens. Is this topic less important in Britain than in the USA? In the USA, group therapy for the aged is moving from previous neglect into a focus of attention.
>
> Grotjahn (1989: 109)

By and large, when thinking about the late-middle-aged phase, group processes have been considered an afterthought or have not been considered at all.

However, recent research studies (Haslam, Lam et al., 2018; Haslam, Steffens et al., 2019) have shown that paying heed to the importance of new group memberships and associated group identities and group attachments have a key role in the process of facing and successfully working through the challenges posed by late-middle age, including the retirement transition. For, when internalised as part of people's sense of self and identity, not only do these enhance the health and well-being of the late-middle-aged but, so too, they allow society to benefit from this population's various group-focused contributions.

These authors addressed a growing body of work and knowledge, which confirms the central role of group memberships, identifications and attachments as key psychological resources that can protect people in periods of major life change, like late-middle age and retirement. Joining new groups, including therapy groups, gaining new group identities and forming new group attachments are key to late-middle-age adjustments, and can also become an important resource further down the track into old age, as we will see in Chapter 7.

After looking into extensive cross-cultural studies, Hildebrand (1986, 1995) concluded that people in the mid-adult range (thirty-five to fifty-four), particularly men, actively seek mastery; they are invested in production and competition; they strive to acquire control over the resources upon which their security and the security of their dependents are based. According to him, in the pursuit of these goals, early- and mid-adults tend to give priority to personal agency over community.

By contrast, Hildebrand also argued that people over fifty-five are less interested in competition, more diffusely sensual and can become particularly interested, not in what they can produce but in that which is produced for them. They look for pleasant sights and sounds, and for uncomplicated social contacts. In effect, late-middle-aged people (especially men) tend to reverse the priorities of younger adults and orient themselves towards community rather than personal agency.

Along those lines, Levinson (1992) claimed that people in their sixties need to work through a developmental stage before entering late adulthood. During this transitional period, late-middle-aged adults have to prepare themselves for the process of becoming *old*. It might be painful for them to realise that they are no longer on the centre stage of life. This loss of power, respect and authority can be particularly difficult for individuals accustomed to having control in their lives.

On the positive side, the late-middle-aged have usually accumulated a wealth of experience and expertise from which younger generations can learn. In addition, they may feel a new freedom to do things for the simple sake of enjoyment and pleasure.

According to Waddell (1998, 2000, 2007), revised psychoanalytic insights into late-middle age and later life tend to emphasise the way in which a person's ability to face loss of all kinds, ultimately death, is rooted in very early capacities to bear psychic reality. As a person gets older, early problematic psychological constellations, if unresolved, are likely to be replayed; primitive defences, if underlying anxieties remain unmodified, are re-erected; child-like needs, if unmet, re-surface.

Also, within psychoanalysis, the neologism *maturescence* (Montero, 2015, 2020) has been proposed to give more specific attention and to understand better the changes of late-middle age.

The failure to master challenges that are typical of a given period of the life-span seems to decrease the likelihood of successfully negotiating future biographical transitions – something that is essential during late-middle age. This notion of sequential influences in the course of personal development has been a central claim of Penberthy and Penberthy (2020), Havighurst and Glasser (1972) and Havighurst (1972), who had originally put across the psychodynamic concept of developmental tasks.

Erikson (1959, 1966) had previously suggested that the fundamental conflict of middle- and late-middle-aged people centres on generativity versus stagnation. Psychologically, generativity (see Chapter 4) has a sense of *making your mark* on the world, through creative and nurturing processes that will outlast the person, often mentoring younger people or sharing with them experiences that may help them develop.

Through generativity, becoming involved in community groups and organisations, a middle- or late-middle-aged individual develops a sense of usefulness or transcendence, and of being a part of the bigger picture. In contrast to this, failing to find a way to contribute may result in shallow involvement with the world, leading to feelings of being unproductive, disconnected and stagnated.

Generativity includes any activity that contributes to the development of others and to the life of future generations. Most of the late-middle-aged patients in this case study felt that the work done in the psychotherapy group, which was video-recorded (and later put into print), had helped them to feel useful and to make a contribution to future generations. One of them put it this way:

> New generations will be able to learn more about human problems and to understand people of our age better.

Undeniably, this psychotherapy group proved Freud wrong over the age-fifty deadline. It also indicated that the problems of late-middle-aged adults have less to do with the loss of sexual function and more with the loss of cherished parts of the self, in the face of a deeper existential realisation of one's own mortality and of a stronger wish to leave a legacy behind.

Late-middle age is a specific life period in which to do substantial work on these ongoing issues, as well as another chance to develop new aspects of oneself. As a sixty-year-old put it:

> We are facing a new opportunity to grow.

Conclusion

Late-middle age can be considered a phase-specific critical period in the life-span, suitable for group-analytic psychotherapy, after mastery of middle adulthood but before settling into old age.

There might be a struggle between the world within and the increasing risk of illness, declining intellectual and economic productivity, intergenerational issues and a feeling of having less to give. In addition, the gradual loss of statuses and of significant attachment figures and peers, as well as a heightened awareness of one's own mortality, may generate states of anxiety and isolation.

In this respect, recent research highlights the importance of reworking group identity, group membership and group attachment, for late-middle-aged adults to focus on these developmental challenges, to grieve their losses, to adjust to major life changes, such as retirement, and to continue growing.

In a number of group contexts, late-middle-aged individuals bring a wealth of experience and wisdom that can be pooled in dealing with universal themes and problems, to enrich their lives and the lives of others. For, when they have an opportunity, not only do people in these age group improve their health and well-being, but so too they may contribute to society and to future generations with their knowledge and richness of experience – something that has been described as generativity.

The clinical group case study presented in this chapter shows that a greater understanding of the developmental pressures, difficulties and opportunities of late-middle age can inform psychotherapeutic group work with this population.

In a well-functioning group, late-middle-aged patients can explore safely, come to grips with their developmental tasks, grieve and work through their losses and difficulties, and face later life in better shape. Group psychotherapy with the late-middle-aged is not only possible but also a cost-effective and highly beneficial form of treatment.

References

Abraham K (1919) The applicability of psycho-analytic treatment to patients at an advanced age. In: *Selected Papers*. New York: Basic Books (1953 edition), pp. 312–317.

Baillargeon R (1982) Determinants of early retirement. *Canada's Mental Health* (September): 20–22.

Beddington E (2021) I do love getting older. Here are five infuriating reasons why. *The Guardian* (22 June). Available at I do love getting older. Here are five infuriating reasons why | Emma Beddington | The Guardian

Beehr TA. (1986) The process of retirement: A review and recommendations for future investigation. *Personnel Psychology* 39(1): 31–55.

Berezin MA and Cath SH (1965) *Geriatric Psychiatry: Grief, Loss and Emotional Disorders in the Aging Process*. New York: International University Press.

Berezin MA (1972) Psychodynamic considerations of aging and the aged. *American Journal of Psychiatry* 128: 1483–1497.

Bion WR (1946) The Leaderless Group Project. *Bulletin of the Menninger Clinic* 10: 77–81.

Bion WR (1961) *Experiences in Groups*. London: Tavistock.

Cohn HW (1986) The double context: On combining individual and group therapy. *Group Analysis* 19(4):327–339.

Davenhill R (2007) (ed) *Looking into Later Life: A Psychoanalytic Approach to Depression and Dementia in Old Age*. London: Karnac.

Denton FT and Spencer BG (2009) What is retirement? A review and assessment of alternative concepts and measures. *Canadian Journal on Aging* 28: 63–76.

Dicks HV (1970) *Fifty Years of the Tavistock Clinic*. London: Routledge & Kegan Paul.

Durkin HE (1983) Developmental levels: Their therapeutic Implications for analytic group psychotherapy. *Group* 7(3): 3–10.

Ekerdt DJ (2010) Frontiers of research on work and retirement. *Journal of Gerontology: B Series* 65B(1): 69–80.

Erikson, EH (1959) *Identity and the Life Cycle*. New York: International Universities Press.

Erikson EH (1966) Eight ages of man. *International Journal of Psychiatry* 2(3): 281–300.

Ezquerro A (1988) Late middle-age and group psychotherapy: a fruitful link? Tavistock Clinic Paper No. 98. London: Tavistock Centre.

Ezquerro A (1989) Group psychotherapy with the pre-elderly. *Group Analysis* 22(3): 299–308.

Ezquerro A (2000) Entramado vincular en un grupo de jubilados. *Clínica y Análisis Grupal* 22(3): 47–56.

Ezquerro A (2010) Cohesion and coherency in group analysis. *Group Analysis* 43(4): 496–504.

Ezquerro A (2017) *Encounters with John Bowlby: Tales of Attachment*. London: Routledge.

Ezriel HA (1950) A psychoanalytic approach to group treatment. *British Journal of Medical Psychology* 23(1–2): 59–74.

Ezriel HA (1952) Notes on psychoanalytic group therapy. *Psychiatry* 15(2): 119–126.

Filippi LS (1983) Psicoterapia psicoanalitica combinata, di grupo e individuale, con soggeti borderline [Combined group and individual psychoanalytical psychotherapy with borderline individuals: Results of fifteen years of treatment]. *Archivo de Psicologia, Neurologia e Psichiatria* 44(3): 289–298.

Freud S (1905) On psychotherapy. In: *Standard Edition of the Complete Works of Sigmund Freud, Vol 7* (1953 edition). London: Hogarth Press, pp. 257–268.

Garland C (1980) Face to face. *Group Analysis* 13(1): 42–43.

Garland C (1982) Group Analysis: Taking the Non-problem Seriously. *Group Analysis* 15(1): 4–14.

Goldfarb AI (1955) One aspect of the psychodynamics of the therapeutic situation with aged patients. *Psychoanalytic Review* 42(2): 180–187.

Goldfarb AI (1971) Group therapy with the old and aged. In Kaplan HI and Sadock BJ (eds) *Comprehensive Group Psychotherapy*. Baltimore, USA: Williams and Wilkins.

Grotjahn M (1955) Analytic psychotherapy with the elderly. *Psychoanalytic Review* 42(4): 419–427.

Grotjahn M (1978) Group communication and group therapy with the aged: A promising project. In: Jarvik LE (ed) *Aging into the Twenty-First Century*. New York: Gardner Press, pp. 113–121.

Grotjahn M (1989) Group analysis in old age. *Group Analysis* 22(1): 109–111.

Guillemard AM (1972) *La Retraite, une Mort Sociale: Sociologie des Conduites en Situation de Retraite*. Paris: Monton.

Hallberg D, Johansson P and Josephson M (2015) Is an early retirement offer good for your health? Quasi-experimental evidence from the army. *Journal of Health Economics* 44: 274–285.

Haslam C, Lam BCP, Branscombe NR, Steffens NK, Haslam SA, Cruwys T, Fong P and Ball TC (2018) Adjusting to life in retirement: the protective role of new group memberships and identification as a retiree. *European Journal of Work and Organizational Psychology* 27(6): 822–839.

Haslam C, Steffens NK, Branscombe NR, Haslam SA, Cruwys T, Lam BCP, Pachana NA and Yang J (2019) The importance of social groups for retirement adjustment: Evidence, application and policy implications of the social identity model of identity change. *Social Issues and Policy Review* 13(1): 93–124.

Havighurst RJ (1972) *Developmental Tasks and Education*. New York: David McKay.

Havighurst RJ and Glasser R (1972) An exploratory study of reminiscence. *Journal of Gerontology* 72: 245–253.

Hershenson DB (2016) Reconceptualizing retirement: A status-based approach. *Journal of Aging Studies* 38: 1–5.

Hildebrand P (1982) Psychotherapy with older patients. *British Journal of Medical Psychology* 55: 19–28.

Hildebrand P (1986) Dynamic psychotherapy with the elderly. In: Hanley I and Gilhooly M (eds) *Psychological therapies for the elderly*. London: Croom Helm, pp. 22–40.

Hildebrand P (1995) *Beyond the Mid-Life Crisis*. London: Sheldon Press.

Jacques E (1965) Death and the mid-life crisis. *International Journal of Psychoanalysis* 46: 502–514.

Jelliffe SE (1925) Old age factors in psychoanalytic therapy. *Medical Journal Review* 121: 7–12

Kalson L (1982) Group therapy with the aged. In Seligman M (ed) *Group Psychotherapy and Counselling with a Special Population*. Baltimore, MD: University Park Press.

King P (1974) Notes on the psychoanalysis of older patients. *Analytical Psychology* 19(1): 22–37.

King P (1980) The life cycle as indicated by the nature of the transference in the psychoanalysis of the middle-aged and elderly. *International Journal of Psychoanalysis* 61: 153–160.

Kulawik H (1982) Kombination der synamischen gruppen-psychotherapie mit der psychodynamischen einzeltherapie [Combination of dynamic group psychotherapy with psychodynamic individual therapy]. *Psychiatrie Neurologie und Medizinische Psychologie* 34(4): 222–228.

Levinson D (1992) *The Seasons of a Woman's Life*. New York: Knopf.

Lofton P, Daugherty C and Mayerson P (1983) Combined group and individual treatment for the borderline patient. *Group* 7(3): 21–26.

Malan DH, Balfour FH, Hood VG and Shooter AM (1976) Group psychotherapy: A long-term follow-up study. *Archives of General Psychiatry* 33(11): 1303–1315.

Mangione L and Forti R (2018) Beyond midlife and before retirement: A short-term women's group. *International Journal of Group Psychotherapy* 68(3): 314–336.

Meerlo J (1955) Psychotherapy with elderly people. *Geriatrics* 10: 583–587.

Montero GJ (2015) Psychoanalysis of maturescence (definition, metapsychology and clinical practice). *International Journal of Psychoanalysis* 96(6): 1491–1513.

Montero GJ (2020) *Psychoanalysis of Aging and Maturity: The Concept of Maturescence*. London: Routledge.

Müller T and Shaikh M (2018) Your retirement and my health behavior: Evidence on retirement externalities from a fuzzy regression discontinuity design. *Journal of Health Economics* 57: 45–59.

Nobler H (1992) It's never too late to change: A group psychotherapy experience for older women. *Group* 16: 146–155.

Paradis AP (1973) Brief out-patient group psychotherapy with older patients in the treatment of age-related problems. *Dissertation Abstracts International* 34(6-B): 2947–2948.

Payne KT and Marcus DK (2008) The efficacy of group psychotherapy for older adult clients: A meta-analysis. *Group Dynamics: Theory, Research and Practice* 12(4): 268–278.

Penberthy JK and Penberthy JM (2020) *Living Mindfully Across the Lifespan: An Intergenerational Guide.* London: Routledge.

Peyró I (2021) Trevor Dadson's last interview. *El Confidencial.* Available at La última entrevista a Trevor Dadson: "¿Qué sabes tú de España si no has leído el 'Quijote'?" (msn.com)

Pines M (1980) What to expect in the psychotherapy of the borderline patient. *Group Analysis* 13(2): 168–177.

Pines M (1987) Bion: A group-analytic appreciation. *Group Analysis* 20(3): 251–262.

Post C, Schneer JA, Reitman F and Oglivie DT (2013) Pathways to retirement: A career stage analysis of retirement age expectations. *Human Relations* 66(1): 87–112.

Salvendy JT (1989) Brief group psychotherapy at retirement. *Group* 13: 43–75.

Segal H (1958) Fear of death: notes on the analysis of an old man. *International Journal of Psychoanalysis* 39: 178–181.

Shultz KS and Wang M (2011) Psychological perspectives on the changing nature of retirement. *American Psychologist* 66(3): 170–179.

Slavinska-Holy N (1983) Combining individual and homogeneous group Psychotherapies for borderline conditions. *International Journal of Group Psychotherapy* 33(3): 297–312.

Trist E (1985) Working with Bion in the 1940s: The group decade. In Pines M (ed) *Bion and Group Psychotherapy.* London: Routledge & Kegan Paul plc, pp. 1–46.

UN (2019) World Population Prospects 2019. United Nations Department of Economic and Social Affairs, Population Division. Available at https://www.un.org/development/desa/publications/worldpopulation-prospects-2019-highlights.html

Van der Kolk BA (1983) Psychotherapy of the elderly: general discussion: The idealizing transference and group psychotherapy with elderly patients. *Journal of Geriatric Psychiatry* 16(1): 99–102.

Waddell M (1998) *Inside Lives: Psychoanalysis and the Growth of the Personality.* London: Duckworth.

Waddell M (2000) Only connect: Developmental issues from early to late life. *Psychoanalytic Psychotherapy* 14(3): 239–252.

Waddell M (2007) Only connect – the links between early and later life. In Davenhill R (ed) *Looking into Later Life: A psychoanalytic approach to depression and dementia in old age.* London: Karnac, pp. 187–200.

Wayne G (1953) Modified psychoanalytic therapy in senescence. *Psychoanalytic Review* 40(2): 99–116.

Weisman ML (1999) The history of retirement, from early man to A. A. R. P. *The New York Times* (21 March). Available at: https://www.nytimes.com/1999/03/21/jobs/the-history-of-retirement-from-early-man-to-aarp.html.

Winnicott DW (1971) *Playing and Reality.* London: Tavistock.

ORCID iD: Arturo Ezquerro https://orcid.org/0000-0002-9910-4576

ORCID iD: María Cañete https://orcid.org/0000-0001-7967-1103

7 Group analysis with older adults

Can creativity survive when time is running out?

Arturo Ezquerro and María Cañete

Introduction

Old age is an integral part of life's ongoing adventure, as well as another opportunity to learn how we can love ourselves and other people better and, also, come to terms with the inescapable reality of approaching death.

There are many ways of growing old; some people are able to take it as a chance for making sense of one's own life history and continuing personal development; other people are anxiously frightened of it as an inexorable defeat on the road to death. In 1599, William Shakespeare put it in dramatic terms:

> Last scene of all, that ends this strange eventful history,
> Is second childishness and mere oblivion,
> Sans teeth, sans eyes, sans taste, sans everything
>
> Shakespeare (1599)

More often than not, age is used for ranking people within a given society. Although advances in medical sciences have led to a longer (even healthier) life span, power and prestige for the elderly have eroded, particularly in the more industrialised western countries. Here, older adults are frequently regarded as unproductive members of society and, in some cases, simply irrelevant or disposable; the poor protection and massive deaths of elderly people during the early stages of the Covid pandemic were too tragic a demonstration of this (Ezquerro, 2020).

By and large, in western societies, there are extensive prejudices about this life period, expressed daily through multiple attitudes and terms that contain pejorative connotations: old codger, old coot, old hag, senile, geezer, crotchety and so on. Such caricatured words are demeaning and biased, representing both overt and subtle discrimination.

This problem has existed for a long time. In 1877, in his lectures on the diseases of old age, the French physician and founder of modern neurology, Jean-Martin Charcot criticised the way elderly patients were treated within general medicine (Howell, 1988).

DOI: 10.4324/9781003167747-8

In the wider context of society, the broad range of prejudices and discrimination directed at older people has been conceptualised under the term *ageism*, which was first distinctly proposed by Robert Butler (1975), in *Why Survive? Being Old in America*, a scholarly analysis of ageing and political manifesto, a call to arms. His book lingered on the *New York Times* best-seller list for weeks.

Butler would later say that the underlying basis of ageism is the dread and fear of growing older, becoming ill and dependent, and approaching death. He called denial a close *cousin* of ageism, since it eliminates ageing from consciousness; he pointed out that, through multiple projections, ageism extends to culture and becomes part of the social unconscious. He went so far as to call ageism a *psychosocial disease* (Bengtson and Whittington, 2014).

A few years before the publication of *Why Survive?*, in an interview for the *Washington Post* with Carl Bernstein (1969), Butler had used the word ageism, suggesting that it was on a par with the evils of racism and sexism, as opposition had arisen to a proposal to build senior housing in Washington DC. It was a theme to which he would return again and again; in fact, his life-long work became a monumental indictment of ageism. He concluded that fears and prejudices regarding ageing would only abate by means of societal reconstruction (Achenbaum, 2013).

Ageism can manifest itself in a variety of ways, through negative attitudes which indicate that older adults are in less than full command of their mental faculties, as well as less competent, less attractive and less valuable than younger adults. This negative view of older people is inter-connected with the reverence for a youthful appearance that characterises most modern western societies and market forces. The growth of the market economy lessened the reliance of the young on their elders' values and resources (Iversen, Larsen and Solem, 2009; Gullette, 2011, 2017; Woodspring, 2012; Jesmin, 2014).

In contrast, traditional Asian societies tend to venerate their elders because they are viewed as having attained special wisdom as a consequence of living so long. Similarly, many Native-American societies have viewed older people as crucial keepers and transmitters of key information about the past.

Moreover, in the colonial period of American history, long life was seen as proof that a person had been particularly virtuous and deserved to be held in high esteem (Bodner, Bergman and Cohen-Fridel, 2012; Maxmen, 2012). In many African cultures, reaching old age is seen as a sign of divine intervention, and the elderly are called *big person* in a number of African languages (Lehr, Seiler and Thomae, 2000).

However, it is important not to make broad, global statements about how older adults are treated in a given society, since attitudes towards the elderly in particular cultures are not uniform.

Generally speaking, cultures that hold the elderly in high regard are relatively homogeneous in socioeconomic terms; in addition, the roles that people play entail greater responsibility with increasing age, and elderly people control resources to a significant extent.

In some of these communities, the concept of retirement is unknown and older individuals continue to be involved in productive daily activities. Societies that change at less rapid a pace than those with fast technological developments see older adults as possessing considerable wisdom, rather than being out-of-date (Comunian and Gielen, 2000; Li, Ji and Chen, 2014; Ritzema, 2019).

Psychoanalysis and group analysis have not been immune to ageism and, for a long time, shied away from working with older adults, placing them in an out-of-the-way group, categorised by decay, ineducability and loss. Later in this chapter, we shall elaborate on this.

According to Feldman (2018), old age tends indeed to be equated with loss: of brain cells, intellectual capabilities, physical and mental energy, sex drive, attachment figures and so forth. On the other hand, he also emphasised that elderly people are increasingly pioneering new fields, achieving new athletic endeavours and challenging the public's perception of the last stage in the life cycle.

For a growing number of them, vigorous mental and physical activity remains an important part of daily life. Thus, chronological age alone cannot define this developmental stage and, in assessing older adults, it is necessary to take into account their physical and psychological well-being; their *functional age*.

There is evidence that, in old age, the brain becomes smaller and lighter, and pulls away from the skull. In fact, the amount of space between brain and skull doubles from age twenty to age seventy (Feldman, 2018). However, in the absence of disease, the brain retains its structure and function.

The number of neurons decreases in some areas, but not as much as previously thought, and recent research suggests that the number of cells in the brain's cortex may drop only minimally or not at all. There is also evidence that certain types of neuronal growth may continue throughout the life-span (Raz et al., 2007; Gattringer et al., 2012; Jäncke et al., 2015).

From a life-span developmental perspective, one of the fundamental questions about old age concerns the degree to which personality may change or remain stable. Feldman (2018) argued that basic personality traits such as extroversion, openness, agreeableness and conscientiousness are remarkably stable throughout adulthood; for instance, most even-tempered people at age twenty are still even-tempered at age seventy-five.

Despite this general stability of basic personality traits, there are ongoing chances to change over time. The significant variations that occur throughout adulthood in people's social and group environments may produce fluctuations in personality. What is important to a person at age seventy-five is not necessarily the same as what was important at age twenty, thirty or forty. There are continuities and discontinuities of development (Ezquerro, 2017).

As we are learning more about neurological, psycho-social and group development, we are in a better position to challenge ageism and change our views and attitudes on old age and its management. Rather than being viewed only as a period of decline and loss, late adulthood can also be seen as a stage in which people face new experiences and continue their development, growing in some areas and declining in others.

In the first volume of his trilogy on *Attachment and Loss*, Bowlby (1969) reflected on the flexibility and resilience that living beings have to acclimatise and survive in an environment of "evolutionary adaptedness". This malleability is especially potent for humans. According to Bowlby, the longer individuals live the more necessary is ontogenetic flexibility, to enable them to adapt to changes in the environment.

It is likewise noteworthy that late adulthood has been increasing in length very rapidly, as people are living longer and longer. Whether we place the start of this period at age sixty-five, seventy or seventy-five, before the Covid pandemic, there was a greater proportion of people alive in late adulthood than at any previous time in human history (UN, 2019).

On the whole, older adults constitute the fastest growing age group in the world, particularly in the more advanced societies. In 2019, people over sixty-five accounted for 9% of the world population. By 2050, they are predicted to have become 17%. This would represent more than one in six people on the planet if, of course, it survives. Within old age itself, the fastest growing segment is in fact that of people over eighty-five. In the last two decades, the size of this older-old group has nearly doubled (Liu, Yang, Lou, Zhou and Tong, 2021).

Older adults have the highest prevalence of physical and mental disturbance of any age group. Their health needs generate the greatest per-capita medical expenses in the population. In connection with these increasingly prominent realities, specialist geriatric services began to develop in the UK in the late 1940s, and psychogeriatric services in the late 1960s. Old age psychiatry was recognised as a medical speciality, by the Royal College of Psychiatrists, in 1989 (Canete, Stormont and Ezquerro, 2000; Liu et al., 2021).

From an overall historical and developmental perspective, we may say that old age is a sort of transition as well: from late-middle age to the possibility of longevity and, ultimately, to death. Certainly, this *winter* of human existence can bring change and growth on a par with, and sometimes even greater than, earlier periods in the life-span (Whitbourne, 2007).

The literature

Research on late life is multifaceted, as individual and group characteristics in this developmental stage vary significantly; older adults may be active and fully functioning, frail or seriously deteriorated, living in the community or in institutions. In general terms, within this broad spectrum, old age progressively brings with it a distinct decline in the sense organs of the body. The sensory decline can have a major impact on psychosocial well-being, as well as on group participation and attachment, since the senses serve as links between the individual and the external world.

Overall, the specialist literature tends to differentiate between the *young-old* and the *old-old*. This does not necessarily coincide with chronological age. The young-old need to adjust to new group connections and roles in society, usually following retirement. They may take up fresh activities and group identities, deriving much satisfaction in developing a novel, perhaps previously dormant, part of themselves (see Chapter 6).

The old–old must also adapt to increasing bodily and mental decline, greater dependency on others and a shorter trajectory to death. The very old may not fear death in the way the young-old do, but they tend to fear more the actual process of dying (Canete et al., 2000).

In a way analogous to how developmental theorists had divided the teen years into the three sub-stages of early, middle and late adolescence (see Chapter 3), Feldman (2018) added a third sub-phase to better described the functional ages of late life. In his view and in broad terms, the *young-old* are healthy and active; the *old-old* have some health problems and difficulties with daily activities; the *oldest-old* are frail and in need of care.

According to this classification, an active and healthy ninety-five-year-old would be considered young-old by researchers on ageing. In comparison, a sixty-five-year-old in the late stages of emphysema or Alzheimer's disease would be considered among the oldest-old, conforming to Feldman's functional-age perspective.

Some 25% of people over sixty-five suffer from mental health problems, affecting their mood, thinking and behaviour. In terms of psychiatric diagnosis, depression is the most prevalent condition. One reason for this is that older people are more vulnerable to cumulative losses, with the death of attachment figures, partners, friends and peers. In addition, their own declining health and capabilities can make them feel less independent, as they progressively lose control, and this may contribute to the prevalence of depression and concomitant suicide risk (Rubenowitz et al., 2001; Menzel, 2008; Vink et al., 2009; Taylor, 2014; Liu et al., 2021).

In terms of neurological or neuro-psychiatric diagnosis, the most common mental disability in old age is dementia, a broad category of serious memory loss accompanied by decline in other mental functioning, which encompasses a number of diseases. Dementia may have many different causes and contributing factors, and the chances of experiencing it increase with age (Feldman, 2018).

In terms of physical illnesses, a majority of older adults have at least one chronic, long-term condition. For instance, arthritis, diabetes, hyperlipidaemia, hypertension, osteoarthrosis, osteoporosis, prostatic hyperplasia and so on. In addition, older people are more susceptible to infectious diseases, since ageing is associated with a weakening of the body's immune system (Feinberg, 2000).

Ultimately, according to the National End of Life Care Intelligence Network (NEOLCIN, 2017), the leading causes of death in elderly people are heart disease, cancer and stroke: close to three-quarters die from these problems.

However, old age does not unavoidably imply pathology. Whether an older person is ill or well depends less on age than on a multiplicity of factors, including genetic predisposition, past and present environmental influences, lifestyle, diet and psychosocial issues. Certain illnesses, such as cancer and heart disease, have a clear genetic component but this predisposition does not mean that a person will develop a particular condition; the risk of becoming ill is raised or lowered by how and when the above factors are combined.

Social services, medical and other healthcare providers working with older adults, have increasingly emphasised the importance of lifestyle choices, not only to spare this population from illness but also to help them remain healthy, extend their active life-spans and enjoy the time left as much as possible (Sawatzky and Naimark, 2002; Gavin and Myers, 2003; Katz and Marshall, 2003; Feldman, 2018).

Delayed psychoanalytic and group analytic contributions

For far too long, psychoanalysis and group analysis neglected thinking about and working with older adults (Grotjahn, 1989). Fortunately, in the last three decades, psychoanalytic and group-analytic psychotherapies have increasingly become available for this population. However, there is still a long way to go.

Within these psychodynamic disciplines, prejudice and neglect started with Freud's (1905) views on old age, which contained a large dose of ageism, as he stated that people over fifty were unsuitable for psychoanalytic psychotherapy and no longer educable (see Chapter 6). Freud postulated that, around that age, mental processes had become too rigidly established for favourable treatment results; he added that the volume of the clinical material would make analysis interminable (Freud, 1905).

In Europe, these Freudian prejudices resulted in an extended neglect of the treatment of older adults by psychoanalytic and group-analytic practitioners virtually until the 1980s. Until then, there was little individual or group psychotherapy provision for this population. Most interventions took place within in-patient or institutional settings, and the main focus was on supportive rather than insight-based techniques (Ezquerro, 1988).

The first psychoanalyst who dared to challenge Freud's ageism was the German, Karl Abraham (1919), who wrote about the applicability of psychoanalytic treatment to patients at an *advanced* age, by which he meant people over forty and, sometimes, over fifty.

Abraham drew an important distinction between the age of the neurosis and the chronological age of the patient. Initially, his ideas on older adults did not have much direct impact on his European colleagues; however, he had a somewhat greater influence in the USA, where a minority of practitioners started to conduct psychoanalytic and psychodynamic psychotherapy with this population (Jelliffe, 1925; Wayne, 1953; Goldfarb, 1955; Grotjahn, 1955; Meerloo, 1956; Berezin and Cath, 1965).

In the European context, there was no clinical publication in the psycho-analytic literature until Hanna Segal (1958) reported an impressive account of a successful analysis of a seventy-three-year-old man, whom she treated for eighteen months following his psychotic breakdown. However, the turning point is attributed to Pearl King's (1974) landmark paper, *Notes on the Psycho-analysis of Older Patients.*

King described a number of successful analyses of older adults and pro-vided an innovative psychoanalytic theory of old age. She put together clin-ical material and theoretical formulations to outline age-specific sources of anxiety and developmental tasks in late life (see Chapter 6).

King (1980) later suggested that the disturbance of some elderly people can often relate to the reawakening of unresolved childhood conflicts, as well as the activation of new developmental challenges – some of which are similar to those of adolescence but in reverse.

Anne-Marie Sandler (1978, 1984) reported on the psychoanalytic treat-ments of some of her elderly patients. She warned about possible unrealistic expectations in the analyst, and did not attempt a full reconstruction of the past or a complete character analysis, but concentrated on age-specific devel-opmental issues.

Both King and Sandler were highly influential and helped change the attitude of many psychoanalytic practitioners, at a time when the Institute of Psychoanalysis in the UK was still not accepting training patients over the age of forty (Cohen, 1982; Limentani, 1995).

In the early 1980s, the British psychoanalyst Peter Hildebrand (1982, 1986, 1995) developed an individual psychotherapy workshop for patients over fif-ty-five at the Tavistock Clinic, a model institution for psychoanalytic psycho-therapy where, until then, people over forty-five had been routinely rejected. The waiting list generated by this workshop led to the first psychoanalytic group for older adults at the Tavistock, as thoroughly described in Chapter 6 and elsewhere (Ezquerro, 1988, 2000).

This piece of work also became the first clinical publication in the journal *Group Analysis* on group psychotherapy with older adults (Ezquerro, 1989). The group, for patients in the age range fifty-five to sixty-seven, produced age-specific themes and fresh issues which indicated that late-middle age can be a distinct developmental stage in the life-span, after mastery of middle adulthood but before settling into old age (see Chapter 6).

Following this group-case publication of 1989, we could only find five articles on group treatment of older adults in the journal *Group Analysis*. Four of these clinical papers described work for patients with various degrees of dementia (Rusted, Sheppard and Waller, 2006; Anderson, 2011; Perren and Richardson, 2018; Hadar, 2018).

These clinicians advocated the use of group-analytic principles, applied flexibly, as the technique had to be adapted to the cognitive and physical disa-bilities of the patients, as well as the culture of care homes and day-hospital set-tings. Some employed a blend of interventions, including art-therapy groups.

Rusted, Sheppard and Waller (2006) developed group-analytic-informed, art-therapy groups for older people with dementia. All the patients were either in day care or in residential care. These group therapists found significant positive changes in mood and cognition, first in the here-and-now of the group sessions and later in the periods between the sessions, particularly regarding mental acuity, emotional involvement, calmness and sociability. The improvements were sustained for over forty weeks.

These findings were compared with those of recreational activity groups, in which positive group changes were also found, but only lasted for approximately fifteen weeks.

Another finding was that, on termination of art-based group therapy, some patients reported increased depressive symptoms, which dissipated by the time they held a follow-up, three months after the group had ended. However, these changes were not observed after the ending of activity groups. The authors concluded that both art therapy and recreational activity groups are beneficial and appropriate interventions for older people with dementia. However, the art therapy groups appeared to offer more subtle and more pronounced positive effects over time.

Anderson (2011) reported on the experience of applying group-analytic principles in a therapy group for older adults with mild dementia. The patients had been selected after requesting an opportunity to discuss in detail the impact of such a diagnosis on their wellbeing and that of their families. The article concluded that group analysis has much to offer to older people, whether suffering from dementia or not, although some flexibility in the technique might be required to accommodate the needs of the more vulnerable patients.

Perren and Richardson (2018) reported on the introduction of group-analytic psychotherapy for older adults with enduring mental health issues, including some cognitive impairment, at the Retreat Hospital in York, UK. The technique had to be modified to some extent to adapt it to the patients' health circumstances.

The authors used an interpretative phenomenological model to analyse the conductors' views on the impact and effectiveness of the group-therapy programme. These group therapists needed to reflect on their own ageism and that of others in the wider hospital context. The groups provided a safe space for members to develop a sense of mutual understanding and belonging, as well as greater freedom to express emotion in terms of both negative and positive feelings.

Hadar (2018) explored important questions regarding the extent to which it might possible to modify the technique, without losing the essence of group-analytic therapy. This author emphasised that, in any case, it is necessary to take into account the presence of ageism in the wider socio-cultural context, including staff working with this population. According to Hadar, raising awareness about ageism should be an important additional task for group analysts.

The only other clinical paper that excluded dementia, published in the journal *Group Analysis*, was a report on a closed psychotherapy group for nine patients, aged seventy-five to eighty-four, which ran weekly over eight months in a day-hospital setting (Evans, Chisholm and Walshe, 2001).

In this group, attendance was regular and seven patients completed the treatment. Although all were used to the structured group activities of the day hospital, none of them had attended a psychodynamic group before. In the early stages, some experienced difficulties with the lack of a formal agenda, but they gradually appreciated the power of bringing their own agenda. After completion, most patients reported increased self-esteem and decreased emotional distress.

Despite this scarcity of publications in *Group Analysis*, some group-analytic practitioners have written elsewhere about their group work with older adults (Evans, 1998; Canete and Ezquerro, 2000; Canete, Stormont and Ezquerro, 2000, 2004; Evans, 2004; Garland, 2007; Panagiotopoulou, 2019).

Evans (1998) argued that a truly group-analytic intervention would not be complete without looking at societal impressions of ageing. She was particularly concerned by the ageist attitude that pervaded the British National Health Service (NHS) at a time when it was strapped for cash (it still is), and by a persistent media blackout of older people: in research by the British Broadcasting Corporation, older people were much less well represented visually than other groups suffering discrimination, like ethnic minorities.

Evans provided clinical examples in which the internalised oppression of ageism manifested itself in some patients by the denial of their own advanced years, and by projections of negative assumptions about old people onto the group. She made therapeutic use of group *mirroring* to help these patients own their projections and discover the healthy aspects of themselves.

Canete and Ezquerro (2000) and Canete, Stormont and Ezquerro (2000, 2004) presented comprehensive clinical material that illustrated age-specific issues and developmental tasks in a group of older adults, in the age range sixty-five to ninety-five years, which ran over a decade in an out-patient NHS setting.

In this project, issues of competitiveness, rivalry, anger and aggressiveness, which are generally present in the beginning of groups with younger adults, tended to be absent or manifested themselves in a gentler fashion. In addition, denial of age became impossible, which helped group patients come to terms with their own mortality and approach death with less anxiety. This qualitative research showed that group-analytic psychotherapy can be especially indicated and beneficial for this population. More about this long-term group therapy programme in the case study below.

Evans (2004) provided evidence for the benefits of various types of group therapy with older adults over sixty-five, such as cognitive, psychodynamic and interpersonal, particularly in the treatment of depression and anxiety disorders. She also reported on her own experience of running groups for this population, conducted on group-analytic principles. Evans advocated flexibility in the application of the therapeutic technique, in order to accommodate the declining abilities of the oldest members.

Garland (2007) concentrated on some tasks of psychoanalytically based group therapy with older adults, such as recalling and working on the meaning of memories, as well as encouraging members to get to know each other, reflect, talk and share thoughts and feelings. In this way, groups for elderly patients provide opportunities for the clarification and expression of unresolved conflicts and difficult feelings, clearly visible and vigorously at work in the psychodynamic setting provided. She accepted that, sometimes, the dependant stance of the elderly (physical disability, incontinence or immobility) may prevent wordy formulations or interpretations.

Garland was particularly mindful of the group therapist's language. She advocated the use of ordinary everyday language to deliver interpretations of some of the difficult feelings of older patients. For example, it would be more appropriate to suggest to some group members that they might be feeling a bit left out, say of the good things they believe the therapist may be up to at the weekend, than suggesting that they could be struggling unsuccessfully with their oedipal anxieties. The latter would probably say more about the therapist's own preoccupations than about the patient's anxieties.

Panagiotopoulou (2019) described the positive experience of treating older adults in psychotherapy groups, conducted on group-analytic lines. This author found encouraging therapeutic characteristics in these groups, since their elderly patients showed a willingness to change, a capacity for empathy with fellow members, a desire for interpersonal engagement, a curiosity about the unconscious, and a capacity to learn from the multiple transferences they brought to the group. The article concluded that group analysis has much more to offer to this population than it has been done so far, and that it should look into its longstanding neglect of older adults.

Other group psychotherapy contributions

Many different forms of group treatment with the elderly have been employed. It is beyond the scope of this chapter to review all the publications on the subject. However, the interested reader can find comprehensive bibliography reviews in Cooper (1984), Griffin and Walker (1985), Schafer (1985) MacLennan et al. (1988), MacLennan et al. (1989), Darnley-Smith (2002), Hamill and Mahony (2011), Kegerreis (2012) and Jain (2019).

In this subsection, we shall mainly focus on psychodynamic group approaches other than group analysis. We will dedicate a further subsection below to a growing modality of group therapy that uses substantially reminiscence and life review.

Quantitative and qualitative research has shown that group psychotherapy is a beneficial and cost-effective treatment for older adults, particularly regarding depression and anxiety. Beneficial effects reported include better mental functioning and reversals in general deterioration, as well as improvements in self-care, home adjustment, interpersonal relationships and quality of social involvement, enhancing morale, self-esteem, self-confidence and the development of self-transcendence (MacLennan et al., 1989; Leszcz, 1990; Porter, 1991; Vardi and Buchholz, 1994; Young and Reed, 1995; Martindale, 1995, 2007; Walker and Clarke, 2001; Jain, 2019; Chilton, Diane, Crone and Tyson, 2020; Saunders et al., 2021).

It is particularly remarkable that a substantial number of research studies have consistently provided evidence that group psychotherapy also improves both life expectancy and quality of life in older patients suffering from terminal cancer (Milton, 1996; Mohammadian Akerdi et al., 2016; Sadri Damirchi et al., 2017; Khezri Moghadam et al., 2018).

The first written account of group psychotherapy with older adults is attributed to Silver (1950), in Canada. He used some psychoeducational principles, providing instructive information, encouragement and emotional support. In the USA, the flexible application of psychoanalytic insights to therapy groups with older patients was pioneered by Linden (1953, 1955), who aimed at restoring social and practical functioning at the expense of deeper work.

He also used some free-floating attention (the group equivalent to free association in psychoanalysis) and was quite directive in encouraging members to express emotion freely (a paradoxical intervention in its own right) and to give mutual interpretations to each other.

Grotjahn (1955, 1978) argued that age-homogeneous group psychotherapy was the preferred form of treatment for older patients, and underscored the task of keeping the communication going in the group. However, in view of the significant limitations of some of his patients, he suggested that the optimal psychoanalytic aim of *working through* had to be reframed sometimes with the humbler task of *living through*.

Krasner (1977) advocated an interesting developmental programme. He started with age-homogeneous groups for older adults and, as they were progressing and feeling more confident, they were invited to join an age-heterogeneous group, so they could use their newly gained insights to work through intergenerational conflicts.

Berland and Poggi (1979) set up a group psychotherapy programme for residents of a private retirement home, ranging in age from seventy-two to ninety-nine. After a trial period of supportive group therapy, the patients demanded more insightful work and interpersonal relatedness. Contrary to some ageist prejudices, the therapists were pleased to realise that the older adults in their groups wanted to change, made therapeutic use of metaphors, and showed that they were capable of forming a deep attachment to others.

A common idea shared by the above authors is that the main impediments on group psychotherapy for older adults come not so much from advanced age but from prejudiced countertransference in the group therapists themselves.

Young and Reed (1995) explored the potential of group psychotherapy in fostering self-transcendence, a developmental task they consider central to old age. These authors argued that psychotherapeutic goals and interventions for older adults, like those for children, adolescents and other age groups, need to be developmentally appropriate. They referred to previous clinical research which had shown that self-transcendence is a valuable resource for mental health in late life. We will look further into this later in the chapter.

Saiger (2001) agreed with that view and described a psychodynamic psychotherapy group for older adults, conducted in an agency setting. This author concluded that group therapists have to be cognisant with their own views on ageing and be attuned with the developmental needs of this population. Some modifications in the usual psychodynamic group techniques are usually required, including supportive, systemic and existential elements, to address fears of disability, ageist attitudes in the wider context and other concerns that are rooted in the individual members' existence.

Agronin (2009) reported on a group psychotherapy programme for vulnerable older adults, conducted on psychodynamic principles, which were applied flexibly when dealing with various forms of cognitive impairment, physical disability and increasing dependency.

This programme was particularly efficacious for depression and anxiety symptoms and compared favourably with individual psychotherapy for this population. Agronin postulated that group psychotherapy is particularly indicated for older adults because it offers opportunities for:

> peer-to-peer interactions that can improve self-understanding, self-esteem, and interpersonal skills and connections. It also can provide support and feedback from peers who are dealing with similar age-specific issues of loss, illness and dependency during times of enormous life transition. Such interaction can enable an individual to talk about symptoms or psychosocial problems that others in the group are also experiencing, leading to greater acceptance…
>
> There also exists the powerful affirming opportunity to be altruistic, to make contributions to others and to experience being useful. Such experiences may prompt an individual with cognitive impairment to sharpen certain cognitive skills that were otherwise dormant.
>
> Agronin (2009: 27)

Schwartz (2019) explored issues of intimacy and sexuality in group psychotherapy with older adults and reflected on the therapists' own attitudes and prejudices when working with this population. The paper examined how the attitudes of society in general, and of group therapists in particular, regarding late-life sexuality and intimacy, may contribute to the omission or neglect of these subjects being discussed in group therapy.

Jain (2019) reviewed the literature on different psychodynamic modalities of group psychotherapy for older adults with major depression. Previous research had validated various group-based psychotherapies for this common and disabling illness in late life, but the techniques applied often needed some modifications to accommodate the increasingly complex needs and declines of older adults. This author found that there is growing support for an integrative model of group-therapy approaches, and incorporated some guidelines for its implementation.

Chilton et al. (2020) investigated the beneficial effects of integrated group-treatment programmes for older adults with a broad range of mental health problems. The programmes included a psychoeducational element, comprising of social support and therapeutic facilitation of peer-group relationships. Semi-structured interviews were undertaken with fifteen service users who successfully participated in this treatment programme.

This research concluded that forming meaningful therapeutic relationships is an influential factor, in countering a range of distressing and incompatible environmental and situational stressors. The importance of integrated group treatment in reducing stigma and exclusion was highlighted.

Life review and reminiscence: a common theme of personality development in old age

In the last part of the twentieth century, a life-span developmental perspective (Butler, 1974, 1975) helped redefine late adulthood as a period of heightened self-examination, retrospection and existential resolution.

Butler in fact suggested that decreasing practical demands and greater proximity to death press people to try for dramatic personal growth in this life stage. According to him, older adults can make the goals of identity consolidation, intimacy and resolution of problematic issues more immediate. He believed that the older adult strives to attain these goals

> through the naturally occurring process of life review, which combines reminiscence, longitudinal perspective and appreciation of the present.
> Butler, in Tross and Blum (1988: 8)

Butler would later consider life review therapy to be an opportunity for enlightenment as well as resolution. In fact, he defined life review as:

> a progressive return to consciousness of memories and unresolved past conflicts for re-evaluation and resolution. It is a normal, developmental task of the later years that occurs with the awareness of finitude and helps individuals face their own mortality.
> Butler (2010: 41)

And he elaborated on that:

> Elders should try through life review to free themselves from being anxious because they are aware that time is running out. Older people ought

to take delight in the elemental things of life such as children, friendship, and human touching (physical and emotional).

Butler (2010: 17)

In his book *Robert Butler, MD: Visionary of Healthy Aging*, Achenbaum (2013) highlighted the therapeutic value of life review, as an effective way to surmount fear in old age. He quoted his master:

We inch along in our fifties and sixties, even seventies and eighties, only beginning to question what we have done and re-evaluating relationships. As we grow still older and approach death, it becomes enormously important to strengthen our intimate relationships, to understand ourselves and our loved ones better, to come to grips with guilt and shame, experience remorse and serve others as well as effect reconciliations.

Butler, in Achenbaum (2013: 203)

According to Butler (2008, 2010), there are four key elements to life review psychotherapy: reminiscence of one's own life, absolution from lingering past guilt, articulation of positive personal values, and resolution of internal and interpersonal conflicts. He used life review therapy in individual and group settings; he found that age-homogeneous groups facilitated this method better than age-heterogeneous groups or individual therapy, as members are bound by common developmental tasks and frames of reference.

However, Buttler considered that, in heterogeneous groups, older adults can confront more directly the inequities of ageist bias amongst younger adults, and eventually achieve the esteem of experienced mentors.

Helping older patients look back and review their life has become an increasingly distinct therapeutic strategy. It is now being widely used by practitioners employing a developmental perspective of old age, confirming Butler's original idea that life review is triggered by the increasingly obvious prospect of one's own death.

By reviewing past events, older adults often come to a better understanding of who they are and where they are coming from. They may also become more able to resolve persistent problems and conflicts that haunted them for many years, such as an estrangement from their children or their siblings, and may eventually face life with greater serenity (Korte et al., 2012; Latorre et al., 2015).

In a psychotherapy group, reminiscence may lead to a sense of sharing and mutuality, a feeling of interconnectedness with others. Moreover, it can be a source of social interaction as older adults seek to share their previous experiences with others who know what it was like. Reminiscence may even have cognitive benefits, improving memory in older people. In turn, these memories may trigger other, related memories and may bring back sights, sounds and even smells of the past (Feldman, 2018).

However, the outcomes of life review and reminiscence are not always positive. People who become obsessive about past events, reliving old insults and mistakes that cannot be rectified, may end up experiencing guilt, depression and anger towards people from the past who may not even be alive. In such cases, reminiscence contributes to poor psychological functioning (Cappeliez et al., 2008).

Whether in therapy or outside therapy, life review and reminiscence can play an important role in the ongoing development of older adults, providing continuity between past and present, and increasing awareness of the contemporary world. These processes can also provide new insights into earlier relational and group contexts, allowing people to continue personality growth and to function more effectively in the present (Coleman, 2005; Haber, 2006; Alwin, 2012).

Although not identical, the terms life review therapy and reminiscence therapy have been increasingly used interchangeably. Both terms involve describing a memory itself; life review therapy is more specific in that it promotes discussing what the memory means to the patient (Liu et al., 2021).

Bissonnette and Barnes (2019) reported on a piece of outcome research into the effectiveness of group reminiscence therapy (GRT) with older adults. They found that GRT helped patients in their group sample by reducing their symptoms of depression and by increasing their well-being and life satisfaction. These positive effects were maintained at three-month follow-up.

Liu et al. (2021) reviewed the group literature on the therapeutic use of reminiscence, from 2000 to 2021, in the treatment of late-life depression, gathering information from ten electronic databases in English and Chinese. They found that reminiscence therapy has a significantly positive effect on relieving depressive symptoms and enhancing life satisfaction in older adults.

This study also showed that beneficial effects and the cost-effectiveness of GRT were higher than individual reminiscence therapy. The results were clear in the short and medium term, after group therapy, but there were no studies on long-term effects of group reminiscence therapy.

Other developmental tasks of old age

We mentioned earlier in this chapter that the British psychoanalyst Peter Hildebrand set up the first individual psychotherapy programme for older adults at the Tavistock Clinic, where patients over forty-five were routinely rejected until the early 1980s.

Hildebrand (1995) argued that psychoanalytic theorists had far too uncritically, and for far too long, accepted a hypothesis of continuous physical and psychosocial development from birth to young adulthood, followed by a long refractory period during mid-life and, then, a final stage of psychic and somatic deficit and social withdrawal before death. This conception was not only oversimplified but also detached from reality, since psychosocial and somatic development in adulthood and in late life is far more complex and multidimensional than had been supposed by Freud and his followers (see Chapter 6).

Erik Erikson (1959, 1966) and John Bowlby (1969, 1973, 1980) were the first psychoanalysts who provided a life-long perspective of human development. Whilst Bowlby put an emphasis on the developmental influence for personality change of meaningful and intimate attachment relationships from cradle to grave, Erikson focused on age-specific developmental tasks across what he termed the eight ages of man (see Chapter 1).

With regard to old age, Erikson suggested that personality changes may occur as a result of new psychosocial challenges, which he amalgamated under a fluctuating tension between *ego-integrity* and *despair*, as part of a process of looking back over one's life, evaluating it, and coming to terms with it.

According to him (Erikson, 1966), individuals who are successful in this final stage of development experience a sense of satisfaction and accomplishment, which he termed integrity. These people typically feel they have realised and fulfilled many of the possibilities that have come their way in life, and they experience few regrets.

In contrast to that, other individuals look back on their lives with dissatisfaction, as they may have missed important opportunities and may not have achieved their targets. These people might become anxious, angry, depressed or despondent over what they have done or failed to do with their lives; in short, they despair.

Robert Peck (1968) suggested that personality development in elderly people is mainly occupied by three major developmental tasks or challenges:

1   *Redefinition of self versus preoccupation with work role.* Older adults have to adjust their values and priorities, placing less emphasis on themselves as workers or professionals and more on other attributes (such as being a grandparent), as well as establishing new group connections.
2   *Body transcendence versus body preoccupation.* Older adults have to adjust to physical decline. If successful, they achieve body transcendence; otherwise, they may become too preoccupied with their physical appearance to the detriment of their personality development.
3   *Ego transcendence versus ego preoccupation.* Older adults have to come to grips with the inescapability of death at not-too-distant a future, which can be anxiety-provoking; at the same time, they may review the contributions they had made to society. When these contributions are perceived as lasting beyond one's own life, older people can experience ego transcendence; otherwise, they may become too preoccupied with oblivion or with the question of whether their lives had any value to society.

In a comprehensive piece of research, Bernice Neugarten (1977) examined the different strategies that people in their seventies employ to cope with ageing. In this study, four distinct types of personality were identified:

- *Disintegrated and disorganised personalities* who are unable to accept ageing and experience despair as they get older. They often end up living in healthcare institutions.
- *Passive-dependent personalities* who are overanxious about the future, becoming fearful of falling ill and of being unable to cope. They may seek out help from family and care providers, even when they do not need it.
- *Defended personalities* who try to stop the fear of ageing in its tracks. They may attempt to act *younger*, exercising vigorously and engaging in youthful activities; but they may create unrealistic expectations for themselves and risk feeling disappointed as a result.
- *Integrated personalities* who are successful in the developmental task of coping with ageing. They accommodate the changes and declines that come with late age; they are also able to review their lives and gaze into the future, including the trajectory to death, with dignity and acceptance.

Neugarten (1977) found that, fortunately, the majority of the people in her research fell into the final successful category.

Waddell (1998, 2000, 2007) looked into the old-age developmental task of facing and working through loss of all kinds, ultimately death. According to her, the ability to successfully deal with such a huge task is rooted in very early capacities to bear psychosocial reality. She emphasised the importance of forming and sustaining balanced *inside lives* that keep connecting with the outside world.

At this point, we should be cautious about the risk of falling into the trap of believing that there can be a completely successful way of ageing. Every-day experience teaches us that it would be more realistic to settle for ways and strategies that are successful enough. How people age depends on personality factors, as well as the psychosocial and environmental circumstances in which they find themselves. Some older adults become progressively less involved with day-to-day events; whereas others maintain active ties with other people, and with groups, and develop areas of personal interest.

Feldman (2018) summarised three major processes and approaches that have been proposed: disengagement, activity and continuity. In short, disengagement theory suggests that getting older successfully is characterised by gradual withdrawal; activity theory argues that successful ageing occurs when people maintain their engagement with the world; continuity theory looks for a compromise and suggests that what is important is maintaining a desired level of involvement.

Another big question formulated by developmentalists is whether getting older also means getting wiser. In order to explore this, we need to consider that wisdom is not the same as cognitive intelligence. Some researchers have suggested that a primary distinction between the two concepts is related to timing: whereas knowledge that is derived from intelligence is usually related to the here-and-now, wisdom has a more timeless quality (Feldman, 2018). Intelligence may permit a person to think logically and systematically, while wisdom provides a deeper understanding of human behaviour and relationships.

According to Erikson's (1966) theory on the stages of human development, achieving wisdom later in life involves revisiting previous crises and reviving psychosocial and group accomplishments.

Simone de Beauvoir (1970), the French philosopher, social theorist and political activist, gave a distinct and beautiful existentialist insight into the developmental tasks of old age, which denotes existential maturity:

> There is only one solution . . . and that is to go on pursuing ends that give our existence meaning – devotion to individuals, to groups or to causes, social, political, intellectual or creative work. In old age, we should wish still to have passions strong enough to prevent us turning in upon ourselves. One's life has value so long as one attributes value to the life of others, by means of love, friendship, indignation, compassion. It is better to live a committed life even when all illusions have vanished.
>
> Beauvoir, 1970, in Davenhill (2007: xxi)

A case study by María Cañete

From the mid-1990s to the mid-2000s, I was in charge of an NHS, long-term group psychotherapy programme that had been originally set up in the early 1990s by Mark Ardern and Brian Martindale, followed by Ruth Porter.

This development occurred in the context of older adults becoming better educated, more psychologically sophisticated and increasingly aware of both NHS and private resources, whilst the disciplines of psychoanalytic psychotherapy and old age psychiatry were coming closer together (Porter, 1991; Martindale, 1995, 2007; Ardern et al., 1998; Garner, 1999; Garner and Evans, 2000; Murphy, 2000; Evans and Garner, 2004; Quinodoz, 2009a, 2009b).

The project consisted of a slow open group for patients in the age range of sixty-five to ninety-five, which people joined and left when ready. I asked for a minimum time commitment of one year; average length of attendance was three and a half years; group membership was eight people on average; the group was run weekly for ninety-minute-long sessions in an out-patient clinic.

I started conducting this group on my own. In 1998, I was joined by Fiona Stormont, who was my co-therapist for two years and contributed to a piece of qualitative research on the group. This was published by the *British Journal of Psychotherapy* (Canete et al., 2000), and it was later translated into German (Canete et al., 2004). Some of the clinical vignettes below are partly based on this research.

For the purpose of illustrating a number of the developmental and clinical issues delineated earlier in this chapter, I will not go through the whole history of the group, in which thirty-two patients were treated in total. Instead, I shall concentrate on relevant, developmentally related themes as they emerged in the group. I will also outline the trajectories of some of the patients, as they struggled with the therapeutic tasks of meaningful reminiscence and integrity-seeking life review.

We did not have strict exclusion criteria, although we were cautious about offering a place to people suffering from active psychosis, especially paranoia. Whilst accepting patients with a history of psychotic episodes, we asked those going through an acute psychotic state to have sufficient psychiatric and social services support before they could join the group.

We accepted patients with personality disorders, major depression, disabling chronic anxiety or addiction problems; but we considered that our group would not be suitable for people with dementia or with greatly impaired communication abilities. We directed these patients to other types of more homogeneous group work, as well as additional health and social care.

From the findings of some of the research studies that were outlined above, I anticipated a better prognosis for those patients who had a good level of verbal communication and social skills. This usually means that they would be able to recall the past, to work through their losses without resorting to somatisation or physical illness and to overcome non-voluntary social isolation. A history of prior successful psychotherapy, whether group or individual, was usually a good indicator of positive outcome. Let us now concentrate on the clinical material.

Reflecting on the group's initial anxieties

I inherited four members from my predecessor, Ruth Porter. As the group had been running for over five years, I expected to find an established group culture. However, I felt that we were starting a process that in many ways resembled the formation of some new groups. For several weeks, members predominantly discussed practicalities about the group and tried to look for things in common.

I wondered if this may have been a defence, as they seemed to be avoiding differences, but decided not to comment on it at such an early stage. Later on, as new members joined and we had a core membership of seven or eight, talk became more personal. Perhaps, the more idled discussions of the previous sessions were necessary for them to feel that, with a new situation and a new conductor, the group could be perceived as a secure base from which to explore.

It soon became apparent that the existing group patients felt especially vulnerable to experiences of being let down and abandoned. I was mindful about it and commented that it seemed to be important for them to feel accepted by a new therapist, perhaps since the departure of the previous therapist may have been perceived by them as a rejection. This interpretation made sense to them and opened a process of deeper explorations.

Real-life events have a bearing on the group's behaviour in the here-and-now. This can manifest itself at conscious and unconscious levels. In the psychoanalytic and group-analytic fields, this has been described as *group culture* or *group matrix* (Foulkes, 1964).

Before I joined the project, group members had endured many changes, including the departure of three therapists and a number of fellow patients. Some of these patients had left when they were ready, contributing to a positive therapeutic group culture. Others had dropped out or died, which generated a high level of anxiety about the survival of the group, and about their own survival.

Thinking of the group's history helped me understand the sense of uncertainty and fragility that I encountered. However, their initial cautiousness, even suspiciousness, gradually gave way to the development of a basic sense of trust, which enabled members to face some of the obvious differences between them.

> **Brenda**, a seventy-two-year-old woman of mixed parentage, had experienced racial discrimination. She was often a *barometer* for the group regarding feelings of unlikeness or rejection. In an age-homogeneous group, she also represented difference.
>
> Brenda had initially felt suspicious and angry with me. She later commented that she had also been unable to trust the group for a while. However, she was now beginning to experience it differently, after the realisation that the group did not persecute her but became consistently caring every week.
>
> At one point, Brenda felt safe enough to disclose details of her transient psychotic breakdown, which was triggered after she discovered her husband's extra-marital affair. She added that he had tried to exploit her vulnerability by demanding that she be admitted, as an in-patient, to a psychiatric hospital. She was adamant that her husband wanted to take advantage of her emotional vulnerability through the divorce proceedings.

Most group members, especially the women, showed support and sympathy towards Brenda and identified with her sense of betrayal and of being abandoned by her ex-husband. Interestingly, soon after this, some commented that they had felt anxious about the continuity of the group, following the departure of my predecessor, and wanted to know for how long I would be running it. My response was twofold: first, I linked their current anxieties with their previous experiences of being abandoned; then, I said I was committed to conducting the group for many years.

Mortality awareness, cohesion and coherency

Brenda's disclosure was followed by other people's disclosures. Most shared their own experiences about separating from their partners and being abandoned by their attachment figures, sometimes by death. Some of them reported on how these losses led to breaking down. This new dynamic of more open exchange was reassuring for Brenda and for the group as a whole.

In fact, members became more *cohesive*, perhaps too much so. The completeness of the group was an important issue for them; the presence of each and every member appeared to be almost a matter of life and death. If a member was missing, they always asked about their whereabouts and became reassured to know that the missing member was *"alive and kicking"*, as one of them put it. When missing members next returned to the group, they were usually welcomed back with a comment that I had not heard in groups with younger patients:

> We were anxious that you might have kicked the bucket.

Interestingly, most members showed great curiosity about language and meaning. They particularly looked into the meaning of some idiomatic phrases, which had been originated in previous centuries. Sometimes, they directly asked whether I was familiar with these old-fashioned English idioms, which were no longer used by younger people and brought to the foreground the age gap between them and me. When I invited members to explore this further, one of them responded:

> At one point in the not-so-distant future, apart from you, we will be pushing up daisies.

Certainly, an awareness of mortality was present in their minds more often that in groups with younger patients. I wondered if there might have been an element of envy towards the younger therapist. Several members commented that, no doubt, death was closer to them than it was to me.

However, they added that being survived by people from younger generations, who knew about them, was somewhat comforting and gave them a sense of life continuity and transcendence. All had been born in the first three decades of the twentieth century. I found myself reading books on the history of that period, which helped me put more context and understanding into their stories.

Of course, similarities in historical background and a growing sense of approaching death generated feelings of togetherness and cohesion. However, I was aware that *group cohesion* may sometimes denote a rather undifferentiated form of getting together. In contrast to that, *group coherency* is the result of more advanced and sophisticated group processes, in which differences, disagreements and conflicts are faced with the aim of being worked through, rather than avoided (Pines, 1986; Ezquerro, 2010).

In this group, members tended to fluctuate, in a sort of pendular movement, from cohesion to coherency and vice versa.

The initial period described above had been characterised by suspiciousness and lack of trust; fears of disintegration and, sometimes, anxieties about survival were prominent. Members gradually overcame these difficulties by emphasising their similarities and achieving a sense of togetherness or cohesion, but without dealing with differences openly. Gradually, they were able to transcend this phase and to look more openly into their diverse range of experiences and personalities. This process of *uncovering* and dealing with their diversity and differences, as well as their common mortality awareness, helped bring about group coherency.

> The arrival of **Ellen**, a 79-year-old woman with a diagnosis of schizo-affective disorder, was met with concern and strong objections. In her first session, she fell asleep and snored noticeably, after having introduced herself to the group saying: "*I am a schizophrenic*".

This peculiar presentation of a newcomer reactivated the old fears of fragmentation. I later learned that Ellen had been over-medicated. When her medication was reduced, she participated in the group more constructively but her impact contributed to one casualty.

> Soon after Ellen's arrival, **Rose**, a youthful 68-year-old woman with a diagnosis of recurrent depression, reported that she was feeling better and left the group. However, her departure was perceived by most members as a bit premature. Some felt rejected by Rose and expressed hostile feelings in the group.

At first, I thought that dealing with differences and achieving a deeper level of exploration or coherency was too difficult for the group. However, after the initial hostility towards Ellen' arrival and Rose's departure, the group shifted from anger to sadness. Members missed Rose, her enthusiasm and liveliness, and they accepted Ellen as a full member. Some commented that her problems might have been exacerbated by discrimination and prejudices towards, both, the elderly and the severely mentally ill, as portrayed in the media with the collusion of society by and large.

> **Martha**, a sixty-eight-year-old retired psychiatric nurse, was particularly supportive of Ellen and told her: "*To me, you don't look or act like a schizophrenic*".
>
> Then, **Ellen** showed the group newspapers photographs and reports about the time when she was a beautiful actress. Reminiscing about past positive experiences in her life made her feel better with herself. She also wanted to reassure the group that she did not have grandiose psychotic fantasies about the past, and remarked that there was a real and healthy side of herself that she needed to re-discover.
>
> The group appreciated that.

Ellen was not the only member to employ reminiscence in the group. Martha, who was very supportive and sympathetic towards Ellen, also made a positive use of reminiscence over an extended period. I will now concentrate on her case.

On reminiscence

Martha had retired three years previously. Soon after her retirement, she started to have a cardiac arrhythmia, causing frequent fainting, which led to an inpatient admission to her local cardiology service. At the hospital, her arrhythmia was controlled, and the treatment was deemed successful for her to be discharged. However, on her return home, she was afraid of going out in case she fainted in the street; she became house-bound and isolated. It was in this context that she experienced depressive symptoms and started hearing voices.

When the nurse from her GP's practice phoned her for a routine follow-up, to check if she had re-experienced heart problems, Martha explained to him that her parents and siblings (who had died long ago) were communicating with her regularly, asking questions about her health status and giving her advice. No wonder the GP immediately referred her to a consultant psychiatrist, who put her on anti-psychotic medication to treat her auditory hallucinations. At the same time, the psychiatrist referred her for group psychotherapy, and I offered Martha a place in our weekly out-patient group, which she accepted without hesitation.

When Martha joined the group, it consisted of four men and three women. Everyone welcomed her and showed interest in getting to know her. Within a few weeks, Martha started to reconstruct her distant past and to review her life through reminiscence. She was the youngest of four siblings in a middle-class Eastern-European family. She said that her childhood memories were those of a happy girl until the age of seven, when she was meant to start formal education. However, this was prevented by the outbreak of the Second World War.

Suddenly, the world around Martha seemed to collapse. Her two older brothers left home with a view to fleeing their country to join the allied forces, but they were taken prisoners by the Nazis. She did not see her brothers, or hear about them, ever again. Sometime after, the city where she lived was annexed by the Russians. Martha, her parents and her sister were forced to emigrate, which was the beginning of a long pilgrimage through several countries in the Middle East and the Far East, over the next fifteen or so years, ending up with her living in Hong Kong, where she undertook and completed her nursing studies. After she qualified, the family obtained a visa to come to London, which became her permanent home.

A few years after her arrival in London, her parents (already elderly) and her sister decided to return to their country. Martha preferred to stay in London, where she got a good job that gave her security, as well as professional and group identity. As she was recalling those events, she commented that when people are young, as she still was at the time, they do not seem to need anyone. She felt satisfied with her life in London and, despite having several suitors, she remained single and committed herself fully to her work.

Over a number of weeks, other group members commented on Martha's traumatic life trajectory, and on how remarkable it was for her to have found her niche in a foreign country, in which she made an important contribution to society through her work. Most members joined her in the task of evoking their stories, having survived the Second World War too. **Brenda** recalled that, like **Martha**, she had also been forced to leave her home country, family and friends behind her.

Martha's individual reminiscence became group reminiscence, which gave her a powerful sense of group belonging, at a time when she was isolated in her own life. In this therapy group of strangers, she discovered the possibility of forming a sufficiently secure group attachment, which compensated for the loss of group connections and attachment relationships in her life. Attending the group regularly, relating meaningfully to other members and, through group reminiscence, making sense of her past helped her come out of her isolation.

Belonging to a caring peer group, to which she became attached and also made important contributions, helped Martha steadily regain her strength of character, her determination and her capacity to care for other people and for herself. She also regained her sense of humour, returned to her local community centre and re-established contact with her old friends. In addition, she felt confident enough to challenge her auditory hallucinations without anti-psychotic medication.

Martha realised that the voices reproduced the content of her imaginary conversations with her deceased parents and siblings. As she was feeling vulnerable, alone and unprotected, following her retirement and cardiac arrhythmia, her attachment needs were reactivated and she missed her family terribly.

However, she became gradually able not to *depend* on the imagined communication with her dead relatives and to rely more on the here-and-now communication in the group. Eventually, she interpreted that her hallucinations were mostly an expression of her unconscious desire to bring her loved-ones back to life and to feel protected by them as she was as a child.

Relationships with their children and grandchildren

At a later stage in the life of the group, members went through a period in which they mainly focused on the negative aspects of the relationships with their children and grandchildren. The new material seemed to reflect something about their own difficult experiences during childhood and adolescence. I tried to provide opportunities for them to explore these difficulties and to improve these relationships.

More than half of the members were grandparents, about which they had mixed feelings. Despite the joy of having grandchildren, some of the new transgenerational realities were painful and, sometimes, perceived as yet another form of displacement or rejection. The in-law families and, of course, the group became *natural* recipients of their hostile projections. However, members usually protected me from their anger at the price, on occasions, of being angry with each other.

In one of the sessions, **Brenda** was angry with **Eddie**, a seventy-nine-year-old man, and accused him of upsetting her with his chauvinistic and patronising attitude. This led to an impasse, until **Tom**, a seventy-four-year-old man, commented that Brenda had previously described her eldest son as a patronising and chauvinistic person. Then, **Brenda** was able to recognise that, in many ways, Eddie reminded her of her eldest son.

At this stage, the group was reasonably solid and able to deal with conflict. Members were more capable of disentangling what belonged to them and what to the transference distortions of the past. Brenda's insight, into her own transference and projections to another group member, helped her reflect on the impact that her psychotic breakdown had on her children.

She regretted that she had become unavailable to them, in much the same way that she had experienced her own mother, with whom she could not form a secure attachment. Brenda also realised that her own children did not establish a secure attachment with her; she was now feeling abandoned by them.

Following Brenda's disclosure, several group members elaborated on their fears of being rejected by their children and, also, of being seen as useless by others in society.

> **June**, an eighty-six-year-old woman reported that, after the death of her daughter-in-law, she went to live with her son to help with the grandchildren. Her first breakdown occurred when her son's new partner moved in with them, which made her feel redundant. The family dynamic became complicated and, paradoxically, her son accused her of trying to take over the maternal role; this comment left her feeling deeply hurt and excluded.
>
> **Tom** joined the conversation. Unlike other members, he had not experienced physical separation from his children, because they were *still* living at home. However, communication with them was very poor and, in his view, they behaved like lodgers.

In contrast to the difficult experiences reported by those patients who were parents, the childless members tended to have an idealised image of parenthood.

> **Martha**, who had no children, stated that it was difficult for her to understand Tom's feelings of loneliness, because he lived with his own children. In her view, they should give Tom good companionship. Then, **Ellen** (also childless) referred to the fact that her first episode of psychotic depression coincided with the realisation that she was too old to become pregnant.

In our group, the patients who had children and grandchildren experienced life as difficult and conflictive; but the childless members tended to talk more often about feelings of emptiness.

I commented that the group was providing opportunities to explore different or even opposite viewpoints and that, according to their stories, children could either be idealised or become a source of pain and problems. This intervention promoted a process through which polarised views were gradually transformed, or *translated*, into more meaningful and less hostile communication – something that had been described by Foulkes (1964) as *ego training in action*.

Over time, childless members could appreciate other creative aspects of their lives, which helped them gain a sense of fulfilment and *transcendence* into posterity.

Intimacy and sexuality

Intimacy refers to the experience of safely connecting with other people, based on feelings of care and affection; it can include social, emotional, intellectual, physical and sexual elements (Jones and Moyle, 2016).

Sexuality is a key component of an individual's identity; it is relevant to, and can still play a significant role in the lives of older adults; they may define and express it through a diverse range of activities and behaviours (Kaplan, 1990; Vincent et al., 2000). However, sexuality remains one of the least understood and explored aspects of ageing (Kehoe, 1986; Schwartz, 2019).

Although human sexuality is an intrinsic part of identity, stereotyping older adults generally leads to ignoring the importance of sexual feeling and fulfilment in relation to their quality of life and emotional well-being (Friend, 1991; Junkers, 2006; Kelly and Barratt, 2007; Hershenson, 2016; Lee et al., 2016; Hadar, 2017).

In this group case, the expression of sexuality and intimacy was present in various forms, although not very often. Members differed widely in their ability to share their own feelings and to hear other people's feelings with regard to sexual issues.

Some, particularly the oldest members, did not feel comfortable talking about their sexuality, possibly under the influence of the societal taboos of their generation. Having said that, the mood of the group often lightened up when they talked about sex; they sometimes giggled and teased each other. Some members were still married or had a partner; others were divorced, widowed or singletons.

Generally speaking, the men in the group seemed more prepared to talk about sexuality and to acknowledge their sexual feelings. On occasions, they brought some fantasies about getting into a warm and romantic relationship that would make them feel loved and cared for, but without putting too many demands on them. At other times, they reminisced about the good moments they had in the relationship with their partners, some of whom were dead.

Those still in a couple considered that the relationship with their partner was not as satisfying as it used to be, but appreciated the companionship and trust they had developed over the years. One member had a bitter relationship with his second wife, but both were too frightened of the prospect of separating.

Most of the women in this particular group did not have a partner and tried to keep an active social life. In general, the women were more reluctant to acknowledge that they wanted or needed a partner. Some commented that they valued their freedom; others were still open to having a new sexual partner, although they appeared to be more concerned with securing companionship than a sexual partnership. Some of the oldest women observed that, for them, *friendship* was more important at this late stage of life.

A common leitmotif shared by all, men and women, was that of maintaining feelings of desire and of being wanted and accepted, particularly in the face of societal prejudices about sexuality in old age.

Ageing, death and the process of dying

Ageing *per se* is a natural process, not a pathological one; it is a consequence of having survived for very long, but it can be physically and emotionally taxing. Some people are more able to accept growing old than others. In the group, the themes of ageing and death usually came up in relation to physical symptoms and decline. At other times, they related to the experience of losing partners, friends, siblings and peers, through death, which was a painful reminder of their own mortality.

Members often complained of being discriminated against in our society. They resented the portrayal of the elderly in the media, whilst in other cultures, older adults are valued as experienced and wise members of the community.

> This theme had a strong *resonance* for **Eddie** who had not come to terms with his loss of status, following his retirement several years previously. He said that things became worse for him after his son took over the directorship of the family business from him. He added that his son would not take any of his advice, which was a form of rejection for him.
>
> **Tom** identified with Eddie and talked about his own decline. He said, with a gesture of resignation on his face, that he felt he could do little more than marking time until he popped off.
>
> **Rose**, who often identified herself with younger people, did not want to join any discussions about ageing. She decided to leave the group to undertake a university course on sociology, as she wanted to develop her intellectual curiosity about groups. There were some concerns in the group about her decision but, also, an appreciation that she was trying to use her remaining years creatively.

Some of the remaining members struggled with a feeling of time running out, and of being under pressure to make decisions about their increasingly limited choices before dying. Sometimes, just the idea of travelling to another country triggered off unbearable anxiety, as the trip may turn out to be a journey of no return. At one point, a member commented that during the very few times he managed to visit his country of birth, he did not feel at home: his family and friends were dead or living far away.

Group members did not usually discuss death openly. They seemed more interested in comparing the actual quality of their lives. However, disabling physical symptoms and dying were matters of concern for them.

> **Tom** and **Brenda** had sometimes commented that they would prefer "*to drop down dead suddenly*", whilst still healthy, because they would not like to be a burden to their children.
>
> **Paul**, a ninety-three-year-old man, could not agree with them. He was physically frail and had lost contact with his family. His main fear was dying alone at home and being dead for days before anyone noticed.

Paul had been a very reliable member of the group for several years. Even during his sudden, final illness, he managed to let me and the group know that he had been admitted to the hospital. In his message, he said that he was in good company and receiving good care.

At the beginning of the following session, the group intuitively knew that something was wrong when they realised that **Paul** was missing. Even before I broke the sad news of his death, several members expressed sorrow. But they were later relieved that he had not died alone.

Discussion

The increasing longevity of the elderly population can be seen as a clear sign of society's success in health and social care. Like Paul, people who reach advanced old age are in many ways survivors, which is an achievement in its own right. Most of them have acquired valuable personal resources and some actually make huge contributions to society, for which they can get recognition or rewards, either before or after they die.

However, older adults' resources and contributions may have little impact on the overall public perception of late life. Modern western societies often appear to be holding up a distorted, denigrating mirror to older adults, making them feel a burden on the young or a drain on resources.

Paradoxically, the energy that social-science researchers and political activists have put into trying to combat ageism seems to have reinforced demeaning societal attitudes towards old people. A group-analytic perspective would not be complete without looking at these prejudiced and discriminatory impressions of ageing.

Even today, many elderly patients do not receive early and adequate care in the community, but are institutionalised in mental hospitals, nursing homes and other care facilities, characterised by medication-prescribing as a sole treatment, as well as insufficient financing and fragmented delivery of psychotherapy services.

Butler (2010) suggested that ageism can be a thinly disguised attempt to bypass the reality of human ageing and death, through which professionals, carers and public often perceive older people as different, less deserving and marginal. Ageism has sometimes contributed to a culture of treating elderly patients with an attitude of *passing time* until the arrival of death.

Things have improved, but there is still a long way to go. In fact, in a recent piece of research, Saunders et al. (2021) found that older adults continue being largely under-represented in psychotherapy and psychological treatment services, and they still suffer disproportionally within established healthcare systems, as shown so dreadfully during the Covid pandemic.

Group analysts and other psychotherapists must be prepared to contest ageism in the consulting room and in the wider context of society. They have to examine carefully the ageist prejudices within their patients, as well as within themselves. This can be quite subtle; a colleague whom we supervised at some point commented that one of her group patients was "*a passive-aggressive character, like most old people are!*"

In our group case study, we found that members were aware of the extensive negative attitudes in society towards the aged, including their own. Overall, they tended to be more caring and self-protective, in the sense that they showed sympathy readily and avoided confrontation or strong overt reactions to other members and to the therapists, when compared with groups that we had conducted with younger adults. There was also less emphasis on here-and-now issues such as analysing interactions with fellow members and with the therapists.

The general atmosphere in the group was predominantly one of mutual acceptance and encouragement. Members showed less anxiety to disclose inner feelings and painful memories than elderly patients in age-heterogeneous groups. It was helpful for our members to share and compare themes, not only in terms of common concerns, but also in the exploration of pleasures and satisfactions that are communal to members of this age group. Our findings were consistent with, although not identical to, previous research (Lakin, 1989; Walker and Clarke, 2001; Saunders et al., 2021).

In a classical study, Lakin (1989) compared psychotherapy groups of older adults with those of younger adults. He found that older adults referred more to differences between themselves and other age groups, demanded and received more guidance from the therapists, and disclosed more intimate details to one another. The latter was particularly striking. Lakin observed that older adults talked with relative ease and no hesitation about profound experiences of bereavement, loneliness, fears of abandonment, problems of widowhood, feelings of rejection and vulnerability and other age-related concerns.

On the other hand, the responses to such disclosures from fellow group members were empathic, but almost stereotypic, as if everyone should expect to experience such losses and feel the same way; this facilitated cohesion and emotional communication. Thus, there was a flow from self-disclosure to reassurance, advice or support, and comforting responses.

By comparison, younger adults disclosed less but, when they did, they elicited more intense responses from other group members (Lakin, 1989). The belief amongst older patients that their problems were common to their age group facilitated disclosure, which in turn reinforced the idea that they were not unique in their misfortune. By contrast, some younger adults believed that their problems were more unique than what they really were, which tended to inhibit self-disclosure.

In our own case study, differences with groups for younger populations became clear from the early stages of the therapeutic process. For example, issues of competitiveness, rivalry and aggression, which are generally present in the early stages of groups with younger adults, tended to be absent or manifested themselves differently in our elderly group. Members did not struggle for power and control openly like the young but concentrated more on the identification of common problems: a process of forming group cohesion, which eventually led to more advanced group coherency (Pines, 1986; Ezquerro, 2010).

Our group members did specific work on their feelings about the disadvantaged status of the aged in society. They did not use the technical term *ageism*, but often commented that they were feeling displaced and made redundant from life. Although they enjoyed being part of a peer group and attended the sessions very regularly, they were also sensitive to being lumped together as a bunch of elderly people.

For them, age alone was not the defining element of their identity; they protected their individuality and past accomplishments. They did not want to be swamped into anonymity and, ultimately, oblivion; but they still endeavoured to grow and to think about the legacy they would be leaving behind themselves.

The predominant view of the specialist literature is that, as members of a disadvantaged minority that is often subjected to social discrimination, elderly patients usually do better in age-homogeneous groups, in which they can commiserate and gain mutual support. However, the benefits of these groups should be weighed against the distinct advantages and disadvantages of age-heterogeneous groups.

Age heterogeneity enhances the possibility of dealing more directly with intergenerational issues. However, an elderly patient who is significantly older than the rest of the group can be put at risk of being left out, or might not be involved enough in some of the issues that are more relevant to younger adults (Moss, 2017).

In this group case study, although all members were older adults, there was sufficient age-heterogeneity anyway, since we had a broad age range: sixty-five to ninety-five, so young-old and old-old. In some way, we had the best of both worlds.

It is also important to emphasise that practitioners working with this age group should not underestimate the rich resources that elderly patients may bring to the therapeutic context. Ignoring their wealth of wisdom and experience unduly fosters dependency. One distinct therapeutic strategy to help older adults use their resources, come to terms with the past, value themselves and achieve ego-integrity is the process of reminiscence and life review.

In our group, as reflected in the clinical vignettes, members gained much insight from reminiscing, recollecting and pondering important past experiences, giving revised meaning to them and sharing common values with people of their own generation. Reminiscence can sometimes connote defensive idealisation and a difficulty in letting go; at other times, continuity with the past can be an antidote to overwhelming despair.

Optimally, as postulated by Butler (1974, 1975, 2008, 2010) and outlined earlier, reminiscence can be conceptualised as a developmentally appropriate and natural component of life review. The re-valuation of one's life may be utilised to promote re-integration of the individual's identity, of who they are, by having them re-connect with who they were. It may become a mainstay of psychoanalytic and group-analytic psychotherapy.

At its best, reminiscence and life review processes flesh out individual members within the group and make them more complete as people. These therapeutic processes may restore feelings of worth and competence through the articulation of past successes and the recollection of prior credentials. A well-functioning therapy group adds an important dimension to the use of reminiscence. What has been of significant subjective importance to any individual can be confirmed by a more collectively objective valuation amongst peers.

A sense of continuity with the future is also crucial for older adults. They often need to develop a sense of continuing existence in a world, in which some part of themselves might remain. They may live on in their children and grandchildren, in the memory of others or in their own productions and creative works, including writing, painting, composing music and so on. Quite simple objects, like photographs and videos, can also help build a sense of continuity, as in the case of Ellen; but past damage may hinder this process.

On the other hand, at its worst, reminiscence may result in a fixation with the past, guilt over irreparable errors, and a heightened, morbid self-absorption leading to social alienation.

Grievous losses are part of the ageing process. These include the loss of personal capabilities, relationships, functions and roles and may result in an impoverished sense of self with feelings of depletion, worthlessness, depression and despair. In a psychotherapy group, appropriate grieving and letting go of the past might be facilitated, promoting better engagement with the current environment. The reminiscence of previously mastered challenges can also help older adults face future uncertainties and shrinking horizons with less apprehension, and achieve existential maturity.

The beneficial effects more frequently reported by patients in our group included improvements in the ways they evaluated and perceived themselves, as well as in quality of their relationships. Most were able to take back their own projections and start seeing themselves in a truer image that included the healthy aspects of themselves as well. Some managed to resolve complex life-long conflicts and move on.

In this case study, existential and survival anxieties were prominent at times of personal and group crises. When emotional security and trust were restored, members became more able to explore differences and confrontation. In turn, this promoted a more mature expression of negative feelings towards one another and towards the therapist. When they were able to work through this challenging tension, a greater potential for change emerged.

It is debatable whether group psychotherapy with older adults may or may not be as open-ended as with the young. In our group case study, we observed that the flexibility of having thinking space, without being pressurised, was beneficial for the majority of members.

Approaching death was often a challenge that some were able to use constructively to be more selective, and to focus on what mattered most for them: the consolidation and affirmation of their existence. On occasion, shortness of time generated overwhelming anxieties, which prevented them from getting on with the therapeutic task.

On other occasions, time restrictions were an incentive to work in therapy rather than the opposite – a real *deadline* may serve to creatively concentrate the mind.

Conclusion

Old age is an integral part of life, with new developmental challenges, facing growth in some areas and decline in others. Elderly people usually experience multiple losses and an increasing sense of shrinking horizons; they are particularly vulnerable to existential anxiety, despair and depression, but personal development and a passionate commitment with life can continue until death – something that is not fully appreciated in our era of rapid social and technological changes, where ageism is a norm.

Around a quarter of older adults suffer significant mental health problems but they are under-represented in the provision of psychotherapy services. The specialist literature indicates that age-homogeneous psychodynamic group therapy can be the treatment of choice for many elderly patients.

This broad modality of group psychotherapy facilitates personal disclosure and sharing of common concerns; affords the identification of age-specific tasks and diverse trajectories; reduces shame, social isolation and fears of rejection; improves mental functioning and interpersonal relationships; enhances self-esteem and self-confidence; provides opportunities for mutual support, creativity and growth.

Age-heterogeneous group psychotherapy can also be beneficial, particularly as it may offer greater opportunities for older adults to explore and work through intergenerational issues; however, they may feel more inhibited to reveal themselves.

To a large extent and for a long time, group analysis neglected developmental understanding and work with this population, perhaps partly as a result of early psychoanalytic prejudices and ageist attitudes. However, the present case study and other group-analytic qualitative research show two main findings:

First, the diverse and flexible nature of group-analytic psychotherapy can be highly beneficial for elderly patients, including those with severe mental illness and mild cognitive impairments. This form of treatment provides a self-sustaining matrix in which older adults can grieve their multiple losses and get on with their new developmental challenges in the context of peer-group belonginess and group attachment, which is key for balanced development and emotional survival.

Second, group-analytic thinking can deepen the therapeutic processes of reminiscence and life review, helping older adults recognise the child, the adolescent and the younger adult still present internally. Meaningful reminiscing and staying in contact with the past can promote a sense of continuity, self-constancy and ego-integrity, for elderly people to review and give value to their own life experiences and to themselves, as well as to come to terms with a heightened realisation of their own mortality.

In this particular group case study, the older members (the old-old) seemed more prepared to accept death than the younger members (the young-old), although they feared more the process of dying. In spite of an increasing sense of time running out and options dwindling, the majority of our elderly patients were able to keep their creativity alive.

Coming to terms with the forthcoming end of one's existence is largely considered the main developmental challenge of late life. However, the ultimate task of old age is not so much a trouble-free death but to live as well as possible all the way to the very end.

References

Abraham K (1919) The applicability of psycho-analytic treatment to patients at an advanced age. In: *Selected Papers*. New York: Basic Books (1953 edition), pp. 312–317.

Achenbaum WA (2013) *Robert Butler, MD: Visionary of Healthy Aging*. New York: Columbia University Press.

Agronin M (2009) Group therapy in older adults. *Current Psychiatry Reports* 11(1): 27–32.

Alwin FD (2012) Integrating varieties of life course concepts. *The Journals of Gerontology: Series B* 67B(2): 206–220.

Anderson D (2011) Group analysis and dementia: reflections on conducting an analytic space. *Group Analysis* 44(4): 385–394.

Ardern M, Garner J and Porter R (1998) Curious bedfellows: psychoanalytic understanding and old age psychiatry. *Psychoanalytic Psychotherapy* 12: 47–56.

Beauvoir S (1970) *La Vieillesse*. Paris: Gallimard.

Bengtson VL and Whittington FJ (2014) From ageism to the longevity revolution: Robert Butler, pioneer. *The Gerontologist* 54(6): 1064–1069. Available at From

Ageism to the Longevity Revolution: Robert Butler, Pioneer | The Gerontologist | Oxford Academic (oup.com)

Berezin MA and Cath SH (1965) *Geriatric Psychiatry: Grief, Loss and Emotional Disorders in the Aging Process.* New York: International University Press.

Berland DI and Poggi R (1979) Expressive group psychotherapy with the aging. *International Journal of Group Psychotherapy* 29: 87–108.

Bernstein C (1969) Age and race fear seen in housing opposition. *Washington Post* (7 March).

Bissonnette BAS and Barnes MA (2019) Group reminiscence therapy: An effective intervention to improve depression, life satisfaction, and well-being in older adults? *International Journal of Group Psychotherapy* 69(4): 460–469.

Bodner E, Bergman YS and Cohen-Fridel S (2012) Different dimensions of ageist attitudes among men and women: A multigenerational perspective. *International Psychogeriatrics* 24(6): 895–901.

Bowlby J (1969) *Attachment and Loss. Vol 1: Attachment* (1991 edition). London: Penguin Books.

Bowlby J (1973) *Attachment and Loss. Vol 2: Separation, Anxiety and Anger* (1991 edition). London: Penguin Books.

Bowlby J (1980) *Attachment and Loss. Vol 3: Loss, Sadness and Depression* (1991 edition). London: Penguin Books.

Butler RN (1974) Successful aging and the role of the life review. *Journal of the American Geriatrics Society* 22: 529–535.

Butler RN (1975) *Why survive? Being old in America.* New York: Harper and Row.

Butler RN (2008) *The longevity Revolution: Benefits and Challenges of Living a Long Life.* New York: Public Affairs.

Butler RN (2010) *The Longevity Prescription: The 8 Proven Keys to a Long, Healthy Life.* New York: Avery/Penguin Group.

Canete M and Ezquerro A (2000) Group-analytic psychotherapy with elderly patients. *Bulletin Oxford Psychotherapy Society* 32: 26–29.

Canete M, Stormont F and Ezquerro A (2000) Group-analytic psychotherapy with the elderly. *British Journal of Psychotherapy* 17: 94–105.

Canete M, Stormont F and Ezquerro A (2004) Gruppenanalytishe psychotherapie mit alteren. In: Hayne M and Kunzke (eds) *Moderne Gruppenanalyse.* Giessen, Germany: Psychosozial-Verlag, pp. 262–280.

Cappeliez P, Guindon M and Robitaille A (2008) Functions of reminiscence and emotional regulation among older adults. *Journal of Aging Studies* 22(3): 266–272.

Chilton J, Diane M. Crone DM and Tyson J (2020) 'The group was the only therapy which supported my needs, because it helped me feel normal and I was able to speak out with a voice': A qualitative study of an integrated group treatment for dual diagnosis service users within a community mental health setting. *International Journal of Mental Health Nursing* 29(3): 406–413.

Cohen N (1982) On loneliness and the ageing process. *International Journal of Psychoanalysis* 63: 149–155.

Coleman PG (2005) Uses of reminiscence: Functions and benefits. *Aging and Mental Health* 9(4): 291–294.

Comunian AL and Gielen UP (2000) *International Perspectives on Human Development.* Lengerich, Germany: Pabst Science Publishers.

Cooper DE (1984) Group psychotherapy with the elderly: Dealing with loss and death. *American Journal of Psychotherapy* 38(2): 203–214.

Darnley-Smith R (2002) Group music therapy with elderly adults. In: Davies A and Richards E (eds) *Music Therapy and Group Work: Sound Company*. London: Jessica Kingsley, pp. 77–89.

Davenhill R (2007) (ed) *Looking into Later Life: A psychoanalytic approach to depression and dementia in old age*. London: Karnac.

Erikson EH (1959) Identity and the life cycle. New York: International Universities Press.

Erikson EH (1966) Eight ages of man. *International Journal of Psychoanalysis* 47: 281–300.

Evans S (1998) Beyond the mirror: A group analytic exploration of late life depression. *Ageing and Mental Health* 2(2): 94–99.

Evans S (2004) Group psychotherapy: Foulkes, Yalom and Bion. In: Evans S and Garner J (eds) *Talking Over the Years: A Handbook of Dynamic Psychotherapy with Older Adults*. Hove, UK: Brunner Routledge, pp. 87–100.

Evans S, Chisholm P and Walshe J (2001) A dynamic psychotherapy group for the elderly. *Group Analysis* 34(2): 287–298.

Evans S and Garner J (eds) (2004) *Talking Over the Years: A Handbook of Dynamic Psychotherapy with Older Adults*. Hove, UK: Brunner Routledge.

Ezquerro A (1988) Late middle-age and group psychotherapy: a fruitful link? Tavistock Clinic Paper No. 98. London: Tavistock Centre.

Ezquerro A (1989) Group psychotherapy with the pre-elderly. *Group Analysis* 22(3): 299–308.

Ezquerro A (2000) Entramado vincular en un grupo de jubilados. *Clínica y Análisis Grupal* 22(3): 47–56.

Ezquerro A (2010) Cohesion and coherency in group analysis. *Group Analysis* 43(4): 496–504.

Ezquerro A (2017) *Encounters with John Bowlby: Tales of Attachment*. London: Routledge.

Ezquerro A (2020) Attachment and survival in the face of Covid-19. *Attachment: New Directions in Psychotherapy and Relational Psychoanalysis* 14(2): 171–187.

Feinberg TE (2000) The nested hierarchy of consciousness: A neurobiological solution to the problem of mental unity. *Neurocase* 6(2): 75–81.

Feldman RS (2018) *Development Across the Life Span*. Harlow, UK: Pearson Education Limited.

Foulkes SH (1964) *Therapeutic Group Analysis*. London: Allen & Unwin.

Freud S (1905) On psychotherapy. In: *Standard Edition of the Complete Works of Sigmund Freud, Vol 7* (1953 edition). London: Hogarth Press, pp. 257–268.

Friend RA (1991) Older lesbian and gay people: A theory of successful ageing. *Journal of Homosexuality* 20: 99–118.

Garland C (2007) Tragi-comical-historical-pastoral: Groups and group therapy in the third age. In: Davenhill R (ed) *Looking into Later Life: A Psychoanalytic Approach to Depression and Dementia in Old Age*. London: Karnac, pp. 90–107.

Garner J (1999) Psychotherapy and old age psychiatry. *Psychiatric Bulletin*, 23: 149–153.

Garner J and Evans S (2000) *Institutional Abuse of Older Adults*. Council Report CR84. London: Royal College of Psychiatrists.

Gattringer T, Enzinger C, Ropele S, Gorani F, Petrovic, K, Schmidt, R and Fazekas F (2012) Vascular risk factors, white matter hyperintensities and hippocampal volume in normal elderly individuals. *Dementia and Geriatric Cognitive Disorders* 33(1): 29–34.

Gavin T and Myers A (2003) Characteristics, enrolment, attendance, and dropout patterns of older adults in beginner Tai-Chi and line-dancing programs. *Journal of Aging and Physical Activity* 11: 123–141.

Goldfarb AI (1955) One aspect of the psychodynamics of the therapeutic situation with aged patients. *Psychoanalytic Review* 42: 180–187.

Griffin M and Walker MV (1985) Group therapy for the elderly: One approach to coping. *Clinical Social Work Journal* 13(3): 261–271.

Grotjahn M (1955) Analytic Psychotherapy with the elderly. *Psychoanalytic Review* 42: 419–427.

Grotjahn M (1978) Group communication and group therapy with the aged: A promising project. In: Jarvik LE (ed) *Aging into the Twenty-First Century*. New York: Gardner Press, pp. 113–121.

Grotjahn M (1989) Group analysis in old age. *Group Analysis* 22(1): 109–111.

Gullette MM (2011) *Agewise: Fighting the New Ageism in America*. Chicago, IL: University of Chicago Press.

Gullette MM (2017) *Ending Ageism, or How Not to Shoot Old People*. New Brunswick,NJ: Rutgers University Press.

Haber C (2006) Old age through the lens of family history. In: Binstock RH, George L, Cuttler S, Hendricks J and Schulz JH (eds) *Handbook of Aging and the Social Sciences*. Burlington, VT: Academic Press, pp. 59–75

Hadar B (2017) Is there hope for change at my age? In: Friedman R and Doron Y (eds) *Group Analysis in the Land of Milk and Honey*. Karnac Books, London: Karnac, pp. 163–176.

Hadar B (2018) Response to Everybody needs a group: a qualitative study looking at therapists' views of the role of psychotherapy groups in working with older people with dementia and complex needs. *Group Analysis* 51(1): 102–109.

Hamill M and Mahony K (2011) 'The long goodbye': Cognitive analytic therapy with carers of people with dementia. *British Journal of Psychotherapy* 27(3): 292–304.

Hershenson DB (2016) Reconceptualizing retirement: A status-based approach. *Journal of Aging Studies* 38: 1–5.

Hildebrand P (1982) Psychotherapy with older patients. *British Journal of Medical Psychology* 55: 19–28.

Hildebrand P (1986) Dynamic psychotherapy with the elderly. In: Hanley I and Gilhooly M (eds) *Psychological Therapies for the Elderly*. London: Croom Helm, pp. 22–40.

Hildebrand P (1995) *Beyond the mid-life crisis*. London: Sheldon Press.

Howell TH (1988) Charcot's lectures on senile dementia. *Age and Ageing* 17: 61–62.

Iversen TN, Larsen L and Solem PE (2009) A conceptual analysis of ageism. *Nordic Psychology* 61(3): 4–22.

Jain N (2019) Group psychotherapy for late-life depression. *Current Treatment Options in Psychiatry* 6: 452–460.

Jäncke L, Merillat S, Liem F and Hänggi J (2015) Brain size, sex, and the aging brain. *Human Brain Mapping* 36: 150–169.

Jelliffe SE (1925) Old age factors in psychoanalytic therapy. *Medical Journal Review* 121: 7–12

Jesmin SS (2014) Agewise: Fighting the New Ageism in America by Margaret Morganroth Gullette. *Journal of Women and Ageing* 26(4): 369–371.

Jones C and Moyle W (2016) Sexuality and dementia: An e-learning resource to improve knowledge and attitudes of aged-care staff. *Educational Gerontology* 42(8): 563–571.

Junkers G (2006) *Is It Too Late? Key Papers on Psychoanalysis and Ageing*. London: Karnac.

Kaplan HS (1990) Sex, intimacy and the aging process. *Journal of the American Academy of Psychoanalysis* 18(2): 185–205.

Katz S and Marshall B (2003) New sex for old: lifestyle, consumerism, and the ethics of aging well. *Journal of Aging Studies* 17(1): 3–16.

Kegerreis P (2012) Work with Older People: A Bibliography. *British Journal of Psychotherapy* 28(1): 117–124.

Kehoe M (1986) Lesbians over 65: A triply invisible minority. *Journal of Homosexuality* 12: 139–152.

Kelly M and Barratt G (2007) Retirement: Phantasy and reality. Dying in the saddle or facing up to it? *Psychodynamic Practice* 13(2): 197–202.

Khezri Moghadam N, Vahidi S and Ashormahani M (2018) Efficiency of cognitive-existential group therapy on life expectancy and depression of elderly residing in nursing home. *Iranian Journal of Ageing* 13(1): 62–73.

King P (1974) Notes on the psychoanalysis of older patients. *Analytical Psychology* 19(1): 22–37.

King P (1980) The life cycle as indicated by the nature of the transference in the psychoanalysis of the middle-aged and elderly. *International Journal of Psychoanalysis* 61: 153–160.

Korte J, Westerhof GJ and Bohlmeijer ET (2012) Mediating processes in an effective life-review intervention. *Psychology and Aging* 27(4): 1172–1181.

Krasner J (1977) Treatment of the elder person. In: Fabricant F, Barronand J and Krasner J (eds) *To Enjoy is to Live*. Chicago, IL: Nelson Hall, pp. 191–204.

Lakin M (1989) Group therapies with the elderly: issues and prospects. In: MacLennan BW, Saul S and Weiner MB (eds) *Group psychotherapies for the elderly*. Madison, WI: International Universities Press, pp. 43–55.

Latorre JM, Serrano JP, Ricarte J, Bonete B, Ros L and Sitges E (2015) Life review based on remembering specific positive events in active aging. *Journal of Aging and Health* 27: 140–157.

Lee D, Nazroo J, O'Connor DB, Blake M and Pendleton N (2016). Sexual health and wellbeing among older men and women in England: Findings from the English longitudinal study of ageing. *Archives of Sexual Behaviour*, 45: 133–144.

Lehr U, Seiler E and Thomae H (2000) Aging in a cross-cultural perspective. In: Comunian AL and Gielen UP (eds) *International Perspectives on Human Development*. Lengerich, Germany: Pabst Science Publishers.

Leszcz M (1990) Towards an integrated model of group psychotherapy with the elderly. *International Journal of Group Psychotherapy* 40: 379–399.

Li H, Ji Y and Chen T (2014) The roles of different sources of social support on emotional well-being among Chinese elderly. *Plos One* 9(3): 88–97.

Limentani A (1995) Creativity and the third age. *International Journal of Psychoanalysis* 76: 825–833.

Linden ME (1953) Group psychotherapy with institutionalized senile women: Study in gerontologic human relations. *International Journal of Group Psychotherapy* 3: 150–170.

Linden ME (1955) Transference in gerontologic group psychotherapy: IV. Studies in gerontologic human relations. *International Journal of Group Psychotherapy* 5: 61–79.

Liu Z, Yang F, Lou Y, Zhou W and Tong F (2021) The effectiveness of reminiscence therapy on alleviating depressive symptoms in older adults: A Systematic Review. *Frontiers in Psychology* 12: 1–13.

MacLennan BW et al. (1988) *Group Psychotherapies with the Elderly*. American Group Psychotherapy Monograph 5. New York: International Universities Press.

MacLennan BW, Saul S and Weiner MB (eds) (1989) *Group Psychotherapies for the Elderly*. Madison, WI: International Universities Press.

Martindale B (1995) Psychological treatments ii: psychodynamic approaches. In: Lindesay J (ed) *Neurotic Disorders in the Elderly*. Oxford, UK: Oxford University Press.

Martindale B (2007) Resilience and vulnerability in later life. *British Journal of Psychotherapy* 23(2): 205–216.

Maxmen A (2012) Harnessing the wisdom of the ages. *Monitor on Psychology* 43(2): 50–53.

Meerlo J (1955) Psychotherapy with elderly people. *Geriatrics* 10: 583–587.

Menzel J (2008) Depression in the elderly after traumatic brain injury: A systematic review. *Brain Injury* 22: 375–380.

Milton J (1996) *Presenting the Case for Psychoanalytic Psychotherapy Services: An Annotated Bibliography*. London: Tavistock Centre.

Mohammadian Akerdi E, Asgari P, Hassanzadeh R, Ahadi H and Naderi F (2016) Effects of cognitive-behavioral group therapy on increased life expectancy of male patients with gastric cancer. *Journal of Babol University of Medical Sciences* 18(6): 42–46.

Moss E (2017) I still want to be relevant: On placing an older person in an analytic therapy group with younger people. In: Friedman R and Doron Y (eds) *Group Analysis in the Land of Milk and Honey*. London: Karnac Books, pp. 177–190.

Murphy S (2000) Provision of psychotherapy services for older people. *Psychiatric Bulletin* 24: 181–184.

NEOLCIN (2017) *The role of care homes in end-of-life care*. The National End of Life Care Intelligence Network. Available at Care home bed provision and potential end of life care (publishing.service.gov.uk)

Neugarten BL (1977) Personality and aging. In: Birren JE and Schaie KW (eds) *Handbook for the Psychology of Aging*. New York: Van Nostrand Reinhold.

Panagiotopoulou K (2019) Group-analytic approaches for the elderly. *Contexts* 85. Available at Group-analytic approaches for the elderly | Group Analytic Society International

Peck RC (1968). Psychological developments in the second half of life. In: BL Neugarten BL (ed) *Middle Age and Aging*. Chicago, IL: University of Chicago Press.

Perren S and Richardson T (2018) Everybody needs a group: a qualitative study looking at therapists' views of the role of psychotherapy groups in working with older people with dementia and complex needs. *Group Analysis* 51(1): 3–17.

Pines M (1986) Coherency and its disruption in the development of the self. *British Journal of Psychotherapy* 2: 180–185.

Porter R (1991) Psychotherapy with the elderly. In: Holmes J (ed) *Textbook of Psychotherapy in Psychiatric Practice*. London: Churchill Livingstone, pp. 469–487.

Quinodoz D (2009a). *Growing Old: A Journey of Self-discovery*. London: Routledge.

Quinodoz D (2009b). Growing old: A psychoanalyst's point of view. *International Journal of Psychoanalysis* 90(4): 773–793.

Raz N, Rodrigue K, Kennedy K and Acker J (2007) Vascular health and longitudinal changes in brain and cognition in middle-aged and older adults. *Neuropsychology* 21(2): 149–157.

Ritzema R (2019) The changing role of the elderly in society. *Family Fire* (3 February). Available at https://familyfire.com/articles/the-changing-role-of-the-elderly-in-society

Rubenowitz E, Waern M, Wilhelmson K and Allebeck P (2001) Life events and psychological factors in elderly suicides: A case-control study. *Psychological Medicine* 31: 1193–202.

Rusted J, Sheppard L and Waller D (2006) A multi-centre randomized control group trial on the use of art therapy for older people with dementia. *Group Analysis* 39(4): 517–536.

Sadri Damirchi E, Ghomi M, Esmaeli Ghazi Valoii F (2017) Effectiveness of life review group therapy on psychological well-being and the life expectancy of elderly women. *Iranian Journal of Aging* 12(3): 312–325.

Saiger GM (2001) Group psychotherapy with older adults. *Psychiatry* 64(2): 132–145.

Sandler AM (1978) Problems in the psychoanalysis of an ageing narcissistic patient. *Journal of Geriatric Psychiatry* 11: 5–16.

Sandler AM (1984) Problems of development and adaptation in an elderly patient. *Psychoanalytic Study of the Child* 39: 471–489.

Saunders R et al. (2021) Older adults respond better to psychological therapy than working-age adults: evidence from a large sample of mental health service attendees. *Journal of Affective Disorders* 294: 85–93.

Sawatzky J and Naimark B (2002) Physical activity and cardiovascular health in aging women: A health-promotion perspective. *Journal of Aging and Physical Activity* 10: 396–412.

Schafer DE (1985) Reminiscence groups and the institutionalized elderly: An experiment. *Dissertation Abstracts International* 46(4-A): 1060.

Schwartz KM (2019) Sexuality, intimacy, and group psychotherapy with older adults. *International Journal of Group Psychotherapy* 69(1): 126–144.

Segal H (1958) Fear of death: notes on the analysis of an old man. *International Journal of Psychoanalysis* 39: 178–181.

Shakespeare W (1599) *As You Like It*. In: Hattaway M (ed) *The New Cambridge Shakespeare* (2009 edition). Cambridge, UK: Cambridge University Press. Available at As You Like It, by William Shakespeare - Free ebook download - Standard Ebooks: Free and liberated ebooks, carefully produced for the true book lover.

Silver A (1950) Group psychotherapy with senile psychotic patients. *Geriatrics* 5: 147–150.

Taylor WD (2014) Depression in the elderly. *The New England Journal of Medicine* 371: 1228–1236.

Tross S and Blum JE (1988) A review of group therapy with the older adult: Practice and research. In: MacLennan B, Saul S and Weiner MB (eds) *Group Therapies for the Elderly*. New York: International University Press, pp. 3–32.

UN (2019) World Population Prospects 2019. United Nations Department of Economic and Social Affairs, Population Division. Available at https://www.un.org/development/desa/publications/worldpopulation-prospects-2019-highlights.html

Vardi DJ and Buchholz ES (1994) Group psychotherapy with inner-city grandmothers raising their grandchildren. *International Journal of Group Psychotherapy* 44: 101–122.

Vincent C, Riddell J and Shmueli A (2000) *Sexuality and the Older Woman: A Literature Review*. Huddersfield: Pennell Institute for Women's Health.

Vink D, Aartsen M, Comijs H, Heymans M, Penninx B, Stek M, et al. (2009) Onset of anxiety and depression in the aging population: Comparison of risk factors in a 9-year prospective study. *The American Journal of Geriatric Psychiatry* 17(8): 642–652.

Waddell M (1998) *Inside Lives: Psychoanalysis and the Growth of the Personality*. London: Duckworth.

Waddell M (2000) Only connect: Developmental issues from early to late life. *Psychoanalytic Psychotherapy* 14(3): 239–252.

Waddell M (2007) Only connect – the links between early and later life. In Davenhill R (ed) *Looking into Later Life: A psychoanalytic approach to depression and dementia in old age.* London: Karnac, pp. 187–200.

Walker DA and Clarke M (2001) Cognitive behavioural psychotherapy: a comparison between younger and older adults in two inner city mental health teams. *Aging Mental Health* 5(2): 197–199.

Wayne G (1953) Modified psychoanalytic therapy in senescence. *Psychoanalytic Review* 40: 99–116.

Whitbourne SK (2007). *Crossing over the bridges of adulthood: Multiple pathways through midlife.* Presidential keynote presented at the 4th Biannual Meeting of the Society for the Study of Human Development (October). Pennsylvania State University, USA.

Woodspring N (2012) Book Review. Agewise: Fighting the new ageism in America. *Health* 16(3): 343–344.

Young CA and Reed PG (1995) Elders' perceptions of the role of group psychotherapy in fostering self-transcendence. *Archives of Psychiatric Nursing* 9(6): 338–347.

ORCID iD: Arturo Ezquerro https://orcid.org/0000-0002-9910-4576

ORCID iD: María Cañete https://orcid.org/0000-0001-7967-1103

Epilogue

Arturo Ezquerro and María Cañete

Thank you for having embarked with us on this exploration into the complexities, intricacies and beauty of human development throughout the life cycle. It is hardly possible to write, or to read, a book like this without thinking, and reflecting, on one's own development and that of the persons we live or work with, including our attachment figures, our colleagues, our patients and other people we care for. Ray Haddock, a prolific group-analytic peer put it succinctly: *"As I read, I found myself quickly moved to reflecting on my work as a therapist and trainer and, more personally, on my own life as it approaches the later stages"*.

Being rooted in conspicuous groundwork, this book project has its own history and whereabouts. On 5 December 2015, we organised an unusual conference, *Group Lives: Tales of Attachment*, at the Institute of Group Analysis. The aim was twofold: first, to commemorate the 25th anniversary of John Bowlby's death; second, to make further links between the worlds of attachment and Foulkesian group analysis (Foulkes, 1964, 1975). It was massively attended – the largest single event in the life of the institution.

The fact that attachment processes are of huge relevance for group analysis had been largely overlooked by the Institute, yet this conference proved that attachment was a key component of the institution's social unconscious. Indeed, our attachment histories are deeply embedded in and constitute an integral part of the social unconscious; which, as Earl Hopper pointed out in his foreword, *"is at the core of the group-analytic perspective"*.

There had been significant contributions that co-constructed bridges between attachment thinking and the group-analytic project (Glen, 1987; Ezquerro, 1991, 2017; Zulueta, 1993, Maratos, 1996; Marrone, 1998; Adshead, 1998). But the task of integrating the work of John Bowlby and of SH Foulkes has been politically complex and challenging: to some extent group analysis had inherited some of the psychoanalytic prejudices towards Bowlby. And Foulkes did not quote or refer to his work in any of his publications.

When John Bowlby (1958) presented the blueprint of his attachment theory to the British Psychoanalytical Society, on 19 June 1957, he was met with an outright hostility that included personal attacks. He was trying to strengthen psychoanalysis with updated scientific knowledge, as expectations

DOI: 10.4324/9781003167747-9

for evidence-based practice were building up, whilst he was coming to the conclusion that Freudian drive theory and Kleinian positions on the death instinct could not be empirically validated. Yet, thirty years later, high-profile psychoanalysts like Hanna Segal still believed that Bowlby *"was attacking psychoanalysis and that his goal was to destroy it"* (in Ezquerro, 2017: 82).

Indeed, an allegiance to a particular theory can represent a complex set of emotional loyalties and may also indicate a commitment to the way one has worked. Thus, challenging existing theories may sometimes be tantamount to threatening the meaning of one's own work. We are all political beings and resistance to theoretical and methodological change often takes the form of political action.

And so, this volume has included insights into the development of one's political self through different ages and stages. In this respect, Jimmy Burns (president of the British Spanish Society) considered the text suitable for a wider readership, beyond the mental health field, *"as societies and communities grapple with challenging personal and group circumstances in the times we live in"*.

Survival, meaningful connections and healthy growth are maximised by the ability of children, adolescents, adults and older adults to explore their environment with confidence. This is heightened by the process of internalising a secure base from relationships with reliable attachment figures. These notions of secure base and exploration are fundamental to attachment theory and to group analysis, and their significance extends to the whole life-course and to every aspect of human existence – including group lives.

The group has played a critical survival role in the evolution of the human species. In light of this, conceiving the group as an attachment figure and secure base is not as implausible as it may initially sound. Like Foulkes, Bowlby was a group person who conceived the human mind as a social phenomenon. In the first volume of his trilogy on *Attachment and Loss*, he advanced the concept of *group attachment*. According to him, the group-as-a-whole can undeniably come to constitute a distinct attachment figure:

> During adolescence and adult life, a measure of attachment behaviour is commonly directed not only towards persons outside the family but also towards groups and institutions other than the family. A school or college, a work group, a religious group or a political group can come to constitute for many people a subordinate attachment figure, and for some people a primary attachment figure. In such cases, it seems probable, the development of attachment to a group is mediated, at least initially, by attachment to a person holding a prominent position within the group.
>
> Bowlby (1969: 207)

During our group-analytic training and beyond, we were able to identify that for many colleagues, and for us, it was important to feel reasonably secure in our attachment with a prominent member of our institute, prior to being able to develop an attachment with a group of peers, such as our therapy group, and with the institution itself. Quite often, trainees may initially start forming an attachment to their analyst, their clinical tutor, their supervisor or another leading figure who might be perceived as stronger, wiser or more able to cope with group life, with the institution as-a-whole and with the world by and large.

Having said that, the literature on group attachment pales into insignificance when compared with the countless publications on interpersonal attachment. And most of it concentrates on attachment processes within the group rather than to the group as-a-whole. Although many colleagues and scholars have indeed studied group dynamics and the processes of group affiliation or membership, the mainstream trend is to keep the group outside the intimate attachment dance. Some believe that accepting group attachment as a distinct concept may dilute the essence of attachment theory.

In contrast, we would like to suggest that group attachment can strengthen and give more meaning and breadth to the, arguably, most far-reaching theory of psychosocial development to date. And for this reason, the second volume of the series, *The Power of Group Attachment,* will study more specifically the concept of *group attachment* as a useful construct for the fields of attachment, group analysis and other therapeutic disciplines, as well as for the understanding of human evolution, organisations, intra-group and inter-group relations, and healthy personal development or otherwise.

The Power of Group Attachment will amalgamate traditional theories with new attainments from the disciplines of developmental psychology, psychiatry, sociology and psychoanalysis, as well as attachment research, within a contemporary attachment and group-analytic context. Special attention will be paid to recent attachment research in group psychotherapy, including Marmarosh (2020), Tasca and Maxwell (2021) and a number of other authors. There will be special chapters on group coherency, as distinct from more undifferentiated group cohesion, as well as on the treatment of severe developmental disruptions and traumatic experiences leading to suicide risk, bipolar disorders and psychosis. The text will complement and expand the present volume. We are working hard on it and can't wait to see it in print.

London, 9 July 2022

References

Adshead G (1998) Psychiatric staff as attachment figures. *British Journal of Psychiatry* 172: 64–69.

Bowlby J (1958) The nature of the child's tie to his mother. *International Journal of Psychoanalysis* 39: 350–373.

Bowlby J (1969) *Attachment and Loss. Vol 1: Attachment* (1991 edition). London: Penguin Books.

Ezquerro A (1991) *Attachment and its Circumstances: Does it relate to Group Analysis?* Theoretical dissertation for membership of the Institute of Group Analysis. Archives Institute of Group Analysis Library, London.

Ezquerro A (2017) *Encounters with John Bowlby: Tales of Attachment.* London: Routledge.

Foulkes SH (1964) *Therapeutic Group Analysis.* London: George Allen & Unwin.

Foulkes SH (1975) *Group Analytic Psychotherapy: Method and Principles.* London: Gordon & Breach.

Glenn L (1987) Attachment theory and group analysis: The group matrix as a secure base. *Group Analysis*, 20(2): 109–126.

Maratos J (1996) Self through attachment and attachment through self in group therapy. *Group Analysis* 29(2): 191–198.

Marmarosh CL (ed) (2020) *Attachment in Group Psychotherapy.* New York: Routledge.

Marrone M (1998) *Attachment and Interaction.* London: Jessica Kingsley.

Tasca GA and Maxwell H (2021) Attachment and group psychotherapy: Applications to work groups and teams. In Parks CD and Tasca GA (eds). *The Psychology of Groups: The Intersection of Social Psychology and Psychotherapy Research.* Washington, DC: American Psychological Association, pp. 149–167.

Zulueta F (1993) *From Pain to Violence: The traumatic roots of destructiveness.* London: Whurr Publishers.

ORCID iD: Arturo Ezquerro https://orcid.org/0000-0002-9910-4576

ORCID iD: María Cañete https://orcid.org/0000-0001-7967-1103

Author Index

Subject Index

231, 233, 239; *see also* development, in late-middle age; developmental tasks; pre-retirement; transitions
rite of passage 96–97, 136; *see also* development, in adolescence
rivalry 37, 49–50, 60, 103, 170, 194, 214, 250, 258; sibling 49–50, 170; *see also* competition; cooperation
Robert Butler, MD: Visionary of Healthy Aging (Achenbaum) 242
role reversal 55, 109
Royal College of Psychiatrists 232

scapegoating 20, 60
schizo-affective disorder 250; *see also* personality disorders; psychosis; schizophrenia
schizophrenia 73, 95, 250; *see also* psychosis; schizo-affective disorder
secure base 11, 29, 60, 72–73, 79, 110, 117, 147, 149, 184, 186, 190, 193, 195, 197, 247, 270; *see also* attachment; exploration; group attachment; group matrix; trust
A Secure Base: Clinical Applications of Attachment Theory (Bowlby) 190
seduction theory 13; *see also* sexual abuse
self-abandon 126, 149
self-absorption 126, 259
self-awareness 19, 28, 53–54
self-care 113, 239
self-continuity 25, 210
self-control 127, 135, 158
self-esteem 28, 60, 68–69, 98, 101, 103–104, 158, 168, 237, 239–240, 260
self-evaluation 60, 98
self-expansion 22, 125
self-focus 22, 125, 131, 133–134, 142, 147
self-governance 149
self-initiation 92
self-integration 209; *see also* integration
self-protection 125, 257
self-recognition 18, 53–54; *see also* mirroring
self-redefinition 26; *see also* identity
self-reflection/self-reflectivity 11, 31, 90, 98, 103, 117, 135, 189–193, 269; *see also* introspection; reflective function; reflective practice group
self-regulation 21, 68, 90, 111, 127, 149; *see also* attachment; regulate the distance
self-report 207
self-responsibility 130

self-transcendence *see* ego-transcendence
self-understanding 54, 125, 132, 147, 240; *see also* mutual understanding; mutuality
sensory-affective integration 54; *see also* integration
separation anxiety 184–189, 192, 219; *see also* anxiety; endings in group therapy
separation-individuation 150, 181–184, 189
separation and loss 34, 75, 184, 186, 192, 217, 219, 253; *see also* depression; loss
sex, drugs and rock'n'roll 129; *see also* sexual revolution
sexism 230; *see also* discrimination; prejudice
sexual abuse 13, 27, 69, 106, 138, 140, 146, 181; *see also* seduction theory; trauma
sexual drives 35, 89, 96, 221, 231
sexual identity 11, 21, 102–103, 125, 133, 142–144, 146, 254; *see also* identity
sexual orientation 130, 133, 140, 143–145, 169
sexual revolution 129–130
sexual transference *see* transference
sexuality, in adolescence 22, 59, 89, 98, 101–104, 128; in adulthood 178–181, 187, 211; and attachment 9, 15, 156, 191, 211; in childhood 13, 59, 167; in consumer society 96; in late-middle age 35, 203–204, 215, 221, 224; and love 125, 126, 129, 254, 255; in old age 231, 240, 254–255; in young adults 22, 125–126, 129, 133, 135; *see also* attachment, love; tenderness
sharing 20, 51, 53, 58, 61–63, 77, 139, 142, 191, 224, 242, 259; *see also* mutuality; reciprocity
sibling rivalry 49, 170; *see also* siblings
siblings 5, 16, 18, 48–50, 57, 59, 80, 138, 170, 177, 179, 187, 194, 218, 222, 242, 251–252, 255; *see also* attachment; competition; cooperation; sibling rivalry
SIMIC *see* social identity model of identity change
the singles market 130
smile 18, 51–52, 54, 76, 162, 169, 172, 185, 187, 189; *see also* attachment; development; eye contact; language, non-verbal
social alienation 259

Milton Keynes UK
Ingram Content Group UK Ltd.
UKHW022007310723
426119UK00010B/62